RE-ORIENTING WESTERN FEMINISMS

The agenda of contemporary western feminism focuses strongly on women's equal participation in work and education, reproductive rights and sexual freedom. But what does feminism mean to the women of rural India who work long hours in someone else's fields, young Thai girls working in the sex industry in Bangkok servicing Japanese, American and Australian men, or Filipino girls working as maids for wealthy women in Hong Kong? Chilla Bulbeck presents a bold challenge to the hegemony of white, western feminism in this incisive and wide-ranging exploration of the lived experiences of 'women of colour'.

Bulbeck examines debates on human rights, family relationships, sexuality and notions of the individual and community to show how their meanings and significance in different parts of the world contest the issues which preoccupy contemporary Anglophone feminists. She then turns the focus back on Anglo culture to illustrate how the theories and politics of western feminism are viewed by non-western women.

Chilla Bulbeck is Professor of Women's Studies at the University of Adelaide, and was previously at the Faculty of Humanities at Griffith University. She is the author of *One World Women's Movement* (1988), *An Introduction to the Social Sciences* (1993, 2nd edn 1997), *Australian Women in Papua New Guinea* (Cambridge, 1992) and *Living Feminism* (Cambridge, 1997). She has written for *Women's Studies International Forum* and *Australian Feminist Studies*. She taught Australian studies at Beijing Foreign Studies University in 1991 and 1993, and was director of the Australian Institute for Women's Research and Policy in 1992–94.

Europe supported by Africa and North America.
Ascribed to William Blake.

RE-ORIENTING
WESTERN FEMINISMS

WOMEN'S DIVERSITY IN A POSTCOLONIAL WORLD

CHILLA BULBECK

PUBLISHED BY THE PRESS SYNDICATE OF THE UNIVERSITY OF CAMBRIDGE
The Pitt Building, Trumpington Street, Cambridge CB2 1RP, United Kingdom

CAMBRIDGE UNIVERSITY PRESS
The Edinburgh Building, Cambridge CB2 2RU, United Kingdom
40 West 20th Street, New York, NY 10011–4211, USA
10 Stamford Road, Oakleigh, Melbourne 3166, Australia

© Chilla Bulbeck 1998

First published 1998

Printed in Hong Kong by Colorcraft

Typeset in Caslon 10/12 pt

Library of Congress Cataloguing in Publication data
Bulbeck, Chilla, 1951– .
Re-orienting western feminism: women's diversity in a
postcolonial world/Chilla Bulbeck.
p.   cm.
Includes bibliographical references and index.
ISBN 0-521-58030-7 (hardback). – ISBN 0-521-58975-4 (pbk.)
1. Feminism. 2. Feminism – Developing countries. 3. Women – Social
conditions. 4. Women – Developing countries – Social conditions.
5. Minority women – Social conditions. 6. Pluralism (Social
Sciences). I. Title.
HQ1154.B848   1998
305.42–dc21   97–25836

A catalogue record for this book is available from the British Library

ISBN 0 521 58030 7 hardback
ISBN 0 521 58975 4 paperback

For Alison, Rebecca, Madelaine and David

Rather than imagining that women automatically have something identifiable in common, why not say, humbly and practically, my first obligation in understanding solidarity is to learn her mother-tongue. You will see immediately what the differences are. You will also feel the solidarity every day as you make the attempt to learn the language in which the other woman learnt to recognize reality at her mother's knee. This is preparation for the intimacy of cultural translation.

– Gayatri Chakravorty Spivak 1992:189–90

CONTENTS

Acknowledgements   x
Abbreviations   xi
Introduction   1   ●
      Justifying the Divide   1
      The Changing Name Brands of Feminisms   7
        Radical, Liberal and Socialist Feminism   7
        The Critique from Women of Colour   9
        Sameness–Difference Feminism   10
        Gynocentric and Postmodern Feminisms   12
        Postcolonial Critiques of Western Feminism   14
      Outline of the Book   16

1 Fracturing Binarisms: First and Third Worlds   18
      Histories of Colonialism   19
        Declension Narratives   19
        Southeast Asia: sex-role complementarity?   21
        Case Studies: India, China, Japan   23
        Modernisation and Tradition: Histories of the Veil   29
      Classifying Women's Worlds: First, Second, Third?   34
        Empirical indicators: 'more than 100 million women
        are missing'   39
      Fracturing Binarisms: Postcolonial Desire   44
        Orientalism   46
        Hybridisation   52
      Conclusion   54

2 Individual versus Community   57
      Constructing and Deconstructing the Western Individual   58
        Speaking the 'Self'   60
        The Ties That Bind   63
      Human Rights or Western Rights?   69
        Universal Declarations of Human Rights   70
        Refracting Rights Through Needs   74

Agency and 'Customary Practices'   79
  Infibulation   80
  Sati   88
Conclusion   93

3 Mothers and Wives   97
  Mothers, Wives and Sisters   97
  Reproductive Labour and its Products   99
    Population Policies   101
    To Have and to Hold: Reproductive Choices   110
  The Powers of Mothers   112
    The Double-edged Significance of 'Black Matriarch'   114
    Sisters in Struggle   117
  Brideprice, Dowry and Patrilocality   120
    Brideprice, Dowry and Domestic Violence   121
    Patrilocality and Mothers-in-Law   123
  Conclusion   127

4 Sexual Identities: Western Imperialism?   129
  'Core' Sexual Identities in the West   131
    Sexual Confessions: Christianity and Foucault   131
    Sexual Expression: Freud and the Sexologists   133
  Masculinities and the Monstrous Feminine   134
    Pollution or Pornography?   136
    Mother–Son Bonds   141
  Speaking With Two Lips to Recognise Third Genders   147
    Homosexual Acts and Homosexual Lives   148
    Third Genders   154
  Sexual Identities Invade the Interior of Colonised
  Subjects?   160
    Little Honeys in China: Prostitutes or Concubines?   160
    Women's Magazines in Singapore and India   162
  Conclusion: Post-sex   165

5 The International Traffic in Women   167
  International Connections Between Women   167
    The International Decade for Women   169
  Trade: Freedom Through Labour?   173
    Unpaid Unseen Women's Labour   174
    Women's Paid Labour: the Free-Trade Zones   176
    Prostitution and Sex Tourism   180
    Aid: International Bounty?   186

The Doubled Vision of Migrant and Indigenous Women   188
     Refugees   188
     Eating Her Words: Multiculturalism   191
   Women's Studies and Women's Politics   196
     Women's Studies   196
     Women's Movements Around the World: New Practices
     for Old Battles   199
   Conclusion   204

Conclusion: Braiding at the Borderlands   206
     Speaking and Subject Positions   208
     Seeing 'Our' 'Selves' Through the Eyes of 'Others'   211
     Coalition Politics   216

Endnotes   222
Bibliography   226
Index   266

Table
Life expectancy, maternal mortality and infant mortality rates:
the poorest performing nations   41

Maps
Images of the world from the Middle Ages to the twentieth
century   36

ACKNOWLEDGEMENTS

My first debt is to Professor Hester Eisenstein who introduced me to ways of looking beyond Anglo feminisms when she was a consultant at Griffith University in 1986. My colleagues at Beijing Foreign Studies University provided the congenial environment in which the seeds of this book took first form. In particular, I would like to thank Professors Hu Wenzhong, Wu Zhenfu and Yu Zhiyuan. Professor Wang Jiaxiang provided valuable insights on feminism in China, including a response to a draft of this book. My female students in the Australian studies classes of 1991 and 1993 discussed gender relations in China with me, both inside and outside the classroom. I remember in particular conversations with Li Wenhong, Ni Weihong and Zhu Xiaodong. Besides supplying a translation for a number of Hindi words in the book, Peter Mayer kindly read an earlier draft and suggested I seek feedback from 'outsiders' to white middle-class English-speaking feminism. This was invaluable advice, leading to the very substantial and useful comments from Doctors Parlo Singh and Indrani Ganguly. Royalties from the sale of this book go to the International Women's Development Agency to contribute, if only marginally, to the improvement of the status of some of the women who appear in the following pages.

ABBREVIATIONS

ASEAN	Association of South East Asian Nations
ATO	Alternative Trading Organisation
CAA	Community Aid Abroad
CEDAW	Convention on the Elimination of All Forms of Discrimination against Women; Committee on the Elimination of Discrimination Against Women
GATT	General Agreement on Tariffs and Trade
IMF	International Monetary Fund
NESB	non-English-speaking background
NGO	non-government organisation
OPEC	Organization of Petroleum Exporting Countries
SEWA	Self-Employed Women's Association of India
UN	United Nations
UNIFEM	United Nations Development Fund for Women
WICH	Women in Industry, Contraception and Health
WID	Women in Development
WLUML	Women Living under Muslim Laws

INTRODUCTION

•

JUSTIFYING THE DIVIDE

> You are facing the Old Royal Observatory, Greenwich. Walk round its
> walls until you come to a brass strip set in the pavement. The smooth,
> gold band in the ground marks the Prime Meridian, or Longitude Zero
> ... Stand to the left-hand side of the brass strip and you are in the
> Western hemisphere. But move a yard to your right, and you enter the
> East: whoever you are, you have been translated from a European into
> an Oriental.
>
> – Young 1995:1

'Learn her mother-tongue' if you wish to feel solidarity, suggests Gayatri
Spivak. Learn about the other woman, not as the stereotype we see in the
popular media, either oppressed by foreign customs or as the exotic other,
clad in colourful difference. From documentaries and news stories, from
advertisements and pleas by aid agencies, western women are bombarded
with images of 'other' women. Often these stereotypes are contradictory:
the strong black matriarch exposed to domestic battery; the veiled Iranian
who took up a gun to fight for her country's independence; the passive
mail-order bride who is nevertheless a scheming gold-digger; the proud
erect image of Winnie Mandela in her traditional headdress but convicted
of corruption. But the purpose of this book is not primarily to learn about
the other woman. This book will fail to deliver the rich detail of women's
lives offered in anthropology courses or area studies (like Asian studies).
Rather, we will explore why and how the stereotypes of 'other' women are
so integral to white western women's constructions of themselves. Contradictory or not, these stereotypes are usually pejorative. Why? What is
their purpose in the construction of 'white westernness'?

As Margaret Jolly (1996:185, 169) suggests, our focus on unfamiliar
forms of feminism, like anthropology's focus on unfamiliar cultures, will
help us challenge and change the familiar forms of feminism we find in
women's studies subjects and our daily lives. This is the meaning of the

play on re-orienting and oriental in this book's title: that we will be viewing western feminism through the eyes of women from the so-called 'third world' (the 'south', the 'east'), asking how women of the 'first world' (the 'north', the 'west') appear through the eyes of others. The unfamiliar allows us to question our understandings of the familiar, for example by comparing infibulation and breast implants. In this sense, the book's purpose departs from that of an anthropological text, for example. The focus is not on understanding how other women live as a project in itself, but on those aspects of other women's lives which challenge western feminism's theoretical and empirical preoccupations. Although we will be exploring research which describes how women live in different cultures, the project is not only about 'them' but also about 'us', how we can see ourselves differently by comparing our taken-for-granted feminist precepts with the writing by women from beyond the Anglophone west. Thus we will use the image of the other to make our familiar faces look strange, to offer new interpretations. As we step into other cultures, we perforce carry our own preoccupations with us. Thus this book carries western feminism's issues and the English language across the borders into other cultures. But it also seeks to carry back across the frontier a cargo that will ask new questions of western feminism: questions that will both challenge the 'imaginative spaces that non-western people occupy' in western minds (Lutz and Collins 1993:2) and the imaginative spaces that 'we' occupy in our own minds. So remember who is taking you on this journey, and why. For those who desire other routes, there are signposts, references to other writers, which I hope offer myriad personal journeys through the literature.

It is the book's project which justifies the juxtaposition suggested in the title of this book: a tiny fragment of the world and its knowledge, 'western feminisms', is arraigned against 'oriental' and 'post-colonial' feminisms and women's writing. This is a book written for white western women, a text which challenges the understandings of ourselves we gain from feminist texts written by and for white western women. In this book western feminisms will usually refer to the work of North American, Australasian and European-descended feminists. Within the west, both indigenous women and diaspora women from Asian and other so-called third world countries have conducted a critique of the 'whiteness' of western feminism. These women often produce writing from the borderlands, work which reflects their home in two cultures. Thus a division, as apparently arbitrary as the Prime Meridian in Greenwich, separates the west from the rest in this book, the self from the other. However, like the Prime Meridian itself, the fault line of this book is born of the history of colonialism, the economics of imperialism, the linguistics of English-language dominance in much of the feminist world, and the pressures of western cultural forms on the lives and psyches of those in the so-called third world. The Greenwich Meridian is not only a geographical convenience; it is no accident that it is in London, at the centre of a former imperial power and maritime nation. In the park below the Old Royal Observatory, among those descended from the 'Angles, Celts, Danes' are a 'varied mingling of peoples, whose ancestors hark back to the Caribbean and Africa, India, Pakistan, Bangladesh, China, Tibet, Afghanistan' (Young 1995:2). This mingling of Londoners is also an outcome of British colonialism; most have migrated from erstwhile colonies. Thus east and west continue to have a real salience, both in our imaginations and in the world of economics and politics.

Nevertheless, the centre from which this text proceeds may seem both odd and tediously familiar to many writers and readers from beyond the white west. They see feminism, as far as they deem it relevant, from a centre which is in India or China, or indigenous communities in Canada or Australia. However overwhelmed by western cultural imperialism, many cultures also construct themselves as a centre of epistemological geography, the space from which they know the world. In Chinese views of the world, there were Han Chinese people and there were barbarians or 'foreign devils'; walls were built to keep the latter out. The characters for China are translated as Middle Kingdom, the centre of the world. Before the twentieth century, outside influences were refused because other cultures were found to be inferior in technology and grace; after Liberation the west was found to be inferior in politics and morality. Chinese language uses the oppositions *wai guo ren* and *Zhong guo ren*, literally 'outside country people' and 'central country people', while 'foreign devil' is even used by Chinese people recently arrived in Australia to describe Australians: 'Using a term like "foreign devil" is 'akin to calling a Chinese person a Chinaman or Chink' (Ye Sang 1996:viii). Although 'foreign experts' may be treated with respect and deference by their junior colleagues and students, foreigners are also 'regarded with contempt', 'loaded with money', 'lazy, weak, and stupid' (Jacka 1994:670). Hindi also has a term for foreigner *firangi* or *firinghee*, which 'implies something of hostility or disparagement'; those who cannot speak Arabic correctly are referred to as *ajami*, foreigners to the faith (Peter Mayer pers. comm.; Mernissi 1993:22). Thus a book by a Chinese or Hindu woman about feminisms around the world would write from another centre; it would not seek or see the same differences as this text explores.

Taking this argument to its logical conclusion, one could claim that there are as many centres as there are women. In a sense there are. But political and theoretical pressures accord particular salience to some differences, for example identities based on class, race/ethnicity, sexuality and, more recently, age. The emerging interest in whiteness and western-ness has been produced by political and ideological pressure from women for whom race has long been salient. White western feminists are now beginning to see themselves as particularised in terms of their ethnicity or culture through a growing interest in 'other' women. Even so, within women's studies courses, 'other' women still often appear as just that, as footnotes of difference on the general themes of white women's lives and experiences. At the same time, women's studies does not and cannot (in my opinion, although this is contested by some postmodernists) dissolve into endless differences. Patterns must be sought, lines of distinction drawn, or nothing much can be said. This book charts the minefield between the overwhelming minutiae and the unacceptable homogen-isation of women's experiences.

Thus the fault line of this book does repress real differences within both west and east as well as the 'mingling' of east in west and west in east. To some extent this grand opposition will be avoided by using other distinctions like religion (particularly Hinduism, Islam, Confucianism, Christianity, Buddhism), nationality (Chinese women, Indian women, Filipinas), class background and geographical location (professional women in the city, peasant women in the country). Clearly these divisions cut across each other, further exposing the false homogenisation of east, or Indian or even women living in New Delhi. Nevertheless, without a book like this, many women's studies students will continue to study English-language western feminisms as though they are (almost) the only feminisms, as though they speak unequivocally for all women. I hope that this book will stretch western feminism out from its eurocentrism towards its borderlands, towards its intersections with women of other cultures. In the process we will see how the lives of some non-Anglo women are differently lived, or at least differently represented. These representations and lives exist not only beyond the countries of the 'west' but also within them, in the women who have come from India or South America as mi-grants, or indigenous women who lived here before English colonisation.

The title of this book uses the term 'western feminisms', although the brand of feminism under challenge from the borderlands might also be called 'Anglo feminism', or feminism produced by English-speaking 'white' women. To some extent the terms 'Anglo' and 'western' will be used interchangeably. Not all western feminisms are English-language-based, however, and there are differences between the theories and practices of feminism in different western countries. For example, Gisela Kaplan (1992:xxi) examines the heterogeneity of the west in her analysis of twenty western European countries' feminist movements, collecting these countries into four groups: the Scandinavian progressive north, the conservative centre, the creative traditionalism of western Europe (France and the Netherlands), radical southern Europe (Italy, Spain, Portugal). English-language feminism, rather than European feminism, has dominated international feminism, while in each country national language archives were supplemented by the ubiquitous holdings of *The Second Sex*, *The Feminine Mystique*, *The Female Eunuch*, *The Dialectics of Sex*, *Sexual Politics* (Kaplan 1992:xxiii–xxiv). The return cultural traffic is more limited. With the exception of 'heavy imports' from France and Germany, European feminism has had little influence on 'big-time feminist theory' (Holub 1994:239).

Even the term 'Anglofeminism', which would exclude much European feminism, also represses national differences: the individualistic, legal rights–oriented and academically nurtured feminism of the United States, the welfare-oriented and trade union–connected feminism of Britain, the femocratic or bureaucratically oriented feminism of the Antipodes (Australia and New Zealand) (Hewlett 1987:xviii; Eisenstein 1996). These internal differences struck me forcibly in April 1992, when I attended the 'We Won't Go Back' (to illegal abortions) rally in Washington DC. In comparison with Australian women's demonstrations, the rally was huge, attended by between 500 000 and 1 million people (*USA Today* 6 April 1992:1) who left a monumental debris of mass-produced signs wielded by the marchers. While marchers were reminded by speakers from non-Anglo backgrounds that abortions which resulted from poverty or forced sterilisations were just as much a matter of reproductive choice as the legalisation of abortions, the dominant refrain was rights and freedoms. Famous speakers, like Jill Eckenberry from *L.A. Law*, Jane Fonda the actor, Senate candidate Geraldine Ferraro reflected on this theme: 'Choice is about freedom, and what is America without freedom?'

As a (perhaps wimpish) Australian, I was struck by the anger of many of the speakers and participants. A black and white women's vocal group from Manhattan, named Betsy, shouted out the slogan 'We are fierce, we are feminist, and we are in your face'. Robin Morgan urged us to buy T-shirts proclaiming 'Rage plus women equals power'. One placard read 'Abort Bush Before his Second Term'. Angry arguments erupted between the pro-choice women and the pro-life women who had erected a 'cemetery of innocents' nearby (representing aborted foetuses and the twenty-three women who had died during legal abortions). I went to the United States believing I knew it intimately from the flood of films, television programs and academic books that pervade Australian popular and intellectual culture. Yet I felt battered and cut adrift by the assertiveness and anger, by the incessant refrain of rights and freedoms. This fashion of feminism was unfamiliar to me (see Bulbeck 1994 for a fuller discussion).

Given its media representation, one might think I would find China more unfamiliar. Mainland China is well known for its one-child policy, a government edict that produces much anguish even among those who accept its necessity: 'nobody thinks it is a perfect policy' but we have to accept that 'it's the lesser of two evils' (Wang Jiaxiang, Beijing Foreign Studies University Women's Group Meeting, 10 December 1993). This terse acknowledgement of necessity is worlds apart from the discourse of rights and freedoms I heard American feminists endorse. Among Chinese feminists I expected to be less at home, to perforce work harder at cross-cultural communication. Yet in some ways their expressions of feminism resonated more with my desired image of Australian feminism. Instead of anger and individual freedoms, Chinese feminists in Beijing, Hong Kong and Taipei stressed compromise and conciliation. Courtesy may have disguised their more forthright opinions of me and my culture, but exchange of ideas appeared more possible.[1]

This brief comparison of the contours of western and Asian women's activism reveals that sometimes we find similarities where they are not expected. While some feminists today are preoccupied with difference as a retort to the universalising claims of categories like 'sisterhood', we are in danger of losing sight of the commonalities and connections between women. As Chapters 1 and 5 warn, however, women of the world are connected *both* through some shared language and ideas *and* in structures of unequal power. There is no pure west and east. People, goods, ideas and texts travel backwards and forwards across the borderlands. This text addresses constantly, though not always comfortably, the tension between commonality and difference. The topics and examples are chosen as areas where a difference between orient and west has been suggested. Our analyses will find that sometimes the differences are inappropriately constructed, or not as great as dichotomous oppositions suggest. Furthermore, we bring those contrasts back to reconceive western difference, rather than focusing our attention on the difference of the other.

In summary, we will seek to challenge the dualism or opposition between self and other in two directions, both by questioning the stereotypes which constitute those women defined as different to the 'self', and by using the words the other has written about white western feminism to ask new questions about ourselves. A key task for this text will be to hold the similarities and differences in view at once, to avoid resorting to either a simple dualism or a simple universalism. One way we will do this is through the notion of connections between women: connections of shared culture and politics as well as connections of economic inequality. These connections point to the claim that many of us are hybrid subjects, neither purely 'westerner' nor purely 'easterner' but a mixture of both: we are in the other but she is also in us, a part of what constitutes our understandings of ourselves and the world. 'Move a yard to your right' and you become an easterner.

But first a brief review of the western feminisms which inform this book.

THE CHANGING NAME BRANDS OF FEMINISMS

Is difference good or bad, biological, social, or historical? Is it a weakness or a strength? Should we forfeit a notion of sexual difference on the grounds that all people, men and women, are not essentially different from each other, but merely culturally constructed as different? Can these constructions of masculinity and femininity be undone?

– Holub 1994:235

This section provides a cursory introduction to the present state of western feminist theorising. Focusing on another tension between similarity and difference (between male and female), we explore the transition from the tripartite classification of liberal-radical-socialist feminism to 'gynocentric' (Seidman 1994:241) and postmodernist feminist discourses. For those familiar with these changes in feminist theory, the last section of this Introduction provides an outline of the book.

Radical, Liberal and Socialist Feminism

Put baldly, radical feminists see women treated as much the same everywhere, and it is badly. There is an independent oppression based on sex, and it occurs across time and tides. As Catharine MacKinnon (1989:10) so aptly summarises it, 'bottom is bottom'. Radical feminism, as this perspective is usually termed, is an 'unmistakably twentieth century phenomenon' which takes 'the subordination of women as its central concern' (Alison Jaggar in Sandoval 1991:7). Radical feminism is also a brand of feminism particularly based in the United States. Through the term patriarchy, radical feminists paid particular attention to oppression based on sex and experienced as (female) bodily disadvantage. Their issues were women's reproductive freedom (for example the right to choose marriage partners and the number and spacing of children), women's bodily autonomy (incest, rape and physical violence towards women) and the representations of women as sexed and inferior (in pornography, advertising and prostitution).[2] Some radical feminists call for sexual, economic, social and/or political separatism from men. Along with other feminist perspectives, the influence of radical feminism can be seen in the discussion of motherhood in Chapter 3, pornography in Chapter 4 and the international traffic in women in Chapter 5.

Liberal feminism, its genesis often associated with Betty Friedan's book *The Feminine Mystique* (1963), has dominated the politics of feminism in the anglophone west. Liberal feminism claims that the capacity to reason is 'part of the human essence', shared by both men and women (Jaggar 1983:37). Differences between the sexes are a result of sexist attitudes more than unequal social structures or real differences between men and women. Liberal feminists thus tend to accept existing economic and political structures and argue for equality of opportunity for women within them. Their policies focus on more women in paid work (for example affirmative action legislation) or in politics. In Australia, femocrats (feminists specifically appointed to government bureaucracies to improve the position of women) generally advocate liberal feminist policies. But attempts to create equality of opportunity have raised issues of sexual difference, for example how primary responsibility for childcare affects participation in the workforce, or how health and emotional disadvantage through exposure to domestic violence reduces women's capacity to perform in the public sphere. Thus liberal feminism has its radical edge. With its sometimes uncritical concentration on the importance of economic development and human rights, liberal feminism has contributed to the discussions of economic development, explored in Chapters 1 and 5, and international women's rights, explored in Chapter 2.

Marxist or socialist feminism asserts either the primacy of class oppression over gender oppression (marxist feminism) or the coexistence of both (socialist feminism) in explaining the subordination of women. While liberal feminists are more likely to believe that attitudinal change will improve the position of women, socialist feminists are dedicated to structural changes, including the abolition of capitalism, which will overcome the vast differences in the economic position between and among men and women. Where the United States has been the major location for theoretical work by radical feminists, Great Britain has a much stronger representation of socialist feminists. Socialist feminists adapted marxist concepts like mode of production (which explained how capitalists appropriated the labour power of workers) to develop notions like the 'domestic mode of production', which explained how husbands appropriated the labour of housewives without paying its full worth. Women's unpaid domestic labour, according to socialist feminists, also benefits capitalists, who can hire workers at lower wages than would otherwise be possible. Socialist feminism has contributed to the discussions of the history of colonialism (Chapter 1) and its contemporary expression in the global economy (Chapter 5).

In the late 1970s marxist feminists developed the above tripartite classification of feminism (also defined as liberal-democratic, radical-separatist and materialist-socialist in Emberley 1993:8). They criticised both liberal and radical feminism for neglecting the class dimension in women's oppression. This class dimension reveals both that working-class women are more exploited than middle-class women and that middle-class women sometimes themselves exploit or benefit from the exploitation of working-class women. Examples which this book will explore include western consumers purchasing commodities produced by low-paid female workers in the free-trade zones of Asia, and western, Hong

Kong and Middle Eastern women hiring Thais and Filipinas as domestic workers. In the 'patriarchy debate' a number of writers sought to conciliate in the 'unhappy marriage between marxism and feminism' (Hartmann 1981; see also Eisenstein 1979). However, since marxist feminists saw class as the paramount form of oppression and radical feminists blamed patriarchy or sex-based oppression, even a marriage of equals was going to please neither side. One response to the patriarchy debate was Catharine MacKinnon's (1987) description of radical feminism as 'feminism unmodified', unmodified by any other -ism such as marxism or liberalism.

The Critique from Women of Colour

From the 1980s, resulting from a decade-long but different sheaf of critiques of feminism, it became unfashionable to divide feminism into this tripartite classification, although you will still find textbooks which do this (this one being no exception!). The first critique, and apparently the easiest to incorporate, came from socialist feminists of colour. If capitalism gave us the oppression of class, then colonialism and imperialism gave us the oppression of colour or race, class oppression written on a global map. This is expressed in the great economic differences in well-being between workers in the west and east or the use of guest labour, immigrants and domestic workers in the west in the lower reaches of the labour force. Indeed, race-based oppression has supplanted class-based oppression as the critique of universal sisterhood: 'class oppression' has become 'definitely *non grata* as a topic' (Barrett 1992:217).

The voices and changing preoccupations of socialist feminists of colour are captured in two edited collections by Miranda Davies: *Third World – Second Sex* vol. 1 (1983) and *Third World – Second Sex* vol. 2 (1987). In both, most writers were connected with socialist movements and saw marxism as the key theoretical tool, and imperialism or postcolonial economic exploitation as the key oppression. Between the first and second collections, however, greater attention was given to so-called 'radical feminist' issues like prostitution, domestic battery, sexual harassment, rape. From two articles by Indian writers in the first issue, the second issue carried seven articles, covering Thailand, the Philippines, Zimbabwe, Brazil, Iran and India (see Bulbeck 1991:80–1). Some women beyond the west now saw oppression as a constellation of 'international oppression, national and personal oppression' (Nawal el Sa'adawi, quoted in Beall et al. 1989:34), of sex, class and race oppression.

This notion of different aspects of oppression led to what Adrienne Rich (1984:289) called the 'fruitless game of "hierarchies of oppression"': which of these characteristics created the *most* oppression? She was responding to the claim that '"bourgeois feminists" are despicable creatures of privilege whose oppression is meaningless beside the oppression of black, Third World, or working-class women and men', thus clearly identifying her quarrel with marxist feminism. In reality, the prioritising of oppression depends on whether one is white or oppressed by one's colour, whether one is heterosexual or oppressed by one's sexuality, whether one is middle-class or oppressed by one's poverty. Thus female academics from Asian nations are sometimes attacked for not 'really' being subordinated: 'I was told I had used my power unfairly by posing as a marginal; that I could criticize the establishment only because I spoke its language too well' (Gayatri Spivak, quoted in Marcus 1990:15; see also Rey Chow, 1991b:98). One can be simultaneously disabled and enabled by the same signifier of status. Thus a woman's use of her married name 'makes graphic at the same time her subordination as a woman and her privilege as a presumptive heterosexual' (Sedgwick 1990:32–3). It is sometimes argued that 'the hierarchies of class, race, and gender are simultaneous and interlocking systems' (Eitzen and Zinn 1992:181).

The response of some radical feminists to the criticisms by women of colour was merely to incorporate non-white women under the umbrella of universal patriarchy, for example Robin Morgan's (1984) collection *Feminism is Global*. Chandra Talpade Mohanty (1992:78–9) criticises such proposals for planetary feminism for assuming that women share a universal experience of oppression from which arises a shared goodwill towards all other women. Furthermore, such global surveys can 'unintentionally set up a hierarchy of "civilized" customs' (Sievers 1992:322), just as surveys like Mary Daly's (1978) attempt to align witch-burning, foot-binding and infibulation.

Sameness–Difference Feminism

We will return to the implications of this multiplication of women's positioning through its role in the postmodern critique explored below. But first, another aspect of the 1980s was a reconstruction of feminism as the minimalist and maximalist positions (Stimpson 1988), or more commonly the sameness–difference debate (MacKinnon 1987:32–45 in the United States and Carol Bacchi 1990 in Australia). The minimalists claimed that women should be seen through a prism which emphasised their similarities with men, while the maximalists believed in women's fundamental differences from men. The liberal and socialist feminists were now aligned under the banner of sameness. Sameness asserted that women, apart from minor physiological differences, were more or less the same as men and should have the same opportunities to participate in politics, paid labour or revolution. Radical feminists, however, focused on differences, but could now be seen as consisting of two strands.

In contrast with the 1970s, when difference was generally seen as the curse of oppression, some feminists now constructed women's difference as positive, perhaps amounting to a 'supremacism' in which women's biological or social differences have provided them with 'a higher ethical and moral vision' (Sandoval 1991:13). In this view, men are seen as relying too much on reason, repudiating their bodies and seeking to control nature. Difference feminists celebrate emotion, the experiences and capacities of the female body: life against death, nurture against aggression, connectedness against individual self-absorption. A more positive notion of women's difference is contributed to in vastly different ways by the French psychoanalytic tradition (particularly Luce Irigaray), American object-relations theorists, and maternal and eco-feminists.

Now called cultural feminists more often than radical feminists, the difference feminists claimed that women's significant differences from men were usually based on some aspect of their physiology or morphology, and necessarily produced quite different understandings of the world. Thus maternal feminists, who also became involved in peace movements, suggested that women's nurturing and reproductive roles made them more connected and peace-loving than men. Eco-feminists suggested the connections between two male desires: mastering nature and mastering women. Carol Gilligan (1982) claimed that girls used an ethic of care to evaluate moral issues whereas boys used an ethic of justice. Girls wanted to maximise welfare but boys learned to follow universally applied rules. Nancy Chodorow, in *The Reproduction of Mothering* (1978), suggested that the primary importance of the mother as the first figure of socialisation meant that boys became men through separating from their mothers, and women more generally. In the process of separation, boys learned individuality and self-sufficiency, but also contempt for women, hatred of the mother who rejected them (in order for them to learn to become men). Girls remained more connected to their primary care object, another woman, but also learned self-denigration, because being a woman is devalued in patriarchal society.

Minimalists continued to campaign politically in governments as liberal feminists, and in labour movements as marxist feminists, seeking economic and political equality between women and men. Maximalists have contributed to academic feminism's turn away from the world of 'things' to the 'words' about them (Barrett 1992). Academic women's studies are now less preoccupied with issues like access to education and work, women and the state, and more preoccupied with analyses of books and films, studies of the meanings and pleasures of sexuality, femininity and masculinity. This trend towards cultural studies in women's studies has been influenced by two other prospective marriages. The first is the influence of psychoanalysis on feminism, which has explored the pleasures of being female, even if femininity is also constructed as a lack, a failure to be male. These pleasures are now ascribed to activities which radical feminists in the past deplored, for example adorning and eroticising the female body (there has been much discussion of the pop star Madonna here) or sado-masochistic role play in lesbian relationships (e.g. see Seidman 1994:244). This brand of feminism is used most fully to discuss the issues addressed in Chapter 4.

Gynocentric and Postmodern Feminisms

The second major courtship – or challenge – to feminism has come from the various post- discourses: postmodernism, poststructuralism and postcolonialism. Psychoanalysis and postmodernism question the notion of a unitary self-aware subject capable of making unambiguous and universal political and moral choices. This is seen as an underlying premise of the 'liberation' or modernist discourses of liberalism, socialism and feminism. For postmodernists, all the 1970s feminisms are similar to each other under the banner of modernism; it is postmodernism which is the new different other.

Pre-modern societies are characterised (caricatured?) as a decentralised and fragmented plurality of self-sufficient and highly stratified communities. Bound by a dominant religious culture, they still respect social diversity and local traditions (Zygmunt Bauman summarised in Seidman 1994:294–8, 315). In modern societies the intellectual ideas of the Enlightenment and science and educational institutions supplant religion and churches by secular knowledge gained through logic and reason. Increasing urbanisation, the economic forces of capitalism, the political ideas of democracy and the significance of the nation-state link communities so that national identity as citizens displaces community or kin-based identity (Habermas 1987:2). Individual freedoms – of thought, to acquire property and so on – become more significant, described by C. B. MacPherson (in 1962, in Francis 1987:12) as 'possessive individualism':

> The French Revolution with its cry for liberty, equality, fraternity; the philosophical systems of Locke and Rousseau with their emphasis on empiricism and the individual's senses as originary loci of knowledge; the self-absorption of Romanticism and its preoccupation with subjective experience; the economic and political shift from aristocratic to bourgeois power; the progressive tendencies of Darwinism, particularly social Darwinism; the consolidation of the Protestant ideology with its emphasis on the accessibility of God to individual prayer and intercession: all these phenomena coalesced to privilege the self-determining individuality of desire and destiny. (Smith 1993:8–9)

Modernism proposed an historical actor, whose purposive activity would bring about liberal, socialist or feminist transformations. Western feminism is part of this philosophical tradition, drawing on humanism, utilitarianism, marxism and liberal individualism to construct its understanding of (white western) women's place in the world (Sandoval 1991:3; Kishwar 1990:3). Thus when Asian-American feminists note 'an identification of feminist practice with Western culture' (Lazreg 1994:11), they might be pointing to this historical connection as well as their exclusion from much contemporary feminist writing.

For the western middle classes endorsing the rational subject, modernism offered comfortable days of knowing the truth or being blighted by false consciousness, of knowledge uncontaminated by the desires of the unconscious, of universal citizenship unchallenged by civil rights movements or indigenous land rights struggles. Modernists proclaimed their particular culture of rationalism and individualism as universal, as the essential attributes of all people. Some time between the 1940s and the 1980s, however, modernism was overtaken by an array of momentous events and phenomena: the anti-semitism of World War II; colonies clamouring for independence from western powers; the Civil Rights movement in the United States; land rights and other movements by indigenous peoples in Australia, Canada and New Zealand; gay, feminist and environmental social movements; mass migration and global tourism. The idea of progress under the banners of democracy, capitalism or science come unstuck in the face of criticisms from those who have not experienced improvement.

Furthermore, these events questioned the certainties of a *universal*, or even national, human identity. Categories like the individual, class, men and women, were no longer self-evident or sufficient to ground politics and morality. Instead people are trained in 'the technologies of the self' as Michel Foucault put it, techniques by which we construct ourselves, our bodies and our souls. Because we make ourselves, we can also unmake and remake ourselves. We are constituted by conflicting, changing and multiple 'subjectivities' or 'identities' as the self is described in postmodern terms.

Under the weight of this postmodern critique, the fault line dividing feminisms now distinguishes those who endorse a modernist view of humanity (and women) from the post-ists who suggest that 'women' as a category is not obvious but 'normative and political'. The liberal, socialist and radical feminist positions are 'gynocentric' (in Seidman's [1994:253] terms, although Iris Young [1990:74, 79, 85] uses the term differently, to describe difference feminism). Gynocentric feminists maintain an identity for women by virtue of a shared biological, psychological or social experience. For postmodernist feminists, gender is performed (for example Judith Butler's [1990] 'performative theory of gender' summarised in Seidman [1994:252]), as is clearly revealed in parodies of gender performance, like drag, which denaturalise the body (Seidman 1994:253).

In the hands of postcolonial writers like Edward Said, Homi Bhabha, Abdul JanMohamed, Gayatri Spivak (most of whom are academics in European or North American universities), postmodernism becomes post-colonialism, a discourse which attempts to heal the 'epistemic violence (to borrow Spivak's phrase) of imperialism' (Emberley 1993:5). The contradictory experiences of those located between a 'homeland' and western academic privilege, or as fourth world peoples in a first world nation, is particularly explored by the postcolonial writers.

Postcolonial Critiques of Western Feminism

In one sense postmodernism has an appeal for women of ex-colonised nations. The rationality of white western subjects was often defined in opposition to the irrationality and non-subjecthood of the colonised peoples, especially women (Mohanty 1991:32), for example as a backward veiled other confined to the harem or zenana. Sidonie Smith (1993:8) suggests a contradiction at the heart of modernism. While it proposes both a universal rational human subject separated off from the vagaries of personal identity, bodily differences and tradition, it also claims that all individuals are unique. This contradiction was held at bay by the presumption of a neutral, middling subject defined against all that was 'colourful', all that was culturally other: 'exotic, unruly, irrational, uncivilized, regional' (Smith 1993:9). It was to this site, the other which defined the universal subject, that women beyond the pale of white western culture were consigned. Postmodernism denies the authority or truth-claims of a universal subject. It avoids the demand of one-way assimilation: 'bear the chameleon's fate, never infecting *us* but only yourselves' (Trinh Minh-ha in Hatzimanolis 1993:128).

But there are reasons why third world women resist the lure of postmodernism and poststructuralism. In their focus on words rather than things, the post- discourses focus at least as much attention on dis-cussions of rape and poverty as the experiences of those raped or poor; they appear to give equal weight to all kinds of 'resistances'. As Catherine Lutz and Jane Collins (1993:219) tartly observe, some of postmodernism's phrases, like 'semiological guerrillas', imply that 'the same concept should serve for the Chinese student uprising and cable TV grazing'. Post-modernism, while it dethrones western rationalism, also undermines the truth-claims of the ex-colonised that they were and are oppressed because of colour, caste, creed. It undermines their experiences of colonialism: 'Says the victim to the oppressor: Look, I bleed too, when I am pricked or flogged'. Furthermore, humanist universalism has been a crucial element 'in resisting racist colonial discourses' (Ram 1993:24; see also Ram 1991a:94; Mohanty 1991:37). Western academics might use multi-culturalism and postcolonialism to retreat from the new realities of global power, but postcolonial writers who adopt the perspective of those who have been colonised realise the battle is not yet won, colonial is not yet post (Said 1995:6; Patricia Johnston and Leonie Pihama [1994:95] make the same point for Aotearoa/New Zealand). The postmodernist writer Judith Butler (1993:223, 228) argues that 'nigger', perhaps unlike 'queer', has not been reclaimed affirmatively. The term still 'reiterate[s] injury', has not been recontextualised. Thus self-naming is contested by a history of usages, 'usages that one never controlled'. As Aileen Moreton-Robinson (pers. comm. 29 May 1995) suggests, indigenous women can construct their subject position all they like but it will not necessarily shift the dominant discourse.

Certainly some postmodernists are aware that discourses are 'held in place by power' (Marcus 1990:13). Their focus is not on the so-called 'real' conditions of poverty or exploitation, which they claim we can never know anyway, refracted as they are through writings or other representations of them. Rather, postmodernism explores violence and power in language, the conditions by which some aspects and voices are repressed while others are expressed. Thus performative acts issue from locations which have more or less power. The celebrant who says 'I pronounce you man and wife' has greater legal effect than the actor who says it, but the celebrant marrying two homosexuals has less effect than the celebrant marrying a man and woman (Butler 1993:225, 223, 232).

Given the multiple bases for subjectivity and the apparent voluntarism of gender performance, politics becomes a series of alignments and coalitions, based on the practical and local issues at hand. In fact our identity is formed in political intervention: 'We cannot know who we are until we act, and our action always takes place in a particular context of relationship to and dialogue with particular others' (Yeatman 1995:55). Postmodernist activists do not join the labour movement or even the women's movement. They join the local residents' action group along with their Chicana and Aboriginal male and female neighbours. Anglo feminists join with Filipina women's groups to resist sex tours by western males. In the Charlottetown Accord Quebecois and First Nation Canadians formed an alliance to change the Canadian Constitution so that the Quebecois could achieve 'distinct society' status and native communities self-government.[3] Gynocentric feminists find such coalitions are not always easy places to be. How can white women support Aboriginal women's resistance to Aboriginal men's violence without endorsing racist stereotypes of Aboriginal men as peculiarly violent? Should white women speak out against the racism of white working-class women, even understanding that economic oppression exacerbates such attitudes? Is it exploitation when ethnic women are hired as domestic servants so white middle-class women can enter the paid labour force (see Pettman 1991:199; James and Saville-Smith 1989:2; Nain 1991:4 for a discussion of these issues). Such problems of alliances and differences preoccupy this book, and form the specific subject of the concluding section.

OUTLINE OF THE BOOK

> Try being Jewish, female and ugly sometime. You'll beg to be black.
> Excuse my French: brown.
>
> – Rushdie 1988:261

The first chapter discusses some of the key parameters and concepts in the construction of so-called first and third world women, focusing on how racism and race relations have contributed to the production of differences between women of the 'west' and 'east'. We will explore and critique various dualisms, like east and west, south and north, traditional and modern. In order to reconceptualise these differences in a more sophisticated register, we will ask whether colonised women's exposure to colonialism is a story of progress, as western liberalism asserts, or a story of loss of women's traditional status and power, as 'declension narratives' claim. The second section examines the problems encountered when classifying women as belonging to the first, second, third (and fourth or indigenous) worlds. In 'Fracturing Binarisms', various dualisms of self and other, for example civilised and primitive, developed and developing, are criticised. A mere inversion of these dualisms, so that the other becomes good and the self despised, is disrupted in 'Postcolonial Desire'.

Chapter 2 takes up issues associated with liberal feminism, that freedom from oppression is based on an expansion and preservation of individual rights, usually guaranteed in laws. In contrast, some women, for example those from indigenous communities in settler western nations, gain considerable strength from their connection with others and mutual obligations which derive from community roles. The chapter explores whether concepts like freedom, rights and agency can be recast to deal with issues of community and connectedness and whether they are appropriate for discussing the meanings of and political responses to practices like polygamy, infibulation and sati.

Chapter 3 investigates another opposition sometimes found in western feminism: women in the west are wives and women in the non-west are mothers. For many non-Anglo women, motherhood does not symbolise poverty and removal to the private sphere, but bestows a new status and associated powers. Even so, there is evidence that motherhood is experienced differently according to practices like patrilocality, dowry and brideprice. Furthermore, and despite global population policies which often exhort white women to have more children and women of colour to have fewer, women around the world seek access to reproductive choices so they can determine the number of healthy children they have.

Chapter 4, drawing on psychoanalytic and social constructionist theories, explores the argument that sexual identity is both peculiarly important and peculiarly fragile in the west. The ways in which homosexual and lesbian practices, as they are called by Anglo-westerners, are performed in other cultures, especially the category of a 'third gender', throw light on some of the rigidities of western sexual identities. Comparisons are made between pornography in the west and pollution in the east as male mechanisms for handling the 'monstrous feminine', the fear of and contempt for women. The chapter also challenges the claim by western psychoanalytic feminists that mothering practices create men's fear and rejection of women by comparing western mothering with the close mother–son bonds and masculinity in Asian and Latin American cultures. Finally, the argument by some women of colour that western sexual identities are invading and disrupting non-western cultures will be analysed.

Chapter 5 derives largely from 'materialist feminism', a feminism sensitive to global economic inequalities reproduced in international connections between women. Besides the movement of cheap consumer goods and cheap female domestic workers to the west, the phenomenon of mail-order brides and prostitution of women in the Philippines and Thailand is discussed as the most recent variant of an international sexual traffic in women. Aid, apparently a benign force against global economic imbalances, has its own contradictions and messages. The diaspora of women as refugees and migrants produces the doubled vision of migrant women from non-English-speaking backgrounds, a doubled vision which can sharpen the focus of western feminism. Finally, international exchanges (or western dominance) in women's studies and political activism are explored.

The Conclusion focuses on exchanges at feminisms' borders. The vexed question of who can speak for whom in relation to issues of identity, difference and politics is discussed. Some of the ways in which the west appears to be seen in the eyes of the non-west are reviewed. Finally the book asks what kinds of political alliances are possible that both accept our differences and recognise our connections.

CHAPTER

1

Fracturing Binarisms:
First and Third Worlds

●

Not so very long ago, the Earth numbered two thousand million inhabitants: five hundred million *men* and one thousand five hundred million *natives*. The former had the Word; the others merely had the use of it.

– Sartre 1967:7

This chapter begins the over-arching task of this book, to critically investigate the various oppositions by which white western women and 'other' women have been constructed. The first question we will ask is 'Did exposure to western values, western economic and political forms improve the status of women in colonised societies?' Generally the answer has been yes, that colonialism has brought 'modernisation' to the 'backward' others. Against this generally progressive tale, recent histories of colonisation, instead of claiming that missionary women 'uplifted' and improved the status of women in the colonies, offer 'declension narratives'. They point to the power women often had in pre-capitalist societies. Whether against 'ancient matriarchies' or pre-colonial societies, the colonists sought to impose patriarchal structures and values on the colonised peoples.

The second question we will ask is what is the first and third world (and second, fourth and fifth worlds for that matter). Can we neatly classify all the countries of the world into these pigeonholes? If not, why do these terms continue to have salience? Given the western tendency to think in dualisms like third world and first world or backward and modern, the final section explores strategies for disrupting such black and white oppositions. Some writers have merely reversed the evaluative connotations of the former dualisms, so that west = bad and east = good. Such postcolonial desire does not overcome the dualism of east and west. We will explore the limitations of a dualist approach through notions of hybridisation, the ways in which east and west are constructed not only in opposition to each other but in an intermingling of one with the other.

HISTORIES OF COLONIALISM

In the Caribbean, the end of colonial rule meant that to the extent that power changed hands 'it went from white men to black men'.

– Nain 1991:1

Chandra Talpade Mohanty (1991:32, 72, 63) suggests that the histories of third world nations are conceptualised as a universal two-step process. Anthropology deals with a timeless period before contact with the west, in which third world women are 'native' or 'traditional' in their religious beliefs or kin connections. Sociology and politics study 'westernisation' and progress for 'traditional' women through education, legal rights, paid work, access to health services, political participation. In contrast to this liberal analysis is the marxist analysis, not of 'development' but of 'exploitation'. According to marxist theory, colonialism and imperialism are expressions of the forces of capitalism beyond national borders. Capitalist relations spread overseas from Europe, supported first by trading outposts for the purchase of slaves and exotic goods (mercantilism), later by colonial conquest of non-European countries (colonialism). In the contemporary postcolonial era, imperialism means that multinational corporations incorporate lower-paid workers in the ex-colonies into capitalist work structures and pay lower prices for raw materials through trading cartels. Colonialism is based on military force and political occupation, imperialism on economic dominance.

But both marxists and liberals share a commitment to development, by which they mean development in its western forms. Where liberals tend to see capitalism, or a 'free-market economy', as the most efficient form of economic relations, marxists see capitalism as a necessary stage in raising living standards before societies can move on to the more desirable stage of socialism, when economic resources will be shared more equitably.

Declension Narratives

'Declension narratives' (Shoemaker 1991:39) of colonialism reverse the story, claiming that colonised women had status and power which they lost under the white patriarchal rule of colonists, both male and female. The idea of ancient matriarchies, often based on the contemporary existence of matrilineage in many societies, has appeal to women of many cultures. Matrilineage means counting descent through one's mother, and is often associated with greater status for women, but not equality (for example see African matrilineal societies discussed by Ogundipe-Leslie [1992:109, 112]). Analyses of 'Venus' figurines and other archaeological remains in Europe or the three-legged cooking vessels of Neolithic China representing women's breasts have led to imaginings of societies which worshipped the life-giving power of a mother goddess, expressed a commonality between humanity and the natural world and celebrated male and female sexual expression. I say 'imaginings' because there is considerable debate on whether these societies were truly matriarchal (Eisler 1988:1–12, 21; Goodison 1990:108–9; Hayden 1986:25, 27) or whether the Venus figurines actually indicate that such societies respected women's reproductive powers (Nelson 1993:51, 53; Russell 1993:95–6; Hayden 1986:23; see also Simson 1995:144; Sternfeld 1995:3; Lindqvist 1991:206; Niederer 1995:11 for debate on the evidence for ancient matriarchies in China).

In declension narratives, indigenous women in the United States, Australia, Canada and New Zealand had autonomy and roles as explorers, political or spiritual leaders, warriors or horticulturists. They had bodily autonomy and control of their own reproduction and freedom from rape and domestic battery, because men were punished severely for these transgressions. Native American Indians claimed a spirit which pervades everything, variously named Old Spider Woman, Serpent Woman, Corn Woman, Earth Woman, or Hard Beings Woman (Allen 1986:13–14). In the Marquesas Islands in the Pacific, high *tapu* women could take a number of husbands, although women were still abused and beaten by husbands (Thomas 1989:80; Gailey 1996:171 for Tonga attributes women's loss of authority to 'missionary and governmental agendas'). African women were involved in state administration and military defence between 3100 and 2345 BC in various locations (Tomaševski, 1995:1). In Nigeria, under customary law the mother might win custody of her children; under colonial rule this flexibility was abolished for father right (Schmidt 1991:751). (See also Ogundipe-Leslie 1992:109, 112 for the effects of colonialism from Europe and Islam on Africa; Johnston and Pihama 1994:91 for the Maori in New Zealand; Hitchcox 1993:146–8 and Buijs 1993:7, 8 for the displacement of Vietnamese women's pre-eighteenth-century roles 'as war leaders, critics, poets, satirists' by both Chinese Confucianism and French colonialism.) Indigenous men sometimes sided with the colonisers to reduce the autonomy and power of indigenous women, perhaps drawing on a pre-existing masculinist undercurrent in their culture (Allen 1986:32, 38 for the United States; Risseuw 1988:185, 287, 332, 354–5 for Sri Lanka; Ounei 1987:85 for New Caledonia; Awekotuku 1991:68–9 and Ishtar 1994:179, 178 for Aotearoa).

Such 'declension narratives' can never be disproved, given the paucity of historical evidence, all refracted through colonising eyes. Furthermore, such histories smack of the 'politics of blame' as Edward Said calls it, in which the white colonisers are blamed for everything. Today women from colonised cultures are more likely to accept that women have been dominated, if in different ways, both before and after culture contact (Sangari and Vaid 1990:17 for India; Ogundipe-Leslie 1992:107, 110, 109 for Africa). Thus, rather than choosing between the 'either' of tradition and the 'or' of development, women in ex-colonised nations produce hybrid practices which combine elements of each, to which we will return in the last section.

Even so, matriarchal myths can serve a political purpose (as they do for the goddess cultists in the west), a 'rediscovery and renaming' of a golden past which demands a more egalitarian present. Thus a polemical variant of Middle Eastern scholarship posits 'a "golden age" myth of uncorrupted original Islam' through which is articulated indigenous feminism (Kandiyoti 1996:10). Similarly, Indian writers have constructed/recovered an idyllic Vedic period (c. 1700 BC), gentle, truthful, otherworldly, passive and reflective in which women were the spiritual and intellectual equals of men. This was a riposte to European writers like John Stuart Mill who condemned the degenerate civilisation, the 'abject position of Hindu women' and the '"effeminacy" of Hindu men who were unfit to rule themselves' (Chakravarti 1990:35). From the 1860s, the recuperation of India's Aryan glories was imbued with nationalist fervour. Indian men were encouraged to develop militant resistance to British rule, and women to choose 'death rather than ravishment': 'Our men are heroes, our women are chaste' (as one historian wrote, in Chakravarti 1990:52).

Southeast Asia: sex-role complementarity?

Where declension narratives refer to past egalitarian societies, much anthropological literature constructs contemporary Southeast Asia as marked by relatively low sex-role differentiation, particularly the island complex of Malaysia, Western Indonesia and the Philippines, but also Kalimantan and Sumatran societies. Patriarchal elements of Brahmanic, Confucian and Islamic traditions were deflected by local traditions of animism, shamanism and spirit mediumship (Karim 1995:38–40). Women's greater autonomy has been attributed to their prominent economic roles, as traders, entrepreneurs and agricultural workers; their central position in the household; the bilateral reckoning of descent and inheritance including land, meaning that women often own property separately from husbands; matrilocal residence, and now neolocal residence. Sex roles are more fluid, allowing men and women to express themselves in the other's gender roles as long as they conform to the appropriate behaviour for men and women who cross boundaries (Brenner 1995:23–4; Karim 1995:36, 49; Errington 1990:3–4; Peletz 1995:81).

Nevertheless, women without independent incomes or resources are more dependent on their husbands (Karim 1995:49). Furthermore, while women may do things westerners value as signs of power, these are not always so valued in Southeast Asian cultures. In western terms, women may be powerful; in Southeast Asian terms they may not. Thus power is seen as economic control and coercive force in Euro-America, while in many parts of island Southeast Asia power is conceived as spiritual rather than economically based, and derives from uncontested acceptance of superior status (Errington 1990:5–7, 42–3). In Thailand women may be central in self-entrepreneurial activity but not in public decision-making, perhaps because Buddhism accords greater value to men (Karim 1995:55). In Java women lose prestige (already possessing less by virtue of being women) because commercial activities require forms of address and behaviour and breaches of linguistic etiquette which lower status (Brenner 1995:25–7). On the other hand the dominant discourses which attribute more spiritual refinement or more reason to men are undercut by everyday discourses, in the mouths of both men and women. Thus it is claimed that men have little self-control in matters of money and sex (Brenner 1995:37; Karim 1995:59 for Vietnam; Hobart 1995:138 for Bali), a claim which may be used to justify greater property inheritance to women, especially as their needs are greater, given men's laziness and women's responsibility for children (Peletz 1995:88–107).

Colonial governments started the process of undercutting gender complementarity, but it has been continued by post-independence governments. Husbands have displaced senior women as household heads (Blackwood 1995:140–2 for the Minangkabau villagers of Indonesia); men more than women have access to paid work and consumer goods, apart from defiling sex work (Klein-Hutheesing 1995:76, 90–3 for the tribal enclaves throughout the region and Stivens 1996:2–3, 6–7, 11, 17–18, 27, 229 for the Minangkabau culture in the Malaysian state of Negeri Sembilan). Maila Stivens notes that women themselves have acted politically to protect their property rights, to participate in the reconstitution of matriliny out of the history of customary law, and in response to the actions of colonial and postcolonial governments. She also notes that women complain of the burdens of housework and childcare, suggesting that while men might claim to value women's reproductive roles, the claim is not enough to make them share these tasks.

Three brief case studies of colonisation will reveal the different ways that tradition and modernity are blended by women in their political struggles. Colonisation is more than an imposition of structures and values by the colonising power. It is responded to differently by various segments of the colonised population, supporting Mohanty's (1991:15) claim that each ex-colonial nation has a different history, that colonialism cannot be reduced to a two-step process from backwardness to modernisation. China was finally transformed by a socialist revolution, Japan by its own adoption of capitalist economic relations, and India by one of the longest periods of western colonial rule before its independence in 1947.

Case Studies

• India

India is described as achieving 'full flower under the Mauryas in the fourth century BC', then succumbing to a series of invasions followed by a renaissance under the Guptas in the fourth and fifth centuries AD (Inden 1990:54). Muslim dynasties from Afghanistan and Turkistan occupied the Punjab in the tenth century, extending to Delhi by 1192; the Mogul Empire spread to a large part of the Indian subcontinent from the middle of the sixteenth century (Jayawardena 1986:74). European traders and missionaries established themselves on the west coast from the end of the fifteenth century, the British East India Company and the British Army gradually extending its control across India and ousting its rivals, a process largely completed by 1823. In 1858, following the Indian Mutiny, the rule of the East India Company was replaced with direct British rule. In the nineteenth century the forces of Anglicisation promoted the creation of a middle-class private sphere, drawing both on Victorian notions of purity and the homebound nature of women and on a revived Indian traditionalism which posited women as 'embodiments of that inner spirituality which lay at the core of national identity' (Banerjee 1990; Sinha 1994:7; Mohanty 1991:20).

The Indian National Congress, formed in 1885, allowed women to become members. Its leaders and followers engaged in a range of resistance activities, for example boycotts of foreign goods and other mass actions of civil disobedience, like the Salt March in 1931 advocated by Gandhi (who took over the leadership of the Congress in 1915). Women were leaders in boycotts against alcohol and foreign goods, donating money and jewellery, to the cause and bursting 'into this fierce light of open warfare'. Male nationalists, pioneered by Raja Rammohan Roy (1772–1833), advocated the abolition of 'certain dreadful practices' like sati and polygamy as well as women's education and property rights (Jayawardena 1986:78, 81). While Gandhi maintained that women and men had equal intellectual capacities, he attributed to women greater nobility which was realised through their silent suffering and humility. For Gandhi, women should occupy a separate sphere from men, that of the home. A two-century struggle against British rule culminated in 1947, when the Indian subcontinent achieved independence, partitioned into India (predominantly Hindu) and Pakistan (predominantly Muslim). The first prime minister, Jawaharlal Nehru, believed that women's independence must be economically based, advocating both full access to education and work outside the home (Jayawardena 1986:95–6, 97–8).

Despite opposition to practices like child marriage and sati from Indian nationalists (including Gandhi's articles opposing child marriages) and the

Women's Indian Association (Sinha 1994:23), it was Katherine Mayo's popular text *Mother India*, published in 1927, which received wide discussion in Britain and the United States. Mayo was 'expressly recruited by a defensive colonial government in India' and served them proud with sensationalist and deceptive portrayals of Indian practices. In reply, several Indian male writers did a hatchet job on United States customs, describing rape, prostitution, venereal disease, lynching by the Ku Klux Klan, practices in Chicago slaughterhouses, American 'sati' which roasts women on the electric chair, and 'the college co-ed from Denver who "sold her soul for a fraternity pin"'. Images of the western woman as either sex-obsessed or a sex-starved spinster (Mayo's unmarried status was frequently commented on by her Indian critics) also circulated (Jayawardena 1995:97). While European women like Annie Besant and Margaret Cousins condemned *Mother India*, if not the practices it described, this example illustrates both how many European women ascribed a barbaric status to oriental women and were ignorant of Indian women's activism, which dated back to the early nineteenth century (Steady 1992:96).

According to Barbara Ramusack (1990:319), 'maternal imperialism' characterised the relations between British and Indian women between the 1870s and the 1930s. Indian women were treated as daughters, or at best younger sisters, even though these 'little sisters' were in many cases women with university degrees (Sinha 1992:109). Josephine Butler could see the common oppression of Indian and British women under the Contagious Diseases Acts (which operated in both countries to allow the compulsory detention of suspected prostitutes): 'Remember them that are in bonds, as being bound with them'. But she also described Indian women as 'helpless, voiceless, hopeless' (quoted in Ware 1992:155–9). From the 1930s, white women's participation in Indian women's struggle was increasingly anachronistic. Thus in 1934 Eleanor Rathbone's offer of support and funds to combat child marriage was debated, and refused (although not unanimously), by the All-India Women's Conference, a new generation of leaders feeling they did not need advice or support from British suffragists (Jayawardena 1995:152, 102, 103, 266).

• China

China has been seen by orientalists as a civilisation which took its fundamental shape in the Han dynasty of the third century BC, unfolded 'ever so slowly' after that, until it eventually fell 'way "behind" the West' (Inden 1990:54). In fact the influence of Buddhism, brought back from India, and of Confucianism had significant impacts on women in China. From the first half of the fourth century women became Buddhist nuns, a retort to the Confucian obligation to obey parents and later husbands. Many nuns were consulted by emperors and empresses on matters of state. The influence of the nuns declined with the 'sinicization of Buddhism' after the Tang Dynasty (Lee 1994:49, 58, 6).

In certain periods before the thirteenth century, women could readily divorce their husbands, there was no foot-binding, widows could remarry, and extramarital dalliances were celebrated (Hinsch 1995:22). However, from the Song Dynasty (960–1279), Neo-Confucianism, or the revival of Confucianism with its 'tenet that man is superior and woman is inferior' (Lee 1994:12), celebrated women who cut off their ears or killed themselves rather than face the shame of surviving rape or widowhood (Hinsch 1995:22, 26; Carlitz 1994:115; Lee 1994:23). But the fact that many women began their education with the _Four Books for Women_, points to women's growing literacy, a concurrent and contrary development which gradually encouraged more equal relations between husbands and wives (Lee 1994:7; Ropp 1993:108). Thus the debate among Chinese women writers about injustices against women preceded the arrival of western missionaries and traders in the nineteenth and twentieth centuries.

The major 'modernising' (or westernising) trend, especially in the arts, is known as the May Fourth Movement of 1919, revealing a need, according to Rey Chow (1991a:72), to 'domesticate' and humanise the power revealed by western invasion and technology, especially in the foreign 'concessions'[1] in Shanghai, Guangzhou and elsewhere. Thus changes in women's status, for example 'companionate marriages' (marrying for love), the abolition of foot-binding and the training of girls to become teachers and doctors, were debated and pursued by female mission teachers, male Chinese reformers like Kang Youwei and Liang Qichao, as well as Chinese women themselves (Graham 1994:34, 35; Lee 1994:7; Ch'en 1992:65; Hoe 1991:228 for Chinese women in Hong Kong). For example, after 1900 mission schools began barring entrance to girls with bound feet unless they were willing to remove their bindings. Chinese officials made the same ruling for entry to government schools in 1907, when public education for girls was inaugurated (Graham 1994:39). Foot-binding thus disappeared fairly quickly, hastened by the Communist Revolution and the fact it was less common in the south where the practice prevented women from transplanting rice in muddy fields (Blake 1994:703–6). The rapid demise of foot-binding in China makes an instructive comparison with infibulation and the re-emergence of sati, to be discussed in the next chapter.

At the turn of the century, although feminism was still tightly bound to patriotism, women students returning from Japan combined with mission-educated women at home to fight against oppression and for equal rights, 'their most illustrious representative' being Qiu Jin (Lee 1994:7). By 1927, International Women's Day demonstrations in

Guangzhou drew 25 000 women and men. When civil war broke out, young women activists, identifable by their bobbed hair, were killed by Chiang Kai-shek's troops, some bound in cotton blankets and burned. Under the Nationalists' influence, the new woman was redefined as having 'new knowledge but old character' (Rowbotham 1992:212–13). With the victory of the Communists in 1949 (over the Nationalists, who retreated to Taiwan), most activist women felt obliged to subordinate their feminist goals to the 'larger' struggle of the revolution (Honig 1992:123).

Since Liberation in 1949, a commitment to women's equality has been part of the communist ideology of progress. Mao Zedung asserted that women were traditionally bound by four thick ropes – political, clan, religious and masculine authority (Jayawardena 1986:192). Because male peasants could not afford a bride, he advocated cohabitation in the commune of Jiangxi. But the risks to women convinced the Party to retreat to a position of sexual puritanism. The women who participated in the Long March, recruiting peasant women by helping with the household chores and 'speaking bitterness' over their common grievances (Rowbotham, 1992:214), did not achieve the high status in communist China that the male long-marchers achieved. After 1949 they were moved out of commanding positions in the army to 'civilian jobs', 'ceremonial roles' or 'work with children', even when they had expressed the desire to stay in the army (Rowbotham 1992:213–14; Simson 1995:146–7; Lee 1994:87).

Official understandings of women's role continue to contrast a feudal barbaric past with a progressive present, even if also deploying ancient matriarchy myths (or 'primitive communism' in marxist discourse), at least until fairly recently (Sternfeld 1995:7). The last decade, however, has seen a steady decrease in women's participation at all political and managerial levels and increasing confinement to health and family planning at the grassroots level. Economic reforms since 1979 have been accompanied by increased discrimination against women in hiring and promotion. Women are seen as 'troublesome' because of pregnancy and the expectation that they will care for elderly relatives, and advertisements asking only for male applicants are common (Wang 1991:177–8). Given these contemporary pressures, a number of my students at the Beijing Foreign Studies University were cynical about the gains won by Liberation. For example, when I spoke about Mao's concern to cut the four ropes binding Chinese women, my students told me that Mao did not live by this rule himself – a comment confirmed by Li's (1994) biography of Mao, detailing his sexual exploits with hundreds of young party women.

• Japan

Japan has been described as a country located 'between the imperializing Subject and the colonized Other' (Caplan 1991:321). Economic 'development' was not enforced by western invasion but chosen by the new rulers under the Meiji Restoration. But this too was a declension narrative, women losing traditional freedom and power, for example in the Muromachi age beginning in 1336 (Iwao 1993:5). The Tokugawa Shogunate, from the twelfth to the nineteenth centuries, imposed a strict four-caste system with the ruling samurai or warrior caste at its head. While the fundamental obligation of a respectable married woman was to produce heirs, women who were not members of wealthy households could take up many roles, including geishas or professional entertainers, entrepreneurs, Buddhist nuns, barren wives, wilful daughters-in-law, artists supported by their natal families. Teenage girls and mothers-in-law were free to travel to shrines and visit their kin, while by the early nineteenth century investment in daughters' education was seen to enhance a wealthy peasant family's status (Walthall 1991:480, 65–6, 49; Bernstein 1991:4–6).

The Meiji period (1868–1912) defeated the Tokugawa regime and constructed an even more centralised nation-state. It introduced compulsory universal education in which girls were schooled in the arts of womanhood (Nolte and Hastings 1991:158), abolished feudal privileges, and promoted industrialisation by introducing technology and work practices from overseas. To purify western values and synthesise them with the Japanese world, the Meiji rulers adopted Chinese Confucianism's emphasis on women's obedience to husbands and seniors, which now became more important than the previous commitment to producing heirs. In fact Confucian ideology discouraged mothers from participating too actively in their children's upbringing as it was felt women lacked the necessary moral qualities. In poorer families, however, both men and women continued to lavish attention on their children, as well as taking an interest in shopping and household chores (Rosenberger 1992:11–12; Uno 1991:30–3).

Japanese women are still addressed with the cross-class term 'Good Wife, Wise Mother' (ryōsai kenbo) which emerged as industrialism progressed. But the wise mother was not confined to the home, as was advocated for her English counterpart at about the same time. The textile industry, which produced 40 per cent of gross national product, had a workforce that was 60 to 90 per cent female (Bernstein 1991:7; Nolte and Hastings 1991:153, 158, 173). On the other hand, the right of some women to vote before the Meiji period was abolished and, indeed, women were not allowed to attend political meetings until 1922 or join political parties until 1945. From the 1910s in particular, Japanese women criticised the Meiji conception of womanhood, arguing for women's political and economic rights and more stridently for state support for women with children (Walthall 1991:69; Nolte and Hastings 1991:155; Rodd 1991:189). With the emergence of militant feminist groups in the 1920s and 1930s, the press responded with the 'Modern Girl', a woman who threatened traditional Japanese values with western clothes and perverse sexuality (Silverberg 1991:258–64). In contrast with women's role in the Sino-Japanese war, by World War II women were no longer urged to work in armaments factories or serve as nurses on the battlefield, but rather were to contribute by producing children (Miyake 1991:268).

Kazuko Tanaka's (1995) description of Japanese feminism's emergence from the 1960s presents an almost western textbook case. Women returned to the workforce from the 1960s but noticed that this did not improve their social status significantly; they were disillusioned with the New Left movements, whose leaders discriminated against women. Like western women, Japanese women turned to consciousness-raising to help women develop a clear self-identity, with sexual liberation as its focus (distributing information about contraception and the female body). In 1974 the feminist movement successfully lobbied against a proposed revision to the Eugenic Protection Law which aimed at prohibiting abortions for economic reasons (Tanaka 1995:347). An International Women's Year Action Group was formed in 1975 and the movement shifted from consciousness-raising to changing social institutions, focusing on health and reproductive rights, discrimination at work, childcare, challenges to the marriage system, combating sexism in the media with feminist publications, protest against war and environmental exploitation, ageing, violence against women and sexual harassment. From the 1980s women's studies emerged, soon followed by the debate over whether it was relevant to all women or appropriated by academic women.

Despite their almost equal levels of education compared with men, Japanese women's participation in politics and management remains low. On 'the most generous measure' women occupied 2.2 per cent of managerial positions in 1989, although, as in western countries, women were better represented as the owners of small businesses, particularly clothing retailers and restaurants but also road construction companies (Steinhoff and Tanaka 1994:86, 89). However, the requirement that Japanese working women serve tea, even to more junior male colleagues, is being replaced by the rule that junior male employees serve tea to senior female executives. Japanese women engage in adult education, local politics and even go out to bars and taverns with other women, something women 'never did in the past' (Iwao 1993:7, 204–6, 272, 101).

These three case histories show that women's movements in colonial times had to work out their relationship with coterminous national independence movements. Indigenous elites often proclaimed their right to independence because they had become civilised in western terms. They were committed to industrialisation, modernisation and democracy, and condemned the practices of a 'savage' past, for example widow-burning, veiling, polygamy, concubinage, foot-binding (Jayawardena 1986:9). Women were often divided over appropriate tactics and alliances with the nationalist movement, especially given the wavering of many nationalists or their claims that the woman question could wait until after the revolution when the 'larger issues' had been settled (Sangari and Vaid 1990:15; Chakravarti, 1990:73). Nevertheless, women participated in national independence movements, and through their alliances with nationalist struggles won the vote, the right to an education or to some of the legal rights enjoyed by men (Jayawardena 1986:12, 41). These rights were not inconsequential, even where framed in terms of women's role as mothers rather than autonomous citizens, an issue discussed further in Chapter 3.

These studies reveal that colonised women were not passive recipients of western feminism or indigenous nationalism. But neither did they refuse all that colonisation demanded, taking and remaking some of its aspects as opportunities (see also Schmidt 1991:749 for Nigeria and Forman 1984:163–4 for the Pacific). We might ask, however, who is writing these colonial histories. Where Adrienne Rich (1984:282) excuses white women in the American slave-holding south as 'impressed into its service', Bell Hooks (1981:124) (who has written under her name Gloria Watson as well as that of her great-grandmother bell hooks) argues that white women merely lacked the opportunity, but not the desire, to be racist. Rich's and Hooks's history of American slavery would thus be vastly different. Besides ethnic identity, theoretical perspective and time of writing also have their influence on the stories told. Nguia te Awekotuku (1991:45), from a radical feminist perspective, says of New Zealand women's struggle to become the first country in the world with female suffrage that 'feminists had to put up a fight to convince the reformers that Maori women equally merited the privilege'. But the price of this collaboration with the Women's Christian Temperance Union, according to Ripeka Evans (1994:56), was acceding to eurocentric rules which embodied 'an assortment of pious demands'. One can see why postmodernists, as well as many other scholars, despair of telling 'truths' about the world, and focus on the role of perspective and position in producing texts. One can also see why writers like Mohanty call on historians of colour to write their own histories rather than have them written for them by (even sympathetic) white feminists.

Modernisation and Tradition: Histories of the Veil

In contrast with the Indian and Chinese case studies, not all nationalist leaders advocate modernisation as the rationale for independence and a sign of progress. Others align nationalism with a return to 'authentic' pre-colonial traditions which are seen as unchanging and almost unconscious. In this case, too, women are the standard-bearers of the nation's culture. It is often *only* women, and not men, who are commanded to uphold tradition. By putting women back in their place (veiled, obedient to father, husband, or son, publicly punished even unto death for presumed sexual transgressions or expressions), men seek to put the world back in order, safe and secure despite rapid changes and economic disorder.[2] Women who refuse to 'return' to 'tradition' are attacked as the dupes of imperialism, manifested as western feminism. But tradition is a slippery term. In riposte to demands that women stop smoking, drinking and wearing trousers, the Iranian feminist Azar Tabari (in French 1992:98) notes that American Indians traditionally smoked tobacco, Hayyam's poetry describes 'a cup of wine and thou' and Iranian hinterland women wear trousers (as do Punjabi women).

Such alignments of women as the protectors of tradition are not confined to the so-called third world. In the west, the revival of Christian fundamentalism expresses anxieties produced by capitalism in crisis and the concurrent disruption of traditional gender roles amplified by the feminist movement (Hawley and Proudfoot 1994:27). But fundamentalist interpretations are not the dominant currency which constructs women in the west. Rather white western women are positioned as liberated in comparison with tradition-bound women of other countries. As Indrani Ganguly (pers. comm. July 1995 in response to a draft of this book) notes, 'not so long ago, our grandmothers were being told that they were immoral because they did not cover up as much as their English contemporaries'. When western women were 'civilised' Victorians because they covered up, exposure was deemed barbaric. Today, the covered veiled woman has replaced the exposed woman as the signifier of the 'other' indicating western woman's superiority. This positioning of self and other is exemplified in the contrasting Gulf War images of the female American tank driver and the veiled Saudi woman who is forbidden by law from acquiring a driver's licence. But there are Saudi women who are university-educated, who have founded women-only banks or who practise medicine in women-only hospitals, while Kuwaiti women have organised neighbourhood-level protests against the occupying Iraqi army (Lazreg 1994:2; Enloe 1993:170–1). This brings us to the role of the veil in defining Arab nationalism.

Like Asian feminisms, Arab feminism has a history of interacting with feminists in imperialist metropolises and of articulating a relationship with nationalist political movements (see Badran and Cooke 1990; Afarq 1992; Nelson 1992; Lazreg 1994). Activist women have addressed the issue of veiling, but not with nearly the energy 1970s western feminists might have recommended.

It is claimed that the custom of veiling arises from the Qur'an's injunction that the believers are to 'cast down their eyes ... and reveal not their adornment save such as is outward; and let them cast their veils over their bosoms' (Lateef 1990:77). This does not clearly enjoin women to wear the full veil, and indeed requires men also to cast down their eyes. Thus Iranian Islamic feminists have recommended that both men and women should wear simple clothing which covers the body in a non-arousing fashion (Paidar 1996:61). In fact veiling is not practised by all Muslim[3] women; even in one location it may vary between a fashionable turban and head-to-toe coverings. Historically and geographically, then, the veil has different forms. It also has different meanings. The veil can liberate women from the 'dictates of male fashion' (Jones 1993:118), while offering 'a truly erotic culture' as an alternative to pornography (as one British Muslim scholar suggests, in Brooks 1995:21). Many wealthy Gulf State women, however, appear to spurn eroticism and follow the dictates of fashion in the domestic space. For example, Geraldine Brooks (1995:12) writes that the wife of the Ayatollah Khomeini hennaed her hair. Where veiling is practised, it supposedly offers women protection when they enter the public sphere (MacLeod 1992:543; see also Jones 1993:118 for Australia). But the veil does not always exempt women from male attention, although wearers claim that a veiled woman can express justified outrage in the face of men's comments and touches which she would invite if unveiled (Odeh 1993:28–9). The veil might also express urban lifestyles and escape from the village where veiling is less common or disguise a lower-class background in universities, by covering women's cheap clothes (Chapkis 1994b:233; Shukrallah 1994:28).

According to Marnia Lazreg (1994:53), colonisation in Algeria meant that men perceived themselves as 'reduced to the social status of women' while women were reduced from decent Muslims to immoral prostitutes used by the French. 'The veil became women's refuge from the French denuding gaze'. During the revolutionary war against French rule, Algerian women 'moved in and out of the veil, as actresses playing roles in different costumes' (Lazreg 1994:127), blending with veiled Algerian women in the market or unveiled school students in French-speaking classrooms. When the French tied unveiling to acceptance of French rule (for example in 1958), Algerian women began to veil and reveil, not as a sign of religious faith so much as 'an instrument for political action ... under which and out of which women and men alike carried out paramilitary assignments' (Lazreg 1994:135). While the Constitution of 1976 guaranteed women some equal rights, in 1984 a family code was passed that institutionalised the unequal status of women in matters of personal autonomy, divorce, polygamy and custody of sons. This was despite the war veterans' appeal to the President of the Republic, Algerian women believing they had earned their rights by participating in the liberation of Algeria (Lazreg 1994:140, 150–6). Today women still wear the *hijab* as a rejection of the persisting influence of French colonialism and western ideas, but more are defining it as a sign of religious readiness, an indication of personal religious commitment (Lazreg 1994:218–19). In

1994 the Islamic Armed Group posted signs on Algiers walls warning women to wear the *hijab* or risk death: two students were subsequently gunned down at a bus stop for not wearing it (Lazreg 1994:222).

The rapid succession of meanings for veiling is also exemplified in Iran's recent history. Under the Shah, women removed their veils as a sign of his modernisation program. As opposition to the Shah's terrorist regime mounted, wearing the veil became an expression of this resistance. Since the institution of an Islamic state, posters and slogans in Iran remind women that the honour of the nation depends on them: 'Lack of coverture is the extreme of westernization, and westernization is the extreme of prostitution!'; 'A wife's uncoveredness is a husband's lack of dignity!' (in Shahidian 1991:27). In 1979 Khomeini had Farrokhrou Parsa (the first woman member of the Iranian cabinet) wrapped in a sack and machine-gunned; she had directed schoolgirls not to veil and had established a commission to produce a non-sexist curriculum (French 1992:65). Mal-veiling (bright colours instead of dark or failure to cover the hair completely) attracts a lashing and imprisonment for up to 25 months (Shahidian 1991:28). Today, then, veiling demonstrates submission to a new nationalist state (Hélie-Lucas 1990:107; Hendessi 1991:71–8), although not all women who believe veiling is a 'mark of decency' are uncritical of Khomeini's interpretation of Islam (de Groot 1996:44). Indeed, Islamic feminists, like evangelical Victorian feminists, have reinterpreted religion to challenge their subordination. Initially silenced, Islamic feminists from the late 1980s have campaigned more openly for women's rights, taking up issues of state remuneration for housewives, monogamy, automatic custody rights for mothers and protection against divorce without the wife's consent (Paidar 1996:60–2).

In 1990 Islamicist activists in Gaza launched a campaign against women in western attire through slogan-writing, throwing stones at women and calling from mosques. They called for women to wear a headscarf as a sign of respect for martyrs. This campaign was reversed by the activism of women's committees, which forced the underground leadership to issue a condemnation (Jad 1995:241, 243). In Malaysia, too, the Islamic revival has been checked by counteracting currents, not the least of which come from the state.

The veiling movement in Malaysia largely affected women in secondary and tertiary education institutions. Some older women criticised younger women's veiling as 'excessive', while rural women remained in their traditional Malay attire. Commencing in 1970, veiling reached its peak in the mid-1980s. While women in 'cloistered dormitories' could be supervised by their classmates, it was more the anxiety they faced entering roles where few women had gone before, afraid they would be priced out of the marriage market by their education (Ong 1995:160–73). Islam offered sure rules in a world made uncertain by economic development, decadent secularism and the excesses of western feminism. Malay women gained ethnic confidence, especially with the rising political and economic ascendancy of the Middle East. Many young women adopted the veil overseas as a retort to western feminism's devaluation of the nurturant wife-mother role. This ironic status reversal proudly threw the image of the 'colonised oriental woman' in the face of western women's caricature of her (Nagata 1995:104–13). By 1990, however, as Aiwha Ong (1995:160) puts it, the black-and-white photographs of Malay campuses had become full colour with pastel robes, embroidered headcloths, discreet jewellery and accessories. The veil had become 'groovy' and fashionable (Nagata 1995:112).

The government condemned full *purdah*, or extensive covering of the face as well as the hair, which is forbidden in many government and private offices and all Malaysian universities, a woman being dismissed for wearing full *purdah* to work (Karim 1995:41; Nagata 1995:110). Thus the state battled with the Muslim authorities, not only over veiling but also family planning and the need for women to enter the industrial sector (Ong 1995:161, 169–73).

These stories reveal that the veil, or any other symbol, does not carry a single unvarying message, even at the same moment. The Cairo woman who feels secure in her veil only requires that security because of the meaning of an unveiled woman. The women who resist the veil in Iran only need to do so because the veil has become so strongly associated with compliant and compulsory femininity. Just as western feminists make political statements when they choose between overalls and shoulder-padded suits, so too do Arab women, often with more dire consequences. They contest politics in the medium of style or the mundane practices of everyday life, and perhaps only with a stray strand of hair (Comaroff 1985:196; Mohanty 1991:38; Odeh 1993:27; Yeganeh 1993:15 for Iran).

In exploring some of the narratives which have constructed and opposed colonising and colonised women, we have set the groundwork for the claim that we cannot readily divide the world into traditional and modern or east and west. We have seen that colonisation has left its mark in the practices and values adopted by women in the former colonised nations; in the final section of this chapter we will see how western women's ideas of themselves are constructed through images of the colonised other. Let us turn first, however, to a critique of the most widely used contemporary classification of international women: first versus third world, worlds once held apart by the now disintegrated second world.

CLASSIFYING WOMEN'S WORLDS: FIRST, SECOND, THIRD?

What the so-called third world nations have in common is their post-colonial status, their relative poverty, their largely tropical locations, their largely non-Caucasian population, and the fact that they were once subjected to Western rule.

– Garber 1992a:11

The term 'third world' originally signified a 'third force' of non-aligned nations which would wedge themselves between the Cold War opposition of first world 'democracy' and second world 'communism' (Longley 1992:20). The second world has been variously defined as the Soviet Union, in which case it has now disappeared, or the communist countries, in which case it is reduced to a clutch of countries like Cuba, China, Burma, Vietnam and North Korea, countries which are often assimilated into the third world. On the whole, it would appear that women's status has deteriorated in post-USSR countries. Rising unemployment for women has been attributed to the imposition of capitalist economic rationales (which suggest that women are less desirable because more costly workers, for example because they take maternity leave). The reassertion of patriarchal claims that women should become home-makers and spiritual guardians of the nation has been embraced by many women, happy to relinquish the crippling double shift of paid labour and domestic duties, made longer by food shortages, inflation, and the fact that communist notions of women's equality rarely applied to shared household labour and protection from violence. Nascent and on the whole tiny feminist movements are tarred with the brush of both socialism and western feminism. Instead women of eastern Europe have been urged to recapture their femininity with a 'return to the home, the kids, the knitting and sewing', often combined with state urgings to have more children (Petrova 1994:268–9).[4]

In those countries which still call themselves communist, women's movements are often mass movements, but they are also linked closely with the communist party. The Federation of Cuban Women, founded in 1960, claims a membership of about 80 per cent of all Cuban women over 14 years old. Until recently it has focused exclusively on issues like education, public health projects, job training, and support of combatants' families rather than gender-specific issues like battery, rape and abortion. Similarly, in Nicaragua the Asociación de Mujeres Nicaragüenses Luisa Amanda Espinosa (AMNLAE), although neither autonomous from the Sandinista hierarchy nor a truly feminist movement, has taken up controversial issues like abortion (which remains illegal), men's support of children after separation, and participation in housework (Randall 1994:24–30).

Trinh Minh-ha (1987:17), quoting commentators like Julia Kristeva on communist China, suggests that the third world still has the positive resonance of a subversive, immense repressed voice about to burst into centre stage of the globe, supported perhaps by the increasing presence of the Southeast Asian economies, now the fastest growing in the world. 'Third world', however, generally signifies 'backward', 'poor' or 'developing' nations, which Trinh Minh-ha (1993:168) contests with her notion of the 'overdeveloping' nations of the west (instead of the 'underdeveloped' nations of the third world). Extending this definition based on deprivation, some commentators describe a 'fourth' and 'fifth' world of women, disadvantaged women who live in the nations of the west. The fourth world consists of indigenous peoples in settler societies in North America and Australia, while the fifth world consists of migrants dispossessed of their heritage (Longley, 1992:20) (migrant women's dialogues with domestic feminism will be explored in Chapter 5). However, the colonisation of South America was also based on the dispossession of the indigenous populations, creating fourth world peoples in these 'third world' countries. Expulsion and genocide was greatest in southern countries like Argentina; in northern countries like Peru, the mestizo, or mixed-race Spanish and Indian people, control politics and the economy to the detriment of indigenous people like the Quechua. In contemporary Latin America, Indian women are sterilised without consent, beg for food in marketplaces, work as maids and have low literacy levels. In fact there are fourth world peoples in almost every corner of the globe, for example in Hokkaido in northern Japan, the minorities around the fringes of China, and the tribal people of India.

The third world has also been described as the 'two-thirds' world, a reference possibly both to the collapse of the second (communist) world and to the fact that at least two-thirds of the world's population live in countries with low average per capita incomes (for example United Nations 1991:12, xiii suggests that more than three-quarters of the world's women live in 'developing' regions). The term 'two-thirds' world focuses on the fact that a majority of women live 'beyond the west' and seeks to displace the pejorative connotations of 'third world'.

The third world is a category produced and reproduced by capitalist imperialism, referred to in the oppositions between industrialised north and developing south, or core and periphery. Powerful global agencies like the United Nations, the World Bank and the International Monetary Fund make distinctions between the first and third worlds which determine global economic policies. The political projects of institutions such as the Central Intelligence Agency and alliances between governments are also shaped by the identification of third world nations. However, and even for these powerful agencies, the third world contains anomalies which are quietly excluded from the all-embracing classification. The IMF does not

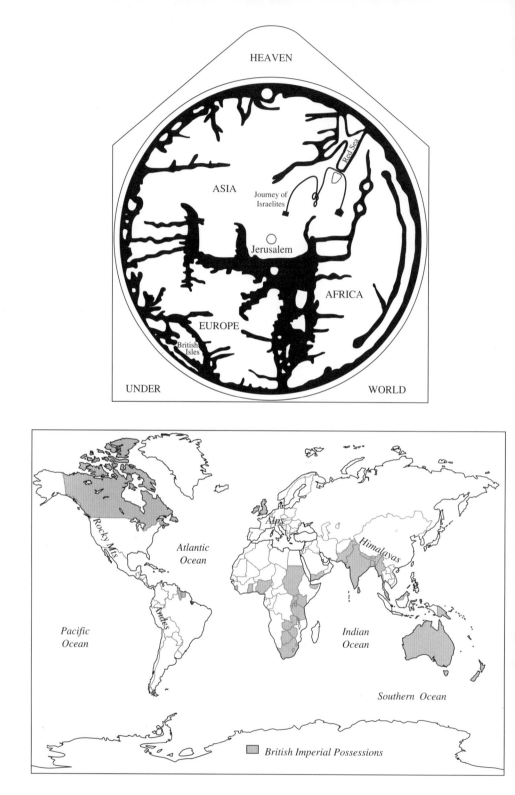

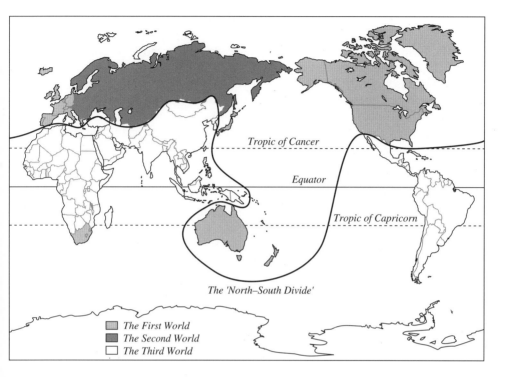

Images of the world from the Middle Ages to the twentieth century. The medieval world picture reveals the significance of Christianity in ordering the world. The Holy City of Jerusalem is at the centre of the world. Asia, Africa and Europe are clustered around it and bounded by heaven and the underworld. By the late nineteenth century, Europeans conceived of the world in more political terms. The imperial world picture shows the 'possessions' which make up the British Empire. Britain as the 'owner' of the colonies is at the centre of the map. By the post-World War II years, decolonisation had shifted the focus of classification to economics. In the postcolonial world picture, third world countries are those viewed as 'poor' and 'underdeveloped', as compared with first world countries, and to a considerable extent second world countries (which are European). Thus China and Cuba should be classified in the second world (as communist) in political terms, but are classified in the third world because they are 'underdeveloped'.

Sources and acknowledgements. Medieval world picture from a simplified sketch based on the *mappa mundi* at Hereford Cathedral, England. Imperial world picture from a simplified version of a school atlas produced for English schoolchildren in the late nineteenth century, in Denis E. Cosgrove, *Social Formation and Symbolic Landscape*, London and Sydney: Croom Helm, 1984, p. 7. Postcolonial world picture adapted from Andrew Webster, *Introduction to the Sociology of Development* Basingstoke, UK: Macmillan Press Ltd, 1986.

tell the Japanese government how to spend its budget. The World Bank is not offering loans to the OPEC Gulf States, Kuwait's per capita income being the highest in the world in 1982 (Fakhro 1990:38). Even though their per capita income is now lower (Bello and Rosenfeld 1990:301), New Zealanders and Australians have not yet become the recipients of aid from the generous citizens of Singapore. And not only western countries have been imperialist aggressors. In its long history of foreign influence and occupation, Korea adopted Confucianism from China during the Chosun Dynasty (1393–1910) and was forcibly occupied by Japan in 1910. Similarly, East Timor was occupied by the Portuguese, the Japanese and the Dutch before its present occupation by Indonesia, which includes systematic bombings and transmigration aimed at matching the numbers of East Timorese with Javanese (Franks 1996:161–3).

Perhaps the greatest challenge to the contrast between first and third world is provided by the no longer Newly Industrialising Countries of Asia: South Korea, Taiwan, Singapore and Hong Kong (at least before 1997 when it returned to mainland China). As a result of high per capita incomes, Hong Kong, Taiwan and Singapore (and the Gulf States) participate in guest worker schemes characteristic of European countries. Japanese feminists identify the benefits they gain from 'the exploitation of other Asian women', 'as do the women of the United States' (Yayori Matsui in Rowbotham 1992:267). Economic superiority is expressed in a racist register by non-white as well as white nations. Indigenous people in Guam accuse the Japanese corporations of being no less racist than white imperialists, bulldozing ancestral bones for a hotel (Ishtar 1994:75). Ilikano male migrant workers from the Philippines were surprised by whippings, amputations and beheadings as punishments in the Middle East. For their part the Arabs said that 'Filipinos are like dogs', loathsome, homeless and scavenging (Margold 1995:276, 288). However, a note on definitions is warranted here. Racial prejudice, when expressed by subordinate groups, should be distinguished from racism, which is prejudice backed by power. Thus while ethnocentrism or racial prejudice is quite possibly endemic to all communities, in white imperialist nations, economic, military and political control stands alongside ideological presumptions, reinforcing the ability to impose one's stereotype or definition of the 'other' on the other. Migrants of colour to the white west experience racial prejudice undergirded by racism (see Friedman 1995:23–4, 26 generally; Hitchcox 1993:149 for Vietman; Peletz 1995:90 for the Malays; hooks 1992:170 and Zack 1993:37 for African Americans).

In some analyses, the third world is not treated all of a piece, even after the removal of anomalous instances such as those noted above. In their textbook survey of *Women in the Third World*, Lynne Brydon and Sylvia Chant (1989:14) reject from their analysis 'atypical' third world countries like China and South Africa. They also use different criteria for grouping countries. A history of British colonial rule conflates South Asia (India, Pakistan, Nepal, Sri Lanka and Bangladesh), while Spanish colonial rule produces South America. The shared religion of Islam unifies Sub-Saharan Africa and North Africa. Southeast Asia is a single region on the basis of high levels of workforce participation by women. The Caribbean has the 'shared history of slavery', along with the 'arguably' greater economic autonomy of Caribbean women (Brydon and Chant 1989:14, 21, 33, 38, 42; see also Momsen 1993:1–3, 6, who relates high levels of workforce participation and education to Caribbean women's historical roles as field labouring slaves). This classification is actually neatly geographical. But the justifications, produced by university teachers for a British audience, are the product of British colonial histories and contemporary international relations. Thus South Asia is known through British colonisation, the Caribbean through British participation in the slave trade. Africa and Southeast Asia are known through contemporary phenomena, in the former case Islam and in the second the high participation of women in the paid workforce.

Brydon and Chant's academic division of the world bears some resemblance to that imagined by the producers and readers of *National Geographic*. The Middle East tends to be conceived as the origin of western religions, a region of nomads and the veil. Africa is a place of poverty and underdevelopment, Micronesia is seen as a child maturing into adulthood, while Polynesia is the place of beautiful women and vagabond men, a paradise more recently turned to pollution (Lutz and Collins 1993:127, 256, 138, 144). Thus, compared with Brydon and Chant (1989:14), who ignore the Pacific completely because 'we have found little material' on this area, Lutz and Collins divide Oceania into two sub-regions. This reflects both their own research interests in Oceania and the undue attention *National Geographic* pays to this region; both of these may reflect, compared with Britain, a greater US preoccupation with the Pacific, given American involvement in the region, especially since World War II.

Empirical indicators: 'more than 100 million women are missing'

If regional classifications suggest more about writers' preoccupations than the countries they are categorising, would not empirical measures of women's status provide an objective basis? Who can argue with women's life expectancy, literacy rates and political representation as a sign of women's advancement? But education may confirm women's traditional roles rather than prepare them for independent lives; women in politics may represent men's interests rather than women's. In terms of other indicators, access to paid labour may denote industrialisation in ways which reduce women's traditional control of production and its products.

As in the Soviet Union, paid work may impose a double burden on women. Thus one also needs to know women's wages as a percentage of men's wages and women's access to land and other resource-producing property. Lower birth rates may reflect either women's greater access to family planning or the imposition of state population control policies. Indicators of reported violence may reveal a greater public awareness and condemnation rather than a greater incidence of violence.

There are further difficulties about the accuracy and comparability of statistics. Polly Hill (1986) explores several reasons why statistics may amount to no more than guesswork. Official third world statistics are biased towards categories which have been derived from economists' descriptions of western economies; towards 'league tables' (United Nations tables ranking the world's countries in terms of indicators like per capita income or calorie consumption); and towards men's work rather than women's (Hill 1986:140–5). They are based on field material which 'has commonly been extracted from unwilling informants by resorting to many convolutions, blandishments and deceits, including sheer guesswork which is not necessarily particularly inspired' (Hill 1986:33). The data may be impossible to collect, for example cassava is stored in the ground until needed as it rots quickly once harvested. 'Capital', like a house, falls down and decays readily in tropical climates (Hill 1986:39). In some marriage systems, a man rarely thinks of all his children as a single category, but rather so many with this wife, so many with that wife (Hill 1986:47); in some parts of India men do not include their female children. Despite these caveats, the United Nations (1991; 1995) has heroically produced a cross-national comparison of the world's women in 1990. In general the world is divided into five areas: the 'developed regions', Africa, Latin America and the Caribbean, Asia, and the Pacific.

Indicators which are commonly used to reflect physical well-being are infant mortality, maternal mortality, life expectancy, literacy, per capita income (Gillett 1990:100). Maternal deaths account for between a quarter and a half of all deaths among women of childbearing age, the WHO (World Health Organisation) estimating that 88 to 98 per cent could be prevented with proper health care (Gillett 1990:100). Let us begin then with these life and death indicators of women's well-being. The following are the 'league' tables for the 'worst' countries in terms of the differences between life expectancy for females and males, maternal mortality and infant mortality rates. Of the seventeen countries where women's life expectancy was less than 50 years, all but three were in Africa; the lowest life expectancy was 44 in Afghanistan and 43 in Uganda (United Nations 1995:85–7).

Fertility rates follow the United Nations' classifications more neatly than the above indicators, varying between 1.2 and 2.2 births per woman

Life expectancy, maternal mortality and infant mortality rates: the poorest performing nations

Life expectancy differential (female minus male, years)		Maternal mortality (per 100 000 births)		Infant mortality (per 1000 births)	
Maldives	–3	Mali	2000	Afghanistan	162
Bangladesh	–1	Nepal	1500	Mali	159
Nepal	–1	Bhutan	1310	East Timor	150
Pakistan	0	Somalia	1100	Mozambique	147
India/Iran	1	Gambia	1050	Sierra Leone	143
Afghanistan/Bhutan	1	Yemen	1000	Malawi	142
Guinea/Malawi	1	Chad	960	Guinea-Bissau	140
Comoros/Zambia	1	Congo/Cambodia	900	Guinea	134
Papua New Guinea	1	Guinea	800	Gambia	132
Yemen	1	Nigeria/Zaire	800	Brunei Darussalam	129
Range for 'developed regions':					
	4–10		4–35		3–83

Source: United Nations 1995:84–8

in the 'developed regions' (with only Albania at 2.7 and the Republic of Moldova at 2.5 outside this range), 4 to 8.5 in Africa (with only Seychelles at 2.7, Tunisia at 3.4, Mauritius at 2.0 and Reunion at 2.3 outside this range), 2.5 to 5.4 in Latin America and the Caribbean (with six countries below this range). Asia and the Pacific, however, reveal wide variability, from the lows of 1.7 in Singapore and 1.4 in Hong Kong to over 6.5 in Afghanistan, Lao People's Democratic Republic, Oman and Yemen (United Nations 1995:28–32).

Adult female illiteracy is the lowest in the developed regions (about 5 per cent), Latin America and the Caribbean (about 15 per cent), followed by eastern and south-eastern Asia (about 23 per cent), Sub-Saharan Africa (about 52 per cent), Northern Africa and western Asia (Somalia and Mauritania but excluding Cyprus, Israel and Turkey) (about 55 per cent), Southern Asia (about 62 per cent) (United Nations 1995:90). Women as a percentage of the adult labour force varies in the 'developed' regions between 48 per cent in eastern Europe and 42 per cent in western Europe, 21 per cent in northern Africa and 38 per cent in Sub-Saharan Africa. In Latin America, the percentage is 33 per cent and in the Caribbean 43 per cent. Asia and the Pacific records figures between 25 per cent for western Asia, 35 per cent for southern Asia, 36 per cent for Oceania, 40 per cent for south-eastern Asia, 41 per cent for eastern Asia and 44 per cent for central Asia (United Nations 1995:109). Similarly the female human development index as a percentage of the male development index (a combined measure of life expectancy, education, employment and wages) reveals the Scandinavian countries at the top, with ratios of 93 to 96 per cent (Sweden, Finland, Norway), followed by largely western countries (for example France at 93 per cent; Australia and New Zealand at 90 per cent; USA at 86 per cent; UK at 85 per cent), with Asian and African countries at lower ratios (Japan at 78 per cent; Hong Kong and Singapore at 71 per cent; Korea at 65 per cent; Kenya at 59 per cent) (Tomaševski 1995:56).

Even though the natural birth ratio is 105 to 106 males to 100 females (Sen 1990:61), given that women tend to outlive men under 'normal' circumstances, it would be odd to find any countries in the world where there are more men than women. In fact, as Amartya Sen (1990:61) so graphically puts it, 'more than 100 million women are missing', 50 million of them in China.[5] By this she means that there are 100 million fewer women in the world than there are men. In terms of women's life expectancy, Sen notes a high correlation with the proportion of women in paid employment, except for China (with its one-child policy, discussed in Chapter 3) (Sen 1990:64). Sen also links women's higher life expectancy to recognition of women's work as productive, ownership of economic resources by women as well as political and civil rights for women, and a 'clear-headed understanding' of women's deprivations and the recognition of possibilities to change the situation (see also Charlton et al. 1989:184ff. who offer a similar analysis in exploring gender relations and various state institutions). Thus Sen is arguing that women's life chances are a reflection of their economic independence and political participation, a similar point being made by the Division of the Advancement of Women (1994).

These statistics reveal something of the differences between women's status in the different regions defined by the United Nations, generally supporting the claim that women are better off in the developed regions (although there are exceptions as noted above). While Southeast Asia might be an economic growth region, women's literacy levels have still not matched those of Latin American women. Africa is often considered one of the poorest continents on earth, reflected perhaps in high infant and maternal mortality rates in some countries, yet in many African countries women's economic participation is relatively high. Variations within regions reveal the limitations of the categories. The statistics also reveal contradictions for individual countries. Thus early-marrying Cuban women (on average 19.9 years old) have only 1.7 children each, while later-marrying Bolivian women (on average 22.1 years old) have 4.6 (United Nations 1995:30, 35). While men outnumber women in Papua New Guinea, women comprise a comparatively high 38 per cent of the economically active population (United Nations 1995:27, 145).

A further problem arises from the wide disparities in economic well-being within nations. The human development index, covering issues like per capita income and life expectancy, is comparable for African-Americans in the United States and for Bangladeshis (Wee 1995). Indeed, women are not universally better off in the third world than in the first. While in European and North American countries about a quarter of academics are female, in many Latin American countries one-third to 40 per cent are; in the Philippines the figure is 53 per cent, while there is much less gender bias in disciplines, both for students and professors (Michel 1995:36). More women are tenured at Delhi University than at Harvard (Sen 1990:62). Until 1980 a Spanish woman required her husband's consent to work outside the home, and until the 1960s a woman under the age of 25 required her parents' consent to leave home (Kaplan 1992:202, 203). While the first women legislators in Oman took their seats in 1994 and women are still not allowed to vote in Kuwait or Saudi Arabia (Pettman 1996:16), women finally received the vote nationally in Switzerland in 1971, although in 1989 one half-canton still did not permit women to vote (Division of the Advancement of Women 1994:431). While Norway was the only country in 1991 to have close to 50 per cent representation of women in its national cabinet, more than one-fifth of the cabinet in the Seychelles and Guyana were women (Division for the Advancement of Women 1992:13–14), but less than 2 per cent of parliamentarians in Japan were female. The first female prime minister of a nation-state was Sirimavo Bandaranaike of Sri Lanka (1960–65, 1970–77). Others include Indira Gandhi in India (1966–77, 1980–84), Golda Meir in Israel (1969–74), Margaret Thatcher in the United Kingdom (1979–90), Benazir Bhutto in Pakistan (1988–90, 1993–96), Khaledia Zia in Bangladesh (1991–), Corazón Aquino in the Philippines (1986–92), while women have been heads of state in Iceland, Nicaragua, Haiti, Bolivia, Argentina, Ireland, Netherlands Antilles, Dominica, Norway, Canada and Portugal (United Nations 1991:32).

As with the United Nations' classification, there will be times in this book when it is useful to speak of countries as groups: for example Muslim countries when speaking of the influence of Islam on women, Southeast Asian nations when speaking of women's expanding role in the free-trade zones, occasionally even Asian nations when speaking of apparent value differences between east and west (as discussed in relation to human rights in the next chapter or sexuality in Chapter 4). Generally, however, this book will use the example of a particular country or locality to challenge western feminist constructions or issues. In a sense this preserves the dualism of 'us' and 'them', although it deploys it in a specific way – to challenge how white western feminism has constructed itself. The next section explores why dualism has such a pervasive purchase in western theories.

FRACTURING BINARISMS: POSTCOLONIAL DESIRE

> Outside the boundaries of the home, I became aware of the 'they' and 'us' in multiple forms. They could mean the government and us the people. They could mean the communists and us the nationalists. They could mean the Americans and us the Vietnamese. They could mean the Catholics and us the Buddhists. They could mean the bad women who prostituted themselves and entertained American soldiers, and us the good women who maintained tradition to the point of refusing to wear western clothes. For the first time, I was bewildered with the terms *Ben Nay, Ben Kia* (this side and the other).
>
> – Thanh-Dam Truong 1994:177–8, Vietnamese writer and worker within the Women and Development Programme, Institute of Social Studies

We can see from the colonial histories of India, China and Japan summarised above that a simple developmental logic from 'backward' to 'modern' does not describe the history of women beyond the west, any more than it captures the history of western women. Second, however, we have also seen that at various times women in Asia and South America have claimed the rights western women claim, for example to an education, to the vote, to control of their bodies and reproductive potential. This second point warns against merely inverting the evaluations of east and west, so that east stands for all that is good, and west for all that is decadent or bad for women. The tendency in European-based philosophy to frame analyses within evaluative dualisms – oppositions of good and bad – is well entrenched, although often contradicted by its own pronouncements as well as the 'realities' it seeks to contain.

Western dualism is generally traced back to René Descartes' (1596–1650) famous formulation 'I think therefore I am'. This proposition offered a firm division between the thinking mind and the 'body' or, more generally, matter that was thought about, a division in which the mind was superior to the body. It also suggested a profound scepticism in knowledge which was nonetheless very egocentric: the only thing of which we can initially be sure is the thinking subject. Thus the man of reason is a product of modernism and the Enlightenment, as discussed in the Introduction. For many years the practitioners of western knowledge were almost invariably white elite males. Their minds studied all sorts of 'bodies', as Moira Gatens (1991:93) puts it: rocks, heavenly bodies, black bodies as well as women's bodies.

Val Plumwood (1993:48–60), using the theme of master and slave, identifies five aspects of dualism as well as the strategies required to overcome each of them. They are outlined briefly below because such strategies are used in this book to query the opposition between the self of white western feminism and the oriental other.

1. *Backgrounding* is the denial of the existence of the other, which thus refuses the centrality of the other in the construction of the self. The master more than the slave requires the other to define his superior identity, while the material conditions in which the master lives are based on exploitation of the slave. To overcome backgrounding, one must learn and acknowledge the contributions of the other, acknowledge *dependency*. Thus Jenny Sharpe (1993:94) suggests that we must explain not how 'European women transformed colonialism but how colonialism has left its indelible mark on European women'; we must write histories of the west which take account of colonial contact. Sharpe is referring to the fact that Anglo women know their ethnicity, their whiteness, their access to civilisation through the ways in which they represent the colonised other.

2. *Radical exclusion* or *hyperseparation* is the attempt to magnify the number and importance of differences, to refuse any shared qualities between self and other. According to Abdul JanMohamed (1986: 89–90), a manichean opposition between coloniser and colonised is based on absolute moral and metaphysical differences, rather than relative and qualitative differences. An empty gulf yawns between self and other, mind and body, reason and emotion. Attached to the distinction first world/third world are a number of other oppositions: west/orient, male/female, white/black, modern/traditional, west/east, active/passive, civilised/primitive, secular/religious, universal/local, culture/nature, intellect/instinct (Marcus 1992:35, 3, 20; Karamacheti in duCille 1994:605). Radical exclusionism defines the 'other' as a complete negation of the self, akin to western philosophy's basic premise that A cannot also be not-A. Radical exclusion is overcome by understanding the overlap and *continuity* between self and other.

3. *Incorporation* or *relational definition* means defining the other purely in terms of the self, for example as a 'lack' or absence of those good qualities in the self. Thus incorporation means that not-A is the deprivation or lack of A; it is not its own independent thing. Thus if A is 'man', and not-A 'woman', woman is defined simply by being not-man; she has no characteristics of her own. As opposed to radical exclusion, she can however be incorporated, by taking on the attributes of man. One overcomes incorporation with 'a non-hierarchical concept of difference' which focuses on the specific cultures and attributes of the other to 'reclaim positive sources of identity and affirm resistance' (Plumwood 1993:60).

4. *Instrumentalism* or *objectification* means that the dominated person's interests are defined as those of the master or in terms of the master's ends. For example one can argue that economic development will be a 'good thing' for colonies and ex-colonies, without understanding the exploitation which accompanies development or the ways in which western consumers benefit. This is overcome by recognising that the other has *independent ends and needs* which are to be respected.

5. *Homogenisation* or *stereotyping* means treating all the others as one other, as all the same. This is overcome by recognising the complexity and diversity of other nations, other cultures, other peoples.

Because this opposition dominates philosophical thought in classifications like sex and ethnicity, the western woman is both dominated in relation to western man, but also a 'master identity' to the extent that she endorses dualistic oppositions. She can be the western self as opposed to the colonised or ex-colonised other (Plumwood 1993:67).

Orientalism

Edward Said (1985a) has famously examined the way in which Cartesian dualisms worked to produce orientalism, or western knowledge of the 'orient'.[6] Not only are western writers the subjects of knowledge and the east their mere speechless objects, but the east is also constructed as inferior, as emotional, passionate, effeminate, irrational. Thus 'oriental despotism' is opposed to the constitutional monarchies or republics of 'the moderate or small nations of Europe'; the caste system and the 'Asiatic mode of production' (basically a form of agricultural production where the agricultural surpluses are taken by central rulers) are opposed to progressive capitalism. In the same vein, Hinduism has been described as a 'jungle' or an amorphous female presence (often linked to the 'dark goddess of the long red tongue', Kali) which threatens to engulf western rationality (Inden 1990:123, 86). Orientalism does not refer to 'mental exercises' but 'urgent social contests' over immigration laws, the legislation of personal conduct, the justification for violence or insurrection and so on (Said 1995:3).

Orientalism might describe with some accuracy the continuing virulent portrayal of the Middle East (Said is a Palestinian now writing in the United States) (Thomas 1994:26–7). However, the history of colonial contact covers six centuries and six continents (including Australia), commencing in the fifteenth and sixteenth centuries with South America. Christopher Columbus, informed by a Christian world-view, saw all South American Indians as the same – 'heathens' who could be made into versions of Europeans through Christian conversion. This belief in similarity (or incorporation in Plumwood's terms) also underwrote missionary endeavours through to the twentieth century. By the seventeenth and eighteenth centuries, however, travellers no longer saw sameness, but itemised differences between human types. At the same time, although preoccupied with classifying the other, white observers saw themselves as essentially distinct. In the mid- to late eighteenth century, anthropological discourses made their appearance, gradually coming to construct difference on an evolutionary scale under the influence of social Darwinism (Thomas 1994:52–3, 70–85) (which also allowed incorporation).

Thus in their extensive analysis of images of the 'non-west' in *National Geographic*, Catherine Lutz and Jane Collins (1993:276, 114, 206, 98, 104, 59) suggest that instead of a dualistic image of orientalism, there is a hierarchy of races from white to Asian to African (light to dark) in terms of civilisation, and thus in terms of similarity to the white west. Over the years the magazine has shifted away from images expressing colonial domination (there are now fewer images with both whites and people of colour in them), while the contemporary relations of economic imperialism are avoided by a general silence on poverty and conflict. Instead the magazine propounds an uneasy humanism, a universal humanity, beneath the colourful flourishes of exotic costumes and customs. But these colourful flourishes carry the message that the non-west, while beautiful, is timeless, without a history or a future. Or as the Australian Murri writer Jackie Huggins (1994:77) notes, Aboriginal women are 'more sensual but less cerebral, more interesting perhaps but less intellectual', 'more exotic but less articulate', 'more cultured but less stimulating, more oppressed but less political'. The west and non-west are still radically different, but some westerners now lament the loss of traditional worlds, and indeed culture itself (Lutz and Collins 1993:242, 248).

Thus Jane Gallop (in duCille 1994:610) suggests, although ironically, 'I want some ancient power that stands beyond the reaches of white male culture. I want black women as the idealized and exoticized alternative to European high culture'. Similarly Gloria Steinem (in Heilbrun 1995:74) remembers her time in India in 1957 as 'bathed in streams and rubbed in coconut oil like an Indian girl, and I was hopelessly lost in caring for these people, those ageless, suffering, dignified people'. The third world offers a 'vessel of "otherness"', containing the spice that can enliven our dull mainstream white culture, a spiritual wholeness that whites lack (Emberley 1993:5; hooks 1992:14). To Jennifer Lawn (1994:295), such claims are similar to those made by men in the men's movement in that 'members of a hegemonic group ostensibly abject themselves to an idealized other, while diverting the terms of the debate from material conditions of oppression to their own psychic malaise'. Such abjection to the other masks the relations of power between self and other, almost reversing these 'realities' for a notion that 'we' are somehow deprived in relation to the other, though in spiritual rather than economic terms.

This postcolonial desire or inversion of dualism has been explored in considerable detail by Rey Chow (1991a; 1991b), who locates herself as a Chinese person who grew up in Hong Kong and emigrated to the United States. She characterises western academics' study of the 'other' as either incorporation or submission. Under incorporation the other is a lesser, backward version of the self. This is the backwardness/development opposition criticised by Mohanty, and discussed at the beginning of this chapter. Submission to the other proclaims its uniqueness, but in a way that denies any similarities with the self. Thus Cathy Davidson (1993:5, 19), who 'dreamt Japan long before I went there', says 'It looks familiar but, an inch below the surface, it isn't anything like the West at all'. The other must be uncontaminated by the west (ideally uncontacted by the west) and is beyond evaluation in western terms (Chow 1991a:30–1).

Postcolonial, or rather colonial, desire is one way in which colonialism has left its indelible mark on European women. Where commentators like Katherine Mayo described barbaric India, there were also women – orientalists, theosophists, followers of gurus – who submitted to India, who privileged its 'authenticity' (Jayawardena 1995:2, 4, 12). These women found south Asian society more attractive than their own, perhaps hoping that Indian culture could civilise western colonisers. They emerged in a late nineteenth-century climate where faith in rationality, development and Christianity was being eroded as religious leaders, scientists and nationalists from South Asia joined intellectual circles in Europe and the United States; and where Japanese, Chinese and Indian art was influencing contemporary European artists. Theosophy, for example, idealised and romanticised Eastern women and ways of life, if not in contemporary forms at least in a former 'golden age'. Theosophy was often linked with women's rights among its female followers, Annie Besant, leader of the Theosophical Society after Blavatsky's death in 1891, advocating better working conditions and more rights for married women in England. In contrast, she suggested that Indian women should be 'good wives and mothers', even though this meant their education and political enfranchisement (Jayawardena 1995:112, 119–21, 123–31). As a sign of her respect for Indian culture, she wore 'sandals in India and shoes in the west' (Jayawardena 1995:135). But those who 'submitted' to the other often found their endorsement of Indian practices more acceptable to Indian men than to Indian women reformers (Jayawardena 1995:134, 190). Those adopting the submission approach may reject democracy, socialism, secularism, and feminism as culturally inappropriate; they may propose a society which should never change through industrialisation and development; they may condemn the use of the English language, computers, cars, television sets (Jayawardena 1995:12–13).

Vandana Shiva, in *Staying Alive*, argues that development is an expression of masculinist western scientific principles which ignore the environmental knowledge of women, the world's primary cultivators.

Historically, women were the inventors of most agricultural tools (like the simple plough and the spade), and practices (like propagation by shoots and cuttings, crop rotation, and irrigation); women found the eight most important cereals (wheat, rice, maize, barley, oats, sorghum, millet and rye) (Shiva 1988:105). This vision of women in harmony with mother earth or Gaia is an important corrective to Enlightenment and Judaeo-Christian notions of 'man' as master of the cosmos. However, it is also easy to claim from Shiva's vision that women should remain 'authentic', in balance with their environment, refusing modern technology, modern goods and modern incomes. Without doubt women's days have been lengthened because forests are cut down and so firewood is further away, but their days have also been shortened through electricity and running water. Similarly, orientalists see eastern things like Chinese silks and calligraphies as embellishments in their lives, but western things like bicycles and trains are central in Chinese lives (Chow 1991a:27). While the 'search for China' is a palliative to the 'frenetic, neurotic west', to the Chinese 'simplicity' often feels like 'poverty' or 'failure' (Eco 1986:284, 285).

China, at least as much as India, evokes submission in white western observers. When finally forced to succumb to western invasion (late in the day by world standards), China revealed both an ancient and secreted culture, with the longest surviving written language in the world.[7] During the nineteenth century the Chinese emigrants to the 'Gold Mountain' in the United States and the 'New Gold Mountain' in Australia were called 'celestials', which means heavenly, angelic, divine (de Lepervanche 1989:42). Arriving in California in 1854, they were likened to Lunarians, looking so unlike 'beings of this earth' (in Rolls 1992:103). China's isolation produced a seductive difference for western observers. So little was known, so much was different, such a large space was suddenly opened on which to project white western dreams and fears.

Although Julia Kristeva is the best known of western feminists to be inspired by visiting China, left-leaning Australian visitors have also made this journey. The Aboriginal writer Oodgeroo Noonuccal said of her time in China in 1985, 'I was so inspired by them. Oh what a beautiful country. I wrote seventeen poems on the track' (Mitchell 1987:207). One of them is entitled 'China ... Woman', in which Oodgeroo (then Kath Walker 1988:17–18) likens the Great Wall to 'my Rainbow Serpent,/Groaning her way,/Through ancient rocks'. Today, China is a woman, standing tall, 'Breasts heavy/With the milk of her labours'. Politically, China is transformed: 'Emperors are entombed/In museums. The people of China/Are now custodians of palaces' (see also Susan Sontag 1979:11–19).

Similar themes of both an alien past and utopian future were evoked by Dymphna Cusack thirty years earlier when she spent two and a half years in China at the invitation of the Chinese Peace Committee (Cusack in

Rigg and Copeland 1985:67). While Cusack has 'always been a feminist', she was nonetheless 'stunned' to discover that the foreign affairs editor of the *Peking Daily* was a woman (Cusack in Rigg and Copeland 1985:67). Even so, Cusack brings her more advanced feminism to at least one household. She meets a 'model worker's' wife, Mrs Lou. The wife is deferential to her husband, but, as Cusack persistently questions her, she gains confidence in discussing her involvement in the Street Committee. Mrs Lou concludes, 'I want to tell you that I shall never forget today', giving her embroidered wedding treasures to Cusack as a parting gift. Cusack notes, 'Mr Lou has on his face the look of a man who has just realized that he has a remarkable wife' (Cusack 1958:48).

China has both a beautiful and a barbaric past, marked by infanticide and concubines as well as a millennial culture (Cusack 1958:4, 3). As Cusack gazes at the 'inverted hibiscus blossoms' of the Temple of Heaven, her guide quotes the statistics of achievement which constructed her hotel. The brave new present and the even braver promised future is built on the destruction of the barbaric in the past. Chinese women 'have stood up, and in their standing up millennial burdens have slid from their backs' (Cusack 1958:262). The stories she tells, the stories she is told, are all of rapid improvements for women in the space of three generations, from selling children because of famine and grandmothers tottering on mutilated feet, to their daughters planning China's future at the All China Women's Congress, to 'fat babies like little burnished buddhas' (Cusack 1958:261, 12). But not all from the past has been destroyed, and this is what marks socialism in China as superior: 'No mere anonymous mass, this crowd. Each unit is individual, stamped with the dignity that comes of an age-old civilization which has nothing to do with literacy or material possessions' (Cusack 1958:260).

Julia Kristeva's (1974) *About Chinese Women* also portrays socialist China as a marvellous combination of the good of the past and the promise of the future. Kristeva's waking dream in China is both of sexual androgyny and celebrated motherhood in which women brandish paintbrushes and machine-guns, shout orders to men, but are 'surrounded as well by a sweet community of children with relaxed, rounded bodies'. The women are workers and mothers, both 'buxom' and 'muscular' with 'strong, boyish calves'. The boys, however, are 'frail, childish, slightly effeminate according to our canon' (Kristeva 1974:151, 158, 180). In identifying China with the feminine, Kristeva locates it outside time in the pre-oedipal maternal phase, a phase which occurs before the acquisition of language and reason (Chow 1991a:7). China, like woman, is unknowable, but also archaic (Chow 1991a:9). More than that, its archaic custom of foot-binding is Chinese culture's recognition of women's equal claims to the symbolic (Chow 1991a:6). This example demonstrates the way in which submission can lead us to value everything in another culture as an expression of something superior to our own culture. As Chow suggests, this is akin to viewing cannibalism or other barbarities with 'awe', as practices outside our own time and also beyond our own judgements.

Submission responses to China are almost impossible for sympathetic western observers to resist. I too have been guilty of romanticising, in my own way and from my own history, my observations of China. I constructed an image of powerful but practical Chinese women, and of their gentle husbands sharing housework and politics. I was struck by one professor who discussed his contributions to the delivery of English education throughout China, all the while unconsciously fondling a large teddy bear. On an occasion when I held a party for my students, two of the young men took their turn at making *jiaozhi* (dumplings), deftly handling the pastry and filling. I brought home a romantic image of Chinese feminism that sought accommodations with others where western feminists more often produce irreconcilable differences (see Bulbeck 1994; and more generally Bulbeck 1991 and Ram 1991a for a critique).

Chow (1991a:xiii) claims that, ironically, although we desire the non-west, we do not attribute desire (and therefore interior complexity) to that which we desire. China is merely desired, having no wishes of its own (like women in some male fantasies): 'our discourses produce a non-west that is deprived of fantasy, desires and contradictory emotions'. In a manner akin to Plumwood's description of instrumentalism, Chow explores this aspect of the submission approach with two examples, *The Last Emperor* and the 'Butterfly literature' of the May Fourth period (see Chow 1991a:34–83). Like Kristeva, Bernardo Bertolucci, director of *The Last Emperor*, likens China to the feminine. He describes the Chinese as feminine, passive 'in the way of people when they are so intelligent and so sophisticated they don't need machismo' (in Chow 1991a:5). The last emperor, Pu Yi, like a woman, is buffeted by events over which he has no control, is lovingly watched and attended, lives in an opulence which is always a parody of the reality around him; yet no one cares about his empty inner self. Bertolucci's 'erotic over-investment' in imperial China, represented by Pu Yi, is similar to the over-investment in women on the screen (Chow 1991a:11). However, while some western academics quickly detect the orientalism in *The Last Emperor*, Chow's mother thinks 'he did a good job', especially for a 'foreign devil' (Chow 1991a:24). Chow's point is that her mother's response precisely indicates the play of fantasy, the nostalgic desire for the past, and the search for identity in changing times. Indeed westernisation may be a form of castration or dismemberment, in which those who have lost their ancient history fetishise and long for a past that cannot be retrieved. Thus Chow suggests that the Chinese have contradictory experiences of both tradition and modernisation. By invoking desire, Chow explores these ambivalent and complicated responses. In sum, China and the Chinese (like westerners) must be allowed to combine the modern and the ancient, the good and the bad, the east and the west, to forge hybrid identities which are neither incorporation nor submission.

Dualistic thinking is not as marked in non-western cosmologies as it is in western philosophy. Indeed Eastern traditions do not separate body and spirit, secular and sacred the way European philosophy does. In Eastern religions spiritual training is not concerned with refusing or transcending the body but with cultivating it, 'to become both more spiritual and more carnal at the same time'. 'Spirit grows from matter' and eventually the divisions 'among body, mind and spirit' disappear (Oppel 1994:87, 88). Sukimo Iwao (1993:10), a Japanese writer reflecting on her time in the United States, suggests the Japanese do not see the world in terms of dichotomous values like private/public, good/bad, male/female. Rather the Japanese see a zone of options between the two ends of the scale. Similarly, my students in Beijing refused the western (and neo-Confucian: Lee 1994:13) conception of yin as the dark female force and yang as the light and powerful male force, focusing more on the cosmic and universal significance of both (see also Barlow 1994:258). Chinese ontology is rich in threes, fours, and fives; for example the Five Blessings of New Year (long life, wealth, health, virtue, and a natural death) or the Four Modernisations (Lindqvist 1991:342, 345). Conceiving of hybrid-isation, or the mingling of A and not-A to produce something which is neither, might then come more naturally to those who have access to non-western ways of viewing the world. In fact the academics most responsible for thinking through hybridisation are scholars in western academia whose early training was in India, South America or Africa.

Hybridisation

A significant source of contemporary writing on hybridisation is Frantz Fanon's *Black Skin, White Masks*, first published in 1953. Frantz Fanon, a psychiatrist from the Antilles trained in France, the coloniser of the Antilles, identified the dilemma for diaspora intellectuals who seek to wear white masks over their black skins. Educated in the language and culture of the colonial power, they must reject their own culture if they are 'to-stand with the white world (that is to say, the real world)' which commands '*turn white or disappear*'. Thus colonised men 'possess' white women to gain civilisation and dignity and colonised women attempt to marry lighter-skinned people to 'whiten the race, save the race' (Fanon 1967:37, 100, 47, 93; Fanon in McClintock 1995:361, 362). But black skins cannot be erased, and 'the educated negro suddenly discovers that he is rejected by a civilization which he has nonetheless assimilated' (Fanon 1967:93). Told to assimilate, to become like the masters, those who look different are still marked as inferior by whites. For the French writer Jean-Paul Sartre, 'anti-racist racism', or celebration of difference, was a stage in the path towards the irrelevance of racial difference. Fanon, however, demanded 'access to the universal *as a black human being*', claimed his continuing difference as part of his acceptance as an equal (Moi 1994:210). New identities nevertheless must be based on the attempt 'to explain the other to myself'; they will be new identities not endlessly recycling old histories. People must move beyond their identity as negro (which speaks to 'the fact that he was enslaved') and as white (which speaks to 'the fact that somewhere he has killed man') (Fanon 1967:230–1).

Indeed, in the process of forging their positive identities, some people of colour have produced an anti-racist racism. This inverted racism 'shun[s] the white-looking Indian, the "high yellow" Black woman, the Asian with the white lover, the Native woman who brings her white girl friend to the Pow Wow, the Chicana who doesn't speak Spanish' (Anzaldúa 1990a:143). Affirming one's racial identity *in opposition to whiteness* condemned the mixed-race or hybrid identity as inferior (see Zack 1993:75). Instead of merely asserting the value of one's pure (but formerly denigrated) identity, postcolonial writers suggest hybrid or mixed identities which encompass the contradictory history of colonisation. An Indian writer working in the United States, Homi Bhabha (1986:173), coined the term 'hybridity' to capture this process, which he calls contra-modernity rather than postmodernity (Bhabha 1991:59), and which 'comes between well established identities and breaks them up' (Stuart Hall in Terry 1995:60). Mimicry, mockery and ironic reversals challenge the west's discourse without adopting fully the discourse of the subordinate colonised group (Bhabha 1994:81). Hybridisation is the fate and contribution of subalterns, for example Indian intellectuals raised in both English and Indian cultures (but see also the Vietnamese film-maker, Trinh Minh-Ha (1992:233–4, 140). Liminal categories like a 'mestiza consciousness', a 'plural consciousness', *la frontera*, a 'consciousness of the borderlands' identify these new conflicting but productive identities (as Gloria Anzaldúa, a Hispanic feminist academic in the United States, puts it: see Anzaldúa 1990a:377). These 'interracial identities' oppose dualistic western thinking with 'divergent thinking, characterized by moving away from set patterns and goals toward a ... perspective ... that includes rather than excludes'. *La mestiza* shows a tolerance for contradictions and ambiguity (Anzaldúa, 1990a:378–9).

However, as with postmodernist theories, postcolonialism has been accused of playing down the power relations between cultures: 'When the rich are grafted to the poor, hybridization is hard to distinguish from pillage; when the strong are grafted to the weak, hybridization is hard to distinguish from conquest' (Anson 1991:65). As Stuart Hall (in Terry 1995:61) says, 'Power always tends to gravitate back to the binary ... The binaries don't go away because hybridity is around, or because we make a theoretical critique of them. So you have to keep asking why the binaries reappear.' Hall is referring to the unequal economic and power structures which continue to affirm one identity, that of being western, over the oriental identity. Thus Parlo Singh, an Australian of Sikh background, explores the difficulties in claiming her hybrid identity. Singh's father cleared land in Australia, was a settler, yet one never represented in Australia's frontier bush tradition. Singh's mother countered the dominant culture's racism with the Punjabi and Hindi languages and stories. Yet 'the ethnicised self of my mother is often portrayed as "too traditional"'. At home the family spoke in hybrid voices, although publicly their voices were excluded and marginalised. Unlike her parents, Singh is asked to speak, although she, unlike women marked as white, must negotiate how she will speak her hybrid voice. When she writes in a 'universal' voice, the 'self of humanism', she is often accused of denying her 'authentic' ethnic identity (Singh 1994a:92). When she speaks her ethnic difference, her white audience sometimes position her as the 'traditional' 'victim' of oppression (although not white women's oppression), speaking from the 'confessional' to disclose the pain and humiliation of sexual and racial harassment. Alternatively she 'really' is not different under her black skin and Indian features. Her ethnicised difference is no more than another '"individual" difference in a society where everyone is effectively a migrant' (Singh 1994a:97, 99). Of course Singh does not leave it there, but the constant refusal of both incorporation and submission requires her to continually negotiate what she wants to say and how.

The notion of hybrid identities reminds us that few of us are islands, a product of a pure uncontaminated culture, given the global exchanges of information, commodities, media messages and people. It is no accident, however, that the major writers on hybrid identities are academics of so-called third world backgrounds now living in the west. They experience their different cultures more acutely than members of a dominant culture do, especially members of an anglophone culture living in the west. Even so, the idea of hybridity is a shorthand for the connections between us, connections which challenge the notion of western dualisms, and of oppositions like third world and first world.

CONCLUSION

There is a difference between a difference and a dichotomy. The first is a comparison and it relates; the second is a severance and it isolates.

– Geertz 1995:28

Fanon (1967:230) tartly observed that he 'should be very happy to know that a correspondence had flourished between some Negro philosopher and Plato. But I can absolutely not see how this would change anything in the lives of the eight-year-old children who labor in the cane fields of Martinique and Guadeloupe'. There are those who labour in the cane fields and those who sit in academic studies and those who throw million dollar parties. There are real economic differences between women, and many of these can be explained in terms of the history of colonialism. There are also differences in the power of naming the other, so that there has been far more naming by white women of women of colour than the reverse (Ganguly 1995b:4).

Susanne Kappeler (1995:44, 48, 83) notes that the 'expedition to the Other is invariably also a journey to oneself', the researcher sharing a desire similar to that of the tourist. The researcher has chosen the interaction, not the researched; if white she probably comes with more resources like education and money than the researched. Similarly the desire to see the same skin beneath its different colours might be the white woman's project 'which renders the other silent', extinguishing her wish. Orientalism was not so much indicated by what Katherine Mayo said but how she said it, and the fact that it was this text rather than those written by more sensitive and knowledgeable Indian men and women which received so much attention (Oldenburg 1994:41). Mayo's text served British not Indian purposes. Similarly, Kristeva's impressions of China reflect her preoccupation with western feminist dilemmas not Chinese ones (Chow 1991b:93; Uberoi 1991:389, 391). Imaginatively, Vietnam, homeland of Trinh Min-ha, is also either a successful revolution or a space in which American soldiers fought. (Think of *Apocalypse Now* or *The Odd Angry Shot*). Both these images deny the 'harrowing difficulties' of a nation now undertaking reconstruction (Trinh 1993:171, 172). Given the purpose of this book, to use the writings by women from beyond the west to query the certainties of western feminism, this appropriation is not such a problem for us. After all, rather than being centrally a book about India or Vietnam, this is more a book about how we see the position of anglophone white women differently as a result of what Indian and Vietnamese women write about us and themselves.

To avoid misappropriating the other, however, requires some sort of compensatory recognition to correct the devaluation of the other. We should recognise the identity of the other as 'a potential source of strength as well as a problem'. 'Those of us from the master culture who lack imagination' can study 'in humility and sympathy' the 'sustaining stories of the cultures we have cast outside reason' with 'better plots, and at least the possibility of some happy endings' (Plumwood 1993:63–4, 196). Kumari Jayawardena (1995:10–11) asserts that 'every woman' has the right to speak out 'against women's oppression and exploitation everywhere', but she must avoid the distortions of a universalism which only takes gender into account or of focusing on racial or ethnic collectivities without addressing class and gender divisions. Thus we must walk this tightrope between similarity and difference armed with knowledge, stories told to us by the other; with honest self-criticism, asking what are our interests as opposed to those of the other; with connection, meeting and hearing the other; and with an understanding of the structures of political and economic domination which have made white voices louder and the voices of the other often muted. We will return to this issue of reading other cultural practices in Chapter 2.

In eschewing dualisms, we recognise the ways in which so many of us are marked by mixed cultures and ethnicities, are producing new hybrid ways of identifying ourselves, us white feminists too. The tension between similarities and connections as well as oppositions and differences in the lives of women means that third world and first world refer to real as well as imagined differences, to both broad patterns of unequal resource allocation as well as caricatures that conceal more than they reveal. The remaining chapters explore and disrupt caricatures of the binary dualism which divides west from east, starting with that between individuals with their rights and communities with their needs, in the next chapter.

CHAPTER
2

Individual Versus Community

•

I'm glad you've read 'Wild Swans'. Although I disagree with the
authors in some respect, the book itself is objective. The author⌐
introduced the social changes of China through telling life stories of │
three generations of her family – maybe this is the most easily
accepted way by foreigners. Today, to most Chinese people even
including those who came into power during the Cultural Revolution,
the life in [the] 1960s is like a nightmare, for you have to hide your
natural selves and follow the fast-changing political trend in order to
escape misfortune.

    – Letter from young Chinese friend to author, December 1994

Tamara Jacka (1994:666) notes that when rural Chinese women were
asked questions about their status or personal welfare, they were frequently either 'completely nonplussed by the question, or will respond in
terms of their family's welfare'. But they also understood exactly what
Jacka 'was getting at' when she asked who controlled the family income or
who did the housework, the latter question provoking laughter 'because
the answer is so obvious'. The comment about *Wild Swans* above reveals
my friend's suspicion that white westerners desire personal narratives
more so than Chinese readers. But because she also notes that the
Chinese have 'natural selves' which had to be disguised during the Cultural Revolution, she is not endorsing the simple opposition between self
and community, between individualism and connectedness, between an
interior life and externally constituted roles, which is often a feature of
western constructions. For her, the Chinese also have 'selves' which had to
be disguised by the communitarian impulses of the Cultural Revolution.

    There can be little doubt that the idea of western individualism,
emerging either with or before industrialisation and democracy, is a much
discussed feature of the westernised personality. It is also connected with
an emphasis on sexual identity as a particular hallmark of the western

individual, an issue we will take up in Chapter 4. Thus Lesley Johnson (1993:10–12, 19) suggests that feminist historians have constructed the post–World War II women's movement as a story of 'growing up', of 'emerging into consciousness, out of silence into speech', out of imposed femininity into the 'truth of their personhood'. Finding one's already given (but disguised) identity was the quest of the movement.

According to Indrani Ganguly (interview 18 May 1994), even the way food is eaten in east and west reveals western commitment to individualism. In Indian offices, it is quite common for people to sit around the table, share their food and exhort others to eat more. In Australia, people rarely share and often 'seem to sit and watch how much someone is eating, and you have women telling other women they're eating too much'. Asian tourists are often perceived by western observers to be uniformly dressed. In Japan, clothing expresses a combination of status and conformity: 'not to be too different from others in your social category, even if that category is only temporary (when golfing wear golfing clothes, when hiking wear hiking clothes)' (Clammer 1992:199). But the very term 'fashion' implies an impulse to conformity in western cultures, to not be unfashionable, while shops stock a limited range of each season's colours, knowing that a different set will be in demand next season. My mother was highly amused when she toured Alaska to note a retired couple from the United States who every day wore matching leisure outfits. They were perhaps expressing a sameness forged through western notions of romantic love.

The opposition between self and community/society is, I would suggest, a western construction, but one which we often use in orientalist ways, assuming that white western women are individuals with personalities and a sense of their rights, while third world women, abroad or at home, are members of the community, connected to society through roles and responsibilities, lacking 'desire' in Rey Chow's terms (see Chapter 1). This chapter explores the reasons for this orientalist dualism and its failure to interrogate the dimensions of individualism as it operates in white western feminist analyses.

CONSTRUCTING AND DECONSTRUCTING THE WESTERN INDIVIDUAL

The New York Times reported that Americans participated in an estimated 100 million therapy sessions with licensed practitioners in the year ending June, 1992, and paid approximately $8.1 billion, not counting prescription drugs, to relieve this national despair.

– Mary Kay Blakely, 'Psyched Out',
– *Los Angeles Times Magazine* 3 October 1993:27

In the massive five-volume *History of Private Life*, edited by Ariès and Duby, contributors claim that the construction of an inner life pre-dates industrialisation and democracy, beginning in the fifteenth century and emerging through practices like the transfer of the religious confession to personal 'confessions' in diaries which became increasingly popular even among the working classes; the spread of private reading which replaced the parchment scrolls held by slave-readers; and changing domestic architecture in which life on the street moved inside the home and away from the life of the street, tavern, mall and church (Corbin 1990:496–9, 570–5; Rouche 1987:541; Chartier et al. 1989:112–13, 128, 130; Ariès 1989:4). Where late medieval city houses faced outwards, rather than inwards to a courtyard as in the East, separate houses or apartments for families, separate beds and then separate rooms for children became more common. The secrecy of the marriage bed was protected by drapes and then walls, and newly-weds were no longer put to bed by a crowd of onlookers (Corbin 1990:480; Ariès 1989:5). From the turn into the twentieth century, the idea of the 'worker-owner' connected home owner-ship, the family wage, protective industrial legislation and the removal of women to the home (Hunt and Hall 1990:82–7; Perrott and Martin-Fugier 1990:124; Perrott and Guerrand 1990:354–6, 420–5).

Exposed breasts and codpieces simulating an erection were abandoned, as nudity, sexual activities and bodily functions were confined to domestic spaces. Births were no longer proclaimed at the town hall. Over the nineteenth century domestic life became redolent with the rituals of Christmas trees and new year celebrations, and annual holidays which were synchronised with school holidays (Revel et al. 1989:392–3; Régnier-Bohter 1987:367–9; Perrott and Martin-Fugier 1990:201, 289, 303–5). Such cosy constructions of a rich private life inside families experienced occasional reversals, for example during the French Revolution, which is echoed in the Chinese Revolution of this century. Thus in France *tu* became a public form of address, while in China *tong zhi* ('comrade' but literally meaning 'same will'), became a normal form of address to strangers following the Communist Revolution. Following the failure of the Cultural Revolution, *tong zhi* has increasingly been replaced by Chinese versions of 'mister', 'miss' and so on. The French and Chinese Revolutions decreed through codes of dress and furniture that private disposition must reflect public commitment. French was the decreed language, marriage was secularised, divorce made more readily available. In France, however, despite the rhetoric of universal citizenship, women who wore red liberty caps and formed clubs were criticised for refusing their (private) roles as mothers, daughters and sisters (Hunt and Hall 1990:14–23, 33), suggesting that the private realm of the family did not wither away completely.

During the nineteenth century a father's capacity to influence his sons' economic future diminished. The peasant passed on his land; from the Industrial Revolution working-class fathers might find apprenticeships for their sons, while the propertied classes passed on their businesses. But by 1870 few fathers could offer such a future to their sons (Stearns 1990:65). Gradually young people turned away from their parents' values and developed countercultures. In the post–World War II families based on the language of intimacy, romantic love and affective equality (often disguising inequality), fathers have ceased to be stern disciplinarians and can hope to become 'buddies' to their children (Orfini 1991:577).

For some observers the diminuition of private patriarchy has been replaced by public patriarchy, or control by the state and other public institutions (Walby 1990). Kristina Orfini et al. (1991:418–34) say that state supervision is most extensive in Sweden, the first country to establish national statistical collections, in 1756. Everyone has access to official documents and redress through ombudspersons. The state regulates parental relations through commitment to children's rights, sexuality through publicity and sex education in schools, allows adopted children and children conceived by insemination from donor to know their fathers, and protects battered women from appearing in court to confront their abusers. In fact I would argue that these are examples of the triumph of individual freedom, guaranteed by state intervention, over family 'privacy' or over private patriarchy, the protection of wives against husbands and children against parents.

This western history of the construction of the rational self-possessed individual, independent of both family and state, influences how western women understand the speech and actions of non-western women, as two examples about speaking indicate. Thus western feminists have accused Maori women of oppression by patriarchal customs because they cannot speak on their ritual meeting ground, the *marae*, while they have also proposed the 'talking cure' of consciousness-raising derived from psychotherapy for women of all ethnic backgrounds.

Speaking the 'Self'

An example of white western women's unreflective application of the notions of individual agency and individual voice is revealed in the New Zealand debate on Maori women's rights to speak on the *marae*. Some white New Zealand feminists have maintained that 'women cannot speak on the marae', a claim which has been used by Pakehas (white or non-Maori New Zealanders) to deny public service appointments to Maori women (Irwin 1991:9). The statement that 'women cannot speak on the marae' is simplistic on a number of counts. Critics collapse two other terms into the word *marae* (the whole domestic complex): the open ground in front of the ancestral meeting house and the area between the hosts and guests during a welcome. In some tribal groups women do have the right to speak on the *marae*. In most clans a woman usually starts the welcoming ceremony when visitors come to a clan's homelands with a *karanga* or call of welcome, to which a woman from the other group replies.

Thus women do speak on the *marae*, but western notions of 'speaking' as authored individual expressions have rendered the welcoming ritual chants as silence. Thus Maori writer Kathie Irwin (1991:13) argues that the greeting on the *marae* is a highly ritualised and formal occasion to which western notions of democratic rights of speaking do not apply, while Mona Lisa Johnson (in Ishtar 1994:178) adds that women can control men through their body language without speaking. Irwin (1991:16–17) is not, however, suggesting that Maori women should confine their speaking to ritual statements. She notes that Pakeha men, with and without knowledge of Maori culture and language, are increasingly speaking on the *marae*. This is a verbal manifestation of the alliance cemented between Maori and Pakeha men in the Maori Council formed in 1962, while women were confined to the Maori Women's Welfare League formed in 1951 (Evans 1994:56). Maori women who advocate their speaking rights have been told there is a 'divine ordinance that the marae atea belongs only to men' (Evans 1994:58), but they were also told not to speak publicly (about this issue) in a Pakeha meeting hall, thus extending the notion of the *marae* to a Pakeha meeting space (Szaszy 1993:78). While critical of Pakeha women's simplistic formulations, these Maori women do however claim their right to shape traditions to meet their current needs rather than adhere to a 'deeply internalised acceptance of powerlessness' (Evans 1994:65; Irwin 1991:16–17). They are claiming their rights to speak, while also correcting eurocentric understandings of their cultural position. Without such adaptations, Maori women face Nguia te Awekotuku's (1991:144) fate: after two generations of women, her family has become *wharengaro* or lost house, has lost its right to speak on the *marae*. Let us turn to the relevance of the talking cure to other than western European-background cultures.

One of the proud slogans of women's liberation in the 1960s and 1970s was 'the personal is political'. This meant not only that oppression begins at home but also that strategies for personal reconstruction and self-discovery were part of women's liberation (for example see MacKinnon 1989:121). But it could be argued that consciousness-raising arose 'naturally' in cultures committed to psychological understandings of the individual, where the 'talking cure' in therapy is a means of stripping away false and damaging conceptions of the self to reveal the true self. From outside white western culture, feminist therapy and consciousness-raising have been seen either as a reflection of obsession with the self or a necessary corrective to the excessive individualism and internalised oppression white women experience from their greater emotional proximity to white men (Huata 1993:122 on Pakeha feminists; the African-American Aida Hurtado 1989:850; see also Joseph 1993:480–1).

Contrariwise, in Mediterranean and Muslim cultures where a woman's sexual honour reflects her family's standing there is fear that 'confessions' will circulate as dishonouring 'gossip' (Rozario 1991:15–26; Al-Khayyat 1990:22; Warnock 1990:25). The matrixes of dishonour may prevent wives confiding in husbands, fearing loss of their natal family honour, or wives speaking of domestic violence publicly because this shames both wife and husband (Al-Khayyat 1990:25–31, 102 for Iraqi wives; Risseuw 1988:276 for Sri Lanka). The Chinese adopt 'silent, stoic forbearance' and keep family affairs private as a protection against information being used against one, by arbitrary rulers both in China and upon migration to the United States (Tan 1994:42–4). In Tunisia, women who speak about the female body, personal relationships, abortion, birth, masturbation and so on are called prostitutes, divorcees, lesbians, robbers of husbands (Accad 1991:241). The greater importance of community acceptance over individual healing is suggested by a Bosnian raped women who rejected offers of counselling: 'I need the understanding of my relatives. I need to go back home' (Lâm (1994:877–8).

Thus in some cultures talking oneself into a cure sits oddly with other cultural practices. Dorinne Kondo (1990:ch. 3) describes her visit to a Japanese ethics camp. Instead of the psychological preoccupation with releasing the true self through speech, in the Japanese ethics school, and other widespread practices like learning the tea ceremony (for women) and the martial arts (for men), the emphasis is upon repetition of bodily motions to achieve social conformity and a disciplined self. The polished *kokoro* (heart) accepts things as they are, without resistance or questioning, sensitive not to its own desires but to the needs of others. Japanese schools advocate 'independence' in children by which they mean 'patterns, skills, and attitudes that enable the child to adopt and perform successfully the labors of the school (and later, work)' (Allison 1996:139).

Where westerners have personal or emotional problems, the Chinese express these dilemmas as physical ailments or interpersonal moral issues: shame, social morality and so on. Where westerners pursue careers, Chinese seek to 'have their bodies settled' (Lung-kee Sun 1991:6, 2–4). In developing a Chinese personality inventory to supplement that devised in the United States, Fanny Cheung et al. (1996) also noted the Chinese tendency to 'somatisation' or the expression of personal and social distress as physical symptoms. Other factors included family orientation, harmony (inner peace and contentment as well as interpersonal harmony), *Ren Qin* (relationship orientation based on reciprocity, courteous rituals, nepotism and so on), defensiveness (externalisation of blame and self-enhancement) and graciousness (patience, forgiveness, acceptance of self and others, self-sacrifice).

However, western-style techniques of counselling have been adopted, or perhaps adapted, in some countries, including China where, for example, the Beijing Normal University psychology centre offers counselling to students with examination fears (Lin Shiwei, 'Centre Solves Problems that are all in the Mind', *China Daily* 26 October 1993:5). Thus Cheung et al. (1996:186) also proposed 'hybrid' Chinese personalities with a 'modernisation' factor (attitudes to traditional Chinese beliefs, family relationships, materialism, hierarchical order, rituals, chastity). The Indonesian language recently incorporated the term 'conseling' as there was no Bahasa Indonesia word for the activity (Murray 1993). Young Minangkabau couples in Malaysia express greater desires for privacy, for example in lockable rooms in their parents' houses; women are expressing stronger opinions about marrying for love rather than accepting arranged marriages; and women construct their growing sense of individualism and personal aspirations within the terms of 'family', aligning notions of self and community in ways which are neither western nor traditionally Malaysian, but a hybrid of both cultures (Stivens 1996:228–9, 237, 243). We will see the intrusion of western notions of the sexualised self into magazines circulating in Asian countries in Chapter 4.

The discussion in this section suggests that western notions of the self and speaking must be interrogated, both because they do not readily apply to people in other cultures and because the critiques offered by people from other cultures suggest some of the limitations of our often unquestioned assumptions about individual agency, assumptions which are akin to a belief in magic according to one non-western observer:

> While the reluctance of some white bourgeois feminists in the United States to fashion societal (rather than individual or intra gender) strategies to end the oppression of women reenacts, in my view, their enveloping culture's pronounced valuation of individualism and self-reliance, their concomitant aversion to admitting personal limitations and dependencies strikes me as emanating from the realm of magic (Maivân Clech Lâm, 1994:879, who grew up in Thailand and is an academic in the United States).

The next section explores further this idea of a self constructed through connection with others rather than separation from them, using linguistic examples and relationally defined identities, and discussing how the idea that the community has more salience in some cultures beyond the anglophone west influences notions of western identities.

The Ties That Bind

When a 'well-bred' Chinese woman finds something oppressive and 'turns inside to "herself"', she runs straight into the two-thousand-year-old definitions, expectations, and clichés of what she always already "is"' (Chow 1991a:57). The internal self is already mapped out for a Chinese woman. A similar point is made by one of the protagonists, Lindo Jong, in *The Joy Luck Club* (by Amy Tan, a Chinese-American writer). Explaining her cunning adaptation of rituals and superstition to escape an arranged marriage, she says 'I remember the day when I finally knew a genuine thought and could follow where it went' (Tan 1990:60–5). In 1993 one of my young colleagues shared with me her conflict between her choice of a fiancé and her parents' response. Although she was clearly distressed by her parents' intervention, she never once cried in my presence, never said it was wrong of her parents to prevent the marriage, and had great difficulty answering my questions about how she felt at different points of the drama (which lasted several months). She identified two choices: suicide, for which she said she lacked the courage, and obedience to her parents. Lorena Sun Butcher (who grew up in Shanghai and Hong Kong) was nonplussed when acquaintances in the United States asked her if she liked her parents. To answer no was such a blasphemy that one would not even consider the question (from 'The Fortunate Daughter', an unpublished biography given as a talk at the International Feminist Book Fair, Brisbane, 6 August 1994).

Such daughterly obedience has often been attributed to Confucianism, a 'humanist' (meaning non-theological) code of conduct which influenced other Asian cultures besides China's. Confucius identified five relations – sovereign and subject, father and son, man and wife, older and younger brother, friend and friend – in which respect for mutual obligations created balance in society generally. For women, however, further controls were required through the four obediences: to father, husband, brother and even son (Lindqvist, 1991:342). Others identify three obediences: to fathers, husbands and sons (for example Brydon and Chant 1989:44). In a revision of ancient texts, taken up below, Lee (1994:49) notes that the 'three obediences' or 'three submissions' are a loose translation of *sancong* or the 'three attachments'. Thus one could argue that Confucius merely meant a woman was to be originally attached to her father's household when unmarried, her husband's when married and her son's when widowed.

Obediences were inscribed in the body: speaking without moving the lips, sitting without moving the knees, standing without moving the skirt, being happy without giggling, listening attentively to parents-in-law while standing, and premasticating food (Barlow 1994:260). One example of bodily inscriptions of respect is the *koutou* (kowtow) or traditional Chinese bow which expresses *guanxi*, social and economic connection, and is usually made to superiors by those inferior in status. In the traditional wedding ceremony in rural Fengjia, the father of the groom kowtows before the offering table, as he repeats, 'Embody respect for heaven and earth, embody respect for your ancestors, embody respect for your father and mother, embody respect for your friends and relatives, embody respect for each other'. With each 'embody', bride and groom also customarily bowed. In 1989, however, Kipnis (1994:208–10) found in his study of the village of Fengja that only some grooms and no bride bowed, one recalcitrant bride even adopting sunglasses and folded arms. Similarly, one of my students, while describing the custom of kowtowing to parents at the Spring Festival, stressed that he only bowed from the waist rather than prostrating himself.

Hong Kong village men accumulate names as they accumulate statuses, including the *ming* name given at one month, a name given by a teacher, a public nickname, a *tzu* taken on marriage to indicate ability to participate in community and lineage rituals, and a courtesy name for business cards which is a mark of social and economic status. Women, by contrast, although named at one month, lose this name upon marriage and are usually referred to by kinship terms or category terms like 'old woman'. Girls' names often express the desire for a son – 'Little Mistake', 'Reluctant to Feed', 'Too Many' (for a second daughter) – or may be generic like 'Little Maiden' (although a long-awaited son might be disguised from the spirits with a girl's name). Her tombstone and flag that leads the spirit of the deceased in her funeral procession will bear only her father's surname, while the man's soul flag will carry his surname, courtesy name and/or posthumous name (Watson 1993:125–6, 120, 127–8). While both male and female names express connection with others, the woman's connection is limited to daughter and wife. A similar lack of variety applied to mainland Chinese names for girls, which were also often generic, for example 'girl', 'sister', 'second girl'. Upon marriage women became known as 'husband's surname-father's surname'-*Shi*. After Liberation, however, more girls were named 'Outdo Men', 'Self-Strength' and 'Independent Eagle'. During the Cultural Revolution girls' names, far more than boys', included the ideogram for red, the colour of Chinese communism. Following the economic reforms of the 1980s, there was a return to names which expressed 'the beauty of and respect for one's parents' (Lu Danni, 1995:107–9).

English, French, Spanish and Russian language word-frequency lists are topped by 'no' and 'I' (Ann 1987:81). In Western Samoa, by contrast, there is no translation for the English word 'self' and no absolute reference point for personal identity outside social context. The *matai* is appointed by consensus among the adults in the village, and is responsible for all household members and maintaining *fa'asamoa* or the Samoan way which stresses the group rather than individual members (Muse 1991: 226, 222, 225). Maori language, although having a personal pronoun, and allowing for a 'personal point of view' normally uses a representative I, located 'within a landscape of whakapapa and whenua relationships; to invoke it in a different landscape is to transform its meanings' (Smith 1994:168). Similar claims have been made for Indigenous Australians (Dudgeon et al. 1990:78); for the Chambri in Papua New Guinea, who see themselves not as 'unique subjectivities – unique clusters of dispositions, capacities and perspectives' but 'the embodiment of their social networks, the embodiment of their relationships with both living and dead' (Errington and Gewertz 1993:237; see also Strathern 1988:339); and for the Tibetans, for whom identity is located in family, class and lineage, and relationality rather than agency is valued (Klein 1995:38–9, 45, 101). Similarly, the Japanese refer to themselves by their relationship: 'Father does not like that' to a child; 'older sister wants you to get up' to a younger sibling; 'company president will come to the noon meeting tomorrow' to his workers (Kondo 1990:27–8), a usage akin to the English 'I'll have to ask the missus [wife]'.

For Takie Lebra (1992), a Japanese-born Western-trained anthropologist, there are four levels of the Japanese self. The interactional self takes account of a generalised other/public opinion or *seken* and is responsible for feeling shame, for example when left behind in the bureaucratic promotion race. The empathetic self is a self almost merged with another in a relationship, for example mother and son. The inner self is constituted by many relationships, giving rise to forms of address like 'uncle' or 'teacher' noted by Kondo. It is this variety that encourages western observers like Cathy Davidson (1993:101) to enthuse, 'One thing I've learned to love about Japan is its freedom from the classic Western notion that a person is a stable, unchanging, continuous entity, some essential self'.

The fourth level of the self, however, suggests that the Japanese are ultimately not so different from North Americans. This is the more stable inner self akin to the white western notion of the true self. Herein resides the real truth, the heart, sentiment, spirit or mind (and described by *kokoro*). While normally indicated by silence, this inner self also allows spontaneous, emotional and impulsive acts under the banner 'be faithful to yourself' (Lebra 1992:114). According to some formulations, there is a fifth level deriving from Buddhist transcendentalism: a boundless self centred in the belly, which is called on in times of life-change (Lebra 1992:114–15; see also Rosenberger 1992:68–9). Contemporary stresses on these traditional constructions of self and behaviour may be realised in western-style alienation and searching for meaning in relationships and institutions (Rosenberger 1992:12). The Japanese self is not like layers of an onion skin, the outer layers appropriate for public occasions and the inner for intimate occasions. Rather, competent members of Japanese society can move between formal and spontaneous expressions within the space of a sentence, recognising the possibility of the latter in the most formal occasions and the chasm which separates all human beings in the most intimate settings. Ritual, circumlocution and public formal occasions are moments for expressing pleasure and even emotions like crying (Tobin 1992:24, 34).

Thus it is not that the Japanese self is utterly different from the western self, but rather that of five levels of the self only one is similar to the western notion of the authentic individual. Daoism similarly allows self-absorbed artistry or excursions in nature (Sun 1991:4), the latter more resonant with the psychologistic western notions of an interior life. Indeed, romantic love is not absent from the Chinese classics, although those who succumb to it usually end in disaster (Chen Fan 1990:194; Indrani Ganguly, interview 18 May 1994, makes the same point for classical Indian romance stories). Furthermore, one psychological test suggests that this inner self is more a feature of Japanese character than Korean or Hong Kong personality (Lebra 1992:112–13). Nancy Rosenberger's (1992:7) review of the literature suggests a widespread assumption that Japanese babies are trained to be other-oriented and interdependent, stressing emotion and intuition, while American babies are trained to be individual-oriented and independent, stressing rational decision-making (a contrast between east and west pursued in Chapter 4). She herself doubts these stark dichotomies, which tend to be framed in white western terms. Thus 'my suspicion is that self as a social phenomenon moving with multiple dimensions of life is as important to our everyday understandings of self and other as it is to that of the Japanese' (Rosenberger 1992:90; see also Tobin 1992:24). Instead of suggesting that white westerners have 'selves' which define their identities while others are but fairly undifferentiated reflections of their connections with their 'others', we should explore if and how identities forged more through connectivity are different from identities forged more through individuation. This is sometimes connected with the notion of community resistance to oppression and the way that individuals define themselves as comrades in resisting oppression which affects their menfolk as well as themselves.

The African-American feminist Patricia Hill Collins (1989:763–5; see also Dyer-Bennem 1994:74–5) draws on the call and response discourse as a model which suggests the stronger ethic of caring and connectedness in the African-American community. This originated in slave days when a holler or call sent a message of fellowship and warned of whites nearby. A collective reply followed. The ring shout used a similar form. It was a form of dance in which the leader would periodically suspend the song, leaving the audience to guess the words by either beginning or ending the phrase. At meetings all who are present must participate, voicing concurrence, objections and elaborations. This is contrasted with the solitary writing and dissection of a passive object practised by white academia. The Gays and Lesbians Aboriginal Alliance (1993:4; see also Watson 1994 and Myers 1986:109) also suggest that a 'group discourse' characterises Aboriginal oral cultures. Rather than paired addressors–addressees, conversation is built on the formulations of previous contributors, a practice which assists in developing consensus. As opposed to the self-making heroine of white western autobiographies, the testimonial is a public and collective discourse, 'for and of the people', which is also 'oppositional', calling on the reader to work for social change (Mohanty 1991:39; see also McClintock 1995:326; hooks 1992:59 for the political role of black women's autobiographies; Cusicanqui 1990 for the Quechua women of the Bolivian Andes).

The requirement to confront the oppression of not only themselves but also their menfolk commends community action to some women activists. Thus Domitilia Barrios de la Chungara (1983:56), who lived with her family at the mining centre Siglo XX about 350 kilometres from La Paz in Bolivia, commenced a hunger strike when the miners were arrested for protesting against worsening working conditions: 'We camponeras, are man's other half'. Grace Mera Molisa, in 1990 private secretary to Father Walter Lini (prime minister of Vanuatu), speaks of white western women's quest for 'personal autonomy rather than questions of collective liberation or communal autonomy' (Jolly 1991:57). These ideas are captured forcefully by African-American writer Alice Walker. Where lesbianism denotes separation and isolation, womanism denotes the generosity that, while preferring 'women's culture … and women's strength', can love individual men and embrace the needs of fathers and brothers, and is committed to the 'survival and wholeness of entire people'. 'Acting womanish' is to be 'audacious, courageous … *wilful*'. The womanist 'Loves struggle. *Loves* the folk. Loves herself. *Regardless*' (Walker 1990:370). In contrast, white feminism suggests a lack of adult status, a retreat to victim status, a tendency to pathologise and thus excuse themselves (Kappeler 1995:54–5, 76). This idea of the womanist's greater strength is captured in Alice Walker's (1990:370) aphorism, 'Womanist is to feminist as purple is to lavender'.

There is a danger, however, in assuming that 'in community is strength'. It is usually only underprivileged minority groups that are described as communities (Anthias and Yuval-Davis 1992:164); the term suggests homogeneity and lack of internal conflict as well as a strength to survive anything – poverty, violence or dispossession. Community is thus a 'very convenient myth for Pakeha' (Potiki 1991:155). In fact 'communities' are often far more complex affairs, as Fred Myers (1986) found in his study of the Pintupi of the Australian Western Desert region. In Pintupi communities there is continuing tension between relatedness and autonomy, expressed in different interpretations of acceptable demands made on kin and in physical fights, of which both men and women speak with pride and animation (Myers 1986:121–2, 160). Parlo Singh (pers. comm. July

1995 in response to this book) suggests that attachment to community can become a form of reverse racism and may even produce the self-hatred which Fanon articulates (Chapter 1). Instead, an outward-looking orientation offers the possibility of productive contact with the host culture and the forging of hybrid identities.

Perhaps, then, the issue is not so much one of self versus society, the orientalist opposition with which we started this chapter, but rather the strengths and combinations of our various connections to society. In the history of the invention of the personal self outlined at the beginning of this chapter, we saw tensions between self, family and state. Perhaps in the white west connections to state are posed as stronger (nationalism) and connections to kin as weaker (smaller and more dislocated families) than in many societies outside the white west. But possibly, too, age-based or non-kin connections like friendships play a part in the (middle-class white) west which is more peripheral and crowded out by kin connections in other societies. Thus some older Chinese intellectuals, who have lived in the west and experienced the Cultural Revolution, suggest that 'friend' has a narrower meaning in China, not generally entailing trust, support and caring. In China 'the family is the only level of trust' (Lewins 1992:61, based on interviews with eighty Beijing intellectuals). However, just as non-western selves are becoming increasingly hybridised by exposure to western techniques of counselling, consumerism and romantic love, so too could white western feminist selves focus on the ways in which we can express our individual needs through connection with and attentiveness to the needs of others. Western feminists could combine strategies which were 'in your face' as I felt the pro-choice rallyists in Washington were (see p. 5) with those which are more conciliatory and collaborative, without immediately thinking this amounts to 'selling out' to the enemy. In the next section we explore another aspect of western individualism, asking whether human rights are universal or a local construction of western Enlightenment history.

HUMAN RIGHTS OR WESTERN RIGHTS?

My dear sisters and brothers, we have made it. We have managed to transcend historical and cultural complexities; we have managed to transcend socio-economic disparities and diversities; we have kept aflame our common vision and goal of equality, development and peace.

– Mrs Gertrude Mongella, Secretary-General of the
United Nations World Conference of Women in Beijing, 1995
in Conference Round-Up, 12 October 1995[1]

While it is understandable that American feminists would 'stockpile legal rights' and seek to express their freedom through 'self-reliance' (Lâm, 1994:879), such insistence refuses real dependencies and connections with others. In this section we will ask whether human rights are an invention of the west or a precious gift to all, whether they are eurocentric or universal. While many so-called non-western nations do have constitutions which guarantee human rights, including women's equality with men, there are indications that human rights mean something more, or are contextualised differently, in other countries. For some, economic and social rights – freedom from hunger, income security for example – are more important than rights to free speech or voting. For others, individual rights must be set within the context of obligations to family, to men, to community and state. As one Chinese observer put it, westerners seek fulfilling relationships, Chinese perform duties (Sun 1991:21). While some of these ideas sound regressive to many western ears, they do expose the sour underbelly of western rights rhetoric. It is much focused on 'I want' rather than 'I owe'.

Universal Declarations of Human Rights

It is often argued that the United Nations' *Universal* Declaration of Human Rights reveals that all the world's nations supported western-style human rights. Only eight of the fifty-six then members of the United Nations abstained from the vote; six were communist countries arguing that economic, social and cultural rights were equally important (Haraway 1992:198). These rights refer to systemic or structured inequality, which legal systems, particularly in the United States, are almost incapable of apprehending. Thus it is a major irony that the only developed country in the world without free medical care and government-funded day care, the United States, 'is jailing *women* for improperly caring for the babies in their wombs' (French 1992:148). Freedom of speech is rarely premised on equal rights to control the media; equality of opportunity to gain an education neglects the lesser cultural and economic resources working-class parents can offer their children. Furthermore, it is difficult to speak of 'freedom to choose' (Schultz 1992:302, 316, 323). Working-class girls might say they would rather marry than have a career, but this choice is often framed in terms of the inaccessibility of professional careers. Why would black and working-class women, who usually have to work from economic necessity, freely choose low-paying jobs? (Bacchi 1990:234–5).

The so-called Universal Declaration of Human Rights is potentially less than universal in another way. Experience has revealed that the Declaration in many respects applied only to men's rights. It has been supplemented with a Convention on the Elimination of All Forms of Discrimination Against Women. The implementation of the Convention is a process whereby national governments ratify it (agree to it), then introduce legislation and other social changes in their countries to implement its goals – a rocky road strewn with many obstacles. Signatory nations are also required to provide progress reports to the United Nations body, CEDAW (Committee on the Elimination of Discrimination Against Women). Only two African nations, Rwanda and Egypt, have fulfilled the immediate obligation of furnishing a report to CEDAW (James 1994:570), while some have ratified it with caveats. Among Muslim states, a common caveat is that the Islamic Shari'a law takes precedence (a law which maintains men as household heads with exclusive rights to allocate property in the family), although it has been suggested that most modern states in the Arab world have made attempts at reforming personal and family law, even if only to tap women's labour potential and turn their allegiance from traditional foci of family towards state, party or leader (Kandiyoti 1991:438). In Tanzania and Botswana, however, the courts have used the Convention to improve the legal status of women. In Tanzania customary law was struck down in favour of the Tanzanian Bill of Rights so that all incidents of land ownership must be equally exercisable by men and women. In Botswana, sexually discriminatory provisions of the Citizenship Act were struck down.

Violence against women also required express prohibition, this not being accepted as an incident of torture and therefore a violation of human rights. In 1993 the UN General Assembly adopted the United Nations Declaration on the Elimination of Violence Against Women, formerly the 'Vienna Declaration':

> The human rights of women and the girl-child are an inalienable, integral and indivisible part of human rights ... Gender based violence and all forms of harassment and exploitation ... must be eliminated. (Sawer and Groves 1994:79; Bullard 1993:1)

The first female UN rapporteur was appointed to collect evidence on violence against women, covering its 'incidence, causes and consequences'. Suggesting that these ideas may have extra-western currency, during the NGO Forum in Beijing, it was reported that a petition demanding that the UN report on the steps it has taken to promote the human rights of women since the Vienna Declaration was sponsored by over 1500 groups internationally (Sara Ann Friedman, 'UN on trial', *Forum '95*, 4 September 1995:15). The Vanuatu National Council of Women have prepared *Woman Ikat Raet Long Human Raet O No?'* (Are human rights also women's rights?). But it should be noted that the Vanuatu Women's Centre is mainly supported by overseas aid monies, particularly from Australia and New Zealand (Jolly 1996:180).

Women's access to equal citizenship rights is largely a victory won this century, although Argentina granted rights of citizenship to all men and women born in Argentina in 1853. The International Alliance of Women for Suffrage and Equal Citizenship was founded in 1917 to secure for women the same right to maintain their nationality as men (Guy 1992:210), a right conferred on married women in the United States in 1934, and on married women in Australia and Britain in 1948 (de Lepervanche 1989:40). In the 1970s in Britain, a British female citizen could still not confer British citizenship on the man she married. When this was appealed in the European Court as a case of sex discrimination, the British government took the equivalent right away from men (Klug 1989:27). Thus even in the most basic matter of citizenship, women's hold on their nationality is often tenuous. Such citizenship rights are increasingly important, given the international diaspora of women, as refugees, domestic servants, wage workers and immigrants (see Chapter 5).

For fourth world women, white legal systems sometimes make them choose between rights to (white) national citizenship and their connections to their communities. In Canada, First Nations (Canadian Native) women used both the Supreme Court of Canada and the United Nations Human Rights Committee to overturn section 12(1)(b) of the Indian Act of 1876. This section denied a Native woman and her children any of the band benefits and welfare rights due to 'status Native' people if she married a non-status man. (Bands are Native Canadian communities with some political, legal and economic autonomy from the wider Canadian state.) In contrast, a non-status woman who married a status man accrued those rights (see Silman 1987 for the full story, incorporating the voices of the First Nations women activists). Resistance from some Native political organisations remains strong to this day, although this may not be solely a matter of patriarchal attitudes, since the Canadian government has allocated no additional resources to bands to support their now expanded communities (Emberley 1993:90). Julia Emberley goes on to ask, 'What then is the place of feminism in relation to Native women's struggle?' Her answer is that we must understand the impact of economic and political inequalities between categories of women, while white women should 'move over' when requested to provide space for native Canadian women's voices (Emberley 1993:93–4). While both recommendations are useful warnings to white feminists, the relationship between community connections and women's rights may offer few ready solutions, as the Indian case suggests.

A similar conflict between community and women's rights has emerged in India, where the post-independence Indian state was created as a secular society. The 1955 Constitution enshrined equality, including sex equality, as a universal guarantee. While the Hindu majority was inscribed within the secular legal system, in the interests of nation-building, the state conceded the demands of religious minorities in the area of personal or family laws, based on the constitutional guarantees of freedom of conscience (Gandhi and Shah 1992:18–19; Parashar, 1992:18–21, 172). Application of religious law, however, conflicts with the constitutional guarantee of equality when religious laws operate against the interests of women.

One of the most renowned examples of this conflict between women's rights and religious custom occurred in 1985. The Supreme Court of India awarded a Muslim divorced woman, Shah Bano, maintenance from her husband beyond the three month period of *iddat*. The court used a provision of the 1973 Criminal Procedure Code actually intended to prevent vagrancy. Although the Supreme Court argued that its decision was consistent with Muslim law expressed in the Shariat Law of 1937 (Islamic Shari'a law as mentioned above), many leaders of the Muslim community disagreed, some also claiming that the Supreme Court had no right to interpret the Quran. The court decision provoked an electoral backlash from Muslim voters against the Congress-I Party, which responded with the Muslim Women's (Protection of Rights on Divorce) Bill. The government argued that this extended the rights of divorced women from those available under the Criminal Procedure Code by increasing the amount which could be claimed and the persons from whom it could be claimed. But it also aligned the divorced woman's rights more closely with those she had in Shariat law (Yasmeen 1991:178, 109; Parashar 1992:173–5, 182; Pathak and Rajan 1992:257–8, 267).

There was debate both in India and overseas about the meaning of these interventions. Shah Bano was accused by upper-class Muslim women of fighting for money from a man who, by virtue of her divorce, had become a stranger. Hindu fundamentalists promised to protect her from Muslim men. Perhaps in consequence, Shah Bano ultimately refused the court's settlement. Some Muslim women's organisations expressed support for the Supreme Court's judgement (Parashar 1992:178). Some argued that Shah Bano won the right to be treated equally, but not in western democracy's terms. Rather her equality was guaranteed by reference to the Quran (Yasmeen 1991:109). Parashar (1992:182) rejects this interpretation, seeing the government as yielding to the demands of Muslim leaders. If the criminal provisions were inadequate to protect women, they should have been changed rather than introducing a special law.

The neighbouring country of Bangladesh offers an example of how feminists are working together to resist the diminution of their rights which results from the application of religious principles. In 1988 Bangladesh changed from being a secular state to a Muslim state. The Muslim majority are now married under Islamic law, which however was recently reformed to allow Muslim women more rights than the minority

Hindu women. Bangladeshi feminists are working to remedy this inequity with the introduction of a uniform family code (Azim 1995). We will return to this issue of interpreting custom against the grain of women's rights or needs in the section on infibulation and sati below. The cases discussed in this section reveal that women in non-western countries are willing to use legal definitions of rights to argue for their needs, but they do so in a more complicated context when it appears they are rejecting their community or when their battles are reconstructed as a sign of oppression by their menfolk, whether Band Indian or Muslim leaders. The next section explores the ways in which some non-western women attempt to negotiate this relationship between rights and obligations by reconstructing rights as something based also on the obligations of self and others, including men.

Refracting Rights Through Needs

> We have to be inside the struggle with the men ... We do not have one world with only us, and another world for the men. So we women have to raise questions together with them.
>
> – Susan Ounei 1992:167, writing of New Caledonia

According to Fatima Mernissi (1991:21–2), although the Muslim states 'thronged into the corridors of the United Nations to sign the Universal Declaration of Human Rights', the 'idea of the individual in a state of nature, in the philosophical meaning of the word, is nonexistent'. Muslims see individual identity as a disturbance of collective harmony, and a traditional Muslim should be submissive to the group. Western-style democracy, people saying whatever comes into their heads rather than yielding to the discipline of tradition and divine law, produces *amma* or disorder. Majority rule cannot coexist with the application of the *Shari'a*, 'the expression of the will of God for the betterment of man'. A political community expresses its interests through *shura*, that is, through the outcomes of consultation with interest groups and scholars (Mernissi 1993:12–13, 184–6; Lazreg 1994:215). By the 1940s, however, Arab feminists were claiming suffrage rights on the basis of their responsibility for future generations, making reference to the 'advanced countries' of the west and the Declaration of Human Rights by the United Nations (Huda Shaarawi in Badran and Cooke 1990:338, 340; Badran and Cooke 1990:347). But this was not only a reflection of western values. There was a long debate during the first centuries of Islam over the struggle for democracy, in the sense of equality, well before the 'importation of the Universal Declaration of Human Rights' (Mernissi 1993:23; endorsed by Jones 1993:124 in the Australian context). Algerian writer Marie-Aimée Hélie-Lucas (1994:402–3) believes that the fight for secularisation and laws based on present understandings of human rights is the only alternative to identity politics based on fundamentalism. Beginning in 1993, Palestinian women and men have been engaged in a process which has led to a 'strong' document, a draft Declaration of Women's Rights (Jad 1995:245).

Western legal systems produce unitary notions of individuality, in which all adults are equal persons before the law, citizens with the same collection of rights bestowed and defended by the state. This is different, as we saw above, to the notions of personhood in many other societies which are constructed through and vary with kin relationships, sex, age, and other factors. In third world countries the language of rights and democracy may be adapted to fit these more complicated expressions. A meeting of 600 women from ten Asian and Pacific nations in 1993 agreed to a new definition of democracy, based not on a form of government but as 'a question of how we relate to each other and how decisions are made'. Although democracy must be an internalised value system, it must 'flow through the family, community, society, the State and at the global level'. Women's empowerment was to be striven for collectively rather than seeking the empowerment of individual women (Centre for Korean Women & Politics Newsletter, 1994 10(1):7). In Japan there is a slogan 'men superior, women dominant' (Iwao 1993:4). Equality is measured over a whole lifetime rather than at any point in time, and Japanese women seek equality through pragmatism and nonconfrontation in a culture which values interpersonal harmony (Iwao 1993:10). Similarly, middle-class Vietnamese women come to rely on the mutuality of social institutions 'out of a sense of rightness rather than fear or submission' (Lâm 1994:877–8).

A word for 'rights' was only introduced into Mandarin in the late nineteenth century. It was seen as demeaning for women to claim their rights, while demands for equality would produce conflict, a western phenomenon not prized by Confucianism, which strives for harmony (Cheung 1989:104; see also Tobin 1992:24, 34; Iwao 1993:15; Liu Yung Ho 1990:73 on western directness). The Hong Kong Council of Women, established in 1947, while committed to 'bringing equal rights to women' and successfully lobbying the government to ratify CEDAW, promising equal opportunity and anti-discrimination legislation in 1994 (Newsletter, Gender Research Program at the Chinese University of Hong Kong, Number 7, September 1994:14, 15), also stresses contributing to society and integrating the needs and interests of men (Ho, 1990:186; Ku 1987:14; Cheung 1989:101–4). Similarly in Singapore the Women's Charter implemented in 1961 was then 'years ahead of similar legislation in the west' and underpins the sense of Singapore activist women that they should have equal access to education and work opportunities as well as protection from male violence. But it also allows for a notion of 'equal but different', especially in the home where women's unique birth-giving capacity is seen as most centrally located (Lyons-Lee 1995:5).

In Taipei it is also not the case that the words 'equality' and 'rights' do not appear in official documents from women's organisations. Rather they are hedged around with statements about the needs of women *and* men, or social benefits as well as women's benefits, or woman's role in the family as well as her individual demands. Thus the brochure of the Modern Women's Foundation in Taipei describes the foundation as committed to women's 'self-recognition, self-fulfillment, self-development'; to their safety and dignity and the maintenance of women's equal rights, helping women find a balance between tradition and the modern family and career so 'they will meet the sunshine and springtime in their lives'. Feminism is worked out in a conjuncture of rapid economic growth, democratic liberalisation and a 'tradition of communal collectivism and Confucian ethics of social harmony', in which the latter 'hampered the development of individualism and the notion of equal rights'. Similar strategies to those adopted by western feminists have been used, however (along with other more local strategies – see Chapter 5 on prostitution). In 1988 the women's groups held a Mr Taipei Beauty Pageant which revealed 'the absurdity of a beauty contest' through gender-role reversal; before the 1992 election candidates were asked to present their views on women's issues; a lesbian group, Between Us, was established in 1990 (Ku 1996: 423, 427).

The very first law passed by the People's Republic of China was the Marriage Law, which was supposed to liberate women from the feudal marriage system (Wang 1991:180). Mao Zedong revived the old saying 'women hold up half the sky', which my postgraduate female students repeated with pride. But research by the All China Women's Federation revealed that, because of lack of penalties and mechanisms for implementing women's constitutional guarantees, these have limited effectiveness (Fennell and Jeffry 1992:28). More recent laws have been passed, including the Law for the Protection of Minors, under which children can sue teachers for beating them, sue fathers for failing to provide maintenance, and even sue step-parents for abandonment (Zhao Gang, 'Children Take Their Parents to Court', *China Daily* 14 December 1993:6). Anti-discrimination legislation passed in 1992 covers the fields of 'politics, culture, education, labor, property, person, family life and so on' which includes equal rights to land ownership for rural women (People's Republic of China 1994:10–11). Part of the Chinese government's program to guarantee the 'rights and interests of women', however, includes 'Regulations on Jobs and Workplaces Inappropriate for Women'. Little wonder, perhaps, that instead of the term *nuquan zhuyi* (women's right-ism), Chinese scholars and many activists use the term *nuxing zhuyi* (female-ism). The latter suggests 'Chinese women's efforts to express their own desires and points of view, but not through fierce political movements'. This 'difference' approach is contrasted with 'sameness' or 'Western women's struggle to wrest their rights from men', rights which some argue Chinese women have already won (Zhang 1995:37).

The postwar Japanese Constitution declares that 'all of the people are equal under the law' (Iwao 1993:11, 2–4). Japanese women believe in equal pay for equal work and equality of opportunity, but they do not wish to be equal to men, who they see as inherently sexually different (Iwao 1993:13). Two examples of this acceptance of difference are menstruation leave and maternity leave, which are also working women's rights in some other Asian countries. In Taiwan, for example, there is a law allowing breastfeeding breaks for women at work, but small firms lay off women who attempt to take advantage of it (Chiang and Ku 1985:24). Female bus conductors struck for menstruation leave in 1928, while intense lobbying by labour unions resulted in three days' (later reduced to two) menstruation leave in the Labor Standards Law of 1947 (Molony 1995:279). According to some commentators, maternity leave seems an unquestioned right to Japanese women, who have been guaranteed maternity leave as well as lighter loads for pregnant women and nursing breaks for breastfeeding mothers since the law of 1947 (Iwao 1993:14; Molony 1995:279–80); others note that only 19 per cent of businesses provided parental leave in 1988. Childcare leave dates from the 1970s, although it was confined to professions with unions conscientiously representing their female members, such as teaching (Molony 1995:280). The Child Care Leave Law of 1992 required all businesses to provide parental leave to the father or the mother, although there is no requirement for paid leave or that an employee will not be disadvantaged as a result of taking leave (Fujimura-Faneslow 1995:148–9). These forms of leave were not framed in terms of women's rights so much as the need to protect their fertility. But there was intense debate in the women's movement over whether these protective measures served largely to discriminate against working women, as a result of which the Equal Employment Opportunity Law passed in 1986 was very weak. Menstruation leave was incorporated into the more general sick leave, although maternity and (unpaid) childcare leave have been extended (Molony 1995:289). For some, this law was seen as 'a form of western encroachment' which 'could destroy Japanese customs' (Molony 1995:283).

These examples refer us to the sameness–difference debate within western feminism discussed in the Introduction. Until this debate emerged, most activist feminists in the United States argued that equality with men was the right to be like them. Because of women's actual differences from men, it took years of legal contortions by feminist lawyers in the United States before women's 'equal' right to maternity leave was guaranteed. Because men did not get pregnant, the courts at first refused to accord women pregnancy leave, and feminist lawyers had to draw analogies with 'disability' or sickness, which men did experience.[2] In response to protective legislation (which sometimes 'protects' women out of higher-paying jobs), equality feminists argue that if occupations are dangerous then men should also be protected from those dangers, rather than excluding women (similar points being made by Indian feminists: Sangari and Vaid 1990:17).

Thus we can see that for many non-western countries rights are not necessarily about being equal or the same; women's rights may include acceptance and guarantees of their differences. This also applies to indigenous women. Dalee Sambo (1994) suggests that 'the right to be different' may be required before equality can be gained. Rights are also more likely to be framed in terms which include obligations or commitment to others. Thus sexual interdependence is not seen as oppression, as white western feminists so often see it, but as right, as a process which constructs the person rather than diminishes her (Lâm 1994:877–8). The Indigenous Australian Eve Fesl (in Rowland 1984:113) claims that 'in order for either men or women to achieve their full potential they need the support of each other', a point also made in relation to feminist nationalist movements in the Philippines and Zimbabwe, as well as the western state of Northern Ireland (West 1992:574).

While women who assert their obligations to men or their families have been criticised by white western feminists, the other half of this relationship claims that men have obligations to women. Given this socially inscribed claim on men, perhaps women of non-western cultures have more success in working with and transforming men than do white western feminists. 'Confucian teachings on the rules of propriety and restriction of one's desires could have lessened overt display of misogyny and thus given women a safer public space once they have managed to move to certain social positions' (Ku 1996:427). To eliminate trafficking in women, the People's Republic of China (1994:15–16) has proposed campaigns for 'high moral standards' and a 'mood of respecting and protecting women'. Western feminists might at first scoff at such pious paternalism, but possibly it derives from a greater belief in reciprocal obligations between men and women. Similarly, it is instructive to contrast the Japanese and American responses to the exploitation by 'their' soldiers of women from other nationalities. The Japanese legal system favours shaming and reintegration, the wrongdoer publicly adopting the role of penitent (Braithwaite 1989:156–65). In 1992 the Japanese government made a formal apology to the Korean women who had been abducted as 'comfort women' to work in brothels for the Japanese Imperial Army troops in World War II (Vickers 1993:21). In the United States, by contrast, concerned lawyers are developing a class action for Filipinas to take against the American soldiers who fathered their children. Thus the Japanese government accepted, at least to some extent, a notion of collective obligation (see Chapter 5), but the United States response is an individualistic legally based one.

However, as Wang Jiaxiang suggested to me on reading this text, Chinese women do endorse strategies which minimise conflict, but not only because they are committed to harmony. They may also see this as the best tactical manoeuvre, just as western feminists fit the grooves of their society's values by demanding their rights: 'Women's desire to reduce conflict is there, but it could also be a tactic to break down very rigid traditional ideas in terms of women's places. So it could be regarded as a means to achieve the final goal' (Wang Jiaxiang, pers. comm. 29 April 1995).

Indeed, acknowledging obligations beyond rights suggests that some non-western constructions of connectedness make people more account-able for their actions than less so. However, and again drawing on the hybrid constructions used by Indian and other feminists who use rights discourse to advance their cause, this is not to suggest that western feminists should give up the purchase offered by human rights. Indeed, as Wang Jiaxiang suggested to me, the Korean and Japanese views on empowerment and rights can backfire, in that they could be used by men as an excuse not to give individual women their rights. Rather all feminists can develop more subtle and complex political actions and social understandings by exploring the tension between individual rights and collective obligations. This stands in contrast to western legal formulations which suggest that only autonomous individuals have the capacity for agency and intention and can thus be held accountable for their actions (Moore 1994a:33). It is to this question of agency that we now turn.

AGENCY AND 'CUSTOMARY PRACTICES'

The strong identification of cultural authenticity with Islam has meant that feminist discourse could only legitimately proceed in two directions: either denying that Islamic practices are necessarily oppressive or asserting that oppressive practices are not necessarily Islamic.

– Deniz Kandiyoti 1996:9

One of the most enduring and translated texts of colonial transition is the story of Anna Leonowens' sojourn as governess in the court of the King of Siam. Her diaries were published in the 1870s, became a novel in 1944, a screenplay in 1945, and a musical in 1951. Unlike many other colonial contact stories, here western civilisation is presented as a woman and eastern barbarism as a man, rendering the protagonists more fictionally equal. Anna's self-appointed task is to bring western dignity and selfhood to the women at court and also, she hopes, to the king. She encourages one of the king's wives, Tuptim, to escape the harem disguised as a priest. Tuptim is recaptured, on which Laura Donaldson (1992:50) comments:

> While no one would or should defend Tuptim's wrongful execution – or *sati*, for that matter – the decisions leading to this end do not necessarily represent an amoral chaos but rather a system of laws embodying profound differences in English and Siamese perceptions of society, the individual, and the idea of justice. We might protest those laws; however, to condemn them as monstrously inhuman is to conflate 'the Orient' with our own recurring nightmare of the Occidental Other. (Donaldson 1992:50)

While Laura Donaldson unfortunately neglects to say on what grounds 'we' might protest 'those' laws, she makes the point that laws which cannot be understood (by 'us') are not necessarily meaningless, unjust or amoral within the context of their own society. Rather they reflect the sense of justice and morality endorsed by the society which produced them.

Exploring that different sense of morality is the task of this section, a task which will I hope sidestep the oriental oppositions of barbarism/civilisation and coloured/white in discussing the rituals of non-western cultures. So ingrained is the racism of this approach that you will often see media reports in which white western men (or women for that matter) contrast 'our' liberated women with 'their' oppressed women (Ware 1992:17), so that apparent commitment to women's rights becomes a container for racism. A pervasive example in Australia concerns Muslim women, for example press outrage over Muslims who murder 'their' women' when they transgress sexual codes or press outrage over the 'mutilation' of women (Jones 1993:108–9).[3]

Infibulation

> I felt the rough hand rub me. I saw the razor blade flash after they spilled alcohol on it ... I saw it coming near me. I screamed. I screamed, and my shouts sounded like the shrieks of a slaughtered baby rabbit. I screamed as it burned and tore through my flesh. ... [She asks] 'Since you love me, why did you sacrifice me?' 'So that men will come running after you without your asking. And when your husband goes away for a long time, you won't suffer at all'.
>
> – Alifa Rifaat, born in Egypt 1930, in Badran and Cooke 1990:75, 77

To equate 'rape, forced prostitution, polygamy, genital mutilation, pornography, the beating of girls and women, purdah' as 'all violations of basic human rights', as Fran Hosken did in 1981, is to claim that all these practices are about sexual control at all times (Mohanty 1991:66). Interestingly, Mohanty goes on to isolate purdah (or veiling and seclusion of women) as the category that should *not* be equated with rape, forced prostitution and so on. The different meanings and practices of purdah were discussed in Chapter 1, where it was seen that veiling is not simply an issue of sexual control, although for some Muslim women this is part of its meaning.

Another good example of eurocentrism is western heterosexual feminists' unthinking condemnation of polygamy (as though every woman would want a husband all to herself). As Victoria Burbank (1994:111) notes in a review of the literature, 'Around the world, conflict, jealousy, and rivalry are associated with the co-wife relationship.' Luo women call their co-wives 'my partner in jealousy'; in Surinam the word for 'fight' is 'to act like a co-wife'. But the crucial issue for co-wives, even if realised as sexual jealousy (or murder when traditional rules of polygamy break down), often appears to be the distribution of resources like food and land when wives and children accumulate these, for example among West Africans and the Sirono of Bolivia (Burbank 1994:111–12). The practice of serial polygamy (divorce and remarriage) in the anglophone west often places ex-wives and current wives in a similar partnership 'in jealousy' based on the man's inability to support two households.

On the up side, polygamy allows one wife to work while the other takes care of the children. Aboriginal women in Arnhem Land describe this as two sisters being 'one fire' (Burbank 1994:115; see also Williams 1993:185 for Plains American Indians). In some cases, in a nice reversal of the preoccupation with heterosexual jealousy, intense erotic attachments emerge between co-wives (Singh 1990:111; Shaaban 1988:61–5; Blackwood 1986:11; Adam 1986:24 for the Azande; Lieh-Mak et al. 1992:100 for Chinese harems, where ivory and lacqured wood dildoes were in use and where the husband may have encouraged such practices to conserve his sexual energy).

More challenging than veiling or polygamy to western notions of individual agency and well-being is the practice of female genital surgery. The practices gathered under the heading of 'female circumcision'[4] occur in twenty-four African (mainly northern Africa but excluding Morocco, Algeria and the Libyan Arab Republic), some Arab and some Asian nations (for example in Rembau in Malaysia and in Singapore, where the sunna method is practised (see below): Stivens 1996:215–16), although it is 'not a practice that is required by any specific known religion' (Nkrumah 1996:28; Abdalla 1982:13). Female genital mutilation ranges from the sunna method of partial clitoridectomy in Egypt (ranging from a symbolic nick in the clitoris to partial removal of the clitoris) to the excision of the clitoris and the labia minora, to the excision of the clitoris, labia minora and parts of the labia majora. This last type includes infibulation, or the fastening or sewing together of the two sides of the vulva to leave a small opening for urine and later menstrual blood. Infibulation often leads to urinary tract infections, extremely painful intercourse and usually requires the cutting of the women's pinhole vaginal opening with a knife by her newly wedded husband. Despite this, many women voluntarily choose reinfibulation, although partly from fear of losing their husbands' affection and limited economic resources to younger wives.

At the Copenhagen United Nations Decade for Women Meeting in 1980, many Muslim women refused to condemn female circumcision as this appeared to endorse western definitions of its 'barbarism'. Orientalism silenced the 'other' woman, her space already defined and 'her subjects objectified' (Lazreg 1990:337). But not all Muslim women have been silenced by western women's strident voices. Nawal el Saadawi is an Egyptian 'intellectual, a feminist, and a political activist'; she is also a medical doctor who was a director within the Ministry of Health Education (Emberley 1993:54–5). She was removed from this position with the publication in 1972 of her first non-fiction work, *Women and Sex*. This did not stop her writing four more books on the treatment of Arab women. For her condemnation of clitoridectomy, *The Hidden Face of Eve* (1980), el Saadawi was arrested and imprisoned in 1981, along with 1035 other leading Egyptian intellectuals (Emberley 1993:55).

Her first work published in English, and written for Anglo feminists, *The Hidden Face of Eve*, is, according to Julia Emberley (1993:16), 'an intervention into the elitist assumptions of First World feminism' assumptions which contribute to constructions of Arab countries as 'uncivilized'. Critiques of the practice are decontextualised from their historical and political surroundings and fail to recognise the feminist activism already occurring in Arab countries (Emberley 1993:55). Like radical feminists, el Saadawi propounds a universal women's oppression when she compares western women's psychological clitoridectomy with the physical experience of Egyptian women (Emberley 1993:56). Furthermore, she expresses class and chauvinist superiority, contrasting the more 'civilised' Egyptian *sunna* practice with the 'barbaric' practice of the Sudan (although she is critical of the Egyptian state for supporting the practice), and she takes on an inappropriate position as the representative spokeswoman for all Arab women (Emberley 1993:58–61).

In an admittedly 'effective passage', el Saadawi (in Emberley 1993:64) describes the villages of rural Egypt where the *daya*, an 'ugly old crone', used her 'long dirty finger nail' to prove the young bride's virginity by pushing up into the vagina to cause a blood flow. If the flow is insufficient, either husband or *daya* may push harder, puncturing the wall of the vagina, perhaps into the urinary bladder. According to Emberley (1993: 64), el Saadawi condemns both husband and *daya* because of their inferior working-class status. But el Saadawi (in Emberley 1993:64) prefaces this passage with 'Numerous were the nights which I spent by the side of a young girl' whose life was threatened in this way. Given these harrowing experiences, one can understand why el Saadawi failed to note the economic needs of the *daya* for payment and the cultural context which explains the importance of virginity. Similarly, Emberley accuses el Saadawi of patronising 'the majority of Arab women [who] don't as yet know how to fight back politically'. But el Saadawi herself says that it is necessary to 'raise the consciousness of the people so that they themselves will do the fighting. It's no good patronising or talking down to them, you must bring them along' (in Emberley 1993:61).

El Saadawi has also written a number of fictional stories on sexual politics, which Emberley (1993:66-7) criticises for their representation of Egyptian women as 'dumb'. By dumb, she means both mute, as in Zayeka at the start of *Woman at Point Zero*[5] (but not at the end), and stupid, as in 'the image of women memorizing the Koran without understanding the words' in *God Dies by the Nile*. *Woman at Point Zero* is based on the life story of a woman condemned to death, a woman el Saadawi met at Qanatir Prison while researching neurosis in Egyptian women. Firdaus is born in a poor family and carries with her two strong childhood memories. One is the first time she earned a piastre from her father by following his orders; the more haunting memory is her only contact with a male not based on an economic nexus, a childhood lover who pleased her before she was given her clitoridectomy. A series of less than happy sexual encounters with men – her uncle, her ageing husband in an arranged marriage, a stranger who appears to offer protection – finally suggest to Firdaus a life of prostitution. Firdaus feels for the first time free; she chooses her clients and controls her own earnings (Saadawi 1983:68). But the illusion is shattered when a client tells her she is 'not respectable' (Saadawi 1983:70). After a search for respectability when she is offered money for sex by her office colleagues and falls in love with a man who treats her just as clients treat prostitutes, except without paying her, she returns to the trade. When a pimp demands most of her earnings, she stabs him and so learns a new invincibility in her power to kill (Saadawi 1983:95). Once imprisoned and sentenced, she goes to her death fearlessly, seeing that she is condemned to die not because she murdered a man ('there are thousands of people being killed every day') but because they are afraid: 'They know that as long as I am alive they will not be safe, that I shall kill them. My life means their death. My death means their life' (Saadawi 1983:100). In my reading of *Woman at Point Zero*, Firdaus is not dumb, but rather makes an eloquent statement of women's limited choices in the face of poverty and clitoridectomy.

In my review of the debate between Julia Emberley, a white Canadian feminist committed to a materialist perspective but *au fait* with post-modernist analyses, and Nawal el Saadawi, a professional Egyptian feminist, it is clear where my sympathies lie. Emberley evaluates el Saadawi in terms of her failure to adopt Emberley's position, a position sensitive to constraints on the freedom of working-class people to make choices in their lives. Thus Emberley chastises el Saadawi for her failure to see the class constraints which limit the *daya's* choices and for speaking for others, foregrounding her shared culture but neglecting the gulf of class. But Emberley, in my opinion, fails to fully appreciate el Saadawi's position, admittedly privileged economically, but also based on a real commitment to overcome the suffering of young girls, so much of which she has seen at first hand. However, there is an important lesson here for evaluating alien practices within their own cultural context. This is the point African-American law professor Isabelle Gunning (1992:240) makes in her notion of 'world-travelling', a mechanism for avoiding both pre-given universals and sinking into a self-censoring relativism.

World-travelling offers a means of approaching 'culturally challenging patriarchal practices like genital surgeries' (Gunning 1992:198) without pre-judging them. World-travelling walks the tightrope between inter-connectedness and independence, between women's shared perspectives and their differences (Gunning 1992:202, 204). In order to achieve these apparently contradictory aims, Gunning (1992:204–5, 212–15, 217–22) recommends three strategies:

1. Understanding the cultural pressures which created 'us', the self. For example genital mutilation (clitoridectomy) was practised until the early decades of this century as a cure for nymphomania in countries like the United States (Dixon 1996:261, note 3).

2. 'Looking at ourselves as others might see us.' Western women also have barbaric or inexplicable practices; for example bulimia and anorexia 'must be close to sacrilege' for women facing malnutrition and starvation. A second element of this task is understanding one's historical relationship to the other, as that relationship would be seen by the other. For example, the pressures of colonialism on countries now trying to forge postcolonial identities might encourage them to turn to traditional practices.

3. Seeing the other as she sees herself in her own cultural context. This requires looking at both cultural analogues in one's own culture and understanding the other's practice in its own cultural context. Cultural analogues are the 'bizarre and barbaric practice of cosmetic surgeries' (Gunning 1992:213) like breast enlargements. Western women are not 'horrified' by these practices because we understand the context and

complexities. Women demand breast surgery just as mothers 'demand' genital mutilation, fearing otherwise that their daughters will not find husbands. In the United States, once the risks of cosmetic surgery became more widely known, the practice continued on the basis that women made informed choices (not that they *were* always informed of the risks) (Davis 1995:37, 130–1). 'The problem of why individuals would want to embark on such a risky undertaking to begin with, however, was not addressed' (Davis 1995:37), apart from some feminists who saw such women as 'cultural dopes', dupes of the beauty myth. But many women chose cosmetic surgery, although aware of the feminist critique, because they saw surgery as the only solution to their problems, problems which they understood as 'a symptom of an unjust social order in which women are forced to go to extremes to have an acceptable body' (Davis 1995:57, 162–3). It should also be noted that women actually had 'little choice of what body to value' (Young 1990:199). All of this could be said of mothers who must feel both the physical pain of their daughters, as they felt their own when young, and yet see no other alternative but genital mutilation to secure their daughters' futures. Furthermore, genital mutilation is often associated with rituals which celebrate a girl's passage to the status of motherhood, which may be one of the few resources a Sudanese woman has: 'marriage . . . is an essential career move'. Among the few alternatives to marriage, ironically, are the midwives who practise clitoral surgery (Gunning 1992:215, 217–19, 222). Similarly, Juliana Nkrumah (1996: 30–2) notes that a Sabiny woman in Uganda cannot perform 'her ordinary economic' activities associated with being a wife unless she is circumcised. Once educational and economic opportunities for women mean that 'women are not economically dependent on men, there will be little need for FGM'.

The United Nations formed a subcommission to inquire into the issue, headed by an African female who was sensitive to its cultural aspects. The group chose not to discuss the issue of patriarchal control (Gunning 1992:244–5). It is important to understand the difference between this approach and that of many western feminists, particularly radical feminists. For them, clitoridectomy, foot-binding and witch-burning are all incidents of patriarchal control, cross-cultural control of women by men. Thus Andrea Dworkin (1994:219) links foot-binding to the masochistic romanticisation of the tolerance of pain, characteristic also of eyebrow-plucking, girdles, nose jobs and so on in western beauty rituals. Instead the group suggested that the traditional functions associated with genital mutilation, which they identified as initiation and a ritual to test the capacity to bear pain, had been undermined by social change which encouraged lower ages for surgery and the increasing use of anaesthetics (Gunning 1992:243).

Neither did the UN subcommittee recommend penal sanctions and a rights-based approach, although they could have invoked the UN Declaration on the Rights of the Child adopted in 1959 (Gunning 1992:231). Given their focus on social changes which undermined the *internal* rationales for genital surgery, the group recommended education rather than penalties. Scattered reports suggest that this is effective.[6]

Other commentators focus on rereading sacred texts to condemn genital surgery, to claim that female circumcision is not a 'real' tradition. Fatima Mernissi (1991:98) argues that female excision was unknown in the Prophet's seventh-century Arabia and that practices like female slavery and the seclusion of women were introduced corruptions to Islam (see also Jones 1993:122, 124 for Australian Islam). Like the Bible, the Quran is open to multiple interpretations. Mernissi (1991:118–19) sees, as evidence of gender equality in Islam, Allah's claim that 'men who guard their modesty and women who guard [their modesty], and men who remember Allah and women who remember – Allah has prepared for them forgiveness and a vast reward.' But Allah also said, 'Your women are a tilth for you [to cultivate] so go to your tilth as ye will', provoking ongoing debates about a husband's right of access to his wife's body (Mernissi 1991:146, 157, 190 who goes on to refute that the Prophet condoned domestic violence).

The international network Women Living under Muslim Laws (WLUML), formed in 1984, links over 2000 women in approximately forty countries among the 450 million women living in Muslim countries and communities around the world, the majority of whom live under Muslim Personal Laws (Hélie-Lucas 1994:394). By exchanging information on the interpretation of laws in different Muslim states, WLUML reveals that 'the idea of one homogenous Muslim world is an illusion' and works to develop alternative interpretations (Shaheed 1994:1009, 1011). This group notes that most legislation in the area of commerce, public service and administration reflects that of the west; Shari'a or Muslim jurisprudence is generally limited to 'the regulation of family and personal matters' (Shaheed 1994:1002). WLUML defends women in individual cases with legal advice, welfare and other services, but only in response to requests for help, expressing a sensitivity to cultural differences in different Muslim nations (Shaheed 1994:997, 1014).

Other Muslim women focus on the health effects of genital surgery rather than the rights of women and girls. But in doing so, the medical approach allows the practice if it can be performed safely without negative consequences (Engle 1992:9–10). This aspect of the debate has come home to many western countries where practising Islamic migrant communities seek medical services for genital surgery. In Australia, with immigrant women from Somalia, Eritrea, Ethiopia and Sudan increasing by 154 per cent since 1991, the government proposes 'education supported by legislation' to prevent female genital mutilation, women as well as service providers being the targets (Office of the Status of Women 1995:32). In 1995 the NSW Parliament passed the Crimes (Female Genital Mutilation) Amendment Act (NSW) which aims to prevent all forms of genital surgery, including a nick in the clitoris. There are four exemptions to the legislation, one of which might allow female genital surgery. Thus it can be performed if necessary for the health of the person on whom it is performed. Second, it may be argued that women who do not receive the operation would be ostracised by their community and so would suffer mentally. Third, it may be performed for medical purposes on a woman in labour or who has just given birth. Fourth, and most interestingly in terms of Gunning's notion of world-travelling, clitoridectomy may be performed as part of a sexual reassignment or sex-change procedure (Dixon 1996:287, 277, 288). Thus removal of the clitoris for sexual reassignment is legal, but a nick in the clitoris for cultural purposes is not.

Female genital mutilation is also illegal in Canada, Sweden, the United Kingdom and France. In France there have been a series of excision trials since 1979, some cases involving the death of the child. Women are the perpetrators, and the defence adopted on their behalf is either that they are compelled by a 'cultural tradition [which] ... in their minds carries the weight of a law that they are bound to obey' or that they have a right to privacy, freedom from state interference (Winter 1994:949, 952–3). Clearly the constructions of agency and rights are close to downright contradictory in these alternative defences. Refusing to recognise the force of a tradition which condemns a non-circumcised woman to the label of 'unclean' and 'masculine' (Winter 1994:941) is just as blind as viewing women as mere dupes of tradition. Rather women are caught in, but also act within, networks of customary expectations, desires for their children and the power of their husbands.

However, as with illegal abortion, making the practice illegal will tend to raise its price and drive it underground into potentially unsafe surgery. Given this, education may be the best strategy in the west as well as the east. Thus excisees who have grown up in France are 'infinitely less likely to have excisions performed on their own children' (Winter 1994:942), while voices of dissent from the immigrant community can be raised in a context which does not mean they are naming their compatriots as criminals.

We will see the same difficulties in discussing the re-emergence in recent years in India of sati, popularly but inaccurately described as widow-burning. The task is to bring 'domination and resistance into the same account' by 'viewing the victim as subject' (Ram 1991a:92, 95).

Sati

It is good to swim in the waters of tradition but to sink in them is
suicide.

– Mahatma Gandhi in Gandhi and Shah 1992:325

As we have seen, Indian feminists are no strangers to the language of
rights. The evaluation that 'the fight for women's rights in India is a
western concept, can only be termed as facile' (Jethmalani 1986:71).
Indian feminism has rebutted the assertion that feminists are 'westernised' or 'manhaters' with images of Asian feminism and Gandhian feminism. Indigenous feminisms are built on 'episodes in mythology, fables, folk
stories, songs and humour [in which] women, in different ways, have
resisted their subordination' (Gandhi and Shah 1992:326, 327, 331, 15).
As in the debates over infibulation, religion, a significant aspect of identity
and meaning construction, has been retrieved from fundamentalist
interpretations (Gandhi and Shah 1992:325). Even so, the adaptation of
religious myths to feminist goals is not without its problems. For example,
it is often the case that when the female dominates the male in Hindu
paired gods, the pair is sinister, but when the male dominates the female,
the pair is benign (Brettell and Sargent 1993:335). Given the religious
diversity of India, one also has to ask 'what sort of connotations the
images of Kali and Shakti have for other religious groupings' (Gandhi and
Shah 1992:326).

The practice of sati is linked to the goddess Sati, the wife of Shiva, who
burned herself before her father to protest Shiva's exclusion from a huge
sacrifice (Hawley 1994:82). Ritually, the sati (the word originally refers to
the widow) sits in the pyre cradling her husband's head, the pyre igniting
spontaneously with the fire of her inner truth. She thus provides her
husband with protection beyond the grave, cancelling any karmic effects
of his shortcomings in life. She also confers blessings and protection on
those who seek her out before the cremation. However, although the sati
is a woman who immolates herself on her husband's funeral pyre, this was
not in fact what the goddess Sati did; indeed the word *sati* merely means
'good wife' (Rajan 1993:56). Thus Indrani Ganguly (pers. comm.) notes
that the practice of sati is 'not endorsed by any Hindu scriptures', but may
be traced to the mass suicides which aristocratic women committed to
avoid capture by invading forces. However, 'we don't know whether a
custom prompted by historical circumstances then gets picked up by the
men in that area to get rid of any women they don't want', in the manner
of witch-hunts in the west. Furthermore, 'under Hindu law, widows can
inherit land; if she remarried then the land went out of the family'.

Apparently also linked to the symbolic significance of sati is the dowry
burnings of brides who are deemed to have brought an insufficient dowry.

In many regions of India it is a mark of a woman's status to be given away with a dowry, so that the practice has spread as a status symbol among non-Hindu groups (Gandhi and Shah 1992:52; Duza and Nag 1993:79; Stone and James 1995:130). But this makes a daughter 'costly', while a son brings in a dowry when he marries. Amniocentesis or sex-testing of foetuses is advertised as 'Better 500 rupees now than 5000 later', referring to the dowry price (Desai 1985:70). Dowry-related deaths run at the rate of at least 2000 each year, two a day in Delhi and one every five days in Bombay (Stone and James 1995:127, a rise from 1000 in 1985; Kelkar 1987:181). Husbands, sometimes with the collusion of their mothers, murder young brides, often in fabricated kitchen fires, and most commonly by soaking them in kerosene and setting them alight (Stone and James 1995:128). The practice has been interpreted as a grotesque version of sati in a modern world increasingly preoccupied with material possessions. Thus dowry deaths are most prevalent in the middle classes, where wives' families cannot afford the dowry payments but husbands' families demand television sets or capital to start a business (Kumari 1989). Even women who have borne the much-prized son are not free of danger; in one study over a third of the women had borne children and another 11 per cent were pregnant at the time of death (Stone and James 1995:131).

A world-travelling response to western horror at the burning of the wife as a kind of sati has been suggested by Veena Oldenburg (1994:43). She notes that kerosene is as ordinary in middle-class Indian kitchens as are guns and knives in American homes: 'Burning a woman in her kitchen is neither fraught with ritual significance nor culturally sanctioned'. It is forensically preferable because it can be made to look like an accident or suicide. She also notes that 1500 women are fatally injured in homes in the United States every year and 2.5 million are the victims of robbery, assault and rape. To match this rate in India more than 5000 women would have to be burned alive annually in India (however Voice of People Awakening 1995:16 suggests 14 000 deaths in India in 1993, 'not counting suicides and those cases unreported'). Furthermore, as Ganguly (pers. comm. July 1995) notes, dowry is often the rationale, but not necessarily the only motive or reason for these deaths. She found in her research on dowry deaths that sometimes women set fire to themselves to draw attention to marital problems, akin to the 'cry for help' of women in the west who attempt suicide, expressing anger or frustrations they cannot clearly name or resolve. Given the publicity of dowry burnings, police respond to accusations of dowry death but not of domestic violence.

The more complex response by Indian feminists to sati, as opposed to dowry burnings, is a function both of its historical and contemporary interpretations. For most British readers sati and child brides were part of the stock horrors of India, as in *Mother India*, discussed in Chapter 1, or in *Jane Eyre*, where Jane says she will not be 'hurried away' in a sati at Rochester's whim (Sharpe 1993:14, 49, 51–2). In the early nineteenth century thousands of pages of parliamentary papers were expended on the 4000 sati immolations, while hardly a word was mentioned of the millions who died from disease and starvation (Yang 1992:77). Local practices, often uncodified, did not necessarily recommend sati (Apffel-Marglin and Simon 1994:29). Sati was highest among the poorest castes, and rose during epidemics, although the rate was never more than 1.2 per cent of widows. Almost half the widows were over 50 years old and often immolated themselves many years after their husband had died, perhaps at the age of 70 or 80. A sati avoided the 'cold sati' of widowhood, terminating a precarious existence made more difficult with advancing years. In return she received the virtue and long-term spiritual rewards of ritual death (Yang 1992:88, 90–2 using local police records).

In 1813, non-voluntary sati was made illegal by the British government, an act which only prevented ten illegal satis and led to an actual increase in numbers because the regulations were interpreted as government approval for sati (Sangari and Vaid 1990:15). In 1829 the British declared sati illegal and punishable, a reform which was devised by Raja Rammohun Roy of Bengal (Yang 1992:74–5). By the second half of the nineteenth century, widow remarriage had replaced the now outlawed sati as the main issue of concern to Indian feminists. This was because the widow often experienced a harrowing existence. She was fallen upon by women from the caste of barbers who stripped her of her jewellery, using rocks to break her bangles (and sometimes her arms). She was refused water and food; she was dragged along the funeral path. She was forced to remain unbathed in her clothes for thirteen days after the funeral. Henceforth she was rarely spoken to as she was considered inauspicious. It is little wonder women preferred to burn themselves, according to one widow (Anonymous in Tharu and Lalita 1991:357–63).

However, a slightly different picture is presented in M. K. Indira's (1976) novel *Phaniyamma*, based on the biography of a 'cold sati' born in 1840 and dying in 1952, who was widowed even before her menstruation. Phaniyamma lives a long and highly respected, although ascetic, life as a servant and a midwife. But she is aware of the sexual discrimination in ritual purification practices, which shape much of her day, and prays not to be reborn: 'I haven't committed any sin in this incarnation. Try not to give me another life like this one' (Indira 1976:86). Similarly, Bālāsatīmātā's husband contracted a deadly fever from touching her hand during the marriage ceremony, leaving her a young widow. She built a hut where she lived on the *sat* (wisdom) she had accumulated, dying at a great age in 1986, after which a shrine was built to her (Courtright 1995). On the other hand, Mīrā Bāī, a Rajput princess, refused to act as a widow when her young husband died, averring that she was married to the god

Krishna, who was still alive. She became a mendicant ascetic (Harlan 1995:204–5).

While some of the Indian elite disavowed sati, others advocated it to assert their ritual purity against British rule. As an 'invented tradition', the rate rose sharply in the late eighteenth century (Yang 1992:76). According to official records, there have been twenty-eight cases of sati in Rajasthan since Independence, although it was only with the sati of the young widow Roop Kanwar in 1987 that the phenomenon caused extensive public debate. In villages where satis occur, shrines are erected which attract pilgrims to annual fairs, bringing 'a measure of wealth to the families and villages involved' (Hawley 1994:81, 84). It has been claimed that according to Rajput custom, because there were no children, if Roop Kanwar lived she would have retained her dowry of gold, money and household goods; thus her in-laws 'had a direct interest in forcing her to commit sati' (Meenakshi 1995:42).

Both advocates and opponents of sati see the widow's action as compelled. For the British then and for Indian liberals today, the widow who goes on the pyre is driven by either physical force or religious compulsion. To the Indian conservatives, she is 'coerced' by western values if she refuses the pyre (Mani 1988:126; Chew 1991:45). These analyses revolve around interpretations of Brahmanic scriptures and the religious nature of *sati*, the existence (or not) of an 'authentic cultural tradition' rather than the perspective of the sati herself (Mani 1988:125, 122; Mani 1990:35).

According to some Indian feminists, one must allow that sati is an existential choice, at least possible, if not always indicated by such coercive measures as the use of opiates, building the sati into the pyre with a wall of wood, or the alternative option of survival as an ill-treated widow. If one does not allow this choice, the sati becomes a victim with no subjectivity or agency. Thus Rajeswari Sunder Rajan (1990:7) argues that the sati's pain (unlike that of dowry deaths or infanticide) is a ritual pain which indicates yogic submission. It is the *meaning* (and celebration) of the death, its focus on women's increased ritual power rather than loss of life which distinguishes it from other so-called choices. Interestingly, British women have historically been awed by sati, noting the sati's 'ability to go beyond the "bounds of requirement"' and express 'spiritual and ascetic tenderness, complete abnegation of herself, unlimited devotion to her family' (Clarisse Bader in 1867) or 'the ultimate power that the Hindu woman had in an otherwise powerless situation' (nineteenth-century observer) (in Chakravarti 1990:44–6). In contrast, the Indian writer Pandita Ramabai in 1886 described sati as the creation of a 'wicked priesthood'. The widow only saw it as a sublime act because of the cruel alternatives (in Chakravarti 1990:71).

It should perhaps give us pause that contemporary interpretations by

Indian women academics echo not the Indian Ramabai's voice but former British voices, expressing an apparent reverence for the ritual and its practitioners. Unlike the white women a hundred years ago, however, today's commentators are perhaps more aware that '*Sati* functions both as the act confirming the stoicism of women and as the practice that epitomizes their weakness' (Mani 1988:139). The sati does not express the free choice of individual selfhood so beloved by some western commentators, including gynocentric feminists; she acts within a context indicating 'more contingent, varied and flexible modes of resistance' (Rajan 1993:11).

Gayatri Spivak (1994) suggests that to understand sati, white western women should try to see it as similar to the context of western martyrdom. Suicide no longer has connotations of martyrdom in the west, except under quite particular circumstances, like politically motivated hunger strikes. Suicide more generally represents failure, either personal or social, although about 35 to 40 per cent of battered women in the United States attempt suicide (Counts 1993:252–3). Thus western observers may have difficulty finding an analogue in our own culture with which to understand sati. Contrariwise, in some other cultures suicide expresses sacrifice and self-abnegation, akin to the sati's suicide. Thus in India three sisters hanged themselves from a ceiling fan because their father could ill afford a dowry for all of them (Rajan 1990:15). In Japan, suicide takes a number of forms, mother-child homicide-suicide, double suicide or *shinju* (sincerity of the heart) engaged in by homosexual and heterosexual lovers, and patriotic *kamikaze* suicide (Oaks 1994:519). Both in the past and present, Chinese women preserved their virtue by committing suicide. Women's courageous deeds in defence of their purity, often ending in suicide, were celebrated as part of Chinese 'history' by local gazetteers and in shrines or tablets. Thus women entered the public zone with their sacrifice for family honour (Chow 1991a:59). In the Ming-Qing period, texts like Ban Zhao's *Nujie* created strong public sanctions against women remarrying and encouraged widow suicide (Lee 1994:6). Thus in the early 1980s, factory workers who were showering when their factory caught fire chose to die rather than flee naked. In 1993 a woman who had been gang-raped by six teenagers 'jumped into a nearby river to escape humiliation and drowned herself' (Ding 1991:113; *China Daily* 13 September 1993:3).

Apparently suicide could also operate as posthumous finger-pointing and revenge in China and West New Britain. People did not ask 'why' but 'who' caused it, suspicion falling on mother-in-law, husband or son (Wolf 1975:111–12). Among the Lusi-Kaliai of West New Britain, where both husbands and wives use physical violence, a battered woman may also expose her husband to her menstrual blood in order to cause him to sicken and die. If all else fails, she can commit suicide. The person held responsible for a suicide is exposed to both large demands for reparation from kin and the possibility that they will kill him by magical means (Counts 1993:252–3, 258).

Even so, suicide is a somewhat self-defeating exercise of power according to western perceptions, an argument I would also apply to anorexia when it is interpreted as adolescent resistance to the demands of womanhood. Similar criticisms of suicide have been made by some contemporary Asian women, campaigning against traditional notions of shame, submissiveness and self-sacrifice. Xie Lihua condemns the 'Model Families' competitions which praise self-sacrificing (but sometimes deeply unhappy) wives (Wang Rong, 'Xie Champions Women's Rights' *China Daily* 11 October 1993:6). Similarly, some Vietnamese women condemn the socialist celebration of self-sacrificing good mothers and wives in Confucian terms. In contrast is the much-loved story of *Kim Van Kieu* which describes a woman who, to save her brother and father from humiliation, becomes a prostitute, concubine, servant and nun before she can return to her first lover. Instead of suicide or life in a nunnery, she loves three men and freely chooses her lovers (Trinh 1992:60).

CONCLUSION

Indrani Ganguly, in response to a draft of this book, suggests that collectivist ideologies have been part of western utopian imagination and practice, in the socialist movement, and in communes, co-operatives and community-based organisations. Just as Asian and indigenous women have balanced rights with obligations, claims to equal treatment with claims to respect for their difference, so too have some auto-critics of western individualism sought to extend the community of care. Maternal and eco-feminists are cases in point. So are contemporary proponents of identity politics based not on individual identity but a shared collective position, even if they fragment earlier claims concerning women's sister-hood. But western discourses are much more uneasy in their attempt to hold these apparently opposing aspects in view at once. Individual rights-claims are a powerful and popular currency. Those who do not have rights are most often seen as the disenfranchised, the incapable, the not yet adult.

Unquestioning acceptance of the freely choosing individual often conceals the fact that western women's wants and desires are quite possibly deformed by the patriarchal structures in which women find their subjectivity. As an example, the sexuality of white western women is constructed in passive, even masochistic terms, and this lends support to the claims made in rape cases that women often enjoy violent sex. The notions of consent and agency do not readily capture these complexities in which 'top-down relations feel sexual' because top-down relations are the only forms of sexual relations women experience. As with resistance to polygamy, the link between sex and resources is (at least implicitly) understood: 'Women also widely experience sexuality as a means to male approval; male approval translates into nearly all social goods' (MacKinnon 1989:147). On the other hand, psychoanalytic feminists, reminiscent of the analyses of sati explored above, suggest that MacKinnon's explanation denies all agency and pleasure to female actors; they are mere dupes of an oppressive patriarchy. The taboo idea that women might enjoy heterosexual (or homosexual) sex with domination-subordination aspects to it (either in fact or fantasy) is now hotly debated. In 1983, however, raising the issue of women's pleasure was criticised because it signalled 'a shift from seeing sex as either "repressed" or "liberated"' (Coward 1983:xii). A more complex notion of women as potentially both victim (repressed) and agent (achieving pleasure) at once was initially resisted for the more straightforward politics of liberation through assertion of sexual independence.

The possibility of women's internal conflict in matters of sex is denied by the 1994 Australian slogan to discourage rape: 'When a woman says no, she means no'. For Ien Ang (1995:62) the slogan expresses 'individualism, conversational explicitness, directness and efficiency – all Western cultural values which may not be available to or appeal to "other" women'. Asian women may use more circuitous but not necessarily less effective ways to achieve their ends. But so might white western women, even unconsciously, thus suggesting the failure of this slogan to capture the reality of many Australian women's (Anglo and Asian) lived experiences. Instead the slogan posits an idealised citizen who knows and can always demand her rights in unproblematic communication, like western individualism's ideal man.

Another example of the complexities of attributing agency to western women is surrogacy contracts. Some feminist commentators say that women cannot enter such contracts as free agents because the very entry of a contract to sell or give away one's baby must be based on coercion, usually economic coercion. But as Rosemary Diprose (1994:112) points out, women must enter a number of work contracts which bring unexpected emotional and physical traumas because of some form of economic coercion, and which, with the exception of prostitution or pornography work, are rarely questioned as a failure of freedom of choice. Instead Disprose tries to make a space to question the 'freedom' of the surrogate mother in entering the contract on two grounds. First, the contract may lead to an objectification of the woman's body, for example by the commissioning couple, who treat her 'lived body as an instrument for the realisation of a child'. Second, if we see the self as ensconced in the body, the self who makes the contract might be quite a different person from the self who has undergone a pregnancy and is now asked to relinquish the child: 'such a significant change of body is a change of mind'. This is suggested in the trauma and psychological disorders experienced by mothers relinquishing children for adoption, especially when they felt they had no choice in the matter (Winkler and Keppel 1984:58–69); it is suggested also by a study of surrogate mothers, in which a majority said that the pain of giving up their children was 'like nothing they could have imagined' (Chesler 1988:117). The problem with this proposal, however, at least in terms of western philosophy's notion of the rational man, is the presumption 'that pregnant women are more fickle than everyone else' (Diprose 1994:113–14, 117).

These justifications may seem somewhat lame, bound as we are in dualistic notions of mind and body and of 'possessive individualism' which decree that adults are marked by the right to dispose freely of their bodies. In England, Australia and Canada, however, court cases and legislation accept that it is 'natural' for a mother, even a surrogate mother, to wish to keep her baby. Thus surrogacy contracts are generally defined as legally unenforceable, while commissioners may even be exposed to criminal sanctions (Morgan 1985:227 for Britain; recommendation of NSW Law Reform Commission 1988:47–60). On the other hand, the United States, with its greater commitment to a rights-based discourse, and perhaps the idea that women should be treated as equally capable of making decisions as men, on the whole deems surrogacy contracts as enforceable against the surrogate mother, following the first fee-paying case in 1980 (Bowral 1983:7; Starke 1988:327; *in re Baby M* 525 A 2d 1128 [1987]).

The surrogacy debate rages on, some feminists asserting that women should be treated as capable of disposing of their bodies as they will; others claiming that mothering transforms a woman into a being with another set of rights. Similarly, Kalpana Ram (1996:131) ruminates on a conversation she had with a white Australian feminist in 1982. She explains to her friend that she 'had to get married'. Her friend immediately sees her as 'the "traditional" Indian immigrant woman, overwhelmed by the collective unfreedoms of clan, kin and community'. But Ram's situation is more complex than this. For her, the marriage expresses 'the simultaneous pleasures *and* pressures of having a more collective sense of one's identity'. The validity of the western marriage contract assumes two and only two completely free (or completely coerced) individuals. It takes no account of an immigrant woman affirming her community links, understanding that her marriage makes way for her younger sister's marriage, of not being blinded to the unalloyed prospects of romantic love. Thus a woman either freely chooses her marriage partner, or she acts under duress and coercion and the marriage may be annulled. There is nothing in between – nothing which takes account of the more experimental relations young people in India are pursuing; nothing which acknowledges that Indian marriage law is very similar to English marriage law, although Indian judges tend to slide away from marriage as contract and reinvoke it as sacrament; and nothing which notes that marriage law in both India and Australia is based on a naturalisation of sexual inequality in which men are assumed to have sexual possession of their wives and women are assumed to desire motherhood (Ram 1996:132–3, 143–4). Focusing on the differences between India and Australia blinds us to the similarities, although Ram does claim a greater sense of collective identity for the Indian woman deciding on her marriage partner. Thus the practices examined in this chapter reveal that locating the notion of agency (choice) within structural constraints and social meanings expands our understanding of decisions made in both the east and the west, of the sati and the woman who chooses genital surgery for her daughter, and of the anorexic and the woman who feels she is nothing without a wedding ring on her finger. It is to marriage and motherhood that we now turn.

CHAPTER
3

Mothers and Wives

●

MOTHERS, WIVES AND SISTERS

I did what was expected of every mother, taking care of the children's daily needs, driving them back and forth between home and school, taking them to music and painting lessons, supervising their homework, doing the grocery shopping, entertaining the occasional guests and so on.

– Associate Professor of Sociology at the National University of Singapore, Aline Wong 1994:22

In *Sex and Destiny* (1984) Germaine Greer claims that Anglo-Saxon societies are peculiarly child-rejecting, contrasting this with the easy presence of children in the social gatherings of Mediterranean societies. Furthermore, motherhood may be a more isolating phenomenon in the anglophone west, where women are expected to be not just the primary carer but the sole carer. Shopping hours, media representations, health, child welfare and education systems impose primary responsibility for childcare on migrant mothers who are used to support from fathers, the school, relatives, neighbours, workplace creches. Even where childcare facilities are available, they are culturally inappropriate or offered only as a relief for mothers in paid work (Ganguly 1994). Following the post–Second World War work of writers like Bowlby on maternal deprivation, mothers were told that their failure to be fully available for their children created juvenile delinquency. Thus from the 1950s, even into the 1970s, mothers who returned to work felt guilty. These factors may explain white western feminism's once vociferous rejection of the prison of motherhood. Additionally, it is likely that more western feminists wrote as daughters in the 1970s, some becoming mothers by the 1990s (see Ross 1995:397–8). We will return to the recent celebration of motherhood by maternal feminists.

In northern European-style societies it may also be the case that, despite her near sole responsibility for parenting, woman's role as wife 'organizes women's secondary status' as dependent on a man and over-shadows her role as mother (Johnson 1988:6, 41). Miriam Johnson (1988:8–9, 26–7) says that girls learn to be mothers from their mothers, but dependent wives from their fathers. Karen Sacks (1979) draws a distinction between sisters (equal members of a community with control over the usually shared resources) and wives (defined in relations of subordination to a husband and his kin). Sacks's model is offered some support by a regression analysis which reveals that in societies where women exercise significant control over resources, men have close relationships with children, men less frequently affirm their manliness through boastful demonstrations of aggressiveness and sexual potency, and women show less deference to men and husbands (Coltrane 1992). In Sacks's model, sisters symbolise the role of independence from men and perhaps also co-operation with other women.

It may be in rejection of wifehood that white western feminism coined the term 'sisterhood'. But the term is also a repression of motherhood as it symbolises relations between more and less powerful women, between mothers and daughters. A relationship between more powerful and weaker women, conceived in age cohort terms, reflects 'the candor with which Italian feminists have dealt with the uneasy problem of relations of power among women' (Holub 1994:254), indeed stressing the disparities between women rather than their equalities. The Italian feminist group Diotima (named after Socrates' 'instructress in the art of love': Holub 1994:242) practises *affidamento* (which, given the context, appropriately means both to inspire confidence and to show promise, both to offer assurance and to rely on). A woman, 'perhaps a younger woman of less experience and of less social and political prestige, privilege, and power, entrusts herself to another woman' who has more prestige, power and status. This is symbolically a mother–daughter relationship in which the more powerful woman mediates the social alienation of the 'daughter' as she engages in patriarchal society (Holub 1994:247–9; see also Holub 1991:137–8). Such 'matronage' (Holub 1995) might sound like 'maternal-ism' both to women of non-western backgrounds, reflecting on their relations with colonialism, and to western feminists who are alienated from the role of mother. The nearest equivalent in anglophone culture is mentorship, a relationship between the structurally stronger and weaker which attempts to improve women's promotion prospects in male-dominated workplaces.

Furthermore, Maria Lugones (1992:407–8) argues that 'sister' and 'sisterhood' are inappropriate metaphors to link white women and women of colour, given the lack of egalitarian relations between the two groups. Similarly, Latinas would not say *hermana* except to describe siblings and close friends. Instead the term *compañera* describes an egalitarian participation in common political struggle. Where African-Americans use 'sister', it has the political meaning that this woman is not an 'auntie' (not the white family's nursemaid) and nor is she promiscuous, another stereotype produced in white society. But if a white woman calls a black woman 'sister', it may produce the suspicion that 'you are reaching past me to my Black man' (Rosezelle in Lugones 1992:409). Thus the term 'sisterhood' demands an equality and intimacy that do not necessarily exist between women of other cultures or between them and white women. The Vietnamese scholar Maivân Lâm (1994:882) coins the hybrid American-Vietnamese term 'older-half-sisterhood'. The term *chi*, older sister, is used by Vietnamese women of the same age-set in non-intimate relationships. It confers a 'presumption of superior knowledge' (older, irrespective of actual age) and 'the privilege of space'. Thus women understand that 'knowledge ... is neither commanded nor grabbed but respectfully approached and deferentially received'.

This chapter explores some of the costs and rewards of motherhood around the world, contrasting the expression of this role in different cultures with the related roles of wife and sister. Although western feminists have seen motherhood as a prison, this might have less to do with anything inherently disempowering about giving birth and taking responsibility for raising children. Rather it might reflect the isolated nuclear family with little kin support, the lack of power or prestige that is accorded to mothers and older women, and the almost one-dimensional focus on economic resources to assess status and power in many anglophone societies.

REPRODUCTIVE LABOUR AND ITS PRODUCTS

> The majority of Third World women see the family and kin networks as valuable prudential institutions, providing supports for widows and accepting responsibility for children. They may see supports for child-rearing as nonexistent in Western society, in which divorced and abandoned women face isolation as well as poverty.
>
> – Conway 1993:252

Some western feminists argue that men attempt to control women's bodies because of their fear and envy of women's reproductive capacities. Male initiation rites allay this fear, constructing a man socially as a counterweight to woman's capacity to make a child biologically. Men repress and express their womb envy in punishment of women, in calling them polluting, in building civilisation as a compensation, in fighting wars to show they too have power over life and death. Furthermore, men have profound fears about the ambiguity of their paternity and their alienation from fatherhood. This explains the history of seclusion of women to the home and the private realm where their movements can be controlled. Men's lives, conversely, span both the household and the public world of religion, politics or cultural pursuits (for example see the marxist psychological feminist analysis offered by Mary O'Brien 1981; or the perspective on white western values offered by Huey-li Li 1993:274, 277).

Where women are not secluded, they may still be commanded to safeguard their virtue and thus maintain their family honour. The system of family honour (protected by men) and shame (which women protect with appropriate behaviour) is found in North Asian, Middle Eastern and Mediterranean societies of Muslim and Christian background (Rozario 1991:15). Her hymen – 'this little membrane is the most important part of her body' (Agger 1994:26) – expresses both her honour and that of her male relatives. Before marriage the obligation to control women rests with her natal family. In general, women's appropriate behaviour (or more importantly what is said about women's behaviour) demonstrates both sexual purity and submissiveness, and may have as its rationale men's lack of sexual self-control. In such societies, young women may feel constantly assailed by guilt, whether or not they have acted dishonourably. First menstruation often provokes fear that virginity has been lost (Rozario 1991:22 for Doria in Bangladesh; Haj 1992:764 and Warnock 1990:25, 70 for Palestine; Al-Khayyat 1990:22, 41 for Iraq; Shaaban 1988:7).

In the west, according to some radical feminists, new technologies and practices like surrogacy and IVF (in vitro fertilisation) perform the function of seclusion in maintaining male control over reproduction. Thus some doctors argue that medical science is superior to natural reproduction, where the woman's womb or will often fails, and have obtained court orders to perform caesarean sections against the wishes of the mother. Women on IVF programs have now begun to speak of the low success rates and the extensive invasion of their privacy and dignity. It is also argued that such developments tend to produce compulsory motherhood, or the expectation that all women will be mothers (see Rowland 1988:171; Corea 1985; 1988; Klein 1989:231; Scutt 1988).

We explored the meaning of surrogacy for women in the last chapter. But it is often the husband and not the wife who desires the surrogate child (and it is his sperm and not her ovum which will be realised in the child). Fathers are increasingly engaging in custody battles to retain their children, although most still fail to support their first families adequately if not compelled by law to do so. The film *Kramer vs Kramer* which pits the self-seeking mother against the self-sacrificing father, the bombing of Family Court judges in Australia in the mid-1980s and the 1987 television advertisement 'Sometimes the best mothers are fathers' all point to the success fathers have had in turning the custody tide. A 1983 Australian study revealed that, in contested cases, between 39 and 67 per cent of awards were to the mother (canvassing several studies). Women without work were not preferred over working women, but white-collar fathers were far more successful than blue-collar fathers (Horwill and Bordow 1983:345; see also Graycar and Morgan 1990:250–1).

This chapter will explore the extent to which women from beyond the west 'want' children. Such desires, or lack of them, are framed within state population policies as well as husbands' demands and contributions.

Population Policies

The needs of the world's poor, on the one hand, and the greed of the world's rich, on the other, are the two forces driving the population-consumption-environment connection.

– Kabeer 1994:203

As an example of world-travelling, Gayatri Spivak (1994) suggests that it is as difficult for women from so-called third world nations to understand a western woman who willingly undergoes abortions because she 'wants rights [over] her own body' as it is for non-Islamic western women to understand genital surgery. Even so, about 33 million safe legal abortions and about 45 to 60 million clandestine abortions are performed annually worldwide, 24–32 induced abortions for every 100 known pregnancies (Kabeer 1994:207). Forty per cent of women live in countries that permit abortion on request, including the United States, Russia (the first country to legalise abortion in 1920 until 1935 when Stalin outlawed it to stimulate population growth; abortion was again made legal in 1955); 21 per cent of women are in countries which allow abortion in limited cases like rape, and 18 per cent are in countries which allow abortion to save the woman's life (Children by Choice Association 1995, Brisbane, flyer quoting the World Health Organisation).

To some extent, at least, different perspectives on birth control are due to the differential impact of population policies on white women and women of colour. As Rosalind Petchesky (1986) so clearly articulated, there is a difference between reproductive freedom and population policies. The former refers to women's choices, the latter to national demands. Population policies are administered by the state, purportedly in the 'national' interest, and consist of 'a formal statement by a government of perceived national demographic problems, solutions, and desired goals and objectives, together with a systematic organizational plan of implementation' (Dixon-Mueller 1993:15). Today, as Kabeer notes above, international population policies are framed in terms of the demand that third world countries control their 'over-population'. This is deemed the source of their poverty, rather than exploitation by the first world through international debts and unequal trade relationships.

Similarly, western commentators tend to see third world overpopulation rather than first world resource consumption as the main environmental hazard. Some third and fourth world women, as we will see, reply with suggestions that they have an obligation to increase their population levels. Clearly such positions readily encourage racism and sexism; they also arouse intense emotional fear and anger in many quarters.

Barbara Rogers (1980:111) argues that early colonial policies were pro-natalist, seeing colonised children as an additional source of labour power. In the slave-holding states, black slaves were forced to give birth unfreely to children who became the slave-holders' property. Since the nineteenth century, however, the cloud of eugenics has hung over population policy debates. Eugenicists believed that 'fit' mothers bore 'fit' children and should be encouraged to breed; unfit mothers should be discouraged from having children, with birth control measures ranging from contraceptives to abortion to compulsory sterilisation. Generally white middle-class women were deemed fit while the working classes, racial minorities, and in Nazi Germany the Jews, were deemed unfit. Thus under Hitler, Aryan women were denied contraception, which was defined as 'racial treason', and women incurred a penalty tax when married for five years without producing offspring. From 1936 women were barred from many of the professions and the quota of female university students was fixed at 10 per cent (Proctor 1988:121, 123).

Some turn-of-the-century feminists, unwisely no doubt, used eugenics to advocate sexual self-control by men and women (particularly working-class men and women) in order to reduce the incidence of sexual diseases (Mort 1987:164, 181–3). The birth control movement in India, led by professional men and elite women in the 1920s, especially in the All India Women's Conference, was based on eugenics and neo-Malthusian[1] doctrines. They welcomed Margaret Sanger, an advocate of birth control from the United States, to speak at meetings across India. While middle-class Indian women and men might be capable of practising sexual self-control, spacing children with more material contraceptive forms was advocated for lower-class Indian women. Most Indian politicians did not wish to consider this possibly divisive issue, a reluctance which continued through the 1940s (Ramusack 1992:180, 188, 183).

Women of colour in the west still experience population policies as an attempt to control the number of children they have, often through the administration of harmful or untested drugs like Depo Provera (licensed for prescription in the USA in 1992 and in Australia in 1994, the delay being due to tumours developing in experimental dogs) or forced sterilisations. Worldwide in the last few decades more than 100 million people have been sterilised. Sterilisations are performed on unsuspecting patients, or women who have been forced to sign consent forms under duress, for example by doctors threatening to drop their newborn babies on the hospital floor (Trombley 1988:177, 189, 234). Thus to many women of colour 'abortion is murder, family planning is genocide' (Radl 1983:40). Aboriginal women in Australia in 1975 resolved to 'stop forced sterilization of black women in Australia while white women campaign for the right to abortion' (quoted in Grimshaw 1981:88).

Sunera Thobani, a woman of South Asian origin born in Tanzania and at the time of writing a doctoral student in Canada, agrees with western feminists that 'the right to abortion is central to gaining control over our bodies' – but she goes on to add, 'as is the right to bear and raise our children with access to the resources necessary to do so'. In her critique of the 'choice' so central to white western feminism's abortion politics, she links imperialism, immigration control and racism in Canada. In Canada eugenicist attitudes are revealed in claims of a 'population explosion' or that Canada will be 'swamped' by immigrants while white women are exhorted to have children through reproductive technologies and attacks on abortion rights (Thobani, 1992:22, 19, 21).

Some Aboriginal women applaud high birthrates:

> the black woman has assumed an awesome burden of responsibility. She is the vessel through which the multiplying must be done ... She is carrying the black community to population levels never before achieved since the first white men set foot on this country. (Sykes 1975:318)

Jeanie Bell (in Coleman and Bell 1986:75; see also Boyle 1983:45) claims that white Australians are 'freaked' out by the growing number of self-defined Aborigines. More gently, another indigenous woman simply asserted, 'We want black kids – the men are fond of children – we all are' (in Burgmann 1984:42).

Despite their historical positioning, not all women of colour refuse contraception, just as not all white women embrace abortion: it is 'wrong, and racist, to assume that African-American women had no interest in controlling the spacing of their children' (Ross 1992:146). Loretta Ross (1992:149–52, 144–5, 153) says that abortion was a traditional method of fertility control in Africa at a time when Christianity viewed it as a sin. Many male African-American leaders and groups adopted pro-natalist responses to depopulation caused by lynchings, poverty and voluntary reduction of fertility. Black Muslims and the Urban League and NAACP both resiled in the 1960s from their earlier support for family planning. There is also evidence that traditionally Indigenous Australian women passed on information on sexual matters through stories, ceremonies and songs and that women today desire access to safe contraception (Daylight and Johnstone 1986:63–4).

A new variant of global eugenics emerged in the largely decolonised post–World War II world. No longer based on the fitness of mothers, it was justified by the discipline of economics. American funding agencies like the Ford Foundation, the Population Council and the Rockefellers financed population studies and projects. In the mid-1960s these agencies claimed that money spent on family planning would contribute up to a hundred times more to per capita incomes than resources invested in production (Hartmann 1987:102; see also Dixon-Mueller 1993:56). From the late 1960s the United States put pressure on the United Nations to support international birth control policies. China replied, 'of all things in the world, people are the most precious', and India argued, 'development is the best contraceptive', which later became a popular slogan (Hartmann 1987:107–8). In 1984 the United States, under pressure from the fundamentalist anti-abortionists, resiled from its position and stopped funding any organisations which provided abortion or abortion advice. Funding was not, however, directed towards development assistance, the United States arguing that development would occur because of free markets and individual initiative (Dixon-Mueller 1993:72–3). The tide has turned again and the dominant theme at the United Nations International Conference on Population and Development in Cairo in 1994 was population control in the third world, even some feminists accepting this position, although others remained staunchly opposed to population policies (Hawthorne 1994:11).

By 1965, fifteen developing countries had adopted explicit demographic policies favouring lower population growth, thirty-one had done so by 1975, and sixty-four in 1988 (Dixon-Mueller 1993:76). In the mid-1980s, developing countries were spending about $1.5 billion in support of their own population programs (including health policies and migration and urbanisation policies), of which about $400 million was dedicated to family planning. The $500 million from developed countries' governments and the 'population establishment' (private agencies and suchlike) was almost entirely dedicated to family planning, while individuals in the third world spent around $100 million on family planning (Hartmann 1987: 111; Dixon-Mueller 1993:76). The World Bank was the third largest contributor to funds by the end of the 1970s (although allocating less than 1 per cent of its lending resources). The largest donor among nations is the United States followed by Japan, with Sweden, Norway, West Germany, United Kingdom, Netherlands, Canada, Denmark, Australia, Switzerland and Belgium also being major donors (Hartmann 1987:113, 112).

In most population policy programs, women are the 'targets' for interventions, although there is usually little recognition of the pressures which frame women's exercise of their reproductive 'rights' or the idea that women should be in charge of their reproductive choices (Dixon-Mueller 1993:57). Not only did methods for women constitute more than three-quarters of public expenditure in 1978, but systemic and surgical methods rather than barrier methods are favoured. Efficacy thus takes precedence over safety (Hartmann 1987:167–8). As an example Norplant was advocated in the late 1980s because it was long-acting, and thus not a drain on embryonic health care systems, and coercive, because the implant is visible beneath the skin and cannot be removed by the user (Hartmann 1987:199–200). In comparison, natural family planning is rarely a high priority. Although revealing a failure rate of up to 30 per cent, it is 'cheap, demands no regular source of supply, causes no side effects that require medical supervision, and encourages active participation of both partners' (which of course can be a problem where men force their wives to have intercourse) (Hartmann 1987:261).

In contrast with these medically driven programs, some feminist commentators argue that better education, income-expansion and good health care are the predictors of successful population policies (Kardan 1991:52). Instead of focusing on women as 'acceptors' of birth control, successful schemes provide integrated birth control information, maternal and health care programs, counselling, screening and follow-up in schemes developed in large part by women for women in clinics or in the community (Hartmann 1987:135; Dixon-Mueller 1993:205). In a word, the focus should be on 'reproductive safety' and 'information sharing' (Kabeer 1994:208, 210). The rapid reductions in both fertility and mortality in Cuba (which now has fertility and life expectancy rates very close to the United States) are explained as a result of low income differentials and the amelioration of sexism through the Family Code legislation (Hartmann 1987:276–7). South Korea halved its crude birthrate between 1960 and 1984, accompanied by land reform and mass education (Hartmann 1987:278). Another perspective is offered by Cho Hyoung (1994:52–3), who suggests that Korean women accepted sterilisations, even though most of them suffered side-effects, as 'a duty of a virtuous wife to her husband and thus to his ancestors' because it was believed men would become impotent if sterilised. Involving men in family planning discussions of 'responsible fatherhood' also seems to increase adoption rates for family planning measures.[2]

Generally however, national declines in birthrates have been achieved with varying degrees of compulsion. In Kenya, despite being the first African nation south of the Sahara to launch an official population control program (in 1967), the birthrate is one of the highest in the world, at an average of more than eight children per woman. The failure of birth control is attributed to the fact that men are unwilling for mothers to be freed from pregnancies but at the same time bear few economic costs in raising children (which is the woman's responsibility); women are encouraged to believe their primary role is as a producer of children. Furthermore there is no companion health care system and there are fears of a genocidal intent behind the scheme (Hartmann 1987:83–7). In Indonesia 'Acceptor Clubs' sell contraception at 'IUD safaris' as a patriotic duty, encouraging the use of government-sponsored contraceptives rather than traditional methods and arguing for birth spacing rather than sterilisation (Hartmann 1987:74–81). In Bangladesh, incentive payments are given not only to acceptors but also to the workers who successfully persuade the acceptors. Because of the poor health care system, 80 per cent of sterilised males and females experienced complications as a result of the operation, for which they had to pay (thus reducing the value of their incentive payment) (Hartmann 1987:131–2, 214, 216, 219). In El Salvador, women are refused government clinic treatment unless they agree to use contraception (Hartmann 1987:135).

While Kerala in India has sterilisation clinics based on incentive schemes, Kerala also has maternal and infant welfare clinics (Jeffrey 1992:197–8; Dixon-Mueller 1993:209). Low infant mortality rates, Keralan women's high literacy rates and high age at marriage are seen as connected, women's education offering 'real alternatives to child-bearing' (Hartmann 1987:282). Kerala is the only state in India where there are more women than men (Jeffrey 1992:5).[3] Perhaps on the basis of a traditional matriliny, now past, it has been argued that the women of Kerala are the most integrated into India's education and health care systems; for example women comprise half the Keralan teachers where the Indian average is 25 per cent (Jeffrey 1992:195, 157). The first Keralan woman to graduate in medicine, Mary Poonen Lukose (1886–1976) in 1915, was also the first woman to head a major department in India, in 1924.

Lest it be thought that only white western nations and their populations pursue racist population policies, race-based reproductive strategies are also advocated by many non-western nations (Petchesky 1986:148–55; Bulbeck 1988:106–8, 132; Momsen 1991:31–5). In some cases women are exhorted to produce soldiers for the revolution. Before their uneasy peace, leaders in both Israel and Palestine expressed fears or exhortations over an 'intensive reproductive "demographic" race' (Anthias and Yuval-Davis 1983:71; Yuval-Davis 1989:92, 96, 99; Yuval-Davis 1996:22). In Nicaragua, Romania, Bulgaria, Czechoslovakia, Hungary and Poland, women have been exhorted to either produce 'combatants for the cause' (Sandinista leader Humberto Ortega in Randall 1994:9) or meet 'population needs' (Zielinska and Plakwicz 1994:94). Women are sometimes forced into this role when abortions are made more inaccessible, as in Poland despite a petition with 1 300 000 signatures (Nowicka 1994:153).

In 1983 the Prime Minister of Singapore, Lee Kuan Yew, revived eugenics in the 'Great Marriage Debate' which used tax breaks and entry into the best schools to urge 'graduate mothers' to raise their reproduction rate from 1.65 children. Less educated mothers were encouraged with cash incentives to reduce their fertility rates from 3.5 children. In fact the two groups thus identified were largely Chinese professional women and working-class women of Malay and Indian background. Concurrently Lee Kuan Yew urged a national revival of Confucianism and Mandarin against the 'decadent individualism' of the west, which he said was responsible for the United States' relative economic decline in contrast with Japan, South Korea, Taiwan and Singapore. The university played its part, changing its admission policy to favour men (Heng and Devan 1992:360–1, 344–5, 351).

Without doubt the most widely publicised population policy to restrict the number of children is China's one-child policy. This is a fairly recent phenomenon. Female cadres complained to the Women's Federation in 1953 about the tight restrictions on contraceptive availability, and this led to a policy expressing reservations about abortion and sterilisation. During the Great Leap Forward Mao suggested that a population of 'one billion plus' rather than the 800 million he had predicted earlier would be no cause for alarm. After the Great Leap Forward failed, population control was again on the agenda as part of the recovery plan (White 1994:257–8, 273–4) leading to the one-child policy in the late 1970s. This policy has always met resistance, two children being preferred. While rural production was organised in collective institutions, local cadres had some impact on individual peasants' well-being and could thus implement the one-child policy with some success. From about the mid-1980s this economic control was lost with decollectivisation, and leaders in Beijing accepted the reality of son-preference. The saying 'Open a small hole to close a big hole' allowed a family in 'real difficulties' (who did not have a son) to produce a second child (Greenhalgh and Li 1995:609, 624). The hole became too big, families with two daughters also producing a third child. By 1993 the policy was basically to allow a second but not a third child if a son did not arrive.

Thus by 1988 two-thirds of China's provinces had incorporated gender considerations into their policies even though the official original policy was gender-neutral (Greenhalgh and Li 1995:609, 617). Girls have 'disappeared' from the birth rolls as a result of adopting out, abandonment and neglect, and ultrasound, which has become an 'open secret' in some areas (Greenhalgh and Li, 1995:628). Even where women who give birth to daughters are not beaten, they may still suffer psychological pressures which cause depression and make them feel they have failed their husband's family. Wang Jiaxiang told me that in the cities, the mother of a daughter sits unattended in her hospital bed as relatives crowd around the more successful mothers in nearby beds. However, many urban Chinese with government employment can hardly afford to forgo the benefits compliance offers. They resent the repudiation of the one-child policy by the villagers, and its non-application to the cultural minorities.

(There is considerable debate on how much coercion is used despite the official claim that ethnic minorities, including the Tibetans, are not subject to the one-child policy; see Dang 1995:370–1 for Shanxi Province and among the Tu ethnic group in Qinghai; Reist 1995:103 for Tibetan women). One of my students wrote to me in 1992:

> In the Spring Festival Programs sponsored by the Central TV station there was a parody carried out by two monkeys and a panda (all from Shanghai Zoo) to ridicule and criticise those who flee to the forests to have the unwelcome babies. Sometimes I really hate those who never seem to understand anything more than having sons to 'continue the family tree'.

sex ratio

The obvious effects of preference for males are now being felt by China's young men, with estimates that single men over the age of 15 outnumber single women by a ratio of three to two. Of the 8 million single people between the ages of 30 and 44, there are 7.4 million men and less than half a million women. Men, however, will not marry women in their forties, who fortunately may today obtain apartments even if single. Women now more insistently demand 'intelligence, education, money' in their husbands and are more willing to divorce and find a better husband. One young man, lounging on Beijing's shopping street, Wangfujing, hoping to catch a girl's eye, noted morosely, 'Without women maybe we will all become monks ... And maybe then the women will feel sorry for us' (*New York Times* 16 August 1994, supplied by Peter Mayer). Patriarchal society's darker side is revealed in the abduction and sale of young women. In July 1994 the Beijing police uncovered a gang who had sold 1800 women in Shaanxi province; the husbands barricaded themselves in their houses to avoid returning their brides. Women are also sold into prostitution; 90 000 were estimated to be working in Guandong province in 1994 (Haworth 1995:20, 18) while women are being trafficked from Thailand and Vietnam into China (Pettman 1996:195). There are more reports of girls being sold as child brides, moving to their future groom's family as young girls and not receiving any education (Schädler 1995:128).

Wang Jiaxiang (Beijing Foreign Studies University Women's Group Meeting, 10 December 1993) notes that most NGOs of the Asia-Pacific region attack China's one-child policy on the grounds that it denies Chinese women their reproductive rights. She herself sounded as outraged as any westerner might be with her description of a 36-year-old mother in shanty-town Manila who had six daughters, each picking the nits out of a younger sibling's hair. Wang concluded, 'so let's stick to our one child policy; if she only had one daughter she wouldn't be this badly off'. Later in conversation she pointed out that women, especially rural women, wanted sons because they lacked government-funded social security for their old age (interview, 15 December 1993). In Yancheng, in northern Jiangsu Province, the chief family planner, Zhong Zuowen, understands this link and has established one-child family co-operatives focused on income-earning (Xion Lei, 'Birth of One-Child Co-Ops Boon to Jiangsu Farmers', *China Daily* 20 December 1993:6). But parents are beginning to realise that daughters can also be good old-age insurance; sons are more readily refusing their filial duties, and daughters are now likely to earn an income which allows them to support parents (Greenhalgh and Li 1995:615, 614). In fact Chinese commentators are concerned at the plight of the one child who might end up with four grandparents to support in a climate where welfare is continuously being eroded (Gavin Jones 1993:281).

Another mechanism for women's old-age security is guaranteeing them rights in property inheritance, such as land. The relationship between this and reduced family size is supported by some limited research in rural Bangladesh and India (Dixon-Mueller 1993:135). Similarly, in Korea, the government was convinced, through judicious lobbying by feminist groups, that if it wanted to achieve its two-child policy introduced in the 1970s (and resisted by families who had two daughters), it would have to provide equal treatment of sons and daughters in family law. A revised family law in 1989 gave women more equality in rights, including equal shares in inheritance (Nam 1995:117–18). The United Nations Conference of Women's Platform of Action (see Chapter 5) condemns strategies which favour both the birth and survival of boy children, recommending, again, both education (108(a)) and criminalisation (125(i)). Although not linked to boy-child preference, the platform also recommends that governments are to 'undertake legislative and administrative reforms to give women full and equal access to economic resources, including the right to inheritance and to ownership of land and other property, credit, natural resources and appropriate technologies' (63(b); 167(e)).

The gist of feminist analyses of the difference between reproductive choice and population policies is that in the former the woman makes fully informed choices about which, if any, reproductive methods she will use. She has access to a full range of safe methods within a wider health service. There is no coercion to limit her family size nor any exhortation to expand it. Even in such a situation, women still do not make 'free' choices in terms framed by western individualism. They still may feel pressured to respond to husbands' desires for a son, either to please their husbands or because they fear punishment; they still may fear for their economic prospects in old age and so desire a large family to shield them.

Thus reproductive choice must be framed in terms of the wider educational, economic and sexual opportunities of women in each society. Let us turn now from government-initiated programs to how women make choices within this range of constraints and possibilities.

To Have and to Hold: Reproductive Choices

Maternity kills half a million women every year. African women are 200 times as likely to die from pregnancy-related causes as women in industrialised countries (Vickers 1991:27). Women know the costs of repeated child-bearing in life, health and wealth. Women also fear consequences from husbands if they make certain reproductive 'choices' (Jeffery et al. 1989:212 for village women in Uttar Pradesh; Al-Hibri 1981:189 for Palestine; Accad 1991:238–9 for the United Arab Emirates where women fear that if they do not produce a child annually they may be repudiated or supplemented with a younger wife). On the other hand, as we have seen above, population policies expose women to another set of health risks.

If we add to the idea of choice that women everywhere should be able to choose the number of children they have, knowing they will grow to healthy adulthood, reproductive choice becomes a big 'ask'. It includes both white women's demands for access to safe abortion and black women's demands for freedom from forced sterilisation. It means that instead of a 'population policy' states must have an interlinked health care system, a 'reproductive rights policy' and a development policy which ensures a universal basic standard of living. Women must also have the capacity to make their reproductive choices free from fear of discrimination or punishment.

A utopian goal of this nature, which is not so far from what western nations deliver to their more affluent female citizens, has little currency in the United Nations or other agencies bent on reducing the world's population. While United Nations declarations have at various times formalised freedom to decide number and spacing of children, they have never ratified an obligation on the state to provide for children, while individuals' 'rights' to be married, divorced or have children cannot be exercised in the face of a partner's opposition. The right of access to information on regulating fertility was first vested in the 'family', later in 'couples', and not until 1974 in 'couples and individuals'. The United Nations has never supported the right to 'control one's own body', an idea which derives from a feminist discourse and is linked to issues like forced sex or marriage, prostitution, female 'circumcision', sterilisation without informed consent, prohibitions on homosexuality, sexual violence, false imprisonment in the home, coerced childbearing and unwanted medical interventions. The Philippines, however, has gone some way towards developing an interrelated policy in its 1989–92 Philippines Development for Women program which sought input from women's organisations and which contained a broad range of sectoral goals and timetables as well as particular demographic goals which focused on women's and children's well-being (Dixon-Mueller 1993:12, 14, 217).

The Asian region[4] has achieved dramatic fertility declines in the last three decades. Two constant refrains occur in the analyses of how fertility declines were achieved. The first is the changing position of women, fertility generally declining with increased education and paid work. More education means that instead of being married shortly after menstruation starts, a young girl will receive secondary and possibly even tertiary education. With an education, she has a greater chance of securing a paid job and perhaps further delaying marriage, and she gains the self-esteem and literacy with which to seek and digest contraceptive information and make contraceptive choices. The opportunity cost of having children also rises as it means forgoing her income. The actual costs of children may also rise as parents wish to bestow equal or better educational and employment opportunities on them. The second refrain is 'economic development'. Monetisation of the economy displaces subsistence production; nuclear families emerge from multi-generation families, which means that individuals save for their own retirement rather than expecting children to support them (Leete and Alam 1993:259; Caldwell 1993:314–15. In Latin America, mothers with seven or more years of education average half as many children as uneducated mothers: Vickers 1993:93).

The lowest fertility rate in Asia is Japan's, which by 1960 had fallen below replacement level, from about five children for each woman in the 1920s (Leete and Alam 1993:263). Although Japanese women's age at first marriage is the highest in the world (Bernstein 1996:326), there has not been a rise in women's workforce participation rates in the higher economic reaches, or their earnings relative to men's or educational aspirations for girls becoming equivalent to those reached in industrialised western societies.[5] About two-thirds of all women have an abortion by age 40 (not much above the United States rate of 46 per cent by age 45: Oaks 1994:511). But this does not necessarily mean that Japanese mothers have low status or do not find abortion a difficult choice. Pregnant women often wear an abdominal sash in the fifth month of pregnancy, which is a public statement of passage to true adulthood (Oaks 1994:519). Shrines are erected to aborted foetuses, probably partly because of the power of the aborted foetus's spirit to cause misfortune to the mother. However, as opposed to Christian fundamentalists in the United States, for example, the Japanese are more likely to believe that personhood is acquired through life-course ceremonies than through any intrinsic right to be born (Oaks 1994:518, 516). Also suggesting the significance of economic factors are the fertility declines recorded in Hong Kong from the 1950s,

Taiwan from the 1960s (Leete and Alam 1993:271) and Singapore from the 1960s (Rele and Alam 1993:18–19). These are compared with the Indian subcontinent, where 'endemic poverty, low levels of education, low status of women as well as ethnic and religious conflicts tend to limit' government attempts to lower fertility (Rele and Alam 1993:22).

But the story is not as simple as this picture suggests. In South Korea fertility decline preceded industrialisation and vigorous government policies, and was not supported by widespread knowledge of contraceptives (Kwon 1993:52–3). In Arab countries, despite rapid economic development, family sizes remain generally at six or more children. This is ascribed to the low status of women and the retention of traditional values (Rele and Alam 1993:23). In Japan elderly couples often still live with their children and often in three-generation households (Leete and Alam 1993:268). Additionally, the thrust of these examples is to suggest that women who have the chance or choice will choose to limit their family size. But this is to impose western notions of what women want on to women in other cultures. Even in the anglophone west there are women who choose large families and women who would like more children if they could 'afford' them. Although their constraints are less burdensome, white middle-class western women also make 'choices' within a set of constraints: for example social expectations about the resources children should receive or that women should now desire careers. The next section explores whether constraints pull in the other direction for women beyond the west. Is there a power and status which comes with motherhood which is not available to single women?

THE POWERS OF MOTHERS

> Perhaps no role presents women with such rewards and anxieties as motherhood.
>
> – Dixon-Mueller 1993:155

> Women are the rightful owners of the country. We give birth to men so in a way we own them.
>
> – Women's Congress, Freetown, Nigeria in Steady 1992:97

A Puerto Rican woman could not understand Ann Snitow's (1990:34) desire to escape motherhood, the role she was born into: 'both sexes believed being a woman was magic ... She means sexual power, primal allure, even social dignity'. The previous section explored the tense relationships between population policies, often refracted through a racist or nationalist lens for third world women, and reproductive rights, the rights to have (or not to have) and to raise the number of children a woman chooses. In many societies, however, the choice of remaining single and childless is well-nigh nonexistent. In South America the figure of Marianismo presents local versions of the Virgin Mary as the role model for women whose central status is motherhood (Sánchez-Ayéndez 1992). Boundless love, self-sacrifice and forgiveness are eulogised in 'Maria the supermadre' and La Madre Abnegada (Franco 1989:155). Few women over 30 are unmarried in Iraq; spinsterhood signals family failure and the girl will not be wanted in her natal home (Al-Khayyat 1990:75). Almost all women in Asia marry (Rele and Alam 1993:23). A group of Asian women's studies teachers 'were almost uniform in their overall commitment to the family', although some questioned patriarchal family practices and all had been exposed to western ways (Karlekar and Lazarus, 1994:8): 'Marriage is the protection of a woman. An ordinary woman always hopes to have a happy family life' (Mei Yuan 1990:8). Even so, more young Chinese women are saying they will remain unmarried if the right man does not come along, despite the difficulties of obtaining an apartment if one is single (*China Daily* 18 October 1993:6).

On the other hand, women in families in much of the world are constrained by unequal laws of inheritance, property ownership, the capacity to enter contracts, custody of children, rights to divorce and a woman's freedom to move about in public, the very laws that western (and eastern) feminists have campaigned against since the turn of the century. In Muslim law a woman inherits one share for every two shares bestowed on a brother (Goonesekere 1986:67; Kaur 1985:150). The Arab concept House of Obedience confers considerable rights on the male head of the house, including the right to bring back by force women who leave because of physical violence (Coomaraswamy 1986:105). Among Muslims in Indonesia and Malaysia, a husband may divorce a woman for adultery but not vice versa. In Taiwan and most ASEAN countries, custody is usually awarded to the father (Kaur 1985:150; Chiang and Ku 1985:16, 18) and the husband has the power to manage and administer the conjugal property. In Thailand, the Philippines and Sri Lanka women lack legal economic capacities unless their husbands consent (Goonesekere 1986:56). In Brazil the husband as head of the household chooses residence, administers the property and can seek a divorce (Pimentel 1986:47). In some countries these unequal burdens do not apply to single women. Thus a wife in Lesotho needs her husband's consent for any property transactions (even if he is away working in South Africa), although a woman past the age of marrying (over 30) is deemed an emancipated spinster who controls her own property (Mamashela 1986:129–30). This section explores the ways in which motherhood can be a fulfilment of both one's reproductive powers and one's obligations.

The Double-edged Significance of 'Black Matriarch'

Titles like *The Anti-Social Family* (Barrett and McIntosh 1982) must have seemed bizarre to women of colour who read them. While women of colour and immigrant women in western nations also experienced unequal housework allocation, domestic violence and reduced autonomy in families, their families could also be a 'site of resistance and relative freedom' (Pettman 1991:196). This included resistance to racist state policies; policies which meant the forcible disintegration of families through apartheid and the removal of children; immigration policies in which, for example, family reunion programs do not comprehend the significance of extended family networks (for example see Moraes-Gorecki 1991:179 on Latin American families in Australia).

The history of the stolen children in Australia, the systematic removal of Indigenous children from their parents, is now being uncovered. It began as early as 1840 in mission schools, expanded into mission homes to which girls especially were abducted, taught a limited vocabulary and sent out to domestic service in white homes. While the children of poor and/or single white mothers were also removed in the nineteenth century, the practice of removing Aboriginal children persisted until the 1970s (Fesl 1989:31; Goodall 1990; 'Workshop Report' in Gale 1983:169).

Different customs, different needs, are often interpreted by Anglo feminists as passivity and backward traditions. Migrant women are thought to 'want families' or 'want men' (Martin 1991:127–8). For migrants to Australia, the family offers a buffer against a strange or hostile dominant culture (de Lepervanche 1991:155; Vasta 1991:174). Some customs and supports are lost to women as a result of migration. Australian-Greek women have lost their entitlement to houses and land, Latin American women their control over household budgets usurped by husbands with more access to English classes, and Turkish women the childcare support of school, relatives and neighbours (Vasta 1991:169, 172; Moraes-Gorecki 1991:185). For Italians and other migrants, then, it sometimes seemed like 'It was "them" and "us" – "them" being that cold, cool Anglo-Saxon world out there' (Giuffré 1992:93). Thus where Anglo-Australian feminism concentrates on shelters and the rights of battered women, migrant women from Vietnam, the Philippines, Yugoslavia and Latin America recommend family and community-based strategies for dealing with the problem (Raquel Aldunte and Gladys Revelo in Migrant Women's Emergency Support Service 1987).

Another example of cross-cultural misunderstanding, and difference, is offered by the experiences of Italian-Australian lesbians. They feel that Anglo lesbian culture demands that they 'come out' to their families. But the possible loss of family acceptance and communion is often considered too high a price to pay, although some do come out as a way of re-educating family and community members as well as challenging wider

Rabbit Proof Fence

social stereotypes (Pallotta-Chiarolli and Skrbis 1994:147, 150, 142–3, 269). Such a dilemma reveals that Italian-Australian culture is determinedly heterosexist, perhaps more so than Anglo-Australian culture. Similarly, Hispanic men and women suggest that 'lesbianism is a sickness we get from American women' (Espín 1992:145). On the other hand, lesbians of colour complain of racism in the white-dominated lesbian community (Gays and Lesbians Aboriginal Alliance 1993:48; Yue 1996:94).

The subculture of resistance to dominant values combines with the affirmation of mothering roles to produce the symbol of the black matriarch, strong African-American and indigenous women who knit their families and their communities together (see Cohen and Somerville 1990 for Australia; Greenman 1996 for the United States). In some white policy-makers' hands, however, the black matriarch is a sign of aberration – of a too powerful mother. The black matriarch stereotype was constructed by white policy-makers in the United States in the mid-1960s; it blamed African-American women for 'emasculating' and marginalising black men in the family, thus obscuring the role of racism in depriving black men of employment (Collins 1990:75). As Jan Pettman (1988:23) suggests, the matriarch stereotype labels both black women and men as failures in terms of patriarchal society's expectations: the woman is too strong and the man is too weak. Because she is too strong, the black matriarch is readily blamed, unconsciously or otherwise, for the black man's 'emasculation'. Furthermore, because of her strength, the black matriarch can understand and bear with fortitude rape and battery at the hands of menfolk emasculated by white American society (Collins 1990:187). Thus Michele Wallace (1990:227), who was 'made a pariah' (hooks 1992:57) for her critique of black masculinity, describes the 'myth of the Superwoman' as the 'inevitable booby prize of a romanticized marginality' which disguises disenfranchisement, exploitation and despair. Such attitudes are also found in relation to Afro-Caribbean women in British welfare agencies (The Violence Against Children Study Group 1990:111–13), and the press in Australia: 'Aboriginal women ... will do almost anything to keep their families together, even if it means tolerating, sometimes for years, violence against themselves' (*Australian* 16 March 1993:17).

Even so, some women of colour have adopted the black matriarch mantle, asserting the obligation on black women to help black men overcome their emasculation at the hands of white culture or powerful black women (for example the African-American Lucie [1984:155] and four Aboriginal women: Pat O'Shane quoted in Burgman 1984:28; Sykes 1990:99; Pat Turner quoted in Grimshaw 1981:92; Boyle 1983). In contrast with the declension narratives discussed in Chapter 1, this view of colonial contact suggests that men rather than women were deprived of their traditional pursuits, for example hunting and ceremonial performances. Conversely, women's role as mothers was supported by the white state, while women gained increased power through education, new political strategies like leaving drinking and philandering husbands or bringing assault charges, and, in some views, a cessation of traditional punishments like gang rape (Mattingley and Hampton 1988:135; Gale 1989; Cowlishaw 1978; Grimshaw 1981:1; Daylight and Johnstone 1986:1–2; Barwick 1970:34, 36–7; Hamilton, 1981:75).

We cannot know which is the more accurate version of Australian contact history. What we do know is that these different histories have contemporary political effects. The Royal Commission into Aboriginal Deaths in Custody, reporting in 1991, adopted the emasculation version of contact history in Australia. In its exploration of high Aboriginal male custody rates in Australia, it linked male violence to the 'crisis of identity' faced by young men and 'anger associated with their loss of a status-sustaining role' (Johnston 1991a:99, 102). There are hints that the myth of the 'black matriarch' also operated to blame Aboriginal women for men's loss of status. Thus the Royal Commission was considerably disturbed by the displacement of young Aboriginal men from council affairs by better-educated Aboriginal women. While young Aboriginal women do have higher rates of participation in education than young men, this has not led to superior employment positions, as even the commission notes (Johnston 1991a:395; Johnston 1991b:435 for the Community Development Employment Programme; see also Moreton-Robinson 1992:6 for employment in the Aboriginal and Torres Strait Islander Commission). Futhermore, the 'perversion' of the powerful Aboriginal woman not only blames her for the emasculation of Aboriginal men but also for her own incarceration, which results from her public drinking and equal participation in physical fights (Johnston 1991a:100).

The black matriarch myth might signal the power of indigenous and African-American mothers and the pride they take in keeping families and communities together under difficult circumstances. This is its positive appeal for women of colour. But it can also have its oppressive aspects. In response to these, instead of accepting the blame for their menfolk's emasculation and hence violence, black women have become increasingly critical of black men who abrogate their responsibilities as husbands and fathers, who criticise African-American women executives who are not warm and nurturing, who express homophobia or bond with white men against women (Collins 1990:116, 71, 194; hooks 1992:102–12 for African-American women; Gays and Lesbians Aboriginal Alliance 1993: 47–8 for Indigenous Australian communities; Arboleda and Murray 1986:131 for Aotearoa). Ngahuia Te Awekotuku (1991:11) argues that indigenous women cover for their men and their weaknesses, both because women are trained to nurture the weak but also because they fear

Soul Food

that speaking out is un-Maori, acting like a Pakeha. We will return to the issue of speaking out against one's community in the Conclusion, when we explore who can or should say what about whom and under what conditions.

Sisters in Struggle

Mangosutho Buthelezi, the leader of Inkatha, 'hails' women as mothers and wives, in their family roles. Yet he praises them also for their public political participation: 'My sisters, you are mothers in suffering humanity ... When others were quaking with fear, when others were intimidated it was you who came to respond to the clarion call of Inkatha' (in Hassim 1993:10). The Inkatha movement has attracted women concerned with the breakdown of social and parental control, afraid for the safety of their daughters and themselves (see also Dworkin 1983 and Stacey 1990 for the attraction of fundamentalism in the United States). In a bad bargain, according to Shireen Hassim (1993:9, 7), these women are also reminded by Buthelezi that they are to be controlled by men and they must be silent at home and abroad.

Much political participation by women, especially as mothers, has been viewed by some western feminists as reactionary or conservative. This raises the question of which political actions make up a women's movement. Western feminists define as 'false consciousness' women's involvement in fundamentalist movements like Right To Life campaigns in the United States. Because left-wing movements have not always taken women's fears for their own and their children's safety and futures seriously, until recently conservative political parties in the English-speaking west have attracted women who have such fears. But women's fear (of crime for example) is often translated into class and race antagonism and women into victims who must be protected by men. In contrast, feminist responses to crime have been more in the 'self-help' vein of rape crisis centres and shelters (Campbell 1987:148–9, 2–4; see also Sawer and Simms 1993:189, 203 for Australia; Townsend 1993:57–8 for Chile). But not all women are interpellated into politics in conservative positions, even if they use their private roles as a justification for stepping beyond the borders of the home.

Latin America has been 'characterized by international peace and internal violence' (Miller 1991:1). Military dictatorships emerged from the late 1960s as a result of Cuba's attempts to spread its communist revolution and the United States' attempt to thwart it. Those who resisted state power were 'disappeared', their bodies dismembered, buried by bulldozers, dropped in the sea. In response probably the most famous public political role of mothers in recent times emerged: *las madres* or the Mothers of the Plaza de Mayo in Argentina, the mothers of the disappeared. Silently protesting the regime's removal of fathers and sons, these women gathered in the plaza weekly, wearing white headscarves embroidered with the names of disappeared husbands and sons, or holding placards with the same information (Rowe and Schelling 1991:228; Alfaro 1994:265; Miller 1991:2). White symbolised peace, 'something which unites all women' as one of them said. They faced repeated dispersal by police and imprisonment. The practice spread to El Salvador, Chile and Guatemala. On the whole, *las madres* were middle-class women, women who sought to fulfil their roles as wives and mothers and expected the state to protect them. When the state failed, instead of retreating into private mourning or going underground into the resistance, they made a public protest, ultimately demanding a civilian government (Miller 1991:2–3). These protests had precedents in Haiti in 1930 when women sang in church their desire for the United States to cease its occupation, and were victorious. In Mexico in 1968 hundreds were killed in a peaceful demonstration and women demanded and held a moment of public mourning in the Plaza de las Tres Culturas where the massacre had occurred (Miller 1991:3–7). Concerned Women of the Philippines was an organisation of daughters of former presidents and cabinet members who exposed the torture of women political prisoners (de Dios 1994:35–6).

Besides their silent vigils, on the walls of Buenos Aires mothers painted more than 30 000 empty silhouettes, each with a name on it (Miller 1991:10). In Chile they wrapped a torture centre in white cloth sprayed in red with the names of those killed within. They made their traditional 'delicate and child-like' *arpilleras* or patchwork pictures, but wrought scenes of torture and soup kitchens in shanty towns (Rowe and Schelling 1991:187, 186). In Brazil a group of women secretly photocopied the court proceedings of the Supreme Military Command which detailed torture and kidnappings. As *Brasil: Nunca Mais* it became the best-selling non-fiction book in Brazilian history (Miller 1991:11). Through their political demands and experience of police oppression these women learned how to negotiate with NGOs, politicians, and international institutions and with husbands who resisted and resented their greater public involvement (Alfaro 1994:266–7).

The role of mothering has also been activated to claim women's righful involvement in peace, security, conservation or even saving the whole planet. In this guise, Japanese mothers – women who accepted marriage partners chosen by others and obediently performed their wifely roles – have taken to the streets (Kondo 1990:135). There are an estimated 13 000 consumer groups, while the umbrella organisation of housewives' associations claims a membership of almost 6 million (Seager 1993:268). These mothers warn the public of industrial pollution sites, while the Seikatsu Club, concerned about food additives in milk, buys milk from cattle farmers who practise ecological farming (Mies 1993:260). In Kenya the National Council of Women has sponsored the planting of over a million trees to ensure wood for fuel (Seager 1993:268).

Such 'affirmation of mother love' can offer exciting images to white western women. In recent years white feminists have also criticised the myopia of a movement which concentrates on entry into the boys' club of work and politics without substantially changing it. The 'female world of love and ritual' (Smith-Rosenberg 1983) has been rediscovered in white women's history. Maternal feminists have claimed women's entitlement to political personhood on the basis of 'mother-work', demanding that the state must provide resources for this vital work which enables children to flourish and that this work should be respected as entitling one to membership of the public community. But 'maternalism is feminism for hard times' in the west, in that it does not allow women the same access to citizenship rights and welfare as soldiers or workers have been able to claim (Brush 1996:454). Thus women in the west who enter the public arena as feminist activists are still bound by the oppositions of female/ male, private/public, emotional/rational, inferior/superior. The role of mother, perhaps because it falls so exclusively on the biological mother, seems to lack the potency it has in other cultures which value fecund women as well as youthful women, which indicates that in these cultures the vagina has not completely displaced the womb as symbol of womanhood.

Whatever the political resonances of mothering suggested by South American and Japanese mothers, there are tantalising and contrary indicators that the role is more romanticised by both maternal feminists and mothers in the west. Maternal feminists, writing in the 1980s, 'did not acknowledge the ways in which the love and care of children is, for everyone, an open invitation not only to unending hard work but also to trouble and sorrow' (Ross 1995:398). In Japan, women do not usually say they have children because it is enjoyable. Raising children is a fraught obligation; because children are seen as an extension of the mother, the child's failure is also the mother's (Iwao 1993:133). In a cross-cultural survey, Cordia Chu (1992:42) found that Chinese women saw giving birth as a duty, 'unpleasant and undesirable periods of their life', while the majority of Australian women identified the experiences as 'an essential aspect of being a woman'. This apparent contradiction might, however, indicate that mothering is a more individualised and privatised activity in the white anglophone west, and therefore less available for conversion into a political status as has been done in other cultures. It also indicates that the pleasures and powers of motherhood vary with specific social and historical contexts. According to some anthropological accounts, a significant basis for a mother's power is whether women go to a husband's family with a dowry, or in exchange for a brideprice, or whether they stay in their own natal family, the husband being the stranger in the house.

BRIDEPRICE, DOWRY AND PATRILOCALITY

'My Wife Does Not Work'

But then,
Who scrapes the sago?
Who tends the pigs?
Grows and sells the food
So that the family survives?

...

Who fetches the water?
Looks after the children?
Who nurses the sick?

Whose work provides the time
For the man to drink, smoke and play politics with friends?
Who minds the children?

...

Whose labour
Unseen
Unheard
Unpaid
Unrecognised
Unhelped
helps development?

Who dares to say
'My wife does not work'?

> – from *Changes, Challenges and Choices: Women in Development
> in Papua New Guinea* (Draft), part 2: a Trainer's Handbook

This section canvasses claims that a woman's power depends on whether she lives with her own family of origin or that of her husband, whether she is given in marriage with a dowry or in return for a brideprice, and whether she is seen as a contributor to the family's productive labour or not. It has been argued that a woman's power is greater in matrilocal than in patrilocal systems, since in the former she lives with her natal family rather than living with her husband's family. In brideprice systems women are exchanged for goods, thus being an economic asset to their natal families. In dowry systems women are given with a dowry, thus being a cost to their natal families.

Brideprice, Dowry and Domestic Violence

Ester Boserup (1970) argued that there was a relationship between dowry and brideprice systems and forms of agriculture. She claims that women tend to participate more in hoe-based agriculture, common to much of Africa, which involves intensive and heavy field labour. This makes women a clear economic asset in production and so they are given in exchange for a brideprice. Plough-based agriculture, common in north Asia, requires much less manual labour and is more often performed by men. Here women are given with a dowry. In plough-based dowry societies, so the argument goes, because women are a burden female infanticide is more common. As we saw in Chapter 2, wife-murders in India have also been related to the practice of giving dowries. But wives who attract a brideprice may also experience unhappy domestic relations, their husbands perhaps arguing they 'own' them and therefore have the right to beat them.

There have been many criticisms of this model which links gift exchanges in marriage with forms of agriculture, status of wives and geographical region. The regional specificity of the link between dowry and women's confinement to the domestic sphere is not nearly as clear as Boserup's theory suggests. Dowry can hardly be said to be characteristic of all of India any more than brideprice is found throughout Africa. Economic straits will force women into the fields while better-educated women choose paid work, although women are less likely to work for wages in those communities which endorse women's seclusion (Raju 1993:12–13, 27–8; Mencher 1993:100–1). Furthermore, the idea that women who contribute to agricultural labour have greater domestic power needs to be qualified. This is more likely where production processes are gender-segregated and the women have their fields, their crops, their accounting units. Field labour may be exhausting rather than liberating (Kabeer 1994:119, 125). Additionally, the contrast between dowry and brideprice suggests that the woman given with a dowry is economically worthless, whereas in fact she gives her body, her work, her children in conjunction with the dowry gifts of her family (Mies 1986:161). There is evidence that the dowry, like the dower in medieval Christian Europe, was the woman's portion of her family estate, given at her marriage rather than at her father's death but hers to dispose of as she wished. This right was whittled away both in medieval Europe and in India with the introduction of a cash component (McCreery 1993:276, 275, who notes that the traditional dowry may include land in the dry zone of Ceylon; Ram 1991b:190–2, 236 for the Mukkuvar fishing people in southern India since the 1950s; Goody 1983:62–3 and Crawford 1984:73 for Europe).

In Gail Rubin's (1975) audacious but much criticised analysis, the exchange of women by men is the mechanism which controls women.

Thus 'paying' for a woman with brideprice may encourage husbands to think they 'own' her and the products of her labour. Both men and women may believe that men have the right to beat a wife who 'fails' in her domestic duties. While some writers support this interpretation and thus condemn the paying of brideprice (for example Gillett 1990:38 for Papua New Guinea; White 1993:160 for South Africa; Ofei-Aboagye 1994:928 for Accra), others suggest that brideprice brings two families together and is a measure of the high value placed on women. Thus many South African women believe it cheapens them if they are given away, saying they are more highly valued and cared for by husbands who pay the *lobolo* (White 1993:160). For some commentators it is the commodification of the exchange, a result of the corruption of custom by capitalism in which customary goods are replaced with money, which has loosened traditional meanings and encouraged a sense of purchase and ownership, similar to the explanation adduced for rising dowry deaths in India (see Nahua Rooney in Gilliam and Rooney 1992:35 and Cox and Aitsi 1988:24 for Papua New Guinea; Oey-Gardiner 1991:106 for Sumatra).

Certainly there is no evidence that violence against women characterises brideprice or dowry societies any more than other societies. Domestic violence rates of between one in three and one in five households in many western societies may reflect a higher incidence of domestic violence in cultures with neither brideprice nor dowry. Such statistics may also reflect a greater willingness to resist and report domestic violence, perhaps because of more extensive state-funded programs for dealing with it. In other societies women may rely more on their kin and neighbours for help. In some Pacific societies, domestic violence has risen over recent years.[6] This has been attributed to the impact of western influences on traditional practices: a lowering in women's status, for example traditional rights to land; the breakdown in traditional mechanisms for controlling violence; and a male backlash against women's greater access to paid employment (Cox and Aitsi 1988:34–5 for Papua New Guinea; see also Muse 1991:228 for Western Samoa).

Since a march of Tolai women in 1963, women are increasingly taking collective action against domestic violence. Some of these actions are adapted from the western feminist arsenal, for example pamphlets on women's rights in relation to violence produced and left in post offices and councils and women's crisis centres (Tuivaga 1988:11). Interestingly, Pacific women activists are increasingly connecting issues of gender violence to women's rights and choices (Griffen 1994:71, 69). A brochure from the Vanuatu Women's Centre proclaiming 'In the Name of Love Stop Violence Against Women' reveals how Pacific feminists call on an array of discourses to combat violence. These include western notions of women's equality and rights, the idea that romantic love is liberating in contrast with traditional 'forced' marriages, and Christianity's rhetorical commitment to familial love and respect. These issues were discussed at a conference on Violence in the Family held in Vanuatu in 1994. The use of a human rights discourse 'tend[s] to situate men on the side of tradition and cultural relativism and women on the side of the human and the universal'. But the debate is not as simple as this: the women say that men are misusing *kastom* (custom) to claim powers over women they did not traditionally have, just as men have sometimes used the Bible to claim a man's right to discipline his wife and children. Rather, Merilyn Tahi suggests that collective values must be changed, but this must be done by men and women acting in concert. If the roots of violence are cultural, so are the means of digging up those roots (Jolly 1996:183, 182). Similarly the Women's Crisis Centre in Fiji points out that wife-beating is hardly a Fijian custom as it occurs worldwide and that not all traditional things need to be accepted anyway (Shamima Ali in Ishtar 1994:131).

Patrilocality and Mothers-in-Law

Bringing up a girl is the same as watering a plant in your neighbour's garden.

– Teluga saying in Vickers 1993:102

[In the history of feminism] is it possible to include the Indian woman who performs sati, not in acquiescence to the demands of tradition but in protest of them? What about Chinese mothers who created a kind of 'uterine politics' that tied their sons to them and gave them protection – often, if not always, at the expense of daughters-in-law?

– Sievers 1992:328

In Papua New Guinea, where wives fetch a brideprice for their exchange, women are still referred to as 'bouncing coconuts' (Denoon 1989:112) because they leave their natal village. Similarly, there is a Chinese proverb that daughters are 'water that is spilled on the ground' (*she-pen huo*) (Furth 1987), while in Palestine a daughter might be described as 'goods on which one loses' (Warnock 1990:28–9). Papua New Guinea has one of the world's highest masculinity ratios, as well as being marked by high levels of domestic violence as discussed above. In China and Palestine as well, the issue of patrilocality, living with the husband's family, may be more significant than the issue of dowry or brideprice in determining the worth of a woman.

In matrilineal societies, which are also often matrilocal, men usually invest their resources and their time in their sisters' children. As a result, argue sociobiologists like Pierre van den Berghe (1979:104–6), men do not control women's sexuality (thus adultery and divorce are common). This is because men are connected to children through their sisters, through the mother, rather than as a father. Matrilineal societies often also evince more respect for the production of life, while men have a sense of strong female figures in their own mothers (Watson-Franke 1993:571, 576). Until after the Communist revolution, the 6000 Yongning Naxi, living on the borders of Yunnan and Sichuan provinces, lived in matriarchal societies in which households were led by the oldest and most capable woman, or sometimes a man. Women's lovers visited them, bringing gifts for the family, stayed the evening and returned to their maternal family next day (Sternfeld 1995:131–3). Such gifts have been described as bride service, a practice in some hunter-gatherer societies like the Kung and Comanche, where young men provide meat to their in-laws, and this entitles them to become equal adults (Lamphere 1993:72). Women have more choice in whether to offer sexual favours in return for meat, as their own brothers also have obligations to supply meat to them. Just as communist China has been (dis)credited with dismantling this matrilineal society, so too has the Spanish conquest been accused of reducing women's power over land and in the house in the traditionally matrilineal societies of the Northern Marianas (Ishtar 1994:89, 88, 90).

The data in Chapter 1 on masculinity ratios, or the proportion of men to women in society, suggest the effects of patrilocality, rather than matri-locality or neolocality, on masculinity ratios, at least for the five countries with the greatest disproportion of men. Thus the Indian law asserting the wife's right to participate in choosing the matrimonial place of residence (Jethmalani 1986:60) is of some consequence to women's status. In fact in Uttar Pradesh, if a wife is to inherit the land, a husband may go to live with his wife's family, although husbands resent this loss of power (Jeffery et al. 1989:30). Alice Pollard (1995), however, suggests that in the patrilineal and matrilineal provinces of the Solomon Islands there may be few differences in the status of women. She attributes the status of women as 'breeders and feeders' to the incidence of the brideprice. Thus no sweep-ing generalisations can be made for patrilocality, any more than they can for the effects of dowry and brideprice.

In patrilocal communities women go as strangers to the family they marry into, households often dominated by the mother-in-law, in which daughters-in-law struggle against each other for household resources. Traditionally the bride's obligations are to be obedient to men and elders in the house and to produce a son, her only chance to one day become a mother-in-law herself. In Indrani Ganguly's (interview 18 May 1994) natal community in India, the husband presents his bride to his mother with, 'Mother, I've brought someone to serve you' (see also O'Harrow 1995:176 for Vietnam). In some societies, the natal family continues to provide a potential refuge or resource (Al-Khayyat 1990:195 for Iraq; Ram 1991b: 176, who also notes the option of neolocality among the Mukkuvar fishing people of South India). The woman's brother may also remain an important source of prestations (presents). Thus in some parts of north India when junior daughters-in-law massage a senior woman's legs she will murmur a benediction: 'May your husband live long, may your brother live long, and may god give you a son' (Raheja 1995:32–3).

A benevolent mother-in-law may offer support to her daughter-in-law (for example support in high-pressure careers: Indrani Ganguly, pers. comm. July 1995, in reply to this book). She can make the all-women domain a place of considerable leisure and fun for women (Jeffery et al. 1989; Ahmed 1982). The daughter-in-law can aspire to the status of mother-in-law herself, which carries the associated prospects of political participation as well as a longer life (see Cornell's 1991:84 interesting statistical analysis of the relationship between bearing sons and living to become a grandmother in pre-modern Japan). Having produced a son, a woman finds it easier to avoid intercourse and further childbearing, while post-menopausal women have more mobility as they do not bring shame on their families when they appear in public. Thus in India, 'the most defenceless stage is the young woman without children'. Indrani Ganguly (interview 18 May 1994) goes on to suggest that older women in India are under relatively less pressure to look young in their sixties and seventies than are Australian women.

The significance of a son is also revealed in kinship terms and children's names. In traditional rural Palestinian communities women and men are referred to as 'mother/father of [their eldest son]' and one word, *bint*, describes a marriageable female, whether she is virgin, girl, daughter or unmarried woman (Warnock 1990:21). In Camp Trad, Beirut, younger siblings are known as the child of 'father and mother of the oldest son'. In pre-revolutionary China it was common to name girls with the syllable *di*, an old term for the wife of a younger brother, thus creating a daughter's name which called for a little brother (for example 'Zhaodi' or 'Laidi') (Lu 1986:41).

More so than in Freud's Vienna, then, there are good reasons for mothers to desire sons, but the desire for the 'phallus' might be the last thing on their minds. A number of cross-cultural reasons have been given for preferring sons: economic support, the son will fare better in patriarchal society, husbands require sons to prove their masculinity, sons are essential for certain religious festivals (for example Confucian and Hindu), sons continue the family line, and women desire sons because of penis envy (Renteln 1992:408). Men are more likely than women to prefer sons, and in the United States girls are preferred for adoption although sons are preferred biologically (Renteln 1992:411). Amniocentesis is marketed to South Asian and Middle Eastern people around the world (Rowland 1992:84–90; Thobani 1992:19). Robyn Rowland (1992:84–90), pointing to the dangers of abortion in death, adhesions and haemorrhaging, notes that in Bombay of 8000 cases of abortion, 7997 were of female foetuses. Thus unless mothers are particularly girl-hating, sex determination seems to be less about women's 'choice' than survival or acquiring the status of mother-in-law.

In contrast, one of the most heartening facts to come my way recently was the results of a survey conducted among Japanese women in 1992. Since 1982 the preference for a daughter if only one child was to be born had risen from 48.5 per cent to 75.7 per cent; the reason given was that daughters are likely to remain closer to their parents than a son (*Women Envision*, January 1994(a):6). There is some evidence from both mainland China and Taiwan that neolocal residence and women's increased earning capacity means that daughters are now more desired, and can be expected to contribute to supporting their ageing parents (Gallin 1991; Tsui 1990). Moreover, my Chinese students suggested that mothers-in-law were no longer a threat. They painted a picture of arrogant daughters ordering their live-in mother-in-law-cum-babysitter-cum-housemaid around while the women went out and made their mark in the public world. Even husbands were afraid of their wives, who had no obligation to stay, given their economic independence (see also Duza and Nag 1993:80–1 for Bangladesh; Singh 1990:120 for India, and Al-Khayyat 1990:116, 194 and Warnock 1990:67 for Arab nations).

For radical feminists, domestic violence against women is a datum of life in every society, and statistics appear to bear them out. But the incidence of violence does appear to vary, not so much depending on whether women are given with a dowry or for a brideprice, but whether they can choose matrilocal or neolocal residence and whether they have access to economic independence. It is not so much the value of their labour in their husband's fields which increases their autonomy, but their ability to support themselves, both providing an alternative to marriage should they wish it and raising their status in the eyes of parents who can now rely also on their daughters in old age.

While a Hindu man's ideal end of life is the renunciation of marriage to focus on his spiritual development, for women, 'ideally and practically, the end of life is marriage' (Harlan and Courtright 1995:14; see also Nicholas, 1995:155). Despite the discussions above, resistance to motherhood and marriage is not new in the east, any more than the women's liberationists of the 1970s invented the idea in the west. During the nineteenth and early twentieth century, perhaps 100 000 southern Chinese women 'did not go down to the family' (Topley 1975). Mostly literate and semi-literate women of the rural Kwangtung delta, they joined sisterhoods and sometimes chose lesbian relationships (Smedley 1995:48) As with women today, marriage resistance reflected women's economic leverage, gained through employment in the silk industry. Their feet were not bound, there was no female infanticide, and girls were taught to read. In the 1930s Agnes Smedley's (1995:48) male escort told her that women spinners were 'too rich', which explained why they became 'proud and contemptuous'. To avoid accusations of sexual impropriety and to save natal families from being haunted by 'hungry ghosts', which daughters became if they died at home, dormitories were established for the sisterhoods.

These women were called 'self-combers' or *sou hei* because they combed their own hair after the fashion in which married women's hair was combed at the wedding ceremony. Self-combers had their own marriage ceremonies in which a woman vowed to remain chaste, saying that she would govern her emotions as a king his people (she ate an egg in which the yolk was golden, the colour representing the emperor). A sister did not have to be a virgin, as she may have gone with her husband while too young to control herself. But a sister was a woman who had not willingly gone with a man. In the early years of the movement, self-combers purchased concubines for their intended husbands, only entering his family when they were menopausal. This produced disruptions, however, as the concubine had become accustomed to being the first wife, and self-combers began to stay in their sisterhoods for life. Families, particularly the women's brothers, were paid much of the self-combers' earnings. The practice declined as technological change displaced women's labour in the silk industry. Some self-combers migrated with their women lovers to Singapore and colonial Malaya, often working as amahs (Hardacre and Manderson 1990:9). *wet nurse or maid*

CONCLUSION

> When the choice is made and the bargaining over furniture, ornaments, number of towels to be given ... all settled with maximum discontent, then the Brahmin priest appears with the tools of his trade. And after a fire has been lit, and the gods appealed to, and the bridal couples' [*sic*] clothes joined in a knot amidst applause from witnesses, when the guests have been fed, and the servants tipped and scolded, when the children have fallen asleep in their party dresses, then the groom takes his bride, a total stranger, and rapes her on a brand new, flower-decked bed.
>
> – Mukherjee 1973:125

This chapter suggests that the value of mothers seems more widely appreciated in many so-called third and fourth world cultures, appreciated with support from fathers, other kin, schools and government, where the western mother is more often left to struggle on alone. For example, for African-Americans, rather than mothering being a biological capacity, it is a social accomplishment, indicated by the term 'othermothers.' Othermothering is a status earned by women with an ethic of care and a sense of the community's culture (James 1992:47). In traditional African world-views, fostering children remedied a 'dysfunctional emphasis on individualism within a communal setting' (James 1992:46). Kristeva and Irigaray have retrieved the mother–child relation in the white west, a relationship repressed into the subconscious as civilisation has repressed its debt to mother the maker, covering it with god the creator or man the self-creator (Grosz 1990:149, 181). However, for western psychoanalytic feminists like Elizabeth Grosz (1989:121, 180), a woman must be more than mother, or she will (psychically) starve or choke her child. The role is too restricting for fulfilment. Some non-Anglo mothers, too, when given the option choose other roles, and do not 'go down to the family'. Thus the struggle for reproductive choice, the right to have and to hold or to remain child-free, the option to enter the public realm as a mother or as a spinster, access to sexual pleasure without paying the price of pregnancy applies in the west and the east. It is to the issue of sex we now turn.

CHAPTER
4

Sexual Identities:
Western Imperialism?

•

The limitations of our current approaches to masculinity are summed up by the ... startling ethnocentrism by which a discourse of 'masculinity' is constructed out of the lives of (at most) 5 percent of the world's population of men, in one culture-area, at one moment in history.

– Connell 1993:600

As Third World women, our sexuality has been subject to public scrutiny and judgment. We are viewed as either oversexed or asexual, immoral or puritanical.

– Basu 1981:71

When colonial conquest included 'conquest' of subordinated women, constructing them often as licentious or promiscuous, white middle-class women drew the distinction of their whiteness, which qualified their gender as being pure, in contrast to the licentious women of colour. More recently white women have 'become' sexually liberated. Against this modern woman is posed 'atavistic' traditions like overpopulation, religious fanaticism, clitoridectomy, polygamy, child marriage (Martin 1991:122; Mohanty 1991:5), some of which were discussed in Chapter 2. The sexually backward ex-colonised woman is revealed in the stereotype of the docile Hindu woman, the *supremadre* self-abnegating Latina, the circumcised and veiled Muslim woman.

In response to this minefield of sexual representation, some women of colour refute the importance of sexual self-expression for more basic issues like health or work: 'who you go to bed with' is a luxury to be indulged in by the 'spoiled bourgeoisie of the rich west' (Carmen et al. 1984:61). Women of Africa 'tend not to emphasize the quest for sexual freedom and promiscuity', a quest which preoccupies the Western feminist (Ogundipe-Leslie 1992:112–13). As one Aboriginal woman (quoted by Joanna Kalowski in Hester Eisenstein 1996:113) pithily put it, 'We'll worry about whether we get pinched on the bum at work when we've got work!'

However, many would agree with Gayatri Spivak (1987:151) that to focus on women's roles in reproduction not only allows appropriation of the womb but also effacement of the clitoris 'as the signifier of the sexual subject'. Some women of colour proudly assert their sexuality, often in opposition to a perceived puritan repressive sexuality in white women: 'Black people *are* really sexy', because of their 'rich and earthy heritage' in contrast with 'puritanical Europe' (Gardner 1994:172). Although middle-class Indians have a 'really puritanical' attitude to sex at one level, scatological and sexual imagery were common two generations ago, while bawdy songs are still sung at the women's rites which precede the wedding (Indrani Ganguly, interview 18 May 1994). The Indian writer Shobha De, 'the Empress of Erotica' (a title used by an Australian reviewer of her books: Singh 1994b:15), writes romance/sex novels just as steamy in their portrayal of sexual adventures as western fiction (for example *Starry Nights* and *Socialite Evenings*). But in De's books, the sexual expertise of Indian men and women contrasts with the tight, repressed western white woman. Agnes Whiten (interview 1 June 1994) also suggests that Filipinos are 'very earthy', aunts quizzing the groom on 'how many times he did it' while on honeymoon, parents exclaiming 'Well look at her, she can't walk straight' (see also Collins 1990:175 for African-American women; Obbo 1992:162–3 for Uganda; Accad 1991:238–9 for the United Arab Emirates).

If any kind of dualistic distinction can be extracted from these tangled histories, it might be the opposition of *ars erotica* and *scientia sexualis*. The European-derived west's version of sexual liberation is modern and progressive, based on a medical or scientific discourse rather than the art of sexual expression. *Ars erotica* is also more likely to have religious connotations than the profane forms of sexual expression found in the west, such as pornography. For example, in India holy prostitutes and temple dancers were engaged to mimic the erotic illustrations on the temple walls (Arcand 1994:206). We will return to the contrast – if there is one – between eastern and western constructions of sexuality in the conclusion to this chapter.

To arrive at that point, this chapter explores a range of cross-cultural explanations of how masculinities and femininities are constructed. What is the role of mothering in constructing masculinities in different cultural settings? Are westerners more likely to define themselves through their sexual identities, see sexual identity as a core aspect of their selfhood? If sexual identity is so important to anglophone westerners, is it the case that, rather than being sexually relaxed, westerners are very 'uptight' about sex? Is this western preoccupation with sexual identity realised in more dualistic notions of sexual identity – man or woman, heterosexual or homosexual, as the example of 'third genders' in some cultures tantalisingly suggests?

'CORE' SEXUAL IDENTITIES IN THE WEST

> Why does a 'nose job' or 'breast job' or 'eye job' pass as mere self-improvement ... while a sex change (could we imagine it called a 'penis job'?) represents the dislocation of everything we emotionally 'know' or believe about gender identities and gender roles, 'male' and 'female' subjectivities?
>
> – Garber 1992a:117

Sexual Confessions: Christianity and Foucault

In terms of the compulsive production, discussion and practice of sexuality in the white west, there is no better place to start than with Michel Foucault. Although westerners were compulsive about sex before Foucault wrote, he told them that they were compulsive, and had been for some time. Foucault (1980:41–9) suggests that four key strategies for sexual regulation and expression were developed in the Victorian period. Women's wombs became a site of medically defined illnesses, while procreative sex became a site of state intervention, as we discussed in the previous chapter. Children's sexuality was increasingly regulated through training in bodily control, for example strictures against masturbation. Finally, there was a psychiatrisation of perverse pleasure, or naming non-procreative sex as perversions or illnesses rather than crimes.

Rather than the Victorian era achieving a repression of sex, it saw an ever-increasing *expression* of sexual issues. Although the message was to refuse sex (at least outside marriage), the telling of the message focused attention on sexuality so that it became an increasingly significant part of people's self-understandings. The religious confession was adapted to psychiatry as 'the nearly infinite task of telling – telling oneself and another, as often as possible, everything that might concern the interplay of innumerable pleasures, sensations, and thoughts which, through the body and the soul, had some affinity with sex' (Foucault 1980:20). It is probably no accident that the confession of guilt in a religious context was transformed into the confession of guilt in a sexual context. Where in traditional societies sexuality is inscribed in the obligations of kinship, western sexual identity is framed by pleasure, fear and guilt, which may still be associated with almost any form of sexual expression. The Christian church remodelled European hunting societies' tolerance for non-reproductive sexual acts. Lesbianism, fellatio and masturbation were condemned. Women were feared for their powers to bewitch men because of their sexual desire (Rouche 1987:533, 481). In this environment, women retreated to nunneries where they refused their bodies' physical and sexual needs, focusing instead on religious devotion (Bynam 1991:120–41, 206).

During the Industrial Revolution, it would appear, women and men became more firmly distinguished in Western European discourses. Before it, women had a number of rights they later lost: the rights of widows to inheritance and of wives to own their own businesses and property, the right to vote and even become members of parliament. In the Middle Ages women managed large convents and controlled vast estates (Vicinus 1985). The gradual confinement of western women to the domestic sphere (at least in the ideal) during the Industrial Revolution paralleled changing conceptions of the woman's body and her contribution to reproduction. It was assumed until 1800 that women and men had the same genitals, except that women's 'are inside the body and not outside it' (Bishop Nemesius, in the sixth century, in Laqueur 1989:2). Thus ovaries were called *testiculi* and a common name for the clitoris was *mentula muliebris*, which meant little mind or female penis. Gradually women were remade into asexual beings whose main physiological purpose was reproduction (Mort 1987:77–9).

If Victorian women were asexual, their clitorises disappearing from sight (literally often in surgery), middle-class Victorian men were also believed capable of restraining their passions with their intellect. In the mid-nineteenth century sexual self-control was the solution proposed for impotence and masturbation, based on William Acton's 1857 notion of the spermatic economy: sperm once expended was lost forever (Mumford 1992:45; see Gilding 1991:97 for turn-of-the-century Australia). 'Social purity' campaigns to protect women from the dangers of pregnancy or venereal disease were also directed at men and were built upon Victorian notions of sexual regulation and self-control. Adolescence was seen as particularly dangerous, because of the proclivity for sexual experimentation and 'self-abuse'. One solution was to send girls and boys to boarding schools; here boys learned a calculative rational masculinity which was required of entrepreneurs in capitalist firms (Perrot and Martin-Fugier 1990:212–16; Corbin 1990:494–5; Connell 1993:607–9).

In contrast with the Victorian middle classes, the working classes and men of colour, particularly in the colonies, were deemed incapable of sexual self-control (thus Indian prostitutes were provided for the British troops in India). Neither were they plagued by impotence (Mumford 1992:44, 47), in the same way that women of colour were deemed too 'coarse' to experience hysteria. It is an ironic extension of the classic Cartesian dualism of mind and body, which makes the whites so refined that it actually weakens their physical constitutions. It found its expression in fears that white women found colonised men more sexually attractive than white men, a repressed fear which persists today in the mythology of the African-American male's large penis (Bolt 1971:136; Ballhatchet 1980:5 on colonial relations) .

Sexual Expression: Freud and the Sexologists

The prevailing standard of masculine sexual behavior changed over time: from the preindustrial era, when manhood depended on the successful reproduction of the family, to the antebellum era, when manhood was achieved by controlling sexual impulses, to the early twentieth century, when to be a man required the display of sexual strength.

– Mumford 1992:57

From the turn of the century, new versions of masculinity and femininity emerged, dedicated to sexual expression. This transformation is told in microcosm through the changing cures proposed for impotence and masturbation. While in the nineteenth century men could cure themselves through self-control, by the 1920s medical intervention (for example enlarging the blood vessels to the penis) was much more commonly recommended as the cure for impotence. 'Psychic impotence' emerged, the result of repressed desire rather than depletion of bodily resources. Masturbation became a 'problem', not because it wasted vital fluids but because it created guilt. By 1912 it was suggested that women's frigidity caused male sexual impotence, and wives were encouraged to humour their husbands by fulfilling their sexual fantasies (Mumford 1992:49–54). Thus sex became psychologised and the message shifted from self-control to expression. Pioneers of the now dominant western medico-psychiatric discourse were Havelock Ellis and Sigmund Freud at the turn of the century. Their work was later popularised by sexologists like Alfred Kinsey and Masters and Johnson.

'Scientific' discoveries asserted that it was unhealthy not to be sexually active (Langman 1992:50). No longer was sexuality something which demonstrated control by the mind or higher feelings over the body; 'natural' and healthy sex required expression, both by men and women. No longer could women choose a sex-free existence, either from time to time or permanently by remaining spinsters. This new ideology was so powerful that most western feminists in the 1960s demanded sexual equality with men in terms of the same rights to sexual expression (through access to contraception and burying the double standard for example). While lesbian feminists argued that heterosexual feminists' preoccupation with the right to have sex with men was a reflection of their heterosexual identities, few voices have been raised in celebration of celibacy (Lake 1991:38–43).

Sexology contributed to the sexualisation of marriage, made possible by the increased severing of sexual activity from reproduction and contributing to a growth in 'affective individualism, the ideal of the companionate marriage, and romanticism' (Stone 1990:259 for England and Castan et al. 1989:115 for Europe). Sexology shifted attention away from fatherhood and motherhood and from parental or kin bonds to a focus on the sexual couple. Between 1957 and 1976 there was a 50 per cent fall in the percentage of American fathers who said children provided a major goal in life, although mothers reported an even sharper decline in their interest in children (Stearns 1990:209). Sexual success has increasingly replaced parental success as the sign of a good marriage. This is another reason, no doubt, why western anglophone parents are sometimes described as less interested in children than parents in other families, as we explored in Chapter 3. When wives displace mothers as the main status for an adult woman, the clitoris displaces the womb, a focus on sexual pleasure eclipses an interest in sexual reproduction.

MASCULINITIES AND THE MONSTROUS FEMININE

> The impulse to subordinate and humiliate women ... is probably a generic aspect of male psychology. Yet it is arguable (although certainly such a view is contentious) that male control of women in pre-modern cultures did not depend primarily upon the practice of violence against them. It was ensured above all through the 'rights of ownership' over women that men characteristically held, coupled to the principle of separate spheres.
>
> – Giddens 1990:121–2

This section explores the connections between menstrual taboos, fear of women's birth-giving powers and psychoanalytic constructions of the monstrous feminine by men, a reminder of the days when they as infants were hopelessly dependent on their mothers. In Chapter 3 we briefly examined Mary O'Brien's (1989) claim that men control women because of their fear and envy of women's reproductive powers. Akin to this is the argument that girls pass 'naturally' into adulthood with the arrival of menarche, a sign that they are life-givers, while men must be initiated through rituals like a risky hunting expedition, often expressing their ability to take life (Rosaldo and Atkinson in Lepowsky 1990:172–3; Sanday 1981; Gilmore 1990:121). All-male bonding ceremonies are claimed, however, not only for the men's initiation hut in the New Guinea Highlands, but for the Nazi *männerbund*, the House of Commons in

Britain, the army, or the Freemasons. 'Bastardisation' ceremonies initiate boys into male boarding schools and men into the army and all-male workplaces (Remy 1990; Carnes 1990; Easthope 1990:66). In similar universalist vein, Pat Whiting suggests that, while varying from the west's 'subtle barriers' to 'complicated Hindu prohibitions', 'menstrual taboos exist in all societies'. They reflect men's envy of women's reproductive capacities and their fear of women's insatiable sexuality. In radical feminist style, she aligns purification rituals among Aboriginal groups with chastity belts and clitoridectomies in the west (Whiting 1972:197–9).

Just as radical feminist perspectives focus on the differences between male and female rather than culturally varying constructions of masculinities and femininities, some psychoanalytic analyses of masculinity and femininity lack cultural specificity. But rather than fear or envy of women's power to give life, men's hatred of women derives from their subconsciously stored fear of their own all-powerful mothers: 'All human societies have a conception of the monstrous-feminine, of what it is about woman that is shocking, terrifying, horrific, abject' (Creed 1993:1). Barbara Creed (1993:105–6) goes on to cite examples from Melanesia, 'the East, India, North America, South America, Africa and Europe', including fears of castration by the toothed vagina or *vagina dentata*; the black hole which can swallow men up in the 'devil's gateway' to be found among the Yanomamo; the Chinese belief that a woman's genitals were the 'executioners of men'; Muslim teaching that if a man looked into a vagina it would blind him (Creed 1993:105–6). Western images include the long fingers and nose of the witch, the Sirens and the Medusa which could kill unwary men, and the female vampire who sucks the blood of her victims (Creed 1993:1–2).

Feminist psychoanalysts posit the monstrous feminine as a retort to psychoanalytic preoccupation with the penis (Freud) or its symbolic representation, the phallus (Lacan). For Lacan the phallus is the key signifier of the symbolic order (crudely the realm of meaning and language). It is the mark of sexual difference between two sexes, who either 'have' the phallus (men) or 'are' the phallus (women representing what men desire, the phallus, and so 'being' it in a sense). But women also (clearly) lack the phallus and so desire completion through men (Moore 1994a:45; Creed 1993:110). According to Lacan, desire emerges from the discovery that we can never be complete, forced on us when we learn of our separation from others. Thus men desire the phallus which exceeds the penis, and women desire the phallus although being it: the phallus represents the completion desired in another but which can never be gained (put very simply). Feminist psychoanalysts argue that male psychoanalysts wield the phallus to keep the 'phallic mother' at bay, the powerful figure in the child's earliest experiences (for example Karen Horney in Connell 1995:11). But the fear of the female castrator is combined with memories of the mother's intimate sensual love, thus producing the deeply ambivalent attitude men have to women in our society (Creed 1993:164). This section asks whether the monstrous feminine is a characteristic of all societies by exploring menstrual taboos in some societies and discussing mother–son bonds in India and Japan.

Pollution or Pornography?

> Tribal people view menstruation as a 'medicine' of such power that it can cause the death of certain people, such as men on the eve of combat, or pregnant women.
>
> – Allen 1986:253

Today's 'subtle barriers' (Whiting 1972:198) against the menstruating woman have their Christian antecedents. In the thirteenth century, intercourse with a menstruating woman was defined as a mortal sin; it was still considered a venial sin at the beginning of the twentieth century. Into the Middle Ages, some European churches were opposed to a menstruating woman receiving communion. After giving birth, a woman was purified or 'reconciled' with the church (in the ceremony now called churching). Women who died before being reconciled were laid out at the door and were sometimes denied burial in the cemetery; in some countries unborn infants were cut out of the womb before mothers could receive a church burial (Ranke-Heinemann 1991:22–5, 77).

The medical profession did little to remove the sense of horror associated with menstrual blood. As the modern understanding of female reproduction developed, menstruation came to be seen as a life-long 'wound', akin to the 'rupture of an acute abscess' (Laqueur 1989:32). Menstruation was described medically as the *failure* of reproduction. This orientation can even be found in some books by feminists who attempt to reclaim menstruation as a positive experience, one describing the 'disintegration' of the lining and the menstrual flow as 'a mixture of tissue, mucus and blood'. One such feminist textbook also aligned the medical 'facts' of menstruation against the taboos of primitive cultures and everyday beliefs of western teenagers (in Apffel-Marglin 1994:24–5).

In Turkish Islam, although both menstrual fluids and semen are unclean, it is their passage from inside to outside which makes them polluting. Ritual cleansing is impossible while such passage occurs, which means women cannot take the journey to Mecca, complete the Ramazan (which goes for thirty days) or become Imams, at least if they are menstruating. Men can participate in religious rituals as long as they refrain from ejaculation (Marcus 1992:67, 83, 126–7). That menstruation is uncontrollable seems to add to the assumed shame associated with it in everyday western understandings informed by medical discourses (Apffel-

Marglin 1994:23) and in psychoanalytic discourses (Julia Kristeva's 'abject woman' contaminated by her proximity to excretions like blood and faeces, corporeal alteration and decay: Creed 1993:8–15).

Islam and Judaeo-Christianity claim allegiance to one *male god*, although the Catholic celebration of Mary undercuts male monotheism in southern Europe and South America. In those societies with a pantheon of gods and goddesses, are women's birth-related powers evaluated more positively? The answer is not so much that menstruation does not invoke associated taboos but that it also often connotes female power, a power sometimes feared by men. The Japanese practise various blends of Shintoism, Buddhism and animism, according to their tastes. Shinto ideals of pollution required menstruating women to eat and sleep apart from their families. However, childbirth and sexuality (desire) were separated into different mythological women, contrasting the passive wife to sexually powerful and voracious sorceresses (Walthall 1991:64; Iwao 1993:4, 112; Robertson 1991:97).

Among the practitioners of Hinduism, the emphasis on pollution occurs more in the Brahmanic castes, while in other castes the emphasis is on danger. Thus in a south Indian Mukkavar fishing village, women are excluded from the beach because they can endanger the catch (Ram 1991b:7, 49; for menstruation as polluting see Jeffery et al. 1989:vii for Uttar Pradesh; Parashar 1992:133; Risseeuw 1988:273 for Sri Lanka). As with the goddesses of destruction, like Kali, or the submissive wifely partner of Vishnu and Shiva, women have the capacity both to generate and sustain life and to destroy and subvert the social order (Ram 1991b:7). The wedding sari is red, both the colour of auspiciousness and linked to menstrual blood and the blood of childbirth (Harlan and Courtright 1995:11). In Buddhism, menstruation is considered polluting, so that Buddha's birth in the *Jakarta Tales* was achieved via a dream and he was born 'unstained with blood, unstained with filth' (Truong 1990:134). On the other hand, in Bali, women not preoccupied with childbirth are both polluting and powerful; they can prey on newborn babes and turn a man's *kris* knife back onto the attacker (Parker 1993).

In Hawaii, *kapu* means 'sacred', 'forbidden' and 'marked', indicating the need to pay attention (Linnekin 1990:15). The word applies to behavioural requirements in relations between men and women (for example, men and women were not to eat together) and between chiefs and commoners (for example, people had to lie face down on the ground in the presence of the higher chiefs) (Linnekin 1990:15–17). Seclusion offers power to women, as a time of freedom from daily tasks, a time, given the likelihood of menstrual synchronisation, to practise their rituals (Buckley 1993:138, 142). The Huaulu huntsmen and fishermen of Seram near Irian Jaya can hear laughter coming 'from the happy women in the menstrual huts', and may wonder if menstrual segregation is a 'sly female invention'

(Valeri 1990:258, 250). Where western discourse focuses on menses as private and linked with reproduction, in Orissa in India, the festival of the goddess Harachandi, in which men and women participate, connects women's menstruation to a seasonal articulation, or *ritu* (which also means menses), between the hot and dry and the subsequent rainy season. But the goddess is not a symbol of women or the earth – a notion that reproduces the western dualism which separates humanity from the non-human world. Rather, as one Orissan woman says, 'we are the same kind as her. She is a woman and we are women'. An Orissan man notes 'we feel that the Mother bleeds through them (women)' (in Apffel-Marglin 1994:29). There is no sense of menstruation as polluting or shameful but rather a celebration that 'she will give forth', as one Orissan man described it (Apffel-Marglin 1994:28).

In *The Crocodile Fury*, women's blood contributes to the power of sorcery: good blood, the blood of a birthing woman, makes powerful charms; but even bad blood, the blood of a menstruating woman, is 'good for catching ghosts' (Yahp 1992:167). Humorously as well as evocatively, Beth Yahp (who grew up in Kuala Lumpur and migrated to Sydney in 1984) details an almost easy tension between the 'west' and the 'east'. The former is particularly represented by the convent, where the nuns encourage the girls to guard and fear their sexuality. The east is embodied in Grandmother and her obsession to regain the powerful ghost-catcher's knife. Women are marked by their cycles, a power Yahp both deploys and mocks. Grandmother as she ages, almost seven cycles times fourteen years old, becomes confused, her main plot to recapture the knife over-written with minor daily injustices: 'cursing the neighbour's daughter for answering back . . . destroying Grandmother's oldest enemy with one fiery stroke' (Yahp 1992:311). Grandmother's life is dense with magical meaning and visions through her third eye: 'This is what my grandmother has taught me: to narrow my eyes and look sideways, and see what she has told' (Yahp 1992:241). Mother, however, as a Christian sees much less: 'No enemy glittered my mother's past life back at her'; rather she sweetly contemplated 'the empty space of heaven' (Yahp 1992:265). The protagonist embraces her sexuality, her crocodile fury, as she moves towards the end of her second cycle: 'I swish my tail and widen my mouth to hiss my thirst' (Yahp 1992:329); she rejects the commands of both the nuns and of Grandmother, who in their different ways tell her to deny her rising sexuality.

Might the pollution of women be connected not so much to their bodily fluids as to the fact that in patrilocal societies women come as foreign matter into families? In such societies the household who takes in a wife takes in a stranger, but one who is necessary if the lineage is to survive. This may help explain the dense associations of impurity and danger with menstruation and childbirth. China from the seventeenth to nineteenth centuries provides another example. Dowry items were subject to 'Sifting Four Eyes', a ritual which protected them from pregnant women (who, carrying a foetus, had four eyes). Birth was a fearful process in the Chinese imagination. When a boy was born, the 'pure sun' saw the birth room submerged in blood. This was bad enough, but when a girl was born, the mother's hair dripped in blood, which flowed into the courtyard (Furth 1987; Teng 1990:167). As in Japan, the passive reproductive wife was accompanied by another female image, the voracious fox-spirit whose sorcery reduced men to ghosts (partly because the woman's yin essence was seen as inexhaustible, while the man's yang essence was strictly limited) (Ng 1987:64). Chinese students in Beijing sometimes distance themselves from such superstitions, but they know them. For example, a man should not have sex with his wife if he has an important business trip the next day; a pregnant woman will steal a nursing mother's milk; a woman must not see anyone except her husband and his parents after giving birth as she will bring trouble (Heather Conley, pers. comm. based on essays by students at Beijing Normal University 1993).

Thus menstruation is often conceived as a combination of pollution and danger, but the weight given to each value varies from society to society. In western medical-inflected discourse, menstruating women are impure rather than dangerous, a construction which has even found expression in some feminist-inspired texts. In Mukkavar women's polluting power can have religious significance, and in Bali it can be turned against men. To-day's western societies have few menstruation rituals or taboos, although they have images of the monstrous feminine. Where some non-western societies negotiate women's difference, both their power and their danger, in terms of religion, perhaps in the west the secular trope of pornography serves as the expression of men's fear of the monstrous feminine. Thus Kristeva suggests that religion once did the work of purification and even celebration of women's capacities, as in Orissa. While Kristeva (in Creed 1993:14) suggests that art supplies this catharsis in the west, pornography is a more vicious expression, one in which women are represented as degraded rather than as dangerous. Thus the monstrous feminine may have found artistic expression in Australians' fascination with Lindy Chamberlain, accused of killing her baby in Australia's red heart (filmed as *Evil Angels*, in the United States called *A Cry in the Dark*) (Wood 1993); and with horror movies (Creed 1993).

It is asserted that pornography, as opposed to these art-forms, makes a separation between 'sex and the rest of human experience'. Western-style pornography, in contrast with erotica in the east, is not located within religion, carnivals or victory celebrations. Furthermore, the perpetrators of sex in pornography have virtually no social attributes (Arcand 1994: 126, 209–10). Said to have emerged in the mid-eighteenth century (Revel et al. 1989:392–3), pornography is premised on massive availability, rather than being rare or reserved for the upper classes, and has become increasingly violent, routinely showing women being beaten, cut to pieces, whipped, or in chains. For writers like Catharine MacKinnon (1987:209), the sadism of pornography is a reflection of the evaluation of women in the west, invading the ex-second world as it takes on western 'freedoms' (Zielinska and Plakwicz 1994:95; see also Harsanyi 1994:44; Petrova 1994:269 for Bulgaria). In South Africa there is some suggestion that white men are responding more enthusiastically to the spread of pornography, but more black African men find it distasteful (Russell 1996:430).

In western pornography, images are racialised as well as sexualised. While white women were still clothed in an aura of purity, *National Geographic* was famous until the early 1970s for its pictures of naked (but dark) women, particularly from the Pacific Islands. In contrast, men's genitals were 'deleted' in photographs or covered with shorts (Lutz and Collins 1993:137, 82). The sexualisation of black women overflows into an actual second rape when reporting a first rape at the police station, or the requirement that models of colour pose 'naked, wearing only a pair of brocade boots' in advertising and fashion magazines (Burgmann 1984:43; hooks 1992:72, 73). Where Asian women are shown in positions of torture, Patricia Hill Collins (1990:169, 167–8, 178) suggests that prevalent themes in pornographic representations of African-American men and women refer to the history of slavery, a linking of sex, violence and bestiality. Black men who were lynched were sometimes also castrated; women and men were auctioned for their breeding capacities, reduced to a large penis or big breasts. This history produces pornographic images of black women as enslaved bodies in chains, or shot from the rear as available animals (Collins 1990:172).

Radical feminism has coined the expression 'Pornography is the theory, and rape the practice' (Robin Morgan in Jaggar 1983: 265). Thus if pornography makes inequality sexy, 'normal' heterosexual intercourse appears little different from rape (MacKinnon 1987:172). Sexology's 'rediscovery' of women's sexuality meant that all women either 'wanted it' or at least 'needed it'. But rape is not peculiar to western societies; indeed it is assumed to be near universal, although exceptions are claimed for a few societies (Sanday 1986 for West Sumatra; Shaaban 1988:230–5 for Tarqui women of rural Algeria). In Hong Kong and Taipei, as in New York, raped women are blamed for wearing short skirts, for flirting, for going home late (interviews with Ching-Li Chang of the Modern Women's Foundation in Taipei on 8 January 1992; Kwan 1990:49; *China Post* 10 January 1992:14).

The contrast between menstruation as power and menstruation as pollution, or between women's sexual difference articulated in a religious ritualised or secular pornographic register, suggests that female sexuality in the former constructions is less debased. While I believe there is some truth in this contrast, it must not be overdrawn. As this book shows, women in Asia are also raped and killed; the ill-treatment of women is not confined to the west. Furthermore, while western ethnographers suggest that women's pollution may also be their power in eastern religions, women in those countries do not always agree. Cordia Chu (1992:101) found a high correlation among Australian and Chinese interviewees between negative beliefs about women and the sense that women are polluting and dangerous. Sri Lankan feminists, whether Christian, Buddhist or Hindu, 'rejected the idea of menstrual pollution and stated that such ideas should be wiped out from the minds of all women' (Seneviratne and Currie 1994:604). Perhaps, then, psychoanalytic constructions of the monstrous feminine serve to retrieve for the female imagination the power of female difference, a power repressed in medical and psychiatric notions of lack and pornographic notions of the abject. Women's enthusiasm for films like *Thelma and Louise* is an expression of our 'crocodile fury'.

Remembering that for psychoanalysts the monstrous feminine was linked to the boy's conception of his mother, where children are raised differently do we see different notions of femininity and masculinity emerge? We will explore this issue with a discussion of mother–son bonds, said to be particularly intense in India, Japan and Latin America.

Mother–Son Bonds

> In one Japanese village a wife suggested that she was unable to tame and infantilise her adventurous husband because he had not sucked her breasts enough.
>
> – Hardacre and Manderson 1990:26–7

> A son's a son till he gets him a wife. A daughter's a daughter all your life.
>
> – Popular saying in Protestant Australian families, in Stivens 1985:24

Edward Said's (1985a; 1985b) concept of 'orientalism' suggests not that Arab men are effeminate, but that the west constructs them so. The 'Orient was routinely described as feminine, its riches as fertile, its main symbols the sensual woman, the harem, and the despotic – but curiously attractive – ruler' (Said 1985b:103). The emerging Indian nationalists were disparaged as 'effeminate' (MacMillan 1988:220), some of them secretly eating meat as they believed this was what made the English strong (Chakrabarty 1994:104–5). Orientalist depictions of Saddam

Hussain during the Gulf War constructed him as masculinity gone mad with violence, but also a man who 'oddly' preferred the submissive position in homosexual encounters (Norton 1992:28). In Tokyo Japanese men carry lemon, pink and mauve umbrellas, and audiences at Tora-san movies 'love to clap in time with the music and to weep' (McQueen 1991:250, 204). In Korea a man hands his earnings to his wife and the Korean athlete who mounts the victory podium gives thanks to his mother (Driesen 1994:327). Indrani Ganguly (interview 18 May 1994) suggests that 'in the west the image of androgyny is based on the male model but in Asia it is based on the female model. So traditionally our men also wore long and flowing garments and they also wore bright colours'.

Although opinions differ (see East Meets West Translation Group 1995:146; Wong 1995:320; Luo Ping 1995:199), most of the younger and older Chinese men I encountered were proud of their cooking skills, while some of them could also knit. Official statistics support the claim that Chinese men do more housework than western men, spending up to 80 per cent of the time women spend on housework (Research Institute of All China Women's Federation and Research Office of Shaanxi Provincial Women's Federation 1991:571, 590). The ancient Chinese intellectuals drew a distinction between the 'stupid masses' and themselves, 'educated' men who pursued classical works, grew orchids, wrote poetry, and dedicated themselves to calligraphy (Lindqvist 1991:310). Such pursuits resonate in many western ears as 'effeminate'. The 'stupid masses' had their revenge in both the Anti-Rightists' Movement and the Cultural Revolution. Intellectuals were brutally attacked, 'shamed' with public trials and sent down to the country to learn from honest labour. The Red Guards spoke of nine classes, workers at the top, and intellectuals at the bottom, described as 'smelly number nine'. One can see here the significance of class differences in the construction of masculinities.

Furthermore, while lemon umbrellas or doing housework may seem feminine to us, this clearly imposes ethnocentric values on others. Theories of child-rearing may be similarly criticised. Instead of this process of detachment, Asian and particularly Indian masculinities are interpreted by western and some Asian analysts as effeminate and infantilised, the result of excessively strong mother–son bonds, sometimes coupled with distant fathers. The son fails to form stable ego boundaries and learns few skills for mastery of the wider environment (Singh 1990:51; Carstairs in Kurtz 1992:37; Singhal and Mrinal 1991:147). Pressing home the point, Robert Stoller (1968:98–103) explains male transsexualism in such terms, contrasting it with the 'correct' (i.e. western) way to raise boys, through separation-individuation, or the detachment of the son from the mother.

Stanley Kurtz (1992) attempts to avoid such a eurocentric interpretation by exploring the significance of multiple mother figures as both the experience of the young boy and connected with Hindu iconography. Western child-rearing practices seek an over-individualisation of the child, compared with the group identification achieved in India (Kurtz 1992:77). Western child-rearing consists of intensive one-to-one training time with the child, in comparison with busy Indian households where the child receives little specialised behaviour-eliciting attention (Mahoney and Yngvesson 1992:55; Kurtz 1992:43–4). More significantly, the mother group – the mother, mother-in-law, aunts and other women in the household – draw the son outward to a 'collective mother', producing a spiritual autonomy as opposed to western identity formation (Roland in Kurtz 1992:31, 41).

Kurtz links the intimate experience of the group mother to the pantheon of male and female gods in Hinduism. The chief male gods are Shiva and Vishnu and his incarnations, the warrior-prince Rama and Krishna. Some of the goddesses are wives or female aspects of male gods. Sometimes their destructive energy is tamed by their husbands, sometimes by appeal to their maternal instincts, for example Kali. Conversely, Kali occasionally stands on the body of Shiva, who may be represented as rising again. In some stories a male figure is reduced to the state of a helpless infant by an engulfing female figure (Gilmore 1990:179–80; see also Kearns 1992:214). Thus, although 'the fierce form is often represented as dark or malevolent, whereas the docile form is represented as light or benevolent', such a simple opposition does not capture the complexity of the case (Harlan and Courtright 1995:9). As Indrani Ganguly (interview 18 May 1994) puts it, Hindu gods are 'domesticated, so they all have consorts and a lot of domestic spats', as do gods in other pantheons, for example the Greek gods). This creates an image of social interdependence rather than 'the individual as the all-knowing and all-powerful god' of Judaeo-Christian religions (Iwao 1993: 281 contrasts these religions with the Japanese pantheon). Furthermore, fierce goddesses like Kali provide images of strong women to accompany the more familiar image of the nurturant woman. There is a subgenre of Indian films which shows avenging women, of which the most famous is *Bandit Queen*, shown at Cannes in 1994, and based on the life of Phoolan Devi who avenged her rape with a massacre and became an outlaw; her autobiography, *I Phoolan Devi*, was published in 1996 by Little Brown.

As in the Hindu pantheon, the Indian child experiences several kinds of mothers. For example, the close mother–son bond is disrupted when the mother-in-law is present, as the mother must ignore her son unless there is a cry for the breast (Kurtz 1992:137, 33, 37). Thus Kali might remind the boy of the demon-mother, the mother-in-law who refused his attentions, while he also learns that Kali can be calmed by a man, her husband prostrate at her feet (Kurtz 1992:110). Both mother and mother-in-law in their joint care might be seen as the benign Durga (Kurtz

1992:106–8). A wonderfully symbolic story from Krishna's adolescence reveals this notion of the group-mother. Krishna's mother and her fellow *gopis*[1] compete incessantly for the affections of the child Krishna. Later Krishna has a chief lover, Radha, with whom he wishes to dance during the great circle dance of all the *gopis*. Realising that the *gopis* will be jealous, he multiplies himself so that each mother dances with 'him'. This is accepted by Radha because she knows that all the *gopis* are a manifestation of herself and embraces *prem* (selfless, divine love which is essentially giving) instead of *kām* (the lustful, selfish love of ordinary social life) (Kurtz 1992:146–7). Thus in worshipping goddesses, Hindus 'recapitulate and reinforce their successful developmental journey through the world of women' (Kurtz 1992:174). It does not, however, mean that rape or dowry deaths are not a feature of contemporary India.

If Hinduism offers an alternative to the monstrous feminine, it has been claimed that in Japan intense mother–son bonds lead to an infantilisation of Japanese men, sometimes to the point of impotence, and possibly leading to a greater incidence of mother–son incest than father–daughter incest (Allison 1994:112, 162–3; Iwao 1993:150–1). The man's relationship with his mother is transferred to both sexual and authority relationships. Men expect their employers to 'mother' them, shield them from blame for mistakes, recognise good work, comment on their new haircut (Allison 1994:98). 'Mama-sans' run local bars, to a large extent patronised by groups of workers who are entertained by their boss at corporate expense. *Mama-sans* are expected to indulge and comfort men (Iwao 1993:151), while the hostess assigned to the men fills glasses and lights cigarettes and must laugh at the rude remarks about her breasts or figure, a mechanism for breaking the ice between the men (Allison 1994:64–5, 49). One commentator said these bars are not about sex so much as being taken care of 'like a baby … washed, caressed … This is the pleasure' (Wagatsuma in Allison 1994:163). And it is a pleasure that is completed with money rather than the lifetime obligation a mother demands.

But if men just want to be pampered, why do they achieve this through the medium of sex, and through the degradation of the hostess, including rape in some cases (Mock 1996:186)? Men explained the attraction of hostess bars by saying it was in a man's nature to be sexual, using the word *sukebei* which means 'lewd, bawdy, lustful, lascivious' (Allison 1994:11). Other forms of night entertainment include prostitution and bars in which women have no underpants, and walk above the clientele over glass floors, swim naked in a tank of water, masturbate clients (Allison 1994:155). Furthermore, Japanese pornography is very brutal, a common motif being the man suckling the breasts of a woman he then violates sexually. Another common theme, which first appeared in an eighth-century text, consists of men slitting the bellies of pregnant women. While the story line repeats western pornography in that the raped and violated woman 'loves it', unlike western tropes, the rapist is contrite, and forgiven by the woman. In a manner akin to my argument about western pornography, Anne Allison (1994:171) suggests that men are expressing their hostility to their mothers.

Although without the same religious resonances as the Indian case, it has been argued that Chicano children have 'a multi-object relational configuration of daughter/ mother/ grandmother/ godmother/ father' (Segura and Pierce 1993:77). But instead of a 'successful developmental journey' into adulthood, commentators suggest that close relationships between mothers and sons in South America and Mediterranean societies create 'machismo' men. Where Asian men are deemed inadequate because effeminate, Latin American men are deemed inadequate because of hypermasculinity or 'protest-masculinity' (Bolton 1979:318). The male must be 'assertive, powerful, aggressive and independent, capable of defending his honor' and competing successfully with men, for example in drinking and physical activities (like murder). He dominates women in the family and sexually conquers other women (Bolton 1979:319).

As in the Japanese case (and as some commentators for India assert), sons are suffocated by mothers' demands, but mothers are too powerful to be rejected explicitly. Instead men repress female identification and express their fear of mature women through machismo. Some Latin American feminist commentators suggest additional effects of 'conquest trauma' in producing machismo, particularly for Mexican men, who displace their class antagonism onto gender relations (Nanda 1990:35; Espín 1992:144; Segura and Pierce 1993:79; Adolph 1971:88; on conquest trauma, see Peña 1991:31; Daniels 1990:317; Zinn 1989:88–95; Anzaldúa 1990a:383). It is significant that Ralph Bolton, a white American male, does not note or notice this connection with colonialism. In fact Bolton is so committed to his theory of machismo that in his analysis of Peruvian truckers' mottoes (painted on their trucks), he neglects some quite tender mottoes in the largest category, romance, love and sexuality. To me, at least, mottoes like 'For you I would give my life' or 'My desire to arrive and see you' (Bolton 1979:330) do not sound like 'hyper-masculinity'.

In associating machismo with conquest trauma, writers are arguing that these forms of masculinity are based on weakness rather than power. They are the expressions of insecure men deprived of their normal capacities to gain an income, marry a wife, be respected in the community. This is probably why Bolton (1979:318) likens machismo to working-class masculinity in the west, where many men may not have secure incomes or community respect. In a Cretan mountain village, the sheep rustlers construct (literally, in tales told in all-male coffee houses) a violent anarchistic masculinity while condemning the staid farmers or town dwellers. Theirs is a losing battle, however, as these latter forms of masculinity are the routes to material wealth (Herzfeld 1985:52, 48, 61,

270). Some Japanese fishermen, as opposed perhaps to impotent salary-men, express their masculinity through violence and humiliation in marital relationships and heroic boozing and whoring (Hardacre and Manderson 1990:26–7).

According to this analysis, the soft new age guy may be an artefact of power. A man who has uncontested authority at home and at work can afford to appear egalitarian as his domination is never questioned (Hondagneu-Sotelo and Messner 1994:214). Similarly it is suggested that Robert Bly's 'Wild Man' movement has particular appeal to middle-class straight men, who have perhaps lost the most although still retaining much, by the workplace transformations of recent years. Reminiscent of images of 'mother-identified' Japanese or machismo men, American men are encouraged to repel the influence of mothers by finding their male mother, through initiation rituals, 'stomping through the bush and hugging other men who have taken totemic animal names' (Kimmel and Kaufman 1994:262, 272).

From the mother's perspective, as we noted in the previous chapter, in patrilocal societies there are good economic reasons to want sons. Economic need can be expressed as erotic attachment, sons being so important to a woman's status, to her very survival in some situations. Furthermore, a wife's husband will be attached to his mother and emotionally unavailable to his wife; perforce, perhaps, the wife perpetuates the same relationship with her son (Al-Khayyat 1990:25–31, 102 for Iraq; Warnock 1990:32 for Palestine; Joseph 1993:473 for Beirut). As one Chinese man said, 'in the end a son must take his mother's side. You can get rid of a wife, but not … your parents' (Thubron 1987:170). Indrani Ganguly (interview 18 May 1994) notes that in Indian families there are mechanisms to dampen the wife–husband relationship, which is seen as a potential threat to connections with the extended family. Thus two generations ago it was bad form for the couple to spend time together during the day, while sexual energy was displaced into a flirtatious relationship with one's younger in-law of the opposite sex. In response to the question of who they felt closer to, 56 per cent of men in an Indian sample said their mothers, 20 per cent their wives, and the remainder equally close to both (Singhal and Mrinal 1991:147).

The analyses outlined in this section posit Asian masculinities at one end of a spectrum as 'effeminate', chicano masculinities at the other end as 'hypermasculine', with white middle-class masculinities in the middle as 'just right'. Put like this, it is clear that orientalism is at work in these classifications. Interestingly, some Asian observers have a reverse evaluation. Where westerners see Japanese culture as 'wet' and western culture as 'dry', 'they see us the way we see them' (McQueen 1991:157). The Prime Minister of Singapore, Lee Kuan Yew, aligned the 'hard' culture of Confucianism with the economic success of Chinese Asian societies;

conversely he claimed that the 'soft' cultures of India and Malaya are too theatrical, contentious, indulgent and loquacious (Heng and Devan 1992:352). These comments remind us that constructions of national masculinities must operate in stereotypes. The point of the exercise has not been to say whether Indian men really do achieve a more mature passage to adulthood through the figure of the multiple mother, or whether Japanese men express their infantilism at their mothers' hands in nightclubs, but to question claims by some psychoanalytic and other feminists that the monstrous feminine is an aspect of all societies, that everywhere women are feared and loathed and envied by men, who are their or other women's sons. In fact, whether the son is constructed through a separation from his mother as in the west or through identification with her as in India and Japan, aspects of fear and degradation of women still seem to operate. Thus the monstrous feminine appears to be not so much a reflection of the mother's separation from the son, as is sometimes suggested in western psychoanalytic theory, as a reflection of the ambivalence men experience in patriarchal societies which devalue women and yet in which most men have experienced the love of women.

In the next section we will explore another apparently universal phenomenon, homosexuality, and its different cultural expressions. The point of this exercise is to ask whether masculinity is a particularly inflexible and fragile construction in the west, requiring aggressive displays of violence to repress insecurity and doubt.

SPEAKING WITH TWO LIPS TO RECOGNISE THIRD GENDERS

> i have it in my mind that
> dykes are indians
>
> ...
>
> they thought caringsharing
> about the earth and each other
> was a good thing
> they rode horses
> and sang to the moon
>
> ...
>
> so dykes
> are like indians
> because everybody is related
> to everybody
> in pain
> in terror

in guilt
in blood
in shame
in disappearance
that never quite manages
to be disappeared
we never go away
even if we're always
leaving
because the only home
is each other
they've occupied all
the rest
colonized it; an
idea about ourselves is all
we own.

– 'Some Like Indians Endure' in Allen 1990:298–301

This section asks whether representations of non-western sexual practices provide a possible rupturing of western dualisms like man and woman, homosexual and heterosexual. Where western men and women who perform homosexual acts increasingly choose to become homosexuals, a lifestyle choice, there is more opportunity to move between these practices in some of the situations discussed below. One of the most intriguing challenges to western dualism is the 'third gender', describing a person who is neither man nor woman, who has specific roles and statuses in many communities.

Homosexual Acts and Homosexual Lives

Almost exclusive to the west is the notion of homosexual identity forged through shared lifestyles. With the rise of western individualism, 'perverse' practices increasingly became identities, leading ultimately to the development of gay communities or lesbian lifestyles, so that one became what one did, for example a homosexual (Plummer 1984:234; Foucault 1980:43). By contrast, in ancient China, 'One can *engage* in homosexual, sadistic or masochistic practises; one *is not defined* as a sadist, a masochist, a homosexual' (Kristeva 1974:63). This distinction adds weight to the claim, introduced at the beginning of this chapter, that gender identity is central in the west's dominant discourses. Furthermore, as Eve Sedgwick (1990:8) points out, contra Foucault, it is in fact not the sodomite identity, the hysterical woman or the masturbating child which has emerged as the definition of sexual orientation but the gender of object choice. So central is (hetero)sexual identity that the defence 'homosexual panic' has been developed, a pathological psychological condition possibly brought on by homosexual advances. A woman approached by a man cannot plead 'gender panic', and nor can one plead 'race panic' when one beats black (or white) people (Sedgwick 1990: 18–19).

Although a central identity, the identity based on sexual orientation is much more open to ambiguity and rearrangement than identities founded on ethnicity or biological sex, for example (but perhaps not class, which is not considered) (Sedgwick 1990:34). While ambiguity makes sexual orientation identity more performative in the postmodern sense, it also makes it harder to prove, so that a response to coming out is often 'How do you know you're really gay?' (see Sedgwick 1990:75–89). Sedgwick's (1990:68) examples also demonstrate that, although western societies contain homosexual subcultures, they also contain intense homophobia and contradictory attitudes to the expression of a gay identity. Courts in the United States rule that one is allowed to be gay, but sometimes as long as you do not tell anyone, at other times as long as you warn prospective employers; at some times as long as you keep it in the bedroom where it belongs, at other times as long as you do not do certain acts even in the bedroom (for example sodomy is outlawed in a number of states). Such confusion and homophobia is a result of two contradictory beliefs, sometimes held simultaneously: that there is a distinct population of persons who are 'really gay' and that all sexual identities have aspects of both same-sex and cross-sex desires. The latter is sometimes repressed and expressed in a scapegoating of the 'really gay' (Sedgwick 1990:36–8, 84–9).

Stephen Murray's (1992a) cross-cultural survey identifies four forms of homosexuality, in addition to the lifestyle choice variety attributed to the west. Only three will be discussed here since the fourth form, homosexual acts purely to earn money, adds little to explorations of masculinity. Age-graded homosexuality is part of a rite of passage to manhood in which young boys graduate to male roles in the homosexual exchange. Profession-defined homosexuality occurs among performers and prostitutes who cross-dress or cross-gender as part of their occupations. Examples include shamans, dancing boys, transvestite singers and prostitutes, and the actors of the Noh and Kabuki theatres in Japan from the fourteenth century (Murray 1992:119–22; Kaplan and Rogers 1990:222–4). In the third form, the man who takes the 'passive' (insertee) role is defined as committing a homosexual act but not the man who takes the 'dominant' (inserter) role. We will explore the relationship of these different forms of homosexuality to masculinity.

Age-graded homosexuality means that older men have sexual relations with younger men, often to mark passages in the younger men's lives or as part of a wider mentoring role. Historically age-graded homosexuality has been discovered in ancient Athens, China, Byzantium and medieval Persia (Adam 1986:22). Its most famous contemporary manifestation in ethnographic accounts is in the Papua New Guinea Highlands. Once considered all of a piece, homosexual practices differ, basically between highly ritualised and age-graded homosexual encounters, for example among the Kiman (Gray 1986:55, 61) to more intimate, apparently loving relations among the Big Nambas or Orokaivans (Jackson 1991:81). One question asked from a western perspective is whether men derive erotic pleasure from these rituals. While some observers suggest they do (Adam 1986:29; Moore 1993:138), one Sambian informant discussed his embarrassment at his preference for homosexual encounters when he was culturally expected to feel 'fear and shame'. He was unable to form a lasting relationship with any of the four wives he was assigned (Herdt 1992:50–9), which points to the expectation that age-graded homosexuality is something men do because of ritual, not something they are because of sexual orientation. Melanesian homosexuality has been explained along monstrous feminine lines (Adam 1986:25; Jackson 1991:81; Strathern 1988:89–114), although sometimes inflected with men's awe and respect for women's birth-giving powers (Strathern 1988:98–100). Such justifications for age-graded ritual homosexuality would explain the absence of ritualised female homosexuality. According to one observer, 'the only relatively clearly documented instance of "institutionalized" lesbianism in Melanesia comes from Malekula Island in the New Hebrides' (Murray 1992d:397).

Generally profession-defined homosexuality has involved younger boys and older men in all-male cultures, like the Buddhist monks and samurais in Japan from the ninth century and the monasteries of Europe in the eleventh century. Although Buddhist monks described homosexual love as *shudo*, short for 'way of the gods' (Murray 1992:xvi–xxv), commentators say it was clearly eroticised (Jackson 1991:78–9). 'China boasts a longer continuous recorded history of male homosexuality than any other nation', dating back to 722–221 BC, and including male brothels, homoerotic art and stories of tender and erotic relations between emperors and their male lovers (Dynes and Donaldson 1992a:xii; Connell 1993:604). The decline in ancient homosexual practices is attributed to the rise of religious or moralistic homophobia, including western influences in more recent times (Dynes and Donaldson 1992a:xiv).

As opposed to western cultures, where homosexual acts denote homosexual lives, in some other cultures men may perform homosexual acts without this being a threat to their heterosexual identity. There appears to be considerable cross-cultural convergence that the role of inserter, as opposed to insertee, retains the aura of masculinity. Ritual homosexuality in Melanesia is said to involve a progression from the less desirable subordinate position of insertee or fellator to the dominant position of inserter or fellated, akin to English public schools (Jackson 1991:79, 83). In Brazil a strong distinction is drawn between the *bicha* (which means worm, internal parasite and is also the name for a female animal), who acts as the insertee, and the *macho* or *homem* or *homem mesmo* (man or real man), who acts as the inserter. The *bicha* is dominated like a woman, chooses female occupations and is referred to as *ela* although he has less status than a woman because of biological lack. Sexual encounters between two *bichas* are regarded as deviant and classed *lesbianismo*. For women the terms are *sapato* (big shoe) or *coturno* (army boot) reflecting an unacceptable masculinity (Fry 1986:141–2; Parker 1986:157, 274). On the other hand, among some homosexual subcultures in the anglophone west at least, both inserter and insertee remain masculine. Thus homosexual identity formation among men in Sydney is consolidated around a relationship with the male body (of both self and other). The men are 'very straight' in this sense of valuing masculine bodies (Connell 1992:743).

The studies discussed above focus on male homosexual acts rather than female homosexuality. This may be an artefact of predominantly male observers, who were less likely to be told of lesbian behaviour. Thus a 1951 study found lesbian behaviour in only 17 out of 76 societies, while a 1984 study found lesbian behaviour in as many as 95 cultures, although one-third were Native North American (Blackwood 1986:9). Out of 99 American Indian tribes who kept written records, 88 mention male homosexuality and 20 refer to lesbianism (Grahn 1986:43). It may be that gender ascription was usually less demanding for women, who therefore did not need to escape their destiny in cross-gender roles. Thus the bedarche (see below) has been explained as the American Indian man who cringes from the role of warrior. But women also chose third genders to become hunters or warriors, while others formed erotic attachments to women (Williams 1993:181, 183). It may be that testosterone and morphology have real effects, whatever cultures do to limit and channel them, so that female anatomy dictates no stark choice between passivity and activity (Mead in Blackwood 1986:7). But the terms passivity and activity are culturally loaded, even if we have seen some cross-cultural adherence to this dichotomy.

Another question which can be asked of this literature is whether the distinction between homosexual acts and homosexual lives is as clear as Murray's classification suggests. It can certainly be questioned by the following examples. In Australia, there were three reports in early 1993 of men forced to have oral and anal sex performed on them, while statistics suggest that men are 6.4 per cent of rape victims and 30 to 35 per cent of sexual assault survivors. The assailants are mostly self-identified as heterosexual, for whom the gender of the victim was immaterial (Burdack 1993:148–7). Both Kinsey (Giddens 1990:13) and more recently Shere

Hite (1994:290) discovered extensive homosexual encounters between adolescents in the United States. Practices appear to have shifted from mutual masturbation in the 1970s to fellatio in the 1990s, reported by 36 per cent of Hite's respondents, although only a minority kiss. Relatively few boys seemed concerned that these practices might indicate homosexuality, although one said, 'At present, I go to a psychiatrist for help in deciding my sexuality' (Hite 1994:290, 293). Thus in the west, too, it would appear that men can perform 'homosexual' acts without seeing themselves as homosexual.

Perhaps, in societies which do not recognise homosexuality publicly, young men and women engage in more public intra-sex physical contact, which might also be associated with intense friendships (Yu and Carpenter 1991:195 for Taiwan). At student dances in Beijing in 1991, the men unselfconsciously danced with each other, as did the women; there were a lesser number of mixed-sex couples (see also Thubron 1987:184 for Shanghai; McQueen 1991:49, 123 for Japan). In Hong Kong in 1979, but not in 1991, and only very rarely in Beijing in 1993, young men could be seen walking with their arms around each other's shoulders. Thus the practice does appear to have lessened as homosexuality has achieved some public recognition. One young man in Beijing told me that girls with arms interlinked did not make him think of lesbianism but that physical contact between boys did make him think of homosexuality. Professor Choi Po-king of the Chinese University of Hong Kong confirmed changing male practices in her society, while other Hong Kong women academics noted that, in comparison with Taiwanese women, Hong Kong women were much less effusive, possibly because lesbianism was more overtly recognised (for example see the study by Lieh-Mak et al. 1992:102–3 of Hong Kong women who self-identified as lesbians).

However, in the Philippines, described as 'one of the most tolerant nations on earth' (Dynes and Donaldson 1992a:xii), intense same-sex friendships are common, and may be homosexual (Hart 1992b:216–19), although this is not necessarily assumed (Agnes Whiten, interview 1 June 1994). As opposed to Chinese culture, there are clear adult homosexual roles, for both men and women. The terms *bayot* (transvestite man, although cross-dressing is confined to the cities) and *lakin-on* lack the pejorative connotations of homosexuality in the west. *Lakin-on* are women who are tough, flat-chested, muscular, challenge men, have a brave look, ride horses or plough fields; they mostly 'only love women' and wear tight-fitting men's trousers. They pick up young college girls and may stab men who try to get too close to them (Whitam 1992:236–7, 242; Hart 1992a:204–9). Young girls may also become 'tomboys' or *callaheras* (girls who love to roam the streets) (de Dios 1994:31), engaging in physical fights and playing boys' ball games. Of one such tomboy, a neighbour said to her mother, 'You were not gifted with a boy child but you had a boy within you' (Del Douglas, interview 21 June 1994).

This review of the literature on homosexual practices reveals that a sharp distinction between westerners 'having' homosexual identities and non-westerners 'doing' homosexual acts does not cover the complexity of practice. But it may well be the case that homosexual subcultures are more prolific in western nations, particularly in large cities. Thus it is claimed that in Turkey, despite a long history of pederasty, only in Istanbul is there a homosexual subculture; elsewhere in the Islamic world homosexuality is defined as taking the receptor role (Dynes and Donaldson 1992a:x–xi). In Japan there were no gay bars until the American occupation; homosexuality has 'remained something that men do, rather than something they become' (Murray 1992c:368). According to Dennis Altman (1992:37),

> in many Third World cities – Bangkok, Rio de Janeiro and Mexico City above all, but also in Soweto, Seoul and Santiago – there are a number of men (though fewer women) who conceive of themselves as 'gay', as we use that term. However, they probably make up a smaller proportion of the homosexually active population than is true in, say, Sydney, Hamburg or Toronto.

In Brazil, under white western influences, homosexuality has changed from the appellation of *bicha* and *sapato* (still common in the country-side) to be defined as a sickness, as occurred in America and Britain at the turn of the century (discussed above). From the late 1960s, homosexuality was increasingly conceived as a chosen lifestyle (Fry 1986:151; Parker 1988:277; Parker 1986:158), indicated by new labels, *homens* and *entendidos* (literally those who know, and have adopted a gay identity). An *entendido* may be either passive or active in sexual encounters but is 'fundamentally homosexual in terms of his sexual object choice' (Parker 1986:158).

Neo-Confucian, Mongol, Manchu and western proscriptions against homosexuality repressed it from the language if not the practice of pre-revolutionary China. Thus, lacking the term homosexual, one of Amy Tan's (1991:350–1) semi-fictional informants uses *zibuyong* meaning 'something like "hens-chicks-and-roosters"' to describe a man who she later understands was possibly gay. While the communist regime was also puritan in matters of sex, by the late 1980s a group of Chinese men, speaking the forbidden language of homosexual desire, expressed their needs in western terms: the right to express their sexuality, freedom to interact with other homosexuals, and a medical scientific explanation for their condition. But their letters also express romantic yearnings: 'The pain in my heart makes me extremely despair', the desire for 'a strong man [to] lie right next to me', as well as misogyny, distaste for women's bodies and their 'irrationality, gossiping, cursing, dependency' (Ruan and Tsai 1992:181, 182, 183).

In Thailand a translation of customary transvestite practices has produced drag shows which borrow heavily from western associations with homosexuality, for example Marilyn Monroe as a gay icon (Hardacre and Manderson 1990:33–4), while a blending of western and traditional Thai tropes has produced 'gym-toned Thai gay men' and *gay-quing*, a sexually versatile homosexual whose partner is a 'Gay-queen'. However, categories are distinguished in terms of masculine or feminine gender position, construed largely in terms of active or passive homosexuality and applying both to the definition of gay women and men (Jackson 1996:110, 115, 117–18).

While these appear to be examples of western sexual identities 'invading' eastern subjectivities, the invasion is built on indigenous understandings and practices of sexuality. In some countries these understandings once confined homosexuality to the role of the insertee, as in South America; in other countries homosexuality has been connected with particular professions, as in the Noh and Kabuki theatres; in other countries there are roles for women and men who choose not to follow the usual feminine and masculine role prescriptions, as in the Philippines. It is to this issue that we now turn, to investigate the idea that sexual identities are more fluid in some non-western cultures, thus providing a challenge to the construction of dualistic identities in the west's dominant discourses. This requires us to consider two assertions: that there is something like a 'third gender' in some non-western cultures, and that western sexual identities are organised around rigid dualisms like man and woman, gay and straight.

Third Genders

> Anthropologists have never assumed that the western concepts of the person and the self are universal, and, almost uniquely among academic disciplines, they have the data to show that this is the case.
>
> – Moore 1994a:29

The term gender identity was invented in the United States and is not found in other cultures (Nanda 1990:138). It suggests both the centrality of gender to one's identity and the fixed nature of that identity. Robert Stoller defines 'core' gender identity as an identity established early in life, although one which may be discrepant with the biologically given sex (Stoller 1968:30–5, 40; Hausman 1992:296). 'I am a male' suggests biological signals, while 'I am manly' is a more subtle and complicated response to social cues. Thus male transvestites retain the core gender identity of a man, but male-to-female transsexuals (the vast majority are male to female) have a core gender identity as women. The concept of 'core' gender identity refers us to humanist notions of the self, a single individual without ambiguity or contradiction. The term would clearly be criticised by postmodernists who focus on gender performance. It is also criticised by social constructionists like Connell (1994), who notes that gender identity is accomplished not only individually but also socially.

The significance of western sexual identities is suggested by the widespread belief that only the very old or very young would choose to be celibate. Indeed women beyond their childbearing years are offered hormone replacement therapy so they can retain their sexual appeal (described by one doctor as their very 'personality' being at stake: in Sybylla 1990:98). Rigid bifurcation also seems to characterise western sexual identities: body/mind, male/female, homosexual/heterosexual. Within these oppositions, western feminists in the 1970s developed another dualism, a distinction between sex as a biological attribute of the body and gender as a social construction of the mind. Thus surgical and other medical intervention in babies maintains a clear biological sex for those born with ambiguous characteristics (Kessler 1990:10), and without which the inevitable question, 'Is it a boy or a girl?,' must provoke discomfort. For Tahitians, by contrast, sexual identity is so insignificant that the sex of newborn infants may not be related as a part of the information which describes the birth (Nanda 1990:141). In much of island Southeast Asia, one does not ask how many brothers and sisters a person has but how many younger and older siblings (Errington 1990:50).

Corrective surgery is also offered to the male-to-female transsexual, but only on condition that s/he demonstrates that he always was a woman inside. The operation is thus performed to reveal 'true' sexual identity (Nanda 1990:143, 138; Raymond 1980), which must not include 'lesbianism, feminism or anal sex', although it appears that clinics are now less rigid in this regard, responding more to 'perseverance and consistency' than appropriate identification as feminine (Lewins 1995:94, 96). Legal access to passports, bank accounts and so on is also denied in a woman's name unless surgery is undertaken to make a 'functional woman'. A functional woman is defined by the fact that her vagina can accept three fingers and thus presumably a penis, aligning 'functional woman' with 'sexual utility' (McColl 1995:51–2, 48, 52).

Male-to-female transsexuals do not usually see themselves as a third sexual category; they are women, and may spurn self-help groups during their liminal stage as a hindrance to this new identity (Nanda 1990:138; see also Hausman 1992:293; Lewins 1995:97–8, who however notes that half the transsexuals in his sample had some association with support groups). But some of them also see that being a woman is a performance, just as being a man required 'pretending' to be male. However it is not pretending or passing to which they aspire, but invisibility, *really* 'being' a woman (McColl 1995:51; Lewins 1995:111). They also understand that gender is inscribed on the whole body rather than merely in the genitals (Lewins 1995:126, 125).

In most traditional societies, and in western society in former times, there were jobs or roles for men and other roles and jobs for women. One did not have to be 'essentially' a woman or man in terms of looks or temperament because the social role defined one's sex. Furthermore, the roles in which one acted may be at least as important as the sex enacted within them. Thus 'a woman acting in the capacity of sister is quite different from a woman acting in the capacity of wife', so that there is not a strong sense of 'the' status of women or their collective definition in contrast to men (Errington 1990:7 for some parts of island Southeast Asia). In such societies, neither biological determinism (sex) nor social constructionism (gender) prevails, but rather women and men are basically the same, although women 'tend not to become prominent and powerful' because of their social activities. Thus a 'Wana woman who becomes a powerful shaman has not broken the rules but beaten the odds' (Errington 1990:40; although Atkinson 1990:84, 90–3 suggests that men's genitals give them a biological edge in becoming shamans). But where there are no specific activities for men and women, sexual difference must perhaps be asserted through notions of essential difference between the sexes. These may be expressed hierarchically – men are superior to women – and driven home with physical force as men become more anxious about the dissolution of gender-role segregation (Johnson 1988:123; Jaggar 1994:144; Moore 1994a:33, 37, 47). In contrast is the acceptance in some cultures of lesbian relations, as long as women also perform their socially assigned role of motherhood (see for example Gandhi and Shah 1992:327 for India; Williams 1993:88 for southern Mexico; and Duncker 1992:70 discussing Audre Laude for the older African-American generation).

Furthermore, the western 'folk model' or 'local philosophy' of identity-formation sees the body as the source and locus of identity, which carries the authentic and 'interior self' (Moore 1994a:47, 33). The body is used to express sexual difference. Homophobic sexuality is expressed in 'poofter-bashing' and heterosexual superiority in physical aggression (on the roads, in bikie gangs, in some cases against women who do not know their place) (Connell 1991:159, 167 for Australia; Kopytoff 1990 for the United States; James and Saville-Smith 1989:14 for New Zealand). In contrast with western preoccupation with the body, 'many of the differences which concern people around the world are internal to bodies, that is within them rather than between them' (Moore 1994b:82–3), and may be shared by both male and female bodies. This is sometimes expressed in the construction of third genders.

It is claimed that some societies allow a third gender, a status which is that of neither man nor woman, and not homosexual either, but 'a distinct and autonomous social status on par with the status of men and women' (Roscoe 1994:370). Ambiguous sexuality or sexual identities are inscribed in Indian religion. Shiva can be both ascetic and erotic; his *linga* or phallus is set in the *yoni* or female symbol; he is often united with his female half or *shakti*. Ancient Hinduism identified a third sex internally divided into four categories (Nanda 1990:20-1). In India today the third sex of *hijras* are a religious community of men who undergo an operation in which the penis and the testicles are removed but no vagina is constructed. The ceremony mimics elements of a woman's wedding (Nanda 1990:26). Dressed in women's clothing, *hijras* perform ceremonies and dances at weddings, at temple festivals, and to celebrate the birth of a child. The dances involve 'an aggressively displayed female sexuality' (Nanda 1990:5). They are also homosexual prostitutes, and may be in social terms wives, mothers or grandmothers (Nanda 1990:xv–xvi). *Hijras* are neither man (because they have demonstrated their impotence and had their genitals removed) nor woman (because they lack the capacity to give birth and act outrageously in ways inappropriate for ordinary women) (Nanda 1990:26, 15–18).

Similarly, in Polynesian societies, like Tahiti, Hawaii, New Zealand, the Marquesas Islands (as well as the *fa'afafine* in Samoa), *mahus* have been described as a 'kind of third entity' who do women's work, and have sex with men. *Mahus* are assumed to be born thus, but can cast off the role 'as one can discontinue being a chief'. In Hawaii and Tahiti, *mahus* are distinguished from gay men because they have a spiritual rather than sexual identity (Nanda 1990:134–7). According to Timon Screech (1993), Japanese culture insistently asserted racial purity (apart from the 'honorary' Japanese, the Chinese) and gave more weight to function (or occupation) than to gender: 'If in the West gender is the *primary* and *least mutable* social division, in Japan that role was played by 'function'. In the West it is easier to switch class than gender[;] one can be classless, but to be genderless is impossible. In Japan the reverse was true' (Screech 1993:134). Thus the Japanese word for person, *hito*, is genderless; Buddhists and monks were accounted neither as men nor women but simply as 'clerics', although the function from which they hailed was always noted in biographies. Where homosexuals and others were categorised as cross-gendered or confused, the *kagema* were 'gender-added boys', an extra gender catering for the sexual desires of either men or women, including monks who were debarred from consorting with women (but could consort with *kagema* because this did not question monks' severance of family ties). The *kagema*, it appears from the evidence, always took the passive role and often wore the purple headcover worn by the female-impersonators of the Kabuki. Thus Screech sees the monks as a third gender where other interpretations describe this as profession-defined homosexuality (see above). This example points to the significance of the gaze through which cultural practices are understood, as does the example of the *xanith*.

In Oman, an Islamic society, the *xanith* (meaning impotent, effeminate, soft) do not undergo castration and have all the legal rights of men. But they dress as women, perform women's household chores and join women on festive occasions, in gossip and at meals (all forbidden to men). *Xanith* are homosexual prostitutes, a role perhaps made necessary by the high moral standard imposed on women (Garber 1992a:349). In sexual encounters *xanith* take the passive role, which is considered the woman's role. At any time they can choose to become 'real' men, marrying and proving their virility by displaying a bloodied handkerchief after the wedding night (Wikan 1992; Nanda 1990:130–1; see also Williams 1988: 258–9). Unni Wikan who described the *xanith* in 1977, called them 'transsexuals' because they wore some female and some male clothing, and were juridically and grammatically men but took on the woman's sexual position. However, Garber (1992a:349, 351) asks whether the term 'transsexual', coined in 1949 to describe the condition of certain European and Anglo-American men, can be translated 'back into a culture which had been closed to the outside world (by Wikan's account) until 1971'.

This question must be asked of all cross-cultural analysis. To describe these third genders as 'homosexual' or 'transvestite' is to neglect the context in which they construct and perform their sexuality. They take on socially inscribed roles rather than gender identities (Moore 1994b:83, 91). Physical characteristics are the sign or effect of sexual difference rather than the cause of gender identity. Morphology is a consequence (not a cause) of behaviour, which then has its own consequences. 'Third gender' roles do not necessarily require a same-sex sexual orientation. Examples include the *bedarche* role for men in American Indian societies who could marry a woman and still remain a *bedarche* and the Chinese sisterhoods of silk weavers who initially took husbands (Blackwood 1984; Williams 1993:186). Neither are these third-gender roles a humanist insistence on revealing one's 'true' sexual inclination nor a dualist insistence on being either a man or a woman. Thus the *mahu* and *xanith* can throw off their roles and become men.

Instead, according to Moore, in traditional cultures 'gender identity' is 'performative' rather than 'categorical' and 'fixed' as in the west (Moore 1994b:91). Does this mean that we can explain such gender roles appropriately within postmodernist discourse? And does this mean that genders are fluid among the postmodernist cognoscenti of the west, performed in a variety of combinations? While 'gender benders' like Boy George have become popular and accepted in the west, their fascination *is* as benders of gender, who remain 'really' either male or female, a point Marjorie Garber (1992a:390) also makes for transvestism or cross-gender role performance (see also Butler 1993:237). McColl (1995:45) suggests that the cross-dresser expresses anxieties about sex and gender roles 'that arise from the changes that body-building and genetic engineering have wrought on cultural ideas of the "naturalness" of sex and gender'. Thus gender bending is bound to the dualisms of male and female, heterosexual and homosexual, even as it challenges the widely assumed connections between body and gender.

Finally, western feminists have made their own attempts to disrupt dualisms like male and female, mind and body, gender and sex. Genevieve Lloyd (1989:20–1) suggests that the mind is the 'idea of the body', and so is also 'sexed' by the body which gives it sense impressions (see also Gatens 1991:25). Luce Irigaray recommends that women envisage their sexuality as 'These Two Lips Which are Not One'. Where men know their sexual pleasure comes from one solitary organ, women feel it coming from two sides, and many places. Women's 'two lips' which 'are one and two *simultaneously*' produce a new representation of women's sexuality. Not having 'one', a penis, may not mean having 'nothing' as Freud suggested. Rather it may mean having one and more than one at the same time (Grosz 1989:115, 116). Similarly some lesbians have rejected what they see as essentialist or humanist explanations for becoming lesbian, explanations which require them to conform to 'monogamous' and 'motherly' heterosexual tropes of femininity. In the 1980s, and influenced by postmodern ideas, a 'queer' self-definition was proposed as a challenge to the fixed and opposite identities produced within and against hetero-sexuality, asserting practices which destabilise both the female body and masculine identity (Martin 1992:109).

To summarise, while there clearly is a greater fluidity of sexual identity in some cultures, very possibly connected to a lesser salience of sexual identity, in all the examples discussed here sexual relations and gender roles are at issue. Societies have developed different ways of negotiating sexual difference, so that in some societies the sexes are very different and in others less so; in white western culture gender seems more mech-anically built on the body, while in other cultures roles serve to support gender. In societies less focused on sex, especially sex defined in binary dualisms, third genders allow for a more fluid and changing expression of role performances which are not centrally gender performances, as such gender bending appears to be in the west. We will explore these issues a little further in the Conclusion, but first let us return to the claim made of homosexual lifestyle choices, that, as with economic and political invasion, contemporary colonialism involves the invasion of the very subjecthood of those dwelling in post-colonies.

SEXUAL IDENTITIES INVADE THE INTERIOR OF COLONISED SUBJECTS?

'How do you know these things?' she gasped. 'Porn', he informed her gravely. 'I study the porn magazine'. She laughed. Thank God for pornography, then, she thought, in the absence of holy erotic temple sculptures, we need secular inspirations.

– Inez Baranay 1995:352 describing a white woman and a Balinese man's sexual encounter

As with the constructions of 'effeminate' Asian and hyper-masculine Latino machismo masculinities, some women of colour are seen as too passive, some too promiscuous. The white woman is seen as at the centre, a reasonable self-possessed balanced sexuality. Clearly 'other' cultures are no strangers to sexual practice or sexual discussions, as the above analysis has revealed. To pose the question of this section is to ask, not whether sex is discussed, practised, enjoyed, but whether it is constructed in terms which reveal the influence of western obsessions with sexual identity or western medicalisation of sex as *scientia sexualis*. Kalpana Ram (1991a: 92) claims that a 'colonial subjectivity' arises from the invasion of the west into the very 'interiority' of the colonial subject (see also Nandan 1992:196 for the South Pacific nations). Thus when Ted Turner launched CNN, he claimed that 'we're gonna take the news and put it on the satellite ... and we're gonna bring world peace, and we're gonna get rich in the process'. The culture-makers of women's magazines in the west are market researchers and advertisers. They are selling commodities like clothing and make-up in particular ways, as an expression of freedom, individuality, leisure, international sophistication, heterosexual attractiveness and even premarital expression, ideas which apparently challenge the conventional social order in countries like India, China and Japan (Rosenberger 1996:2, 24 speaking of women's magazines in Japan). But are the watchers and readers of western images mere passive recipients of a promised bag of goodies where democratic values and consumerist desires are indistinguishable? Two case studies reveal the hybridisation of sexual identities in China, Singapore, India and Japan.

Little Honeys in China: Prostitutes or Concubines?
In 1991 a student class in Beijing presented a skit which contrasted western sexual desire (represented by a male) and eastern reticence and modesty (represented by a female). During the May Fourth Movement

particularly, Chinese intellectuals grappled with western concepts, adopting neologisms for society, culture, intellectuals, individualism. A sexological perspective also suggested a new word for woman, *nüxing*, literally 'female sex' but suggesting 'sex opposition and sex attraction'. *Nüxing* was deemed unsuitable by communist writers, who saw it as 'febrile' and indicating 'bourgeois women's preoccupations'. They invented the 'kin-inflected category of' *funü*, a womanhood achieved through 'revolutionary practice' (Barlow 1994:263–9). With the easing of communist ideological control, *nüxing* has reappeared, but now suggests 'biologically inferior', subject to romantic love, pertaining to gender psychology and so on (Barlow 1994:277).

From a western perspective, the asexual nature of Chinese society struck me forcibly when I was there in 1979, so that I suffered my own version of 'gender vertigo' (Connell 1990:470–1). Professor Wang Jiaxiang, while comfortable using the English words for 'the lower part of the body', rarely reads or says those words in Chinese. Foreign literature translated into Chinese is censored of the explicit sexual scenes, as are the movies. One of my friends, a woman in her mid-twenties, suffered considerable embarrassment when I asked her to translate the Chinese terms for various methods of contraception (this required her to use terms like condom, IUD, sterilisation and, most difficult for her, *coitus interruptus*). This may be a function of marital status or personality, as another of my friends of the same age, but married, blithely told me about the unreliability of free government-made condoms available from clinics. In 1991 tales of illegitimate pregnancies and students' affairs with married men were communicated in hushed and horrified tones. By 1993, however, Chinese-language newspapers were bemoaning the phenomenon of 'little honeys'. These women, often college-educated, become mistresses of Chinese businessmen (often from Taiwan or Hong Kong). Some are calculating and save enough money for a comfortable retirement when replaced. Others fall in love and commit suicide when their lover loses interest in them. The same mixture of responses seems to characterise the 'Chinese girlfriends' of the young (and sometimes not so young) western bucks who teach in Beijing's universities. Some girlfriends say they are open-eyed, but are willing to risk their virginity for a chance, however slight, to emigrate to the west. Some deeply regret falling in love and giving up their virginity in a lost cause. Aware of women's calculus in sexual matters, some young Chinese men complain of the growing demands by girlfriends for material tokens in exchange for sexual favours ('We throw our money after them ... Sometimes my friends spend *half a month's salary* on one meal. That's to get the girls to do what they want': Thubron 1987:60–1).

Clearly sexual practices and orientations have changed in China; superficially they have become more 'westernised'. Thus in classes for newly-weds, instructors now suggest that women can approach the relationship as a source of enjoyment and not merely a duty, while commercialised and eroticised images of the female body are becoming more common (Evans 1995:383, 389), as are abortions among unmarried women, at least in Beijing and Shanghai (Xiao et al. 1995:245). Ding Xiaoqi (1991:112) bemoans the trend towards divorce, women demanding orgasms (ten years ago a survey suggested that 97 per cent of women never experienced orgasm), wearing bikinis and entering the fashion industry, attracted by 'the allure of the self-expression involved in this profession'.

Additionally since the 1980s, sexual issues are dealt with in 'scientific' discourses, in sexual disorder clinics, in marriage guidance counselling, in research on 'sexual psychology' and sexual crime (like 'peeping toms'), in sex education for adolescents (Xiao 1987:17; Fennell and Jeffry 1992:20–1; Lin Shiwei, 'Centre Solves Problems that are all in the Mind', *China Daily* 26 October 1993:5). On the other hand, young women told me that 'true equality', such as they believe western women have, makes women deny their real essence: their femininity and their dependence on men. Thus although there is now greater emphasis on sexual self-definition, and some of it arises from western influences, Chinese femininity is still a thing apart, drawing on a history of romantic tragedy, concubinage and the competent revolutionary woman as well as on western fashions.

Women's Magazines in Singapore and India[2]

The standard of female beauty as white, western and wealthy is promulgated by magazines like *Cosmopolitan*, which is translated into seventeen languages (Chapkis 1994a:230). In white society largeness is no longer associated with largesse but with lack of self-control (Bordo 1990:94), and there are signs that these new meanings of ample figures are seeping into the minds of younger middle-class women in other cultures. Today Maori tourist shows concentrate on 'fineness and fairness, along with an affected delicacy of movement' instead of the 'big women, really big, and graceful' who once performed 'forceful dance styles'. These gifted performers have internalised Pakeha myths that they are 'too fat', 'too black' or need to shave their legs (Awekotuku 1991:92, 132–3). Indrani Ganguly's (1992:2–3) survey of immigrants to Australia found that many upper-class Argentinians believed women were ideally 'slim' or 'thin', although Tongan women disagreed. Vietnamese women thought a 'flat, thin' body the ideal, although a little more weight after marriage was a good sign: 'A moon face is the sign of graciousness' (Ganguly n.d.:17). Fair skin was considered preferable by women from most countries surveyed, in contrast with an acquired darker skin preferred by Anglo-

Australians and Argentinians. Some Vietnamese women favoured cosmetic surgery to make their eyes look 'more western' (Ganguly 1992:3).

There is both cultural resistance and accommodation to white western standards of beauty in this sample of immigrants to Australia. Thus western standards are often integrated with traditional images. In Singapore *Her World* reproduces glamorous images of women who are recognisably Asian but who are 'Europeanised' in terms of low-cut attire, make-up and eye shape. In October 1994 ('If I Were a Young Woman', *Her World* 1994:117–26), a number of leading Singapore women gave advice to young women. These women were bank vice-presidents, company managing directors, senior public servants and professional women. They advised young women on how to combine motherhood and career, both being deemed an expected part of a woman's life (although only one adviser suggested life might be possible without marriage and motherhood). Younger women were advised to use the government's matchmaking agency, to use condoms if engaging in premarital sex, to deliver their babies normally (some women choose Caesarean sections because they think normal delivery loosens muscles and produces a 'less exciting sex life') and to use HRT in menopause (from Mary Rauff, gynaecologist, *Her World* 1994:125). Readers were also advised to 'stay away from heavy make-up', 'chunky accessories – and gold, gold, gold' and to 'Change your spectacle frames every year' (Sylvia Lian, *Her World* 1994:125). Indirect methods of conflict resolution were suggested, for example accepting that an argument with mother has been forgiven if she warms up your dinner when you come home, or leaving your husband in charge of the household for a while if he denigrates the way you run it (Esther Tzer Wong, *Her World* 1994:118). While Singaporean female university students want more equally shared housework and family decision-making, they phrase this not in terms of 'love' but 'mutual respect' and mutual obligations (Lyons 1994:3–4).

The ideal woman on Delhi television is as charming as western women, but she produces sons to ensure patriliny, engages in traditional rites and rituals and dies unsullied, if abandoned (Krishnan and Dighe 1990:51–2). A deviant male does not care for the family, puts self above community and country, is violent towards women, is not an income earner and allows his wife to dominate him (Krishnaraj and Chanana 1990). An article on 'Modern Day Marriages' in the Indian magazine *Feminina* (its masthead declaring it to be 'For The Woman of Substance') notes the influence of western thinking in marriage choice. Religion and lineage have been displaced for 'interpersonal vibes', education, financial independence and emotional responsibility for oneself (Ritu Bhatia in Sand 1994:18). Such marriages may be preceded by living together and end in divorce or single parenthood. In a current affairs magazine, an article entitled 'The Changing Woman' describes women who 'are becoming the kind of men they wanted to marry' (Jain 1992:36). Changing women include fourteen airline pilots of Indian Airlines, deans of hospitals, politicians who made it without the help of male political relatives, and the 130 000 women in 1988–89 who set up small-scale industries. Prahlad Kakkar notes that films and women's magazines like *Savvy* encourage more explicit sexual talk of 'the need for sexual fulfilment', 'impotence and perversions', 'adultery, wife abuse and her sex life', and women's willingness to ask for what she wants in love-making (Jain 1992:41, 43).

Sexually degrading representations of women have been attacked – literally with eggs, cowdung and tar thrown at offending billboards. Women's movement activists have engaged in critiques of beauty contests and 'chick charts' and 'uglies' lists drawn up by male students at a college in Delhi (Gandhi and Shah 1992:69, 75, 50). When two women police constables married in a Hindu ceremony, most women's groups refused to comment publicly beyond saying it was a personal matter, possibly fearing a backlash. There was much private discussion, but Nadita Gandhi and Nandita Shah (1992:158) ask, 'Why have we not been able to discuss the compulsory nature of heterosexuality, non-penetrative sexual methods and lesbianism?' Is it cultural reluctance or a belief that these issues are far removed from the daily struggle of most Indian women? One answer is that mainstream Indian political life (as in many countries in both west and east) more readily accommodates women's interventions in defence of the dignified or victimised woman, as attacks on pornography suggest, rather than producing an Indian woman who seeks sexual expression apart from men (Rajan 1993:136–8).

To some Chinese observers, western constructions of sexuality are overdetermined, focused on the romantic dyad and constantly verbalised (Sun 1991:12, 28, 11; Chen Zhingming et al. 1990:113). The same point is made for Japan, where most people distinguish the fleeting nature of romance (expressed in extramarital affairs by both sexes) from the long-term arrangement of marriage (Iwao 1993:111, 61). In contrast, the demands placed on an American marriage must make it 'full of sustained tension and energy, which could be quite strenuous'. A good Japanese marriage, on the other hand, is 'like air', vital for survival but hardly felt (Iwao 1993:77, 75). Women hope for the 'three highs' in marriage: high income, higher education and physical height (Iwao 1993:67), but not high love.[3] As with the Chinese reluctance to discuss personal matters, in Japan putting feelings into words is thought to diminish them so that there is much reading between the lines (Iwao 1993:98). The divorce rate is rising as in China, but remains well below the United States rate (1.26 per cent compared with 4.8 per cent: Iwao 1993:113). The pressures on marriage in Japan include women's greater financial independence, and greater assertiveness and impatience with men who are 'bright and well educated, gentle and kind, but vulnerable and spoiled' (Iwao, 1993: 273–4). But the generation educated after World War II has taken on some notions of dyadic companionship, so that a lecture series, School for Bridegrooms, trains men in how to be 'good husbands and wise fathers' (Iwao 1993:66–7), while more young couples marry for love or companionship, wives expecting husbands to share leisure interests and child-rearing (Imamura 1996:3). Seven men have formed a men's liberation movement which offers a critical reading of the heroic samurai and addresses the problems of the early-dying overworked salary-man (Connell 1994). Some men have become primary carers of children; some seek new family-oriented roles as they worry about their future after retirement; some have formed the Association of Men Opposed to Prostitution in Asia. Such men tend to be viewed as 'oddities, "drop-outs" from the competition for success, or as traitors to the male sex' (Yamaguchi 1995:253).

The history of colonialism, the seductive power of media images from the west, and the alignment of material commodities with progress, means that western images probably have an advantage over indigenous ones. Both invasion and hybridisation are at work in the powers of persuasion and resistance across cultural borders. Western forms of sexual identity and expression are derided, devalued or transformed. Commitment to kin connections rather than the exclusive love dyad, to rational calculations in sexual exchanges rather than helpless romanticism, and to indigenous styles of fashion and beauty persist.

CONCLUSION: POST-SEX[4]

> The seeds of hegemony are never scattered on barren ground. They might establish themselves at the expense of prior forms, but they seldom succeed in totally supplanting what was there before.
>
> – Comaroff and Comaroff 1991:25

The so-called third genders of non-western societies are made up of elements of male and female roles and biologies. They are not something entirely different, like kangaroos for example. Similarly, postmodernists do not, on the whole, suggest that westerners should challenge gender identities by presenting asexual images. If this were so, Madonna would hardly be one of the most written-about icons of sexual disruption. Thus she stops short of outright contestation of sexuality as a mechanism of desire (Kaplan 1993:161, 155). Nor do postmodernists suggest that instead of defining ourselves through our sex we choose another medium, for example our spirituality. To indigenous people in Australia, 'humans are more spirit than matter'. Women in white western culture are so defined by their sexual being that rape is a total abnegation of their selfhood. For Murris, while rape is not pleasant, it does not violate a woman's spirit (Watson 1994). Indeed, speaking of women reclaiming the monstrous feminine but perhaps equally applicable to gender performances like Madonna's, Marina Warner (1994:11) is sceptical of women's power to perform their sexuality in parody: 'these postmodern strategies all buckle in the last resort under the weight of culpability the myth has entrenched'. Like Victorian attempts to repress sex, attempts at inversion merely magnify the demons of female pollution or the significance of sex in our lives.

Thus white western women and men might learn something about the sexual prison in which they construct their identities from considering other attitudes towards sex, many of which are far more liberating than the compulsive obsession with youth, looks and sexual activity in the west (at least for women who lack these!). Just as western sexualised images invade Japan, China and Singapore, so too have Japanese gay and lesbian groups appropriated the erotic histories of homosexual practices by monks or actors to explore their sexual identities and expressions. Instead of their preoccupation with sexual identity, westerners might also consider the performative aspects of gender flexibility which suggest that sexual practice and orientation can be picked up and put aside, and is often a relatively insignificant definition of the self in society. Perhaps, too, western society is developing its own mechanisms for moving beyond the requirements of compulsive sexual expression. 'Post-sex', possibly provoked by the threat of AIDS but also interpreted in the light of postmodernist ideas, does not view sex with disgust, as did the medieval Christians, but rather with 'a trendy indifference' (Arcand 1994:241). Post-sex also suggests a lighthearted attack on sexual preoccupation while allowing greater space for other avenues of identity construction – spiritual, kin-related, cerebral, and so on.

CHAPTER 5

The International Traffic
in Women

•

Women and girls constitute one-half of the world population and one-third of the official labour force, perform nearly two-thirds of work hours, but, according to some estimates, receive only one-tenth of the world's income and less than one-hundredth of world property.

– International Labor Organization, 1978 in Hill 1987:340

INTERNATIONAL CONNECTIONS BETWEEN WOMEN

National boundaries have recently been loosened by international capitalism and challenged by ethnic strife in Africa and the former Yugoslavia, but people have long been on the move. The slave trade moved millions of people, while South Asians moved to East Africa and Fiji as indentured labour. From 1500 to 1800 comparatively small numbers of Europeans moved to the colonies, this number increasing dramatically between 1815 and World War I. Ten million Russians moved to Siberia and Central Asia, 12 million Chinese and 6 million Japanese to East and Southeast Asia. During World War II many Europeans were displaced across state borders and many migrated after the war. More recently there has been a reverse flow of people from south to north, often following the contours of colonialism, as temporary or permanent labourers in Europe, and later the Gulf States and Japan. People moved from Egypt and other Arab states to the Gulf States, from poorer South and Southeast Asian countries to comparatively rich neighbours; in the Pacific Samoan, Fijian and other Pacific Islanders have made significant communities in Auckland, Honolulu and Sydney (Pettman, 1996:65–6). The status of a country in this international flow can change as its economy improves. Italy was a state of emigration after World War II but now attracts migrants from north and sub-Saharan Africa (Pettman, 1996:66). Some 45 to 50 million people are on the move internationally each year. Of these, women are a significant proportion of labour migrants, while 80 per cent of the estimated 17 to 20 million refugees are women and children (Pettman, 1996:66; Vickers 1993:30).

Cynthia Enloe's (1989) *Bananas, Beaches and Bases* is an ambitious claim that, far from feminist politics being personal, it is international. Women's unpaid domestic labour supports diplomatic husbands; sexual services convince American soldiers posted overseas that they are manly; international politics focuses on the balance of terror between nations rather than the imbalance of inequalities between men and women in the nations of the world (Enloe 1989:196–8). In this chapter we explore three kinds of global connections between women: economic, political and cultural.

Women's economic connections are forged through what is sometimes called the global economic order, in which multinational corporations have produced an international division of labour as they search for the cheapest workers for their factories and the richest markets for their products. The exploitation of the female labour of recent immigrants to western nations is duplicated, sometimes exceeded, in the free-trade zone sweatshops of the third world, the sweatshops which helped create the 'miracle' of the 'Asian dragons'. As women in Hong Kong, Singapore and the United States go back to high-powered professional and executive careers, women from Indonesia, Thailand, South America, by dint of commanding lower wages, become their household help. When white western women travel overseas as privileged tourists, their rooms are cleaned by hotel maids who receive lower incomes and tips than hotel porters. 'Sex tourism' connects Thai and Filipino prostitutes with white wives and girlfriends.

Rey Chow (1991b:98) asks western women (who include herself) to face up to colonial history and postcolonial politics and economics. This has given white feminists the space to speak our exclusion as women, but it is a space built on oppressions and victimisations, 'many of which are performed at territorial borders'. Where this chapter defines relations of economic exploitation between women, it draws on a marxist feminist legacy. For socialist feminists in the west and east, the eradication of poverty is the first giant leap in the long march towards women's betterment. An evocative instance of this idea comes from a peasant women's movement in India. When they finally gained access to land in their own right, the women stated: 'We had tongues but we could not speak; we had feet but we could not walk. But now that we have land we can speak and walk' (Kelkar 1995). This chapter also discusses the international traffic in women, in sex tourism and prostitution, using a radical feminist perspective that connects the circumstances of women through universal sexual exploitation. Another aspect of international traffic is migration and refugee movements.

The doubled vision of non-anglophone women in the west is also explored. This leads into discussion of more hopeful connections between women of the north and south, the potential for shared political activism in international forums like those of the United Nations, and the halting attempts at cross-cultural understanding, for example through the international development of women's studies. We start with the United Nations and conclude with women's studies and women's politics at more local levels.

The International Decade for Women

> Once I found a place to eat and was reassured I wasn't 'chowing down' to a meal of Snoopy or any of his relatives; a toilet that a) flushed and b) didn't result in cramps in the thighs from squatting, I got down to the task of attending the Forum.
>
> – Jenny Dunn, Children by Choice vice-president, 'Beijing Report', *Children by Choice Newsletter* December 1995:8

The United Nations International Decade for Women brought women from all over the world together three times, in 1975 in Mexico City, in 1980 in Copenhagen and in 1985 in Nairobi. Women met again in Beijing in 1995 to review the achievements of the decade and plan future action. During the decade many governments were encouraged to address and publicise issues that concerned women (Miller 1991:188). In the United Nations itself, a number of organs expressly dedicated to the needs and experiences of women were spawned, for example the Commission on the Status of Women and the Division for the Advancement of Women. Even so, women are not well represented in the upper reaches of the United Nations.[1]

The most important commitment of the United Nations to come out of the Decade for Women was the System-wide Medium-term plan for Women and Development 1990–1995. The plan focuses on eliminating legal and attitudinal discrimination, improving access to productive resources, income and employment, improving access to social services (including family planning), participation in decision-making (measured quantitatively), and improving international information collection, training and co-operation (Pietilä and Vickers 1990:105). It was through this plan and the assessment of its goals that increasing poverty for women and loss of gains in literacy and other areas were discovered. This was part of the rationale for a further meeting in Beijing.

The Mexico meeting revealed the chasm of difference (indifference?) which separated women of the north and south. Domitila Barrios de Chungara, leader of the Housewives' Committee in Peru (see Chapter 2), remembers being 'confounded by the concerns she heard expressed: the problems of prostitutes, the lesbian experience, the need for equal rights, the idea that men were responsible for war, that men abused women. "We spoke very different languages, no?"' (Miller 1991:200). She rejected the idea of fighting against one's menfolk, instead endorsing the socialist goal of common struggle (de Chungara in Miller 1991:200). Instead of access to abortion, a concern of western feminists at the forum, she felt that strength of numbers was the principal weapon the miners and the House-wives' Committee possessed (Miller 1991:200). The World Plan of Action which emerged from the Mexico meeting bore the imprint of an alliance between the Soviet and East European delegates and representatives from Africa, Latin America and some Asian countries. It recognised the impact of colonialism and neo-colonialism as 'among the greatest obstacles to the full emancipation of and progress of developing countries and all the peoples concerned'. It did not specify women or include sexism as an obstacle, despite hours of debate (Miller 1991:202).

At the Copenhagen Meeting in 1980, infibulation or female genital surgery became the main divisive issue, with western women attacking it as 'barbaric' and 'backward' (see Chapter 2). In this climate, many Muslim women refused to condemn female circumcision because it placed them as dupes of western feminists and imperialism. Their speaking space was taken up and the issues defined in ways that made their contribution impossible. By the end of the decade, however, 'a cross-fertilization of ideas had occurred' (Miller 1991:201). More feminists of the west were aware that drinking-water, daily bread, and the right to organise were important to women (and their menfolk) in the third world. More women from countries in the south and east began to see why so many western feminists constructed men or patriarchy as the enemy. There were issues of power between men and women which would not be solved automatic-ally within either a socialist or liberal agenda.

Even so, as the quotation at the beginning of this section and press coverage of Beijing reveal, women still came to Beijing with ethnocentric presumptions about atavistic customs and economically backward countries. When addressing the government forum at Beijing, Hillary Clinton focused on human rights as women's rights, pointing to 'female infanticide, dowry burning, rape, genital mutilation, and the denial of the right of women to plan their families, including being forced to have abortions or being sterilized against their will' ('Hillary Clinton: End the History of Silence', *Forum '95* 5 September 1995:1). One can see again the barbarism/civilisation opposition at work. We the United States are advanced, you the 'east' are not. Happily, paragraph 225 of the platform, on violence against women, refuses Hillary Clinton's dualism and captures the effect of world-travelling (see Chapter 2). It states that 'any harmful aspect of certain traditional, customary or *modern* practices that violates the rights of women should be prohibited and eliminated' (italics mine).

The Platform of Action which emerged from the conference is not itself a legally binding document on governments but is tied to other binding documents. These include those on women's rights in relation to violence (Vienna, 1993) and the population and reproduction policies conference (Cairo, 1994), while the platform also evolves from both the summit on environment and development (Rio de Janeiro, 1992) and on social development (Copenhagen, 1995).

The United Nations NGO Forum and World Conference of Women in Beijing in 1995 has been described as 'the largest conference the UN has been involved in', with 4995 official delegates, 4035 NGOs accredited to the UN, 446 UN staff, 363 VIPs and 30 000 NGOs at the NGO Forum (Kathy Townsend, *CAPOW Bulletin* November, 1995:4).[2] Towards the end of the forum, a two-kilometre banner, the result of contributions from women of 122 countries, was carried around the forum site and then hung on the Great Wall (Margaret Hinchey, 'Women Weaving the World Together', *CAPOW Bulletin* November 1995:33). According to Bina Agarwal (1996:87; see also Otto 1996:23), 'the single most critical issue' at the NGO Forum was economic crisis: women of the south reeling under structural adjustment; women of Eastern Europe confronting economic insecurity with the break-up of the Soviet system; women of the west confronting economic rationalism's impact in cuts to health, education and welfare. About 500 of the 3000 odd panels dealt with economic issues. In this climate, 'romantic sisterhood' was giving way to 'strategic sisterhood' to confront 'the global crisis of economy and polity' (Agarwal 1996:88).

Despite the concerns for economic issues expressed at the NGO forum, it seemed to many that the central issue for debate was sexual orientation. At the 39th Session of the Commission on the Status of Women, a Central American nation asked that gender be bracketed in the draft platform, claiming that 'gender' 'is a ploy by the West to include homosexuality and bisexuality'. Before the Beijing meeting a 'contact group' at the UN headquarters in New York reached agreement that gender was understood in its 'ordinary generally accepted usage'. Although specific mention of sexual orientation was removed from the platform, it is encompassed by reference to 'other discriminatory factors' ('Conference of Commitments', 'Fourth United Nations World Conference on Women Beijing 4–15 September 1995: Infosheet No 8', June 1995:4; *Forum '95* 4 September 1995:1). North American Protestants, the Vatican and Muslim fundamentalists (not all Muslim nations any more than all Christian nations) combined to promote an anti-homosexual agenda, to emphasise the superiority of the heterosexual married couple family form and to oppose many of the rights claimed for the girl child (Otto 1996:26).

Many commitments have been expressed in abstract or formulaic statements, despite the attempt by the Australian delegation to make Beijing a Conference of Commitments in which each country pledged itself to practical and measurable outcomes. In a document of 362 paragraphs, covering twelve areas, specific targets were identified in only three areas. These were universal primary education by the year 2015 and closing the gender gap in secondary education by the year 2005 (paragraphs 82(b), 83(a)); reducing maternal, infant and child mortality and malnutrition rates (107); and to 'ensure that clean water is available and accessible to all by the year 2000' (256 (l)). (The Draft Platform was made available by the United Nations Information Centre in Sydney for Australia, New Zealand and the South Pacific in 1995).

While other paragraphs clearly contain statements with which women activists can make claims for action, the language is often supplicatory rather than mandatory. This is particularly obvious in the mechanisms for reducing poverty and resource inequality, perhaps suggesting the dominance of western voices (and those of the no-longer newly industrialising Asian 'dragons') in the platform. Thus the platform concedes that more women than men live in poverty and most of them live in the developing countries. It commits countries to 'people-centred sustainable development' and recognises 'the structural causes of poverty' (paragraphs 15, 18, 16, 26). Nevertheless, structural adjustment programs are described as 'beneficial in the long term' (20), as is liberalisation of world trade (18). International agencies and western countries are requested (usually nicely) to contribute tiny fractions of resources to a process which can best be described as equalising the exploitation of men and women in developing countries. It is true that the platform tells governments to 'seek to mobilize new and additional financial resources' to reduce poverty, while implementation of the Paris Club debt forgiveness terms is recommended (61(c)). This recommends that banks should accept their responsibility in lending money to third world countries for risky projects by writing off some of the debts. Banks and governments have made some debt-for-development swaps where they donate their entitlement to repayment in exchange for government-funded health, water and reforestation programs. However, in the face of transnational capitalism, which brings us relatively cheap food, clothes and computers produced by exploited women and children elsewhere in the world, these recommended flows of 'aid' will remain but a trickle in the face of 'trade'. Indeed, the major proposal for eradicating poverty is via a reallocation of defence expenditure (e.g. 15, 350). Thus, on the whole, 'equality' means that women are compared only with 'similarly situated men' rather than with women in other classes or other countries (Otto 1996:8, 13, 18).

The language of the platform confirms that women from beyond the west have taken up the language of human rights. It also confirms that the notion of rights is often adapted to express interdependence and collective goals. Thus 'the Platform for Action emphasizes that women share common concerns that can be addressed only by working together and in partnership with men towards the common goal of gender equality around the world' (3). Probably the main way in which this is proposed is through the 'empowerment' of women, their representation on decision-making bodies. Where the 'slogan' of the Decade of Women was 'equality, development and peace for all women everywhere in the interest of all humanity' (as paragraph 3 of the Declaration in the Platform of Action puts it), empowerment has become almost a co-equal goal by 1995:

> Empowerment of women and equality between women and men are prerequisites for achieving political, social, economic, cultural and environmental security among all peoples'. (43)

Denied access to traditional power structures, women have made their voices heard in 'alternative structures, particularly in the non-governmental organization sector' and 'grass-roots organizations' (186). The platform recommends bringing women's voices into central decision-making forums in all the major areas (except violence) addressed by the platform: poverty, education, health, inequality in economic structures, armed and other conflict, human rights, communication systems, the environment. There is also a separate section on decision-making power. Whether phrased as 'full', 'equal' or 'gender balanced' participation (equal opportunity in the human rights section is all that is demanded), women are to be present in the banking sector, environmental decision-making, media regulation and so on.

While an equal representation of women on committees or in occupations is not the same thing as an equal representation of feminists, advocating empowerment of women seems a safer way to meet Gunning's proposals for world-travelling than forcing women's diversity into the straitjackets of rights or other discourses favoured in the west. It also means that women will be in a position to turn a 'motherhood' statement into strategies and programs (if women can turn the above motherhood statements on empowerment into practice). One can imagine that if the International Monetary Fund or World Bank were guided by the voices of peasant farming women from the developing world, even the issue of women's unequal access to the world's (and not each country's) resources would be debated and perhaps addressed (see Agarwal 1996:91). The next section explores the economic connections between women internationally.

TRADE: FREEDOM THROUGH LABOUR?

The weavers have no mobility since they must sit on the bench in front of the looms for several hours at a time. Concentration is extremely important. If one knot loses its density, the defect could be found during the inspection by the supervisors ... There is usually inadequate light in most rural homes, and the weavers' houses are damp, dark, and cramped. The average working life cycle of a highly skilled weaver is estimated at 13 years since the weavers lose their eyesight, in part, due to improper lighting ... Due to the weight of carpet, looms sometimes collapse on the weavers, causing death or permanent injury ... Many pregnant women often have Caesarian or even still births, both attributable to weaving ... In Klar some of the weavers are engaged in services such as housecleaning and laundry at the upper class summer homes in town ... Another weaver ... said, 'Whenever I am short of money I become sigheh to a man [temporary marriages or *mutah*]. You see, I know this old lady who knows a lot of lonely men and she arranges the meeting.'

> – Ghvamshadhidi 1995:147, 146 on the conditions under which
> Persian carpets are produced in Iran

While some women in the west worry about cracking through the glass ceiling, a Japanese woman at the Beijing Forum said that western women might have a glass ceiling, but at least they can see through it. In Japan they call it the bamboo ceiling. Other women, in both the east and west, can see neither glass nor bamboo ceiling. They spend their long working hours on the concrete floor. The working lives of these women are explored in this section because they connect women of the west and the third world in relations of economic inequality.

Unpaid Unseen Women's Labour

Until Ester Boserup (1970) published *Women's Role in Economic Development*, it was thought that women were reproducers and not producers, and that therefore men should write development plans in which men were the recipients of development monies. Women received assistance as mothers (health care and nutritional programs) or as auxiliary workers dependent on men (handicrafts production) or as potential mothers (population policies). The declaration which announced the First Development Decade (1961–70) made no specific reference to women. A brief mention was made of encouraging 'the full integration' of women into the development process at the start of the Second Decade. By the 1990s the UN has declared the need to 'empower' women for development if high returns are to be achieved (Kabeer 1994:1, 3, 2, who provides a thorough overview of gender and development issues). As Barbara Rogers claimed in 1980, it was 'not so much that women needed development, but that development needed women' (Kabeer 1996:25).

Thus emerged WID (Women in Development) or 'liberal feminism writ global' (Kabeer 1994:27). The focus on women's productive potential, however, often exhorted women into more productive activities without recognising their long hours of unpaid domestic labour, their important contributions in the subsistence sector and the unequal access to resources and power between nations (and women) of the first and third worlds (Kabeer 1994:28, 33). An example in microcosm of these processes is the collectively run dairy in Kaira in India, which included women as members. The dairy added two hours to the women's twelve-hour working day, took away the milk, ghee, butter and whey women had kept for home consumption, while the profits were appropriated by the men who led the co-operative (Jain 1993:52).

National statistics often supported the belief that women were non-productive, an idea that was challenged by the World Survey of women, conducted by women, which found that women's contribution to gross national product was much higher than the national accounts suggested.[3] National accounts as representations of a nation's economy have policy implications. If they do not include the contributions of women, then women will not be seen as worthy recipients of economic development assistance. The best that women can hope for is the 'gift' of aid as a welfare measure. National accounts put no value on forests and resources until they are destroyed (become an input into production); peace is not valued but preparation for war is; and women's labour is far less often valued than men's (Waring 1988:20–9). When applied to the World Bank's recommendations for the Pacific nations, the move to cash cropping expands the national accounts but creates dependency on food imports; logging and mining raise the gross national product, but deforestation causes land erosion and the run-off from mines destroys fisheries (Emberson-Bain 1994:iv–v, vii). Thus some analysts suggest we should invert the normal evaluations which assume the export-oriented sector is the most important and focus our attention on the less vulnerable domestic sector which produces for the home market – and often the things that people really need, like food, clothing, shelter (Waring 1988:243).

Now that women's work is more visible, a picture is emerging of women concentrated in the more marginal informal labour market. Women prepare food and drinks for sale, are small shopkeepers of perishable goods, do cleaning, washing and childcare, provide sexual services. Some United Nations and other schemes have responded to this fact by providing revolving loans which allow women to buy capital for their small-scale enterprises, like sewing machines, raw materials, or goods for trade like school uniforms. The loans also finance training in sewing, knitting, tie-dyeing, batik, welding, brick-making, leather work, cement-making, water jar construction and so on. The repayment rate for UNIFEM (United

Nations Development Fund for Women) loans was 85 per cent in 1986 (Vickers 1991:71). In Papua New Guinea, Wok Meri is an indigenous revolving loan scheme. In the Eastern Highlands, money is made, saved, invested and loaned to 'daughters' in need, accompanied by a cycle of ceremonies (Reay 1975). At the Beijing NGO Forum a speaker for the International Coalition on Women and Credit, with similar goals, described one woman, Milagro, who started with $50 and a sewing machine. Now she co-operates with hundreds of microbusinesses and exports her clothes. The organisation also puts pressure on banks to change their lending priorities. Such a career ladder is rarely available to the women working in Southeast Asia's free-trade zones.

Women's Paid Labour: the Free-trade Zones

Southeast Asia is a rendition of Chandra Mohanty's claim that anthropologists see one thing and sociologists another. Where anthropologists construct the images of gender bilateralism discussed in Chapter 1, political economists construct the oppressed female worker in the free-trade zones. Not all free-trade zones are in Southeast Asia, and neither are those who have suffered the internationalisation of capital all women. Indeed sweatshops have been discovered in New York employing illegal immigrant workers, and wages paid in some factories in Scotland are lower than those paid in Hong Kong (Chase-Dunn 1989:80).

The so-called 'economic miracles', the Asian tigers or Asian dragons of Taiwan, Korea, Hong Kong and Singapore have been built largely on a female workforce. To benefit from wage differentials in north and south, multinational corporations have set up factories in third world countries, particularly for the labour-intensive elements of production. In the 'free-trade zones', there may also be tax incentives; unions are often illegal, while regulation of safety and other working conditions is minimal. Until the late 1980s, Korean industrial development focused on shopfloor improvements rather than design innovation (basic research was borrowed from overseas), although this has changed in more recent years. Korea has the longest working week in the world (in one firm, POSCO, the working week was 56 hours over seven days with one day off each month: Amsden 1990:30), although with rising wages (due to labour shortages) Korean companies are now locating new factories overseas in cheaper-wage countries.

Among the 'Asian dragons', women are the preferred manual workers in the export-oriented industries (see also de Dios 1994:36 for the Philippines). This is not only because their wages are 50 to 62 per cent those of men, but also because they are more compliant, just as productive, and deemed more suited to repetitive and detailed work because of their 'swift fingers'. Women are also more easily laid off in times of recession (Bello and Rosenfeld 1990:25, 216, 308), while any potentially 'troublesome' aspects of their employment like maternity leave are not an aspect of their working conditions. Instead, the free-trade zone employers rely on the subsistence sector to raise the worker, and maintain him or her in times of unemployment, sickness and old age (Larrain 1989:115–17, 138–42). Thus the subsistence sector subsidises the transnational capitalist, who does not have to pay the real costs of the production and replacement of the worker. This made it possible in 1985 for 64 per cent of female workers in Korea to earn below the minimum cost of living (Bello and Rosenfeld 1990:26). In South Korea's and Hong Kong's microelectronics assembly firms, most women will be forced to leave their jobs before they are 30 because of deteriorating eyesight (see Bulbeck 1988:99 for further discussion) and there are virtually no prospects for promotion or economic independence (Bello and Rosenfeld 1990:308 on Singapore; Nam 1994:61 on Korea).

Working conditions may be appalling. In one factory in Taiwan there is no air-conditioning and asbestos fluff covers and clogs the whole body (Bello and Rosenfeld 1990:217). In 1991 eighty young women workers from the rural provinces of China were burned to death when a fire broke out in a Hong Kong-owned factory in Dongguan. The women had been locked into their dormitory atop the factory (Knight 1994:23). Most women 'will continue to pass their personal lives isolated and hidden in dormitories and rented rooms', surviving on 'instant noodle soup', while 'a movie or even a beer is a rare' luxury (Bello and Rosenfeld 1990:219, 26, 25). Dormitories are more like barracks in their lack of privacy, their overcrowding, their formica benches for beds, their lack of running water, heating or cooling, and the control of workers' private lives (Bello and Rosenfeld 1990:26, 218).

Perhaps based on women's resistance and struggle through Korea's long years of Japanese occupation (see Kim 1996), in Korea women were the leaders of the labour clashes of the early 1980s, exposing themselves to arrest and 'stripping, kissing, fondling, threat of rape and rape itself' in police interrogations (Nam 1994:64–5, 60). The Korean Women Workers Association advocates an eight-hour day and higher wages, maternity leave, menstrual leave, breastfeeding and day care facilities. It organises against gender discrimination in the union movement and at work, including sexual harassment, and advocates shared responsibility for women and men in the home (Louie 1995:421–2). In many countries, Christian and Buddhist religious institutions campaign against sexual harassment, offer legal advice to workers, provide boarding houses or food co-operatives (Rosa 1994:92), while the Committee for Asian Women organises exchanges between women workers in various Asian countries to explore the international effects of globalisation on women's working conditions (Louie 1995:422). A group of Korean women union leaders, when told they would be sacked when Japanese-owned factories closed, went to Japan to negotiate with the parent company. Japanese workers, moved by their action, joined in their struggle; the Korean workers eventually won compensation in a retirement allowance (Matsui 1995b:155–6).

Despite their dreams of marrying a 'man with a necktie' (a white-collar worker), women have few prospects of escape through marriage (Louie 1995:421; Bello and Rosenfeld 1990:26), even if low wages and competition for the few well-placed men encourage a tangled blend of prostitution (Bello and Rosenfeld 1990:219) and sexual harassment. Thus women workers are accused of loose morals and are liable to rape. Aihwa Ong (1987) notes that the young Malay women who work in the electronics industry are taunted as 'electric girls', both in the streets, the press and by government spokesmen. This triple pun reflects their jobs in the electronics industry, their search for the bright lights and their (supposed) unrestrained sexuality. Repudiating such constructions, many women workers adopt a heightened cult of purity and passivity – giving their wages to their families, praying more often and monitoring co-workers' dating activities (Ong 1987; see also Enloe 1989:165).

The World Bank is attempting to re-create the 'Asian economic miracle' in the twenty-two Pacific countries (over 60 per cent of the population is in Papua New Guinea and 20 per cent in Fiji: Underhill-Sem 1994:3). Recommended policies include reduced government expenditure on the social wage. Governments are under strong pressure to sell their state-owned enterprises, while export-oriented manufacturing ventures based on generous tax incentives as well as 'the unmitigated exploitation of unorganised (and mainly female) workers' (Emberson-Bain 1994:152) have been established. Notable among these are garments in Fiji and automotive wire assembly in Western Samoa (Slatter 1994:21), as well as fish-processing where women may have to stand for up to eleven hours a day in overheated and deafening work conditions (Emberson-Bain 1994: 162, 160). Where women are the sole breadwinners, men have not necessarily taken on childcare and other support roles, while levels of domestic violence, child malnutrition and behavioural problems in children have increased (Emberson-Bain 1994:155).

Although it is the 'electric girls' who have captured the imagination of feminist and other writers (Stivens 1994:377), domestic workers may work in more hazardous, isolated and lower-paid conditions than even the free-trade zone workers. In the late 1980s the average hourly rate for Singapore production workers was $S3.50, and for domestics $S1.45, but this was based on an ordinary day, not the 5 a.m. to 11 p.m. most of them work (Bello and Rosenfeld 1990:313). Particularly before World War II, African-American women were employed as 'mammies' in white households in the United States; in Australia Aboriginal girls were employed in domestic service until the 1960s. Brutal treatment often accompanied employment (Huggins and Blake 1992:55). As among western employers, female employers in Asia have a range of responses to their domestic workers. In 1985 the Women's Centre in Hong Kong opened its doors. Not without initial resistance from some Chinese women, the Women's Centre offers legal advice to Filipino maids complaining of ill-treatment. The co-founder of the Women's Research Program at National Taiwan University, Nora Lan-hung Chiang (1994:163) 'regards' her two full-time maids as 'helpers'. Vivienne Wee (1995) notes that 51 per cent of Singaporean women have access to high-income jobs because of the wage subsidy provided by the lower-paid Filipino maids.

Increasingly domestic workers cross national borders to find their employment, heightening the risk of economic and sexual exploitation as escape requires the negotiation of foreign borders (Robinson 1991:49 for Indonesian women in Saudi Arabia; Bello and Rosenfeld 1990:313–14 for domestic workers in Singapore). In the Philippines, the three biggest foreign exchange earners are textiles and garments, dominated by women, and the earnings of overseas contract workers, half of whom are women (de Dios 1994:47) and most of whom work in Singapore and Hong Kong. Sri Lankan and Indonesian women are more likely to work in the Gulf States (Enloe 1989:192).

This section is headed 'freedom through labour', borrowing from the marxist idea that economic independence and self-actualisation are achieved through this route. Indeed there are reasons why a woman with a wage may have certain freedoms and opportunities that a woman without one lacks, especially as wages have risen over the years. Women might escape customs they find inhibiting when they leave the countryside for the free-trade zones (Robinson 1991:36). One should not, however, assume that all third world countries can follow the route of the Asian tigers into rising incomes for workers. A new General Agreement on Tariffs and Trade (GATT) means that tariff rates which stood at 60 per cent in the 1970s will be reduced to 5 per cent. Indeed GATT has been replaced with the World Trade Organisation which will adjudicate disputes, in which it appears increasingly certain that protective labour laws, environmental protection measures and other attempts to regulate 'free trade' (or free exploitation of labour) will be declared an infringement of free international trade.

Next we look at prostitution, only recently seen more in terms of labour than sexual exploitation. Where radical feminists aligned prostitutes and wives in the sexual service of men, except that prostitutes were paid by the hour and wives sometimes not at all, a liberal or marxist analysis now prevails. The term sex worker has replaced prostitute, acknowledging that prostitutes sell a service, and in a trade often made more dangerous if it is illegal. Thus most feminists join with sex workers in calling for decriminalisation of the industry to increase the safety of its workers. Nonetheless, prostitution is a particular kind of work, the supply of sexual services, in which overwhelmingly the sellers are women and the purchasers men. This says something about sexual relations, whatever one might want to say about sex workers. Analyses of sex tourism, then, deal with both the economic aspects of the trade, a significant foreign exchange earner, and the sexual and racial relations created between men and women in different countries.

Prostitution and Sex Tourism

> The show programe for this night. Pussy pingpongball pussy shoot banana pussy smokecigaretters. Pussy writeletter. Lesbian show. Boy and girl fucking show ... Bigdildo show ... Long-eggplant push into her cunt. Pussy drink water bottle show. Blue movies film too girl and snake sexy dance.
>
> – Tout's card, Bangkok in Odzer 1994:7

> Make love take three minute. Make rice take eleven hour in sun. Skin turn black; body have pain.
>
> – Thai bar girl in Odzer 1994:225

Prostitution has been defined as the explicit exchange of sex for money. Does this definition apply to the temple prostitutes of India who gained autonomy and wealth (Srinivasan 1988) or the high-status courtesans in Japan (Allison 1994:165), pre-Liberation China (Hershatter 1992) and Cochinchina (Poivre 1993:77), skilled artists as well as lovers, who commanded high payment? In both post-Liberation China and Taiwan, prostitution has not retrieved its high status and nor are working conditions conducive to describing prostitutes as sex workers. It is estimated that there are 100 000 illegal (that is under-age) prostitutes in Taiwan, a disproportionate number of them drawn from the indigenous population. Girls are kept locked up by brothel owners, malnourished, and fear police harassment if they seek protection. The Taipei Women's Rescue Foundation works to stop the sale of teenage girls in the country, rescues teenagers in the city, represents victims in court, provides rehabilitation at halfway houses, advocates legislative changes and studies and publicises the issues (Interview with Chang Lan Shin, a social worker with Tapei Women's Rescue Foundation, January 1992).

In post-Liberation China, brothels were closed down and prostitutes sent to reform schools 'where they went through the ideological remoulding, the reform through labour, and medical treatment' (Shaanxi Provincial Women's Federation 1991:5; see also Cusack 1958:250–8). Officially there were no prostitutes in China before 1989, when the government admitted the existence of the 'problem'. In 1991 the formal count of prostitutes was 2 million. Treatment still involves 'rescuing' 'victims', who are sent to rehabilitation camps for two to three years. While traffickers might be 'caught', clients usually only incur a fine and do not have their papers marked as prostitutes' papers are (People's Republic of China 1994:15; Official from the All China Women's Federation, based on two surveys in a city and a rural/provincial area, presentation to Beijing Foreign Studies University Women's Group, 3 January 1992). Prostitution is attributed to the needs of single men, the sexualisation of Chinese culture by western influences, the traditional acceptance of polygamy and concubinage, and the growing gap between men's and women's wages, although women are deemed responsible for seducing men.

As prostitution is explicitly condemned in the Quran, temporary marriages serve the place of prostitution in other societies by providing a palliative for the sexual needs of men who cannot afford to support a wife. Once he reaches adulthood, unless he becomes insane, a man's legal persona is fixed until death; a woman's depends on whether she is a virgin, divorced, married or widowed (Haeri 1989:96–7). Divorced or widowed women (for example as a result of the Iraq–Iran war) are an economic burden on their families, while their sexuality is considered insatiable. Such women are drawn by the none too secure income-earning alternative of temporary marriage, the definition and use of which has been expanded to cover activities for which western men might visit prostitutes, for example group sex (Haeri 1989:96–7). In temporary marriage, theoretically a woman enters a voluntary contract to exchange legitimate and exclusive access to her reproductive powers and her obedience for a brideprice and financial support for a specified period. She has more rights to determine the contract, but less status than a permanent wife (Haeri 1989:147, 96–7, 28, 40, 41, 46, 147, 54, 66–7).

Sex workers are also part of the international migration of labour. For example most immigrant sex workers in the Netherlands are from Thailand, second from the Philippines, then Malaysia, Indonesia and Taiwan (Brussa 1989:234). Thai and Filipino prostitutes work in Japan, some emigrating as thinly disguised domestic workers, many as undocumented workers who are often controlled by the Yakuza, with 'numerous reports of mysterious deaths, beatings, torture, and enforced prostitution' (de Dios 1994:47; Jantraka 1994:99; Peredo 1991:52). Alternatively, the clients migrate temporarily, as sex tourists, associated particularly with Thailand and the Philippines. Sex tourism has spilled over into Tahiti and Guam, Filipina sex workers moving there after the closure of the US military bases (Ishtar 1994:197, 75). Sex tourists from Britain travel to Brazil, some African and Caribbean countries, and increasingly are choosing Ho Chi Minh City, Hanoi and Phnom Penh, where sex tourists claim the girls are 'less commercial' than the now spoiled women of Thailand (Davidson 1995:42, 63; Enloe 1993:27).

In both Thailand and the Philippines (under Marcos), government officials have explicitly stated that female sexuality is to be regarded as an economic asset for national development (Truong 1990:148, 128). Although brothels in Korea, Thailand and the Philippines are associated with United States military bases, in Thailand and Korea the majority of clients are local men (Manderson 1992:453; Louie 1995:423). In Thailand, although prostitutes are considered to be of 'low birth', which condones beatings and killings, a man may take many kinds of wives – those bought, those who provide household services, and those who are temporary or momentary (Truong 1990:189, 136). Wives often feel that prostitution is a less threatening alternative than second or minor wives (Manderson 1992:466–7). There is some truth in the tales told to tourists, that prostitutes are performing a service for their poor rural families. Prostitutes can achieve reintegration into their villages or become nuns in mid-life (Truong 1990:178; Manderson, 1992:457, 470). But there is also ample evidence of abductions or parents selling daughters into the trade. A fire in Phu Ket in 1984 revealed the burnt bodies of young girls chained to their beds (Truong 1990:181–2). In the Philippines and Thailand there has been an increase in child prostitution, especially with rising fears of AIDS and a demand for virgins or 'clean' young girls (it is estimated that 80 per cent of Thai prostitutes are HIV-positive: Jantraka 1994:99). The youngest male sold into the 'flesh trade' in the Philippines was six and the youngest female seven (Peredo 1991:50).

In Pat Bong, a tourist-oriented neighbourhood of Bangkok, 400 000 more women than men are residents, while male tourists outnumber female tourists by three to one. In the mid-1980s, 85 per cent of the tourists visiting the Philippines were men, arrivals increasing from 166 000 in 1972 to over 1 million in 1980. Up to 9 per cent of women in Thailand between the ages of 15 and 34 are in some form of prostitution (Enloe 1989:35, 38; de Dios 1994:36; Truong 1990:181). The men come predominantly from the United States, Australia, Germany and other European countries, and Japan. They give different reasons for their behaviour and are differently viewed by the sex workers. The Japanese choose packaged tours, which avoids negotiations with individual workers, tend to engage only at the sexual level and maintain a greater distance than other clients, and are thus nicknamed 'duck' in Thailand and 'monkey' in the Philippines. They also tend to express a 'racial and nationalistic arrogance' (Allison 1994:165–6), statements in the Japanese press referring to the 'oriental charm' of 'Asian women' which is an 'exoticism for Western and Japanese' men (Matsui 1995a:317). The Australians and some of the

British resort to welfare justifications based on helping the 'poor girls' send money home so younger sisters can get an education and 'break the vicious cycle' (Manderson 1993:18; Davidson 1995:59). A survey of masseuses in Bangkok revealed that 55 per cent planned to establish small businesses or become tailors, while 12 per cent planned to engage in agricultural work, 2 per cent to become a housewife and 3 per cent to go home (Odzer 1994:239).

As Julia Davidson (1995:43–5, 49) notes, it is not only the attraction of cheap, exotic and compliant sex workers which lures the British 'Macho Lads' to Thailand. Because of the differences between the British and Thai economy, they can live like lords for several weeks, in their hotel accommodation and purchasing power of the pound, which also buys a woman's companionship, cleaning, massaging and sexual favours. Those who use British prostitutes also comment favourably on the form of the contract: Thai women are 'more like girlfriends' in that every favour is not contractually negotiated but rather the woman's services are hired for a time, often at a price only determined at the conclusion of the encounter (Davidson 1995:45, 47–8, 51). In contrast with these beautiful, nice girls, many European prostitutes are seen to be impersonal 'low life'. Of course, these British men are responding to the fact that first world prostitutes generally command a higher wage than do third world prostitutes. To deflect attention from their role as buyers of sex, the British sex tourists sometimes rationalise that Thai prostitutes want to marry a European.

In the last chapter we explored the ways in which white western sexualities invade eastern sensibilities. The practice of prostitution in 'sex tour' destinations would appear to be another example of such invasion. But western sexuality is also hybridised in its encounter with the exotic, producing new evaluations of both white western women and Asian women. Thus for some American sex tourists, the imagined mixture of Singapore girl, masseur, and geisha girl is far preferable to the overbearing and lazy American woman (Krich 1989:385; Manderson 1993:18). As a British sex tourist noted, 'Would a charming, beautiful, young woman want me in England? No. I'd have to accept a big, fat, ugly woman. That's all I could get' (in Davidson 1995:58). The Japanese sex tourists also compare subservient Thai prostitutes with their whining wives (Allison 1994:166); Australian men compare assertive and unfeminine Anglo-Australian women with Filipinas (*The Age* 30 December 1992:4); Latin American men describe Anglo-American women as 'lazy, footloose, unfaithful, and generally insubordinate to men's authority' (Peña 1991: 33). But some of the British sex tourists did note, 'You can talk to Western women, but they don't look good. With Thai girls it's the other way round' (Davidson 1995:58).

But there is also suspicion that the prostitute's submissiveness is merely an act; hence the term used of some Asian women: 'She's pulling a Butterfly' (Garber 1992b:124: Madame Butterfly is based on the western stereotype of Asian women as 'modest' and 'submissive'). Prostitutes must also be sexually available before they can demonstrate that they are sexually submissive, and this is exposed most clearly in the strip shows (Manderson 1992:452, 460–2). The strip show format was translated into the degrading depiction of a Filipina wife in the Australian movie *Priscilla Queen of the Desert*, an image of excessive, tasteless sexuality rather than submissive compliance. Furthermore, Asian women are defined as 'gold-diggers', partly because among some, especially those divorced with children, the chance of a new life overseas has its appeal. Some Filipinas believe western men will make better husbands, not given to violence or rejection of women. In fact the evidence in Australia tends to suggest greater domestic violence in these cross-cultural marriages, no doubt contributed to by the contradictory but racist stereotoypes of subservient/licentious/acquisitive women.

How then are western feminists to assess the sex tourist industry? Certainly Cleo Odzer's (1994:309) claim that prostitutes are 'pioneers in advancing women's autonomy by breaking from the mould of suppressed and passive females' raised the hackles of two Thai conference participants. They claimed that Odzer was 'being ethnocentric for advocating sexual liberation for Thai women'. This is perhaps not surprising, given Odzer's (1994:219) further assertion that Thai women 'have no opportunity for effectiveness or power' and control family finances only to 'buy rice and pay the butcher'. Where Odzer (1994:309) claims that her time in Bangkok allowed her to see life 'through a double perspective', 'seeing the illusions of both' her society and Thai society, her summation of Thai women suggests a reproduction of the submissive Asian stereotype rather than a world-travelling sensitivity to Thai women's lives.[4]

In the racist and sexist portrayal of the 'Sarong Party Girl', co-authored by an expatriate and a Singapore national, the Sarong Party Girl is described as a 'kampong girl with dollar signs in her eyes' who sends out 'desperate radar signals to expatriates' for a 'meaningful relationship' based on 'expatriate salaries'. While expatriate men denigrate her for her sexual availability, expatriate wives are represented as among the Sarong Party Girl's 'natural enemies', jealous of her slim young body (Aitchison and Chan 1994:53, 16, 51, 68–9).[5] In the 1980s some Anglo-Australian women responded similarly to the phenomenon of the 'mail-order bride', of Australian men marrying Filipinas, with jealousy that Filipinas were stealing 'our' men. They, too, were sometimes suspicious that Filipinas were not marrying for love, unquestioningly assuming this was the best basis for producing 'family life and stable marriage' (Robinson 1996:56). The image of the Filipina 'gold-digger' has been questioned by Melba Marginson's Collective of Filipinas for Empowerment and Development, formed as a result of the murder of a Filipina bride (Marginson 1992:122). Filipino women have been involved in establishing refuges and other support services for Filipinas caught in violent cross-cultural marriages. Furthermore, despite the stereotypes, the average level of education of Filipinas in Australia is higher than that of Australian-born women.[6] Australian feminists have worked with Asian women, developing projects to redress the power imbalance between Asian women and Australian men. Following Germany, the Australian government passed a law in November 1993, providing a fourteen-year gaol sentence for Australians overseas who have sex with a child under 16 years old, and a seventeen-year gaol sentence where the child is under 12. The Australian government has also established a counselling service in the Philippines for intending migrants. The service passes on the names of Australian men who have previously sponsored a Filipina, in the hopes of reducing serial sponsorship and migration, which may indicate either a history of domestic violence or sponsorship for the purposes of employment in Australian brothels. The government will also allow women to retain eligibility for permanent residence if their relationship ceases because of proven domestic violence (Office of the Status of Women 1995:32).

Not only rich western men, but western female tourists too, can deploy their economic resources in exchange for sexual favours. In Bali, North and West Africa, the Caribbean and South Asia, western women's search for the exotic includes affairs with local men. In Bali's 'economy of pleasure', young *cowoks* (meaning 'guy' or eligible man) act as guides and become 'boyfriends', receiving gifts and expenses from their 'girlfriend' tourists. Young Japanese girls who seek sex with western men in Japan or overseas are described as 'yellow cabs' (presumably by western men) (Pettman, 1996:201; see also Davidson 1995:42; Jennaway 1993; Cohen 1971 on young Arab men). But there are differences between men and women as 'sex' tourists. First, given the dominant evaluations of sexually active men in these cultures, men seeking sex or servicing female tourists are not risking their reputations or chances of marriage by their actions. Second, women's interactions as sex tourists suggest relationships closer to escort work than prostitution. Clearly, however, white and Japanese women who have sexual liaisons with *cowoks*, young Arabs or western men, as well as the professional women in Canada, Singapore or Saudi Arabia who employ domestic servants, are benefiting from their economic superiority in the global marketplace. Indeed, almost all women in western nations buy goods like clothes or computers made in free-trade zones, and thus participate in the exploitation of other women. But western women may well ask 'What else can I do?' For some, the answer lies in aid, giving back something of what has been gained. Let us turn to some of the traps in this apparent bounty.

Aid: International Bounty?

The old idea behind aid, that instead of giving a man a fish you should teach him how to fish, is triply flawed: firstly it's a woman, not a man; secondly it is the rich who control fishing, and thirdly fishing stocks are being depleted world-wide.

– David Armstrong, ex-chief executive officer,
Community Aid Abroad, in Blackburn 1993:351

No doubt in the industrialised world it is widely believed that money flows from rich nations to poor nations to assist in the struggle against poverty. Ten years ago that was true. In 1979 a net $40 billion flowed from the northern hemisphere to the developing nations of the south. Today that flow has been reversed. Taking everything into account – loans, aid, repayments of interest and capital – the southern world is now transferring at least $20 billion a year to the northern hemisphere. If one includes the deteriorating terms of trade between raw materials and manufactured goods, the transfer may be as much as $60 billion a year (Vickers 1991:4). Furthermore, aid has its price. It may be tied to conditions which require the purchase of donor country's goods or technologies, or it may be really a soft loan which must be repaid (Blackburn 1993:272). Japan's overseas development program has included projects which serve the wealthy of foreign countries rather than the poor (for example a luxury hotel in Bangladesh, a 500-bed hospital in Sri Lanka where a network of primary health care in villages is needed) or Japanese companies rather than local people (a road for a Japanese logging company in Malaysia) (Matsui 1995b:153–4). France and the United States give aid in the Pacific, seeking silence on nuclear testing; Japanese aid is given 'in return' for driftnet fishing rights and the dumping of toxic wastes.

In the 1970s, banks in the First World had a surplus of deposits, much of which they loaned to third world governments to help them along the path to 'development', for example with large-scale schemes like hydroelectricity plants. The theory was that industrialisation would produce increased exports with which to repay the loans. The promised industrialisation did not materialise at the rate envisaged, while export income from raw materials was insufficient. Since the 1980s, governments of the south have been coerced by the IMF and World Bank into 'austerity measures', the reduction of welfare expenditure so that more money is available to repay foreign debts. Such reductions in welfare have had deleterious effects on family health, women's literacy, family income support and so on (Vickers 1991:28, 27). A further strategy for debt repayment is a move to cash cropping, which displaces subsistence production. In sum, between 1973 and 1987, the mean income of families in the poorest fifth of nations fell by 10.8 per cent and the richest fifth gained 24.1 per cent in real terms (Vickers 1991:23).

Aid is a small return to peoples of the south in exchange for the cheap goods produced by their labour and the unequal terms of trade between nations. Until recently – the change was partly due to the UN Decade for Women – development aid (as opposed to palliative aid) generally went to male recipients. Although today aid agencies are more aware of women's specific needs and contributions to society; much of this aid still sees women as targets rather than agents of policy, evidenced in terms like 'family planning acceptor', 'recipient', 'family labour' (Miller 1991:202; terms used by both male and female planners in Jakarta in one study: Dawson 1994). NGOs in industrialised countries provided about 10 per cent of the total aid from those countries in 1985, the majority being church-based organisations (Blackburn 1993:4, 40). Community Aid Abroad in Australia (somewhat like Oxfam in Britain) has shifted from aid as philanthropic giving, even if based on community-to-community connections, to seeking both the empowerment of recipients and the education of donors in the global structures of inequality which make aid necessary (Blackburn 1993:20, 6–7, 50–1, 77, 174). In 1981 CAA's Project Selection Criteria further recognised the 'especially oppressed position of women in most communities' as well as the need for technologies in 'harmony with the local environment and culture' (Blackburn 1993:181).

The path of aid is laid with mines. The hand extended in generosity can seem like maternalism, especially when it comes with the harsh reminder of imperialist tongues. Refusing to give – because 'they' will feel patronised, because corruption means 'they' don't receive it – is to refuse the unequal connections between women of the world. Some aid agencies do attempt to implement 'women's empowerment', 'planning *with* women' to increase their 'self-confidence and capacity to organise for change', as Dawson (1994:80) put it. Examples include UNIFEM's revolving loan scheme discussed above, support for programs to reduce domestic violence in the Pacific, discussed in Chapter 3, and education programs in relation to genital surgery, discussed in Chapter 2. However, when such programs work with local women, this often means members of the indigenous educated elite. It is difficult to determine whether (all) the women in Papua New Guinea or other Pacific nations, or (all) the women in Africa want programs to reduce domestic violence or educate women about the health effects of infibulation rather than money to buy land or start a business.

Some aid agencies have also entered alternative trading, or the production and distribution of goods which is not based on exploited overseas labour. Community Aid Abroad's is the largest Alternative Trading Organisation (ATO) in Australia, and Oxfam and Traidcraft are the largest in the United Kingdom. Not only do they investigate and expose exploitation of labour by other suppliers, but they also help producers with marketing, stock control and design advice (Mitter

1994:41). ATOs present images of skilful and productive rather than starving third world people, and help women towards economic independence when they buy from them (Ogle 1994:18–19). ATOs, along with trade unions and producer co-operatives[7] in the north and the south (for example SEWA the Self-Employed Women's Association of India) (Mitter 1994:36; Jhabvala 1994:132–3), also lobby governments to require that imported goods are marked when they are produced in unacceptable labour conditions, for example using child labour or where free-trade unions are not allowed to exist (Atkinson 1995:9). However, although this 'ethical market' now reaches 10 million people in North America, ATOs are small international players. For example, globally ATO trade in coffee is about $50 million compared with over $50 billion by just three corporations (Mitter 1994:41; Ogle 1994:17).

THE DOUBLED VISION OF MIGRANT AND INDIGENOUS WOMEN

> Where do you come from, *originally*?
> My mother's womb – how about you?
>
> – C. Allyson Lee, 'Recipe' in Yue 1996:87

Most of the debates between 'third world' women and white western feminists have been articulated by diaspora women, women either living or trained in the west, women who bring 'the migrant's double vision' (Bhabha 1994:5) to their analyses. These women are more likely to find a voice in western feminist journals and other academic forums than women writing within the third world. But, as they admit, they also speak from a particular position, between two cultures and not completely of either. It is also possible that when Hispanic, Indian, African, Arab but western-educated women speak in English they 'do not talk the same language'. Perhaps they cannot fully translate their worlds, and end only in communicating the 'experience of exclusion' (Lugones in Lugones and Spelman 1990:28). Perhaps that exclusion is doubly felt, from both the west and their indigenous culture. This section explores some of the effects of living at cultural crossroads.

Refugees

> When we first began using the word 'postcolonial' we used it ironically ... it was the exact beginning of recolonization ... It is very frightening to me, this celebration of globalization in a world where non-alignment is no longer possible and the divisions are becoming exacerbated.
>
> – Spivak in Stephens 1996:35

Not only do women and children make up the vast majority of the world's refugees, but it has been estimated that torture 'is common and widely used in the exercise of power practised in one-third of the countries of the world' (Agger 1994:64). Sexual discrimination and torture, such as lapidation for losing one's virginity, are gradually becoming recognised as persecutions which produce female refugees, although such recognition is at the discretion of signatory states to the Convention (Martin 1993:23, 24: Aldunate 1995:6). Without this recognition, a man who witnessed his wife's sexual assault would have had the basis for a claim to refugee status, while his wife did not (Indrani Ganguly, pers. comm. July 1995).

Besides the problems faced by all migrants, for example cultural and language barriers, refugee migrants face post-traumatic stress disorders occasioned by the violence done against them, by persecution and by camp life, which often includes lack of resources and the danger of armed attack. Torture is both horrifically cruel and detailed in its relatively minor persecutions such as not being allowed to wash when menstruating and being fed infrequently so that 'you throw yourself over' food. (Latin American political refugee woman in Agger 1994:71). Some Latin American political refugees were told to 'spread our legs, and they put their rifles between our legs' (in Agger 1994:70). Vietnamese boat women suffered abduction and rape by pirates while trying to escape (Vickers 1993:22–3, 28). In the refugee camps in Asia, women, especially single mothers, may be exposed to sexual attacks from officials and men in the camp (Martin 1993:5, 19). Partly because of lack of work in the camps, Vietnamese men often become involved in gangs and violence against women. As a result, women required a male protector or sought independent access to economic resources through prostitution (Buijs 1993:8).

While the definition of refugees suggests involuntary relocation, host countries and their governments are often suspicious. In January 1995, while I was writing a draft of this chapter, Australia received an unexpected influx of boat people refugees, Vietnamese-descended people from southern China. Such 'boat people' are accommodated in detention centres, sometimes for years, as their applications and appeals for refugee status drag through the courts. Australians were treated to television images of refugees being dragged up aircraft gangplanks, their legal paths exhausted, and white Australians saying, 'Send them back' and 'Bomb their ships'. As part of the strategy to process (i.e. return, the cynics might say) the 1995 influx of refugees to Australia, Nick Bolkus, then Minister for Immigration, recommended removing the one-child policy as a condition which allows application for refugee status. When West Germany accepted Palestinian refugees, they were housed first in barracks-like conditions and then dispersed around the country with little regard for family connections (Buijs 1993:5). Their dependence on welfare was virtually assured as they were denied work permits for first two and later five years (Abdulrahim 1993:63).

Women have so often been raped as part of the process of war that it can hardly be described as 'extracurricular'. In fact raping women is not only the spoils of war which maintains the morale of victorious soldiers but also a weapon of fear which causes women to flee and thus to destabilise the invaded population (Copelon 1994:205). There are precedents for seeing rape as a 'war crime', the United Nations Security Council reaffirming it as a 'crime against humanity' when part of a systematic attack on a civilian population on 'national, political, ethnic, racial or religious grounds' (Copelon 1994:204). During World War II the Japanese 'deceived or disappeared' 200 000 to 400 000 women into 'comfort stations' (also referred to as 'sanitary public toilets'). Eighty per cent of these women were Koreans, although some were Chinese, Taiwanese, Filipino, Indonesian and Dutch women (from Indonesia); some were Japanese, for example the daughters of poor families sold into prostitution (Watanabe 1994:4). The purpose was to 'motivate as well as reward' Japanese soldiers, and prevent them from repeating incidents like the 'rape of Nanjing' in 1937, when the victorious Japanese troops committed wholesale rape and murder of the women of Nanjing in China. This practice stood ill with the claims by the Japanese that they were saving Asia from western colonisation (Watanabe 1994:7). 'Each woman was made to serve an average of thirty to forty soldiers per day'. Those who refused were beaten and tortured, for example two women who refused were hung from a tree, their breasts cut off and when they died their heads cut off. These were boiled in water and the other women made to drink the broth on threat of their lives (Watanabe 1994:9–10). An estimated 70 to 90 per cent died and none of the surviving women who have been traced have been able to bear children (Copelon 1994:205).

Korean Confucianism taught women they should commit suicide to protect their chastity, and this prevented women from speaking of their experiences for many years (Watanabe 1994:10). From the mid-1970s, however, Japanese women in the Asian Women's Association began to protest against Japanese sex tourism, in the process discovering the case of the 'comfort women'. Meanwhile, the women's movement in Korea and Japan in the 1980s encouraged a more open discussion of women's sexuality issues (Watanabe 1994:11–12). Japanese feminist groups have linked the case of comfort women to contemporary sex tourism, the Japanese-Korean women's groups attributing sex tourism to the imbalance in the international economy and the systematic commodification of women's bodies (Watanabe 1994:13–14). In 1991 Korean women filed a lawsuit against the Japanese government, demanding an official apology, some compensatory payment, a thorough investigation of their cases, a revision of Japanese school textbooks identifying this aspect of colonial oppression of the Korean people, and the erection of a memorial museum (Watanabe 1994:3). In reply the Japanese government established a fund to collect money via private donations for Korean comfort women, but it has not admitted fault or offered official compensation.

In 1971 when Pakistan occupied Bangladesh, the troops raped an estimated 30 000 to 200 000 Bengali women to 'improve the genes of the Bengali people'. The women were ostracised by 'their own men when they returned to their Muslim villages' (Kabeer 1991:40–2; Copelon 1994:197; Brownmiller 1994:182). Mass rapes by policemen of groups of women in India have been seen as part of state reprisals against underclass political movements in rural areas, an issue which has provoked continuing women's activism in response (Kumar 1995:68–9). Half of the indigenous Yuracruz women of Ecuador were estimated to be raped by mercenaries of an agribusiness company seeking to 'cleanse' the land (Copelon 1994:198). In Bosnia-Herzegovina the rape of Muslim women by Serbian forces was called 'ethnic cleansing'. Serbian soldiers shouted 'Death to all Turkish sperm' (Azra in Stiglmayer 1994:109) or beat young women who failed to become pregnant for not revealing the contraceptives they were using (Kadira in Stiglmayer 1994:119). Rape is connected to pornographic practices. The Serbian forces filmed as they raped (providing voiceovers for some incidents and televising them as rape of Serbian women by Croatian men). Tanks were plastered with pornography and men invited their friends to come and watch, 'like in a movie theatre' as one women said (MacKinnon 1994:75–6, 78). One woman was 'forced to keep her Serbian captor's penis hard in her mouth from midnight to 5.00 A.M. for fourteen nights in a Serb-run concentration camp' or be killed (MacKinnon 1994:78). Some men, neighbours of the raped women, refused to participate: 'they're dead now, they refused . . . and so they killed them' (Kadira in Stiglmayer 1994:120).

Eating Her Words: Multiculturalism

> Australia is still being used as a dumping ground for many other world cultures.
>
> – Oodgeroo Noonuccal 1989:1
> comparing the first invasion and later immigration

Most refugees, at least before children are born, want to return to their countries, but 'in peace and dignity' (Martin 1993:64). Sometimes homelands become reconstructed in an 'idealised perception of the society of origin' (Buijs 1993:3). Some women adapt to western conditions, and come to believe in the greater freedom of a woman who has an independent income and drives a car (Eastmond 1993:46–7). Some Palestinian men in Germany have devised a way to live in two cultures. They first marry a Palestinian wife and then divorce her through the German state, so they can marry a German wife. The German divorce is not recognised by the Palestinian community, and so the man is able to be polygamous. He now has access to residence and work permits, so that extra resources accrue to the Palestinian household. The men help their German wives with domestic chores but not their Palestinian wives; they hold drinking parties in the German wife's home and community activities in their first domicile (Abdulrahim 1993:74). In contrast, the women relocated from Palestine to Berlin lost freedom and status. In the camps they had more often been employed than was possible in Berlin, while the notion of a joint political struggle allowed women freedom of movement and interaction in Palestine. In response to the perceived promiscuity of German women, Palestinian men demanded Palestinian women be modest and restrained, shifting self-definition from a political register to a more conservative religious register (Abdulrahim 1993:66–7, 71). The second generation adapted to the host society's possibilities, girls often doing better at school because they had less freedom of movement than their brothers, understanding that German women's refuges would allow escape from parental claims, although the cost could be ostracism and deportation (Abdulrahim 1993:68, 70). Let us explore in a little more detail this double world of migrants, often produced in the writings of second-generation migrant women.

Most migrants to Europe are considered to be temporary guest workers who will return to their own country, although an exception is the post–World War II migration to Britain. Until the 1971 Immigration Act, it was relatively easy for people from India, Pakistan, the Caribbean and other British colonies or former colonies to enter Britain (Bryan et al. 1985:157). The 1970s produced both greater politicisation among these migrants and mounting hostility from racist groups in a climate of growing unemployment. In the 1980s women from these communities began telling stories of their often painful interactions with white British feminism, which they experienced as racist and exclusivist (for example Beverley Bryan et al. 1985; and Hazel Carby 1982). Workforce participation rates are high for women of Caribbean background, although they are overrepresented in unskilled jobs. Non-Muslim Asian women and white women have similar participation rates, including representation in professional and managerial jobs (Bhachu 1993:103–4).

In the 'new' nations of the United States, Canada, Australia and New Zealand, migration has been a significant source of population expansion. For the United States, most of this extensive nation-building migration had ceased by World War II, by which time Chinese, Irish, southern and eastern European migrants had created distinctive neighbourhoods in cities like New York. Today a combination of legal and illegal migration from across the southern border is giving a clear Latin American flavour to cities like Los Angeles. For illegal migrants particularly, labour exploitation is a common hazard. As they lack legal status, they cannot readily complain about unpaid wages or dangerous working conditions.

In terms of theorising the effects of migration, ideas like the 'melting pot', assimilation and so on had their first testing ground in the United States. The melting pot referred to theories of racial assimilation, in which the various races would become intermixed to achieve a homogeneous culture. What was not usually made explicit was that the mixed ingredients of the melting pot would largely reflect the dominant culture. Critics of this theory, which were few before the 1970s, suggested 'pluralism', in which everyone received their rights, not as abstract individuals, but as members of minorities, as Sartre put it (in Zack 1993:162). One might call this the salad bowl theory of racial mixing, as Jock Collins (1992:114) describes multicultural policies in Australia; groups retain their individual cultures (colours and flavours) but form part of a harmonious whole. Before the development of multicultural policies during the 1970s, Australia officially dealt with its immigrant population through policies of assimilation (to the dominant culture) and then integration (which had the same goal as assimilation but recognised that migrants required specific services in order to complete their integration into Anglo-Celtic Australia).

For Australians of non-English-speaking background at least, multi-culturalism has been the major (if flawed) vehicle for incorporation into government institutions and Australian cultural life over the last two decades. Multiculturalism is a policy which attempts to compensate for the deprivation of language, history and homeland, by celebrating the two cultures in which migrants remake themselves. It seeks to eliminate prejudice, assuming in liberal fashion that this is built on ignorance, by increasing second-language training in schools and adding multicultural activities to school curricula and public life. According to its critics, the name multiculturalism is no accident. No attempt is made to change the structures of economic opportunity, which varies between ethnic groups, except by providing English classes. Multiculturalism has also been criticised for paternalist overtones (Hatzimanolis 1993:133–6).

While women now outnumber men as immigrants to Australia (Cony-beare 1992:30), they come largely as dependents, overrepresented in the family migration and spouse/fiancé categories, while men outnumber women in the skill and humanitarian (refugee) categories (Young and Madden 1992:5). For those without English skills, manual labour in factories or doing piecework at home is often undertaken in conditions rivalling the sweatshops in the Asian free-trade zones (Collins 1988:173; Probert 1989:120). WICH (Women in Industry, Contraception and Health) discovered in the factories they visited that women could take perhaps two toilet breaks daily, forcing them to wear layers of sanitary napkins; faced extremes of temperature; ate while working because of targets or dirty or nonexistent canteens. A team of bilingual workers visited factories and eventually enabled the working women to either participate in existing union structures or develop their own committees (La Marchesina 1994:259, 262–3, 267). Stories of discrimination are rampant: 'If they were more intelligent or better educated they would become bored'; 'Australians would push us around ... They used to pick on us. Call us names. The women were worse' (in Ganguly 1995a:41). Since the 1980s the incidence of below-award wage outwork has increased with the restructuring of Australian industry and greater exposure to overseas competition through the removal of protective tariffs.

Today, then, and almost unique among the nations of the world, Australia contains within its shores over a hundred ways of being feminine, womanly or feminist. These include the dominant practices of the Anglo-Celtic-descended white population, drawn principally from Britain, but also New Zealand and North America; those of the longest surviving culture in the world, that of the Aborigines and the other 'fourth world' group, the Torres Strait Islanders; and those of women who have come from Europe, Asia, Africa and South America. Until recently, Australian feminism hardly recognised these other voices, but gradually these voices of difference are commanding a space in literature, politics and women's studies, forging new meanings for autonomous womanhood in the new-old nation of Australia. According to Indrani Ganguly, however, community and government sectors of feminism have been more responsive to the issues confronted by women from non-English-speaking backgrounds than has academic feminism, so that there is only one course offered in Australian universities which focuses on the issues of such women (Ganguly 1995a:37, 52; see also Huggins 1994:78).

The images of the other which this book has sought to contest are attributed to migrants from Asian and other nations, characterised as either the 'exotic other' or the 'oppressed' other, victims of 'barbaric' practices like arranged marriages or female circumcision. Migrants face the structural barriers of foreign language and customs, non-recognition of their qualifications, and racism, all of which diminish their competence to interact with potential employers, schools and welfare agencies, particularly when children must act as interpreters. But migrant women come from many different backgrounds, a number of cultural groups being more academically qualified than Australian-born women. Some, for example from countries like Sri Lanka or the Philippines, have more political experience than the average Australian-born woman and are more vocal in trade unions, despite the widespread belief in lower union participation rates for migrant women. As we noted in Chapter 3, many are surprised by the lack of childcare facilities in Australia, and find reliance on the nuclear family (more particularly the mother) strange.

Feminist movements in many women's countries of origin are sometimes 'of a more radical nature than feminism in Australia' (Ganguly 1995a:45, 42, 48).

While families of non-English-speaking background (NESB) are often criticised by Anglo-Australians for being patriarchal (as though Anglo-Australian families are not), some migrant women do lose traditional rights when migrating, for example Greek women's entitlement to houses and land as part of their dowry, or Latin American women's control of domestic budgets. Furthermore, the public face of Italian women's submission – *la bella figura* (putting on a good face for the public) – often disguises private domestic power. But Australian mores also offer opportunities for some migrants: Greek women talk of escape from the constraints of in-laws and the village community, Italians of the capacity to leave a bad marriage. 'In reality, NESB women's issues are neither totally similar nor totally different to that of Anglo-Australian women, but a mix of the two' (Ganguly 1995a:45, 39).

Multicultural writers are often called on to be 'authentic', to express their cultural difference rather than human issues in general (Gunew 1993:10, 12). Some writers escape this command by becoming cultural 'looters' (Yvonne du Fresne's term) of their host culture. Their doubled vision 'casts a devastatingly satiric eye on the dominant Anglo culture' (Gunew 1993:14). A light-hearted example of this is Joanne Travaglia and Elizabeth Weiss's (1992) assessment of both the traditional Italian gifts of *bomboniere* and of feminism. Instead of pure and frilly sugar-coated almonds (the traditional sweet) as gifts, they suggest a copy of *The Female Eunuch* at baptism, tampons at confirmation, and a university degree instead of a wedding (Weiss in Travaglia in Weiss 1992:126–9). They also make fun of chic multiculturalism in yuppie Australia, in an imagined discourse on *bomboniere*:

> 'Well yes', you can casually throw over the Balmain Brie and Fettucini alla Annandale. 'I have a fine collection (pass the chinotto, Damien). It was handed to me by my mother when her last mirror-backed cabinet smashed under their weight. (More foccacia, Tamara?) Some of them have been in my family for generations. They represent the movement from the traditional communal village lifestyle as shown by the simpleness of the tulle, to urban living and the consumer society as shown by ...'. Well, you get the picture. (Travaglia in Travaglia and Weiss 1992:123–4)

A practical example of doubled vision are the East African Sikh women in London who, through their income-earning capacity, build up their own dowries. They have greater control over these resources than they would have over dowries bestowed by parents. Like increasing numbers of young women in India, while they accept arranged marriages, seeing little of attraction in European-style 'love matches', they now demand a right of veto (Buijs 1993:9, 12). Thus to form an identity is to take from each what one wants, 'to enjoy, but not be helplessly possessed' (Giuffré, 1992:96). But it requires comfort in both cultures, it requires a host society which respects other cultures. As was noted in Chapter 1, this is a condition of hybrid identities.

WOMEN'S STUDIES AND WOMEN'S POLITICS

> Ola, she had thought, seemed to get his best ideas over food ... 'Do you know what guerilla fighters do more than anything else? Skirmishes and battles occupy a very small portion of their time. They *talk*.' Ola stopped long enough to have a spoonful of fruit. 'Talk,' he continued, chewing rapidly and swallowing, 'is the key to liberation, one's tongue the very machete of freedom'.
>
> – Walker 1989:348

So far this chapter has explored the international traffic in women, the 'vast diasporas of deterritorialised populations', immigrant workers, guest labourers, refugees (Ram 1991a:93) who experience 'the "unhomeliness" inherent in that rite of extra-territorial and cross-cultural initiation' (Bhabha 1994:9). In this last section we turn to a traffic in more privileged women, middle-class professionals and intellectuals who come and go between the worlds, lending their analyses and reflections to the task of enriching women's studies and women's political interventions.

Women's Studies

> 'Why should a promising young sociologist like you spend so much time and energy on such trivial matters as women and poverty?'
>
> – Question asked by a senior colleague in 1979 of Cho Hyoung (1994:51), professor of sociology, Ehwa Women's University, Korea

Around the world, research has suggested the overwhelming significance of education for improving the access of women to the paid workforce, to reproductive choices and better health, to awareness of their legal rights, to a fuller cultural life, and even to feminism.[8] Partly as a result of initiatives introduced by the UN Decade for Women, the ratio of female to male illiteracy was reduced to 4:3 in 1980, whereas it had been 2:1 in the developing world in 1960 (Momsen 1991:35). But there are indications that female literacy is again declining, perhaps because parents are unwilling or unable to spend shrinking resources on daughters who will marry out of the family, especially when fees rise (India), governments expend less resources on education, particularly in the countryside (China), teenage pregnancies or women's requirement to work on farms disrupt schooling and men reject 'over-educated' women as wives (Africa) (Desai 1993:33, 39 for India; Njeuma 1993:127 for Africa).

Studies and projects which originate in the west often take the simple approach that more education is a good thing for women. Scholars in the east (now more often called the south), however, critically evaluate the content of that education. The role of colonial education was to produce 'competent clerks and administrators', not 'creative thinkers'. In rural India the school curriculum is irrelevant to people's daily life (Shaheed and Mumtaz 1993:61, 69). In Africa women need agricultural education and political skills to maintain their rights over land (Conway 1993: 250–1). In Brazil whites make more money than blacks for the same level of education, and the differential increases with the amount of education (Rosemberg 1993:227).

Furthermore, a growing critique of the gendered nature of educational curricula is 'characteristic of the international women's movement throughout the third world' (Mazumdar 1993:21). Studies reveal the preponderance of images or stories which relate to boys rather than girls in school textbooks, generally about 10:1 (Gail S. Fu, newsletter of the Gender Research Program at the Chinese University of Hong Kong, No. 7, September 1994:12; People's Republic of China 1994:10; Desai 1993:38 for India). One study of Hindi textbooks, however, found that the ratio of boy-centred to girl-centred stories was 21:0, while no lesson referred to the role of women in agriculture (Desai 1993:38; on women represented in agriculture see also Shaheed and Mumtaz 1993:69 for Pakistan; Kinyanjui 1993:143 for Kenya; for role stereotyping in African textbooks see Njeuma 1993:128). The Jakarta Declaration for the Advancement of Women in Asia and the Pacific (issued by the United Nations Economic and Social Council, June 1994:38) recommends that 'every attempt should be made to eliminate the depiction of gender-stereotyped roles for women through revision of syllabus and course content, conscientization of teachers and parents, and innovative affirmative action programs for girl students'.

Developing from the example of Afro-American studies, and now supplemented by Latin American studies, women's studies has achieved its greatest numerical preponderance in the United States, where it was taught in about 500 colleges and universities in the mid-1980s (there were also 50 research centres for women) (James 1992:3). Particularly over the last decade, women's studies courses have been established in many third world nations. These include women's resource centres to support women's studies programs in India and Pakistan; fieldwork which links feminist theory and practice, for example in the sex tourist locales of

Manila; and graduate programs, although when it was set up in 1982, the program in Korea was the 'only advanced degree program in Asia', a description which applied until 1990 (Desai 1993:39 for India; Zafar 1994:83 for Pakistan; de Dios 1994:41 for the Philippines; Hyoung 1994:54 for Korea; see also Mbilinyi and Meena 1991:846–51 for Botswana, Nigeria, Tanzania, Uganda; Vargas 1993:147 and Miller 1991:247 for South America; Fujieda and Fujimura-Faneslow 1995:161 for Japan).

The question of western feminist imperialism is often raised by women's studies teachers beyond the United States. Thus most of the writing on Arab women is by women who are members of western women's studies programs; indeed much of it is written in English and is not available in Arabic. Women's studies is, however, taught at Ahfad University in Sudan and the American University in Cairo (Kawar 1991:308). In the late 1970s 'certain self-appointed theoreticians' classified the emerging Indian women's movement along western lines, as 'bourgeois feminist, socialist feminist and radical feminist': 'We were supposed to have split even before we got a real opportunity to get together' (Kishwar 1990:3, 40).

Madhu Kishwar goes on to note how the results of research in the west are used as justifications for activism in India, without any indigenous research to assess their relevance to India. She offers the examples of activism around the spread of reproductive technologies, demands for refuges and shelters for battered women and the hole in the ozone layer when most people do not have clean water (Kishwar 1995:16). Even where funding is available for local research, its content is often determined by the agenda of funding agencies, who ignore 'more pressing priorities' (Kishwar 1990:6–7):

> African scholars are forced into certain forms of intellectual endeavors that are peripheral to the development of their societies ... I have visited villages where, at a time when the village women are asking for better health facilities and lower infant-mortality rates, they are presented with questionnaires on family planning. In some instances, when women would like to have piped water in the village, they may be at the same time faced with a researcher interested in investigating power and powerlessness in the household. (Pala 1977:10)

While a western training may well produce a reasonably uncritical adoption of western values, it seems unlikely that third world academics – literally world-travellers if they return to their native lands – would not seek to adapt their western education to local conditions. Such adaptations will be supported as more local research and theorising on women's status occurs in countries beyond the west. Thus the Chinese example suggests that women's studies teachers accept the legacy of western feminist texts but also assert the importance of local conditions, issues and research. After the first Institute for Women's Studies was established by the All-China Women's Federation in 1983, a number of provincial branches established similar research arms, committed to 'Marxist women's liberation theory' (Li and Zhang 1994:141, 142). While feminism is still seen as 'part of bourgeois ideology' by many, women's studies in Chinese universities draws on and adapts western feminists texts. 'Feminology' (female-ism according to Zhang 1995:37) reflects 'that Chinese women's studies has its own background and circumstances unique to Chinese history and social reality' (Li and Zhang 1994:148). In the one feminist theory course taught in Beijing, 'Min Dongchao has found that the most popular section of the course concerns how women can get to know themselves' (Fennell and Jeffry 1992:11), a superficially western-flavoured quest. There are 500 women's studies groups in China and research has expanded into areas which previously received little attention: reproductive health, violence against women, women's human rights and so on (Wang Jiaxiang 1996).

Amrita Basu (1995:2) disputes claims that women's movements are a result of women's education and expanded job opportunities during industrialisation. Instead she suggests that in many countries women's movements 'tend to be weak where state control permeates civil society'. Let us turn then to women's movement politics, and its different contours in different social settings.

Women's Movements Around the World: New Practices for Old Battles

The feminist movement and the demands of women in any particular country grow out of the reality of that country, and it is wrong to say that what we want is what everybody should want and what we don't want nobody should ask for.

– Wang Jiaxiang 1991:180

Feminism is influenced by the culture which nurtures (and opposes) it, so the preoccupations of women will not be everywhere the same. Where religion is a significant belief system, women struggle to interpret it to meet their own ends and for their own experiences, as we discussed in Chapter 2 in relation to female circumcision. Where democratic states talk of citizens' rights, women deploy their own notions of women's rights in riposte. Where population policies collide with reproductive choices, women develop contesting images of maternity. Nonetheless, a multinational feminism is likely to be stronger and certainly presents a richer tapestry than any insular variant. Images of the other provide the warp and weft of dreams and possibilities.

In some countries women's organisations are enviable structures, topped by a national peak council with links to grassroots organisations in almost every community. Papua New Guinea's National Council of Women, with its top-down approach, is one such organisation. When placed alongside the bottom-up approach of church networks, it makes a flow of communications possible between Port Moresby and the villages (Nakikus et al. 1991:41; Bonnell 1982:30–1). China, the largest nation in the world, is served by the All China Women's Federation, with links into every province in China, as well as numerous villages. As it is affiliated with the Chinese Communist Party, the official voice of China's feminism is refracted through party policies, and its pronouncements often also reflect marxist ideology. In contrast, according to Xie Lihua (1995:71) African women's groups are 'as numerous as mushrooms after a spring rain'; they do not focus on nationwide programs but are producer groups, special interest groups (for business and professional women for example), and occasionally grassroots groups (see Hubbard and Solomon 1995; Oduol and Kabira 1995; Abdullah 1995).

More than 140 states have women's machinery in bureaucracy and government (Pettman 1996:14; for example Njeuma 1993:129 for 'some African nations'; Zafar 1994:83 for Pakistan's Ministry of Women's Development established in 1989). But femocrats as women's advisers or in women's affairs departments are constrained by government policies to be less radical than some of their sisters would like. The Taiwan Women's Department was established under the Central Committee in 1953, and chaired by Madame Chiang Kai-shek. It presented a 'maternal image' of women and advocated the 'feminine virtues' of charity workers, loving mothers, obedient daughters and devoted wives (Chiang and Ku 1985:28). A more radical strand of feminism developed from the 1970s, led particularly by Lu Hsiu-lien and Li Yuan-chen. They attacked the pardoning of men who killed wives suspected of adultery, exposed rape, sought new divorce laws and the protection of teenage prostitutes, and successfully resisted the construction of a dangerous chemical plant (Ku 1987:15–22).

Women activists outside (and inside!) the west often eschew the title 'feminist', perhaps proclaiming in declension narrative fashion that gender inequality is a foreign import or experience, specific to 'European culture'. Among the fifty contributors to a book on Chinese women's experiences of preparations for the UN women's forum in Beijing, only a handful called themselves feminist: 'proudly' in Zhu Xiaodong's (1995: 123) case; 'happily' in Li Ping's (1995:256–7) case; as an 'honorary feminist' so dubbed by her Finnish friends because she had 'done so much for women' in Luo Xiaolu's case (in Wong 1995:302). While one commentator says that Chinese feminism in Hong Kong should 'avoid the polarisation of women against men as advocated by some of the militant feminist groups in the West' (Cheung 1989:101), this has not meant that women's groups have not established refuges and been active against rape; one militant group formed in 1984 even called itself the Association for the Advancement of Feminism (Cheung 1989:100; Ho 1990:187, 190). The leaders of the African National Congress Women's Section have insisted 'there is nothing wrong with feminism. It is as progressive or as reactionary as nationalism', and placed gender issues on the political agenda in 1990, as part of 'national liberation'. Even so, at a Congress of South African Trade Unions, the women's demand to transform labour relations in the household 'was brusquely flicked aside' with the label 'bourgeois imperialist feminism', while lesbian and gay activists have been condemned on similar grounds (McClintock 1995:384; Kemp et al. 1995:146).

Madhu Kishwar (1990:2), long associated with the Indian journal *Manushi*, explains that the title was chosen to indicate concern 'not just with women's equality, as the term "feminist" would imply, but with the protection of human rights of all the disadvantaged or discriminated groups in our society'. While Kishwar advocates a new social consensus to prevent sati, dowry, and pre-natal sex-determination tests, consensus must be supported by appropriate economic structures. She was one of the many women and men who publicly pledged to neither be given with nor receive a dowry. She now realises that women need inheritance rights; dowry should come in the form of investment property rather than consumer goods and laws should prevent dowry harassment rather than dowry *per se*. She suggests picketing to oppose sex-determination clinics rather than draconian laws, producing reform in one's own life as Gandhi did before seeking to reform others. 'Our politics and social reform strategies must attempt to be inclusivist rather than exclusivist, aiming towards the ultimate end of minimising social conflict rather than resulting in greater disharmony'. This includes talking with in-laws and husbands about a woman's marital rights as well as encouraging her to assert her rights. It is also important to understand that the 'virtuous oppressed' (Kishwar 1995:16) is an ideal and that one offers assistance to real people, who have their faults and weaknesses; activists should not use activism to 'resolve our personal problems' or 'as vehicles for our own empowerment' (contra US feminism's slogan, the personal is political). Instead activist work should be undertaken 'in the spirit of unconditional giving, in the same way that people do *seva* [service] in a *gurudwara* [Sikh temple]' (Kishwar 1995:17).

Another example of Indian women's activism occurs in Indian villages. The Indian government first established Maliha Mandals in the 1950s 'as part of a program to meet the development needs of rural women' (Auluck-Wilson 1995:1031). In the predominantly Hindu village of Peth in Maharashtra, when a woman's body was found in a well with deep gashes in her head and genitals in 1989, the organisation was rejuvenated. The Mahila Mandal that formed even included marginalised caste women through a unique structure of three office-holders in each of the executive positions of president, secretary and treasurer who collectively implement the organisation's decisions and maintain unity where caste divisions could easily divide the women (Auluck-Wilson 1995:1032). A group of ten to fifteen members went to any home where violence was reported, taking photographs of the violence perpetrated on the women and recording the exchanges and later playing them in the village square. Women began to use the threat of the Mahila Mandal against husbands' abuse. Meanwhile, some dominant caste men who had been targets of intervention prevailed upon local landlords to refuse to pay the wages of all marginalised caste members if the Mahila Mandal continued its activities. The Mahila Mandal switched its tactics and secured free legal aid to take seven cases of domestic abuse to court, while also winning eight cases of alimony and three of inheritance rights. The Mahila Mandal then turned its attention to other issues. They opened a local high school because parents would not allow their daughters to attend the high school in the next village. They prevailed upon a private hospital in the nearest city to establish free daily clinics, which the hospital supported as the interns needed more experience in rural medicine. In late 1993 the Mahila Mandal won five out of nine seats in the village council election, which meant they were able to close down the remaining illicit liquor suppliers in the village (one supplier had changed to a dry goods store when the Mahila Mandal promised to patronise his shop). Describing their mountain of poverty, never-ending work, violence and despair, members concluded 'When all the women lift, the mountain will move' (in Auluck-Wilson 1995:1038). Elsewhere in India Mahila Mandals have been rejuvenated and refocused on women's issues (Basu 1995:75).

Not only does this story testify to the courage and inventiveness of the village women, but it shows how the women addressed first the immediate issue – domestic violence and dowry-related deaths – but moved on from that to address structural issues, for example the role of low education and literacy levels in limiting women's life choices. They also expanded their political base to stand for election in 'mainstream' political organisations. The issues they took up are part of a familiar litany of feminist activism: bodily security, health, education, political participation.

Western feminists are now less likely to engage in the militant tactics deplored by some Asian observers. In contrast, in Korea the 'new women's movement' was born in 1984 with the Committee to Ensure Women's Survival. They protested instances where women's rights had been violated in 'sit-down strikes and confrontations with the police' (Lee

1993:100). In India women march to liquor stores, smash liquor pots (Steady 1992:96) and parade liquor dealers through the streets in their protest against alcohol-related domestic violence. In 1982 women evicted men from the women's compartments of Bombay trains for a fortnight (Gandhi and Shah 1992:49). In 1992, as part of a strategy for the public shaming of men, women marched into the house of a man who had slowly poisoned his wife to death, stripped him naked and marched him through the streets. Such actions are often forced on women by the refusal of police to intervene, possibly because of bribes, or even illegal actions by policemen themselves. Thus it was the rape of a tribal girl by two policemen which launched the national campaign against rape (Kelkar 1995).

Other connections between the actions of an often repressive state and women's movement politics are offered by the example of South America. Socialist feminism 'became the predominant strain of feminist thought in Latin America in the twentieth century' (Miller 1991:14), although women's movements in Latin America are also drawn from human rights organisations, urban poor women, feminists and middle-class professionals (to which are added Catholic church-based movements in Brazil: Soares et al. 1995:311). Activist women often linked their analysis of patriarchal oppression to military dictatorship (Frohmann and Valdés 1995:280, 294). Despite interaction with both American and European feminisms, it was not really until the 1970s that sexual issues like lesbianism and domestic violence against women gained significance. Resistance to both state violence and domestic violence is captured in the slogan 'Democracy in the country and the home' (Miller 1991:248). Similarly, the banners over traffic lights in St Croix in the Caribbean proclaim 'World Peace Begins at Home' (Morrow 1994:580–3). These slogans, also repeated in India (Kelkar 1995), sound superficially like 'the personal is political'. However, where participants in consciousness-raising groups often focused on changes to their personal lives (see Henry and Derlet 1993:183 for Australia; Shreve 1989:220–1 for the United States), the slogans in India and South America seek to connect domestic politics with national politics.

The International Decade for Women taught white feminists that their priorities, interpretations and political solutions were not always shared by third world women. But it also brought women of the south together, to form political alliances and share strategies. Women from seventeen Muslim countries exchange information which gives them new alternatives (Hélie-Lucas 1987:13). After attending the Asian Women in Struggle for Justice Conference in Bombay in 1983 Edith Tores of the Philippines became a militant feminist (Brydon and Chant 1989:245) and builds on a proud history of *feministas* going back to the early 1900s. Japanese women have worked with Korean women over the 'comfort' women and with Filipino women to resist the exploitation and abuse of Filipinas who are forced to engage in prostitution in Japan (believing they would be working as secretaries and such like). The Asian Women's Association held a mass protest when the prime minister of Japan visited the Philippines in 1981, denouncing the economic exploitation of women in poor countries by men in rich countries (Matsui 1995a:310–13, 318). Indigenous women around the world use the United Nations as a forum to air their grievances, international connections accelerated by the International Year of Indigenous People in 1993 (Langton 1988; Yeatman 1992:458–9).

CONCLUSION

Against the hope for global connections between women are instances of racism in the white women's movement. Roberta Sykes was publicly and virulently attacked by white feminists when she opposed the legalisation of abortion (Rowland 1984:65). Chapter 3 explained why black and white women might place themselves on different sides of the reproductive debate; clearly these white feminists did not take cognisance of that history. For some indigenous women, white femocrats act like modern missionaries, handing out largesse to their underprivileged sisters (Sykes in Rowland 1984:63–4; Huggins 1994: 74). As late as 1994, a self-defined black feminist, Melissa Lucashenko (1994:23), said, 'The major obstacle to totally effective Black feminism is white racism in the feminist movement'.

For some writers from beyond the white west, alliances are only possible if white women give priority to race-based struggles. This is understandable in a country like Australia, where being Aboriginal is reinvoked daily in racist discrimination, in a way that being female is not. In a reversal of their criticism of third world women as a category of knowledge, Mohanty et al. (1991:ix) embrace the notion 'third world women' as a category of politics, a unity based on the shared history of oppression, shared by 'the colonized, neocolonized or decolonized countries (of Asia, Africa and Latin America) . . . and . . . black, Asian, Latino, and indigenous peoples in North America, Europe and Australia' (Mohanty et al. 1991:ix). Even white women 'can align themselves with and participate' in the 'imagined communities' which make up the third world, but for these writers the precondition is to accept that the oppressions of gender, even if a part of the analysis, cannot displace the oppression of imperialism (Mohanty et al. 1991:4).

While women writing from oppressed groups are acutely aware of the needs of their menfolk, women writing from oppressor groups are more likely to seek alliances with women across cultures. As Jan Pettman

(1992:12) suggests, we should both accept our diversity and call up a 'strategic essentialism' when men seek to silence women by claiming an alliance with 'their' own women, against other women. Cross-cultural alliances, however, are only likely to succeed if they are based on some understanding of why other women take the political positions that they do. 'The unequal relations among women' cannot be reduced to 'a universal sisterhood composed of an essential plurality of differences' (Emberley 1993:92). In the end there is inequality as well as difference: some women are better off in the economy and more securely placed in the dominant culture than others. In exploring those inequalities, this chapter has provided some reasons why white feminists should seek alliances based on a clear-eyed politics rather than a dewy-eyed romanticism.

On the other hand, for many white feminists at least, the tension between women's lives and those of men must remain the centre of a feminist text and politics. This will be deemed wrong-headed by those for whom race or class or sexual preference are the great dividers in society. But we have to start somewhere, and this is where most feminists start: with women. They then unravel and complicate the category, until sometimes it disappears altogether. Even so, at a mundane level women as a political and theoretical category has continuing salience. Almost everybody in the world remembers and is reminded daily to which gender they belong. This does not, however, excuse 'universalising' or 'essentialising' women and their predicament. The Conclusion explores some of the ways women from beyond the white west 'complicate' the taken-for-granted nature of 'woman' by revealing how 'woman' often means 'only women like me, the speaker', and how we can try to build a 'coalition politics' on our understandings of women's complexity.

Conclusion:
Braiding at the Borderlands

•

> One of the very small girls understands at three years old, the teaching of the sweetgrass braid - how weak one strand is, how easy it is to break it up, and it's gone. She knows, however, that many strands, braided together, cannot be torn apart.
>
> – Osennontion (Marlyn Kane) in Emberley 1992:93

While teaching in Beijing in 1991 and 1993, I sometimes became silently impatient with the contradictory demands of my female students. 'They don't want to be "iron women", uncomplainingly shouldering the burdens of career and household, but they want equality; they don't want demanding or difficult jobs but they want promotion; they dislike physical activity and outside work'. 'Dammit', I remember thinking, 'don't these students realise that life isn't like that for women?' Suddenly I realised that my impatience was built on my totally implicit acceptance of an equality framework when thinking about women's rights. In Australia feminists tend to accept that women must play by the overt rules of meritocracy (even if men do not); women's advancement is based on being as good as or better than men. My Chinese students were asking to be treated like their less-qualified male classmates, to receive the advantages life offered even if they did not 'deserve' them in terms of some notion of equal reward for equal merit or equal exertion. And, of course, they were also using the idea of women's difference, weaker and more feminine, to support some of their wishes. In a more feminist vein, one of my students, Zhu Xiaodong (1995:127–30), compares her own position with that of her grandmother, who had never worn a skirt or permed her hair and accepts that 'her children suffered a lot' because of her commitment to 'in no way fall behind' her male colleagues. When Zhu Xiaodong told her grandmother she had released to the mass media the names of departments and companies who had discriminated against women by hiring less-qualified male graduates, her grandmother protested that 'female university students should be held responsible for this phenomenon' because they were 'always putting their families first'. For Zhu Xiaodong her grandmother's sacrifices had been unfair: instead of 'changing ourselves to gain society's recognition, we should change the way society views us'.

This conclusion explores how the norms of other cultures can disrupt and question the taken-for-grantedness of our own. If you are not a white middle-class western feminist, you have been reading this book as an outsider, at least some of the time. The text speaks most obviously to a white audience, about the experiences of the 'other', even if including the voices of the other. When women of colour were first asked to speak, they felt they were expected to take up certain positions. Almost a decade ago, Trinh Minh-ha (1987:14) suggested that women like her were treated as both dangerous (yellow peril) and endangered (exposed to a loss of authenticity):

> Now I am not only given the permission to open up and talk, I am also encouraged to express my difference. My audience expects and demands it; otherwise people would feel as if they have been cheated: We did not come here to hear a Third World member speak about the First (?) World. We came to listen to that voice of difference likely to bring us *what we can't have*, and to divert us from the monotony of sameness.

The 'other' enables scholars working in exhausted (white) fields to cross over into new ('Other') territory (duCille 1994:623).

However, Parlo Singh (1994a:93, 95–6), an Australian academic of Indian background, contends that while 'othering' of women like herself has been part of the project of white western humanism, the 'project of modernity has been so comprehensive that there can no longer be a position of the "Other"'. 'We all have become entwined in the centre of cultural production.' Thus a key issue for those in the dominant ethnic groups is to identify their own ethnic identities and how these are created in relation to marginalised ethnic identities. What has been said by women 'othered' or hybridised by western cultures provides startling revisions for white women, some of which this book has explored. I hope that women in dominant cultures can also learn to move backwards and forwards between cultures as the subordinated no doubt must, almost daily. One aspect of speaking between cultures is the issue of speaking and subject positions: who can say what about whom when.

SPEAKING AND SUBJECT POSITIONS

It is now time for feminist scholars to ask Native American women –
indeed, all groups of women they study – what their agendas are and
how feminist scholars might lend themselves to the task.

– Green 1980:267

In China Dymphna Cusack (1958:13) asserted that 'my brief experience
has taught me that language is no barrier. Minds leap to each other with
instinctive sympathy'. But Cusack (1958:261) has a moment of doubt:
'The reality is deeper. Perhaps it could be written only by a Chinese
woman who has herself experienced it. Only she can know the inmost
truth'. Should white feminists, then, remain silent concerning the experiences of others, leaving them to tell 'the inmost truth'? Linda Alcoff, a
Panamanian-American feminist, takes up 'The Problem of Speaking for
Others', which must perforce include speaking about others. If we speak
only for groups of which we are a member, in the upshot each individual
may speak only for herself. If we refuse to speak for others, we may refuse
a powerful platform from which to support struggles against oppression;
we may indeed 'retreat into a narcissistic yuppie lifestyle', masking it with
our 'respectful' silence. Such a retreat avoids the pain and 'emotionally
troublesome endeavour' of 'constant interrogation and critical reflection';
it also denies the real connections between women (Alcoff 1992:9, 17, 22,
20, 21). Furthermore, according to Edward Said (in Attwood 1992:
xii–xiii), disentitling white women (or white men) from speaking about
the other is likely to produce a discourse from below which is just as
'exclusivist, as limited, provincial, and discriminatory in its suppressions
and repressions as the master discourses of colonialism and elitism'.

This problem has been raised in Canada over the issue of intra-
community violence in both First Nations and immigrant communities.
In mainstream white discourses such violence is often attributed to cultural 'backwardness', so that western men become 'gems of enlightenment
and kindness' by comparison with South Asian men (Yasmin Jiwani in
Razack 1994:916). In response, says the Coalition of Immigrant and Visible Minority Women of British Columbia, 'no culture condones violence',
although 'culture' is used by men from different backgrounds as a 'cocoon'
against criticism. Similarly, some First Nations women's groups claim that
rape of aboriginal women should be treated just as seriously whether the
perpetrator is an Inuit man or a white man. For others, however, such a
position effaces the significance of a history of colonialism which has
produced white cultural supremacy and unequal access to resources, and
which has contributed to male violence and must be addressed to help
overcome violence. Some First Nations people call for culturally specific
solutions to violence, like 'healing circles'. But these sometimes replace

any other form of punishment, allowing the perpetrator to remain in the community (Razack 1994:917, 902, 908). The Ontario Native Women's Association combines traditional and white Canadian solutions. They advocate healing *all* members of the family but also assert that 'the needs and safety of the abused woman and children are more urgent at first' (in Razack 1994:911).

In Australian indigenous communities there are tales of gang rape; 'of brothers "selling sisters" (to both black and white men) to pay gambling debts or for beer; of 8-year-old girls being shown hard pornography and being asked to perform the act depicted' (Judy Atkinson's position summarised in Bell 1991:388); of 'the daily parade of women with band-aged heads and broken arms' (Langton et al. 1991:373). The idiom for women bashing is 'Blackfella loving', jealousy indicating love (Lucashenko and Best 1995:21). In 1989 an article by Diane Bell, then professor of anthropology in Australia and now in the United States, and Topsy Napurrula Nelson, female elder of the Pawurrinji Aboriginal group, was published on the previously taboo issue of intra-racial rape in indigenous Australia. A group of urban Aboriginal women protested that Nelson could not, because of academic inequalities, be a true co-author (Nelson [1991: 507] denied this: 'I had no Aboriginal to write this. Diane is like a sister; best friend. She wrote this all down for me. That's OK – women to women; it doesn't matter black or white'). White women were told not to speak about such issues: 'It is our business how we deal with rape and have done so for the last 202 years quite well' (Huggins et al. 1991:506–7). They were also angry that many Aboriginal women working for and sometimes writing about Aboriginal women's safety and addressing rape in their communities were not acknowledged in the article, and indeed have not been given the same recognition or invitation to speak where a white feminist has (Pettman 1996:41).

For her part, Diane Bell (1996:253) has suggested that 'our heresies have become received wisdom' for women working in Aboriginal communities and developing their own legal groups to respond to intra-racial rape. Indeed, Melissa Lucashenko and Odette Best, describing themselves as 'Aboriginal feminists', criticise the lack of public attention given when 'the murders and bashings are Black-on-Black', as compared with Aboriginal deaths in custody (Lucashenko and Best 1995:20, 19). White silence may arise from a notion that indigenous communities are 'a harmonious, peace-loving people living as one with Mother Earth' (Lucashenko and Best 1995:20), or from fears of charges of racism. They point also to the effects of colonisation (which I suspect cannot even begin to be imagined by those of us who have not experienced them), compounded by white colonisers' glorification of violent masculinity, and the importance of addressing structural inequalities in seeking solutions for indigenous violence. However, violent Aboriginal men include 'senior

bureaucrats, academics, footballers, highly respected research consult-
ants, and senior community leaders'; like senior white men they lead
'double lives of respectability and brutality'. Thus 'what we are saying is
that despite the living conditions of Aboriginal men, despite the racism,
the alcohol and drug abuse, the poverty and the general lack of hope
characteristic of our lives, women bashing is wrong in Aboriginal Law and
must stop' (Lucashenko and Best 1995:20).

Like the First Nations women of Canada, Aboriginal women in Australia
are refusing both the straitjacket of 'authentic' Aboriginality which locks
indigenous people into a fabricated past, and the demands of assimilation
which says their best solutions are white feminists' solutions (Lucashenko
and Best 1995:21). For example, since Aboriginal women traditionally 'are
by no means simply passive victims' in the context of Aboriginal violence
(Johnston 1991b:100), women in central Australia have produced a
powerful reworking of the black matriarch myth and an expansion of
white feminism's conception of strong womanhood. Women's night patrols
are conducted by big women, sometimes armed with sticks, who defuse
potentially violent situations. In such ways, indigenous women challenge
sexist behaviour, 'reinventing and revitalising Black feminism' (Lucashenko and Best 1995:22; see also Salomon-Nékiriai 1996:22–3 for New
Caledonia).

While Lucashenko and Best suggest that refusal to speak about the ill-
treatment of women in other cultures may be patronising and devaluing of
these other women's experiences, not all indigenous women in Australia
adopt a feminist position or suggest they would welcome white feminists'
support, as we saw in relation to intra-racial rape. Thus white feminists
must pay attention to how we speak out, and when. Both Ann duCille, an
African-American academic, and Alcoff note the different effects of the
same information spoken by differently positioned speakers. DuCille
(1994:600) argues that many present academic discussions of black
culture are not new to African-Americans, but that 'black culture is more
easily intellectualized (and canonized) when transferred from the danger
of lived black experience to the safety of white metaphor'. Alcoff (1992:
27) suggests that when the Panamanian Opposition criticise Noriega as a
corrupt dictator it has a meaning which is lost when President Bush does
the same thing. Bush frames the United States as the protector of democracy against the backwardness of the third world, rather than addressing
the role of United States imperialism in producing conditions conducive
to autocracy in Panama. We must think of speaking/writing as 'an *event*,
which includes speaker, words, hearers, location, language, and so on'
(Alcoff 1992:26).

As members of a dominant group, white feminists have the obligation to
consider the connections of *power* between them and women of colour.
Elspeth Probyn (1993:140) calls this speaking 'with attitude', seeking not

merely to speak about oneself or the other, but 'speaking within the space between my self and another self'. This can only be done by being clear how our self-definition requires a necessary other to bound it, to contrast with it, and so excludes the 'other' (Probyn 1993:145, 7). In the spaces between women who define themselves as different, we run the risk of transgressing sensibilities and overreaching the limits of our capacities. The space between self and other might seem to become a widening and deepening abyss as one attempts to bridge it (Probyn 1993:145, 161). Thus one has to start with the familiar, increasingly enlarging its boundaries. Isabelle Gunning's notion of world-travelling thus seeks to recognise the similarity of the other with the self – 'shared values and perspectives' (Gunning 1992:202) – as well as the independence of the other – the differences between women. Much of this work is done through seeing our own culture differently, through another's eyes. What, then, are some of the differences women from beyond the west's dominant culture see in western women?

SEEING 'OUR' 'SELVES' THROUGH THE EYES OF 'OTHERS'

There has to be a simultaneous other focus: not merely who am I? but who is the other woman? How am I naming her? How does she name me?

– Gayatri Spivak in Hardacre and Manderson 1990:17

In 1994, after paying her respects to the Indigenous Australian people of the Geelong area, Lilla Watson, Murri artist, lecturer and writer, noted that 'I speak from the perspective of a mature culture', and 'our experience of colonisation may provide useful insights and tactics for feminists'. 'For the first time in our history we have been asked to describe ourselves to the colonisers.' Before 'we have never felt the need to describe ourselves to anyone', because there was no other to create difference. Lilla Watson then went on to suggest several ways in which Murri and white women might have different cosmologies. In Chapter 4, I noted her comments on the effects of sexualisation of white female identity in producing white women's horror of rape. Murri women are not easily controlled by fear of male violence, which establishes a victim mentality, and respond instead with revenge and public humiliation. White women in Brisbane shelters report that Murri men respect the fact that this is a 'woman's place', while white men demand to see their wives.

Decision-making operates on a consensus which balances men's and women's business. Women's business includes techniques for managing conflict, land and the natural world. Women's, men's and public business may be conceived as three overlapping circles in indigenous cultures, where important public issues require the input of both sexes. However, women have autonomy in their own sphere. Even a five-year-old niece of Watson's could say to her father and uncle, who would respect her request, 'Please leave the room, this is women's business', when she wanted to show a box of flowers and feathers to Watson. In contrast, white women are represented as the inside circle of three concentric circles, surrounded and contained by the circle of men's business and then the public world. Men both constrain and contain white women's business, representing it as unimportant, and control public business. The women's movement has pushed out beyond the men's circle to some extent so that they now abut the circle of public business, but only by accepting co-option into 'equality' and 'individual rights and freedoms'.

It is perhaps the doubled strength of a sphere of women's business and an acceptance of women's right to participate in public business which encourages some indigenous women to reject white feminism (Wirrpanda 1987:75; Oodgeroo Noonuccal as Kath Walker in Mitchell 1987:209). Women from other cultures have also been amused by white western women's constructions of their autonomy. One Japanese woman laughed (behind her hand) that American women could believe they were liberated and would still consult their husbands before buying a house (Davidson 1993:72). Some Japanese women expressed surprise that American women can claim to be feminist in a country with high rates of rape, domestic violence and infant mortality: 'A typical Japanese woman wouldn't put up with that' (Davidson 1993:77). Luo Ping (1995:202), although impressed by the gentle Swedish men pushing baby carriages, notes that in the west 'women do not have the basic rights to their own surnames ... they don't even have abortion rights'. Some NESB women in Australia consider that it is Anglo-Australian women, and not them, who are 'traditional': 'Australian girls work only until they are 25, then they get married, have babies, stop working, get fat, and watch TV all day' (quoted in Ganguly 1995a:40).

Chapter 4 discussed the greater centrality and fragility of sexual identity in the white west, a perception shared by some commentators from other cultures. Throughout this century, 'third world' women have noticed western women's preoccupation with beauty, often described as superficial, written on the body. In the 1830s when the British were describing with horror Iranian men's 'excessive desire for beardless teen-agers' and the existence of 'eunuch- and whore-houses', Mirza Fattah, a member of an Iranian delegation to Europe, commented on the failure of European men to satisfy European women's insatiable lust, so that women kept dogs for this purpose (in Tavakoli-Targhi 1994:109, 107). In Algeria, some newspapers describe the western woman as 'a piece of merchandise, subject to men's desires', 'freed from her home' to be thrown into the public world where she is exposed to 'sexual aggressions'. Furthermore, 'one can no more distinguish men from women' (Boatta and Cherifati-Merabtine 1994:194). In 1909 Bahithat al-Badiya of Egypt rejected white feminist attacks on the veil by claiming the European woman 'makes a wall out of her face – a wall that she paints various colours' (Badran and Cooke 1990:233). A Chinese male comments on the brassy sexuality of American women with their 'heavy foreign perfume', 'artificially painted face', 'blood-red lips' – all 'ridiculous' in his eyes (Xing 1990:222). In 1978 two Indian women, Girija Khanna and Mariamma Varghese, reported on Indian women's 'healthy attitude to sex' because they did not make a great issue of sexual satisfaction in marriage or engage in adultery. They also noted the 'mental maturity' that allows 90 per cent of Indian women to refuse to indulge 'madly' in fashion (Caplan 1979:464).

In almost direct contradiction of these images, white western women are criticised for being unfeminine by the standards of some cultures, perhaps a reflection of more gender-neutral dress and a proclivity for exercise at least in some quarters. In combination with their more muscular bodies, western women are also sometimes seen as too forthright. 'As for Swiss women, they are the frankest as well as the least feminine in the world' (Mei Yuan, 1990:3–4). Japanese Nomura-san, a retired Takarazienne (an all-female theatrical company which plays male and female roles) said, 'We often watch Western women to understand better how to act like a man' (Davidson 1993:89).

In China a woman who is labelled a feminist is conceived of as a sort of 'monster', a 'mannish woman' (Ding 1991:111). The adjectives used to describe feminists by eight younger members of Singapore's women's association Aware (Association of Women for Action and Research) included 'militant, lesbian, bra-burning, anti-men ... sexually promis-cuous ... really not women, really aggressive, women who don't shave their legs ... ranting and raving' (Lyons-Lee 1995:3). To Hira Jhamtani (1991:99) of Indonesia, women's liberation accepts masculinity as sup-erior and prescribes the masculinisation of the female (see also Bhasin and Khan 1986:1 for India and Cheung's 1994:60 response to United States feminism in the 1970s).

While one of my Beijing students in 1993 drew an analogy between the beauty myth and foot-binding, my students could hardly come to grips with silicone implants and anorexia, so prevalent in the west. They tentatively suggested that, in contrast to their own stable sense of self-worth as females, western women must be lacking in self-respect and dignity. Similarly Indrani Ganguly (interview 18 May 1994) noted, 'I was really quite shocked to find out how far very intelligent and otherwise quite independent women would starve themselves, to conform to pretty unrealistic expectations'. There have been a variety of explanations for the prevalence of anorexia among middle class western adolescent women, suggesting both grotesque conformity to white western beauty standards and a rejection of motherhood (possibly because they are in a mother-rejecting culture). Thus Liu Yung Ho (1990:76) is astonished that breastfeeding in public is against the law in the West, and yet women wander around in public in 'low-cut tops and even bikinis'. (Breastfeeding is allowed in public in Australia, guaranteed on the basis of anti-discrimination legislation. But many men find it distasteful.)

Linked to the beauty myth, then, is the idea that white western women are forever young and sexy individuals, while women elsewhere graduate to connectivity and motherhood. When one political refugee woman in Denmark noted 'Will you hear the truth? I do not like your life, for sexual freedom is not good. We think about sexuality in a different way from people in the West. We feel that it is holy', Agger (1994:27) reflects that when women's purity as a 'social symbol ceases to function', 'the institution of marriage becomes threatened'. The lack of family feeling in the west is sometimes associated with a compulsive pursuit of 'love' and romance (Mei Yuan 1990:5), the dyadic couple's relations displacing those with children (Wu Ping 1990:126–9). Divorce is explained as a product of this individualism (Xie Shihao 1990:162). Chen Fan (1990:193), however, comes to the reluctant conclusion that 'quite a few Chinese couples have virtually separated, but they remain together for the sake of so-called virtue'. But for some observers, these differences are overdrawn. An Arab woman asserts, 'it is not true there is no family feeling in Europe' (Shaaban 1988:128). Shang Rongguang (1990:166-7, 171) suggests Americans are 'normal, not much different from us Chinese' in 'the common values of family, friendship, and love shared by all peoples'; 'they care as much about their relatives and friends as the Chinese do'.

White women have also been asked to reflect upon the politics of sexual liaisons with men of colour. For some these are an expression of race superiority, which stigmatises the woman of colour as less desirable (Badran and Cooke 1990:235; Collins 1990:191; Huata 1993:123). For others, black men might also be saying 'f— you whitey', sending a message to white men, rather than expressing affection for white women (Australian Aboriginal respondent in Burgmann 1984:27).

Although a dominant group rarely has to confront this, just as 'Aboriginality' 'arises from the experience of both Aboriginal and non-Aboriginal people who engage in any inter-cultural dialogue' (Langton 1993:82, 81), 'so does whiteness' (Parlo Singh, pers. comm. 1995). Both whiteness and Aboriginality arise from its definition in opposition to and in relation with the 'other'. Given this, it is surprising how difficult it is for Anglo-westerners to define their racial identities. Michael King (1985) set this quest rolling in the Antipodes with his autobiography which explored the notion of 'being Pakeha'. In his edited collection on the same theme, all fourteen contributors bar one (Jim Traue 1991:70) defined being Pakeha at least in part through a dialogue with Maori-ness: 'One essential ingredient of Pakeha-ness, as far as I am concerned, is contact with and being affected by Maori things' (King 1991:9). Connection with the land is a common theme, occasionally asserted as just as important for Pakehas as Maoris. 'I don't think any Maori could love his or her tribal lands more passionately than I love the hills of my childhood' (Catley 1991:40); 'I think the landscape is more crucial to our identity than it is in older nations, where culture suffices' (Head 1991:23).

Inspired by these books, Duncan Graham (1994:19) asked a group of prominent Australians to address the issue of 'being Whitefella'. Again, although possibly cued by Graham's (1994:21) checklist of questions, most writers traversed familiar public territory, covering the need for racial justice and their early ignorance of things and people Aboriginal. But this is clearly preferable to the response of some white people who claim their own subordination in the face of equality legislation, for example David Duke's founding of the National Association for the Advancement of White People (Roman 1993:72) or an Anglo-Celtic Australian male who wrote in 1989 that the ascendancy of multiculturalism and feminism has meant the marginalisation and oppression of his identity in much the same way as Aborigines are oppressed (in Hatzimanolis 1993:131). Some echoed the New Zealand contributors in referring to land, one further speaking of Aboriginal cultural knowledge giving access to 'our other selves' (Laurie 1994:61). Similarly, Veronica Brady (1994: 136–9) drew a parallel between her Catholic perception of the 'sacred' and Aboriginal perceptions, noting her childhood sadness for a land imprisoned in asphalt, but also warning against romanticising traditional Aboriginal culture. Ted Egan (1994:74) suggests 'she'll be right' and just 'being one of the mob' are attitudes ascribed to white Australian culture but inherited from Indigenous Australian culture.

Similarly, Ruth Frankenberg's (1993:32–3) interviews with women in the United States revealed that 'while their feelings about racism were frequently intense, the issue did not feel as though it was about their own identities'. They had learned a 'color- and power-evasive repertoire', so that they felt 'either one does not have anything to say about race, or one is apt to be deemed "racist" simply by having something to say'. Being white was 'formless', only taking 'shape in relation to other people' (Frankenberg 1993:196), bland like bread, lacking in vitality. Other cultures are about 'culture', meanings, colour. White culture was an 'unmarked marker' of the norm, but a despised norm, partly because it was tainted by power (Frankenberg 1993:198–200), 'power from unearned privilege' (McIntosh 1992:78). Without knowing one's own culture, solidarity work is impossible, as Joan Wingfield (in Ishtar 1994:242) suggests: 'Everybody's got a culture. You White people have got a culture. What is it? Where is it? Do you know? Because it's important if you're doing solidarity work with Indigenous women to know where you are coming from'. This lack of knowledge, this 'infantilization of judgement' makes whites either racist or anti-racist, but only in the abstract, lacking engagement with real individuals and issues (Lugones 1990b:53). While white culture clearly is about race privilege, it is about other signs of difference as well. When speaking about an indigenous other, whiteness may be expressed in terms of race privilege. But in daily living, the contributors to *Whitefella* are possibly as unable to locate their ethnic identity as the women with whom Frankenberg spoke.

It thus appears likely that subordinated groups in predominantly white nations know both their own culture of origin and that of the oppressor better than the oppressor knows either. In fact Frankenberg's respondents who were most able to articulate a white culture had lived with people of colour. Even so, one of them, Cathy, felt 'eclipsed by the enormity' of Miranda's Chicano culture. Miranda learned little of Cathy's culture, Cathy feeling this would have been tantamount to imposing assimilation (Frankenberg 1993:121).

Women from beyond the white west have provided some reverse and even contradictory stereotypes, as perforce they must be, whereby 'women readers in the "First World" are able to re-evaluate the cultural assumptions which inform their own readings' (Nasta 1991:xvii). From the perspective of the other (whoever our other may be) we can look back with fresh eyes and question ourselves: 'It would seem that if the outsider wants you to understand how she sees you and you have given your account of how you see yourself to her, there is a possibility of genuine dialogue between the two' (Lugones and Spelman 1990:25).

We turn now to how this dialogue must straddle both women's differences and our similarities, how it must acknowledge our infinitely determined lives while also finding the convergences which can ground political and theoretical work, to talk and act about women as though they were a category which made some sense.

COALITION POLITICS

> [Other indigenous women] can understand a lot better than most Whites ... We're not all the same, we have differences but they can accept the differences without trying to change us to being the same as them ... Many Whites don't accept differences.
>
> – Joan Wingfield in Ishtar 1994:154

My arguments here are encapsulated in Susan Stanford Friedman's (1995) comparison of two discourses about difference within feminism. The first we met in the Introduction, a script of denial from white women ('I'm a feminist so how could I be a racist?', 'I'm oppressed so how could I be an oppressor?'). This elicited from women of colour a script of accusation, that white women trivialised or distorted the differences of race in women's lives. During the 1980s and 1990s, scripts of confession ('I'm so guilty that I can't do anything but think about how guilty I am') 'mushroomed in response'. White feminists dwelt on their 'frozen guilt' but in the process produced 'a fetishization of women of color that once again reconstitutes them as other caught in the gaze of white feminist desire' (Friedman 1995:10, 11). We met this response in Chapter 1 in the section on 'Post-Colonial Desire' and Rey Chow's notion of submission.

There are two major problems with these scripts (besides the way they paralyse the speakers into political passivity). First, the implied binarism means that we lose the multiplicity of possible conversations between others: a Korean to a Japanese woman, a Greek-Australian to an Indigenous Australian, a Hindu to a Muslim woman and so on. Second, they focus almost exclusively on aspects of oppression and privilege based on ethnicity (Friedman 1995:14). Instead, Friedman (1995:17) recommends that we construct and define our identities in a fluid manner, in response to those changing others with whom we are in dialogue: feminists of colour are 'women without a line. We are women who contradict each other' (Cherrie Moraga in Sandoval 1991:15). When an Indigenous Australian woman speaks to me, she quite possibly feels her indigenous identity just as I feel my white identity; we may or may not find some shared experiences of being female. But when she is with another Indigenous Australian woman, she is more likely to feel whether she is Koori or Murri, how she is kin-connected to this other woman.

It is a commonplace of our everyday relations that we are something different in bed with a lover, at a family dinner, with our workmates and in political activist groups. The significance of thinking about these differences within a feminist framework is twofold. First, not all identities are equally powerful, in terms of the resources or respect they command, and we must remember this. The lessons of marxism (loosely defined) remind us that we cannot wish all differences into the same impact: some of us have more money, more power, more influence, more comfort, than others. And one's comfort is connected to another's lack of comfort: 'That which divides us may also connect us, but will not easily unite us' (Monk et al. 1991:241). 'It is not difference that is feared, Cherrie Moraga notes, but similarity'. The oppressor 'fears he will have to change his life once he has seen himself in the bodies of the people he has called different' (in Razack 1994:913). Maria Mies and Vandana Shiva (1993:12–13) argue for the (universal) 'subsistence knowledge' necessary for survival, and which is superior to western enlightenment knowledge. They claim there are universal fundamental needs 'for food, shelter, clothing; for affection, care and love; for dignity and identity, for knowledge and freedom, leisure and joy' which they propose should replace so-called universal but in fact western rights (Mies and Shiva 1993:13). As eco-feminists with a material-ist (marxist) understanding of exploitation, they claim connections be-tween consumerism in the west and disasters like Bhopal and Chernobyl, biotechnology, genetic engineering, feminist spirituality and peace move-ments (Mies and Shiva 1993:19). Thus they eschew western dualisms for a new kind of universalism, or interconnection based on human needs.

Second, the possibilities of connection and the impossibilities of differ-ence determine the political coalitions we are capable of forming with other women, determine both the other women with whom we may work and over what issues. But we cannot begin to separate the differences from the similarities until we understand the history, the culture, the resources, the world-view of other women. The first steps of that task have been taken in this book. It means moving beyond the half-truths of stereotypes, for example in the opposition between sexually defined white woman and the 'black matriarch'. It means understanding the cultural embeddedness of different practices, like veiling, sati or polygamy, questioning both ethnocentric descriptions of these practices and the universal applicability of individualist rights-based discourses, even if finally we want to criticise these practices from a feminist standpoint. It means understanding where the dualisms between first and third worlds come from, how they are based on real but connected inequalities between women in the pathways of global economic exploitation.

A practical example of the various approaches white women take to an issue concerns claims that NESB women suffer more domestic violence and use support services less than women from Anglo-Australian backgrounds. This is usually explained in terms of the 'patriarchal nature' of those women's cultures ('bad' culture, if you like). But it may also be explained in terms of greater respect for the family and community ('good' culture). In fact there are considerable structural disadvantages faced by non-English-speaking migrant women to Australia which may both explain the higher incidence of domestic violence and the reluctance to use mainstream services. These would be structural disadvantages for English-speaking women if they went to live in a foreign non-English-speaking culture, in Vietnam or Latin America, for example. These disadvantages include the stress of relocation, the fact that until 1991 women who were the partners of primary applicants for migration but who separated from their partners were liable to deportation (and many women may still not know of the legislative changes), comparative lack of access to English classes in comparison to men, lack of recognition of their qualifications, lack of an extended family to offer support in situations of domestic violence, the cultural unsuitability of Anglo-run refuges and the widely reported male bias of Australia's judiciary which does not encourage confidence in its ability to support women (Ethnic Policy Unit 1993:1–2).

Another example of how power relations between ethnic groups change, and in that shift alter the prospects of cross-cultural dialogue, is offered by Ann duCille (1994:613). Reading Adrienne Rich's *Of Woman Born*, duCille was positive until she encountered the silent nameless 'Black mother' who nursed the young Adrienne but 'has no identity of her own' and does not exist beyond her connection with Adrienne. Rich both denied the subjectivity of this woman and her 'material poverty'. Reflecting on her own classes where students from different backgrounds can 'disagree without being disagreeable, and . . . learn from and with each other', duCille (1994:616, 624–5) wonders what would have happened if she had been able to read Rich's book in manuscript and tell Rich, not the readers of *Signs*, her problems with 'my Black mother': 'However idle they may appear, for me these speculations about what might have been offer a measure of hope about what yet might be' (duCille 1994:625).

The politics of difference is expressed in Bernice Johnson Reagon's distinction between 'home' and 'coalition'. An African-American from Georgia, Reagon was active in the civil rights movement and sings in the group Sweet Honey and the Rock. She contrasts coalition-building with the nurturing but 'little barred room' of home. Home, like nationalism, enables identity formation and establishes shared interests, but it also produces xenophobia (Reagon 1983:358). Only those who share the same identity, who are oppressed or oppressors in the same way, can join the 'homeland of the mind' (Jenny Bourne in Kappeler 1995:231). For a long time, middle-class white feminists thought all-women gatherings were home gatherings. But then some 'other' women – women of colour, disabled women, working-class women and so on – sought entrance. This proved that what women do together is coalition work and not nurturing work: 'Coalition work is not work done in your home. Coalition work has to be done in the streets. And it is some of the most dangerous work you can do' (Reagon 1983:359).

With identity politics, 'to know friend from foe we do not need to analyse their actions and the political implications and consequences; we only need to consult their identity' (Kappeler 1995:239). Ien Ang (1995: 57–8, 73, 60; 1996:39, 42–4) makes the same point using the concept of multicultural nation. Multiculturalism is deployed by Anglo-feminists to 'invite' other women in, thus expressing rather than undermining privilege. The home is assumed to be based on 'commonality and community', when 'there are moments at which no common ground exists whatsoever'. Thus feminism can only be 'a *limited* political home, which does not absorb difference' but which 'leaves room for ambivalence and ambiguity'. By ambivalence Ang means an affective state where we invest two mutually exclusive desires with intense emotional energy so that neither can be abandoned. Thus we must achieve 'acceptance through difference, inclusion by virtue of otherness'. Unfortunately, the 'real tensions' associated with living in a culturally diverse society and the 'feelings of resentment and animosity they can induce' are repressed as 'racist' rather than expressed. To avoid being labelled racist, some white liberals do not discuss difference, for example difficult issues like clitoridectomy or intra-Aboriginal rape. Even asking someone ethnically marked as different 'Where are you from?' can elicit an angry response from some people, tolerant repetition of an answer often given from others, and from others again, a genuine pleasure that someone has shown an interest in their ethnic specificity. The white interlocutor must learn to take the risk the question carries, must learn to understand why there might be a range of responses, and not to respond to an angry or bored response with her own anger.

Coalition work is necessary because the reality of life is that many kinds of people live in the world. We must accept and include women from different ethnicities and backgrounds, because that is to accept reality and to minimise the chance that other women might endanger us and our projects (on coalitions and alliances, see Anzaldúa 1990b:23–4; Pheterson 1990:36–48; Albrecht and Brewer 1990:4–5; Alperin 1990:28; Bunch 1990:54; West 1990:161, 166–7). Through coalitions, we strive to know more, while at the same time risking not knowing and rejection (Probyn 1993:163). It is only possible to enter this realm by shattering the 'unitary sense of self'; coalitions mean being 'threatened to the core' if they are to work (Reagon in Sandoval 1991:23). But there have been coalitions, or at least constellations, of women expressing both their difference and their connectedness under the banner of female, not the least powerful of which has been women working together at United Nations meetings. But women express their difference and their connectedness at music and arts festivals, in the work of collectives and project teams (Frye 1996: 1006). We now take it for granted that many voices and colours will be encountered in a women's bookstore or at a women's studies conference.

This might seem a mundane, even obvious, conclusion for such a far-reaching text. If this is so, it is because of the work done by women of colour who have raised the issues which undergird this book. While it is now obvious to most feminists that the word 'man' rarely meant women, it has taken men a longer time to see the point (some still don't). Similarly, it has taken a considerable epistemological toil for white feminists to see that for many years they said 'women' but were thinking only of themselves. We can see how such an excessively inclusive use of the term was no doubt based on white women's inability to see the specifics of their own race and culture. Even if 'we' (white feminists) can now see these things, that does not guarantee that we will speak appropriately, especially when we enter the complex terrain of speaking to other women.

I hope, however, that white western readers of this book have acquired the capacity for 'world-travelling' (of 'understanding how other women might see you') combined with 'loving perception' or 'seeing each potential friend at home, in her own cultural context', as Marilyn Frye (in Gaard 1993:310) calls it. World-travelling is based on knowledge of the cultural specificities of other lives, a knowledge towards which this book makes a start. But such knowledge must be read in multiple shuttles. Orientalism or Rey Chow's notion of submission studied the 'other', but only to distance it from the self. World-travelling brings back knowledge of the other to question practices in our own culture, for example anorexia, breast implants or abortion. To add a postmodernist twist to this earnest endeavour, Argentinian-born Maria Lugones (1990a:401, 398) suggests playfulness, openness to playing the fool and to self-(re)construction from our world-travelling. Lugones suggests using stereotypes to parody, mime and mimic characteristics in ourselves.

Thus coalition work is the product of accepting differences between women as well as similarities, and, hardest of all, working out which is which at any one time. A pointer for doing this is the suggestion by Indrani Ganguly (1995b:4) that when white women see difference, it is often to construct the other woman as more oppressed or backward. White women are more reluctant to see difference as differences of power between women. When white women see similarity, it is to muster support for a particular (white feminist–defined) cause. Similarity is ignored, however, in the effort to prove that other women are more oppressed. Coalition work does not mean submission to the other. As Maria Lugones (1990b:52) asserts, it can be 'politically correct' to prefer one's own culture and kin, not as 'better than other people's' but 'dearer to me than other people's'. Coalition work certainly does not advocate incorporation of the other. It means walking the tightrope of connection, distance and power. As Elspeth Probyn (1993:163) says, in recognising our uncommon humanity, we know that 'without her I am nothing'.

NOTES

Introduction

1. Lenore Lyons-Lee (1995:6) reports similar attitudes among feminists in Singapore's Aware (Association of Women for Action and Research) when younger members felt that 'Aware was pandering too much to the patriarchs'. After a meeting between the two groups, most younger members had a clearer understanding of the need for a conciliatory approach as well as 'a sense of respect for the wisdom of their elders'. Several, who could not agree with AWARE's direction, disengaged from it.
2. For example, early radical feminists made claims about 'the *forceful* suppression of women's inordinate sexual demands' given women's capacity for multiple orgasm (Mary Jane Sherfey in Jaggar 1983:89), 'the tyranny of their reproductive biology' (Shulamith Firestone in Jaggar 1983:92), that female anatomy allows male rape (Susan Brownmiller in Jaggar 1983:90), which is represented in pornography eroticising women's pain, humiliation and murder. One can understand the focus on the female body by radical feminists as the basis of universal oppression. All women appear to have much the same kind of body: 'It is on the basis of their shared experience as bio-culturally female beings that women have started to speak in their own voice, distancing it from masculine experience' (Rosi Bradiotti in Moore 1994:85). Bradiotti urges a materiality based on 'the corporeal ground of our intelligence' and sees political action emerging from the requirement to control our own bodies and the desire to 'touch the unity and resonance of our physicality' (in Moore 1994:86).
3. The proposed change was defeated at a referendum in 1992, six out of ten provinces voting against it (*Times Higher Education Supplement* 23 October 1992:44; *Independent* 24 August 1992:10).

1 Fracturing Binarisms

1. The 'concessions' were agreements forced on China after its defeat by the British in 1842 and the Japanese in 1895. Concessions were signed between China and, principally, Britain, France, the United States and Japan. The first concessions allowed extra-territoriality (foreign law prevailed over Chinese law in concession districts). Over the years the foreign powers gained the right to build churches, hospitals, factories and so to create, virtually unhindered, their cultural and economic institutions on Chinese soil (Clifford 1991:16–18).
2. Arizpe 1990:xix for Latin America; Shaaban 1988:92–3, 105, 123, 126 for Lebanon; Mernissi 1991:23 for the Arab world; Ong 1987 for Malaysia; Obbo 1989:85–6 for Idi Amin's 1972 command that women wear long dresses in imitation of traditional clothing; Heng and Devan 1992:348–9 for Prime Minister Lee Kuan Yew's recommendations that Singapore return to concubinage and child marriages; Hawley and Proudfoot 1994:32–3 for the upsurge of 'religious machismo' in the United States, the Army of Shiva in India and

among Gush Emunin Jews. Note that Kalpana Ram (1991b:xvii) suggests that colonised men have also been forced into a culture of compromise in their dress, work, and resistance to colonial rule. Where women have been asked to uphold tradition, men have been forced to cast tradition aside in order to appear ready for independence.

3. Marie-Aimée Hélie-Lucas (1994:393) claims that Muslim means 'the social reality of the Muslim world as it is – people, countries, states, laws and customs', while Islam means 'religion as such, theological reflections and interpretations of the Quran', 'so that there are Muslim states not Islamic ones'.

4. For a discussion of women in post-Soviet Europe, see Einhorn 1993; Lykke et al. 1994:112; Jogan 1994 for Slovenia; Petrova 1994:268–9, Harsanyi 1994:42 and Nicolaescu 1994:118 for Romania; Wolchik 1994:101 for the Czech and Slovak Republics; Zielinska and Plakwicz 1994:98 for Poland.

5. Bahrain, Kuwait, Oman, Qatar, Saudi Arabia and United Arab Emirates have between 48 and 91 women for every 100 men, although these rates are part-ially attributable to large immigrant male populations of guest workers. Other countries where there are between 90 and 95 women per 100 men include Nepal, Bangladesh, India, Pakistan, Hong Kong, Papua New Guinea, Vanuatu, Turkey and Afghanistan (United Nations 1991:11).

6. While 'the Orient' and 'the East' are now equated with 'Asia', in fact the orient as something other than Europe has undergone transformations. When the Ottoman Turkish empire ruled much of Europe, a Christian Europe was dis-tinguished from an Islamic Asia (which included Greece, the Levant, Albania and Bulgaria) known as the 'Near East'. Today this same area, with the addition of Muslim-dominated North Africa and the subtraction of European lands, is called the Middle East. Later Caucasian or European racial stock countries, which also practised the monotheistic religions of Islam and Judaeo-Christianity, were opposed to 'Hither Asia' as Hegel termed it: India, China, Japan, Central and South-East Asia (Inden 1990:50–1).

7. The Chinese today refer to their 'four thousand years of recorded history' (Song in Fang and Hay 1992:155).

2 Individual versus Community

1. Provided by UN Information Centre, Sydney, on internet, listowner-beijing-conf@tristram.edc.org, 17 October 1995.

2. For example, see the cases of *Struck v Secretary of Defense* 409 U.S. 1071 (1972); *Geduldig v Aiello* 417 U.S. 484 (1974); *General Electric Company v Gilbert* 429 U.S. 125 (1976).

3. Not only westerners are orientalist. From another cultural centre, one Chinese commentator condemns the tradition-bound British and 'century-old customs' like 'the black veils worn by women in the Arab world, the burning alive of widows with their dead husbands in some Indian states and many other horrifying practices (Zhou Lishing 1990:29).

4. The term is put in quotation marks here because, as Emberley (1993:57) suggests, female circumcision is a 'phallocentric' term which fails to distinguish this experience from male circumcision. However, infibulation is not an acceptable substitute because it only describes one type of female circum-cision. Another term in use is female genital surgery.

5. Published in 1975 in Arabic as *Firdaus*.

6. See International Women's Development Agency, *9th Annual Report* (1994:6) on the Inter Africa Committee established in 1984 which works in twenty-six African countries; Robertson (1996:628–30) for Kenya.

3 Mothers and Wives

1. Malthus claimed that under uncontrolled circumstances, when food resources increased people had more children so that population was always pressing at the limits of resource availability. Such a hypothesis found a ready reception in the eugenics movement.
2. In Bombay a rise from 15 per cent to 71 per cent (Kabeer 1994:213). Programs have also been introduced in Hong Kong, Ireland and Sierra Leone.
3. A sex ratio of 1032 women for every 1000 men as opposed to 933 women for every 1000 men in India as a whole (Jeffrey 1992:5).
4. Here defined as the geographical area between Saudi Arabia and the Philippines which contains 59 per cent of the world's 5.3 billion people (with the largest populations being in China, India, Pakistan, Bangladesh, Japan and Indonesia).
5. Women earn 57 per cent of men's wages, one of the largest differentials in the developed world, and a differential which increases with age (Allison 1994:108; see also Hardacre 1994:124; Iwao 1993:160–1).
6. In the early 1980s in Papua New Guinea assaults against women rose, as did the incidence of unpaid maintenance (Rarua 1988:84–5). Sixty-seven per cent of rural wives in Papua New Guinea and Fiji have been hit by their husbands (Margaret Nakikus et al. 1991:86; Sabina Fuluvii at the 'Women in the Pacific: Health and Development Workshop', Brisbane, 22 October 1992). According to Jolly's (1996:178) research, violence was not prevalent in the 1970s in the South Pentecost societies (Vanuatu).

4 Sexual Identities

1. The *gopis* were the wives and daughters of the *gopas* or cowherds. Krishna was raised among the *gopis* of Brajabhumi.
2. My thanks to Lenore Lyons-Lee and Indrani Ganguly for providing me with the magazines on which this section is based.
3. A comparative survey of American and Japanese couples reveals these differences. Where 84 per cent of American men and 87 per cent of American women rated being in love as very important, only 67 per cent of Japanese men and 68 per cent of Japanese women did so (Iwao 1993:70).
4. I am grateful to my colleague Barbara Sullivan for this term.

5 The International Traffic in Women

1. In 1991 there were two women out of eighteen on the Economic, Social and Cultural Rights Committee, one out of eighteen on the Committee on the Elimination of Racial Discrimination, two out of eighteen on the Human Rights Committee, and two out of ten on the Committee against Torture (Vickers 1993:113, 112). In May 1990 the UN's Economic and Social Council resolved to ask the General Secretary to take measures to ensure that 35 per cent of professional posts were to be held by women in 1995.
2. The 32 200 registrations for the NGO Forum on Women included 14 800 from Europe and North America, 12 300 from Asia and the Pacific, 3200 from Africa, 2000 from Latin America and the Caribbean, and 3200 from Africa. The Australian NGO International Women's Development Agency funded several indigenous women and refugee women in exile to attend the forum as well as campaigning (unsuccessfully) for Tibetan women in exile to attend. They thus responded to the privileging of certain ethnic groups and those with a secure

citizenship as Conference and Forum attendees (International Women's Development Agency, *10th Annual Report 1994–1995*, Fitzroy, 1995:5).
3. Thus Egypt's statistics suggested that 3.6 per cent of the agricultural workforce were women; the World Survey showed that in lower Egypt half of the wives levelled and ploughed land while 55 to 70 per cent took part in important agricultural production activities. The Peruvian 1972 census suggested that 2.6 per cent of rural women were economically active; an interview study revealed that 86 per cent of women took part in agricultural field work (Pietilä and Vickers 1990:15). Indeed, in one-half of advanced horticultural countries, farming is exclusively women's business; in only 23 per cent is it exclusively men's business (Shiva 1988:105).
4. Furthermore, Odzer (1994:218) had an affair with a married Thai man, 'demanding he relinquish his family life when I had no intention of considering marriage'. She does note that prostitution is a result of poverty and inequality between men and women (Odzer 1994:309).
5. My thanks to Lenore Lyons-Lee for alerting me to this publication.
6. In 1986 22.7 per cent of Filipinas in Australia had a tertiary degree compared with 4.1 per cent of all overseas-born women and 3.3 per cent of third-generation or more Australian-born women (Jones 1991:54, 162). In 1993 13 per cent of NESB women held tertiary qualifications compared with 10 per cent of Australian-born women (*ANESBWA* (Association of Non-English Speaking Background Women of Australia) *Bulletin*, August 1995:2).
7. Producer co-operatives of homeworkers and other small producers extend the claims made by unions for wages and working conditions to include maternity leave, group insurance and retirement benefits to the home workers (Mitter 1994:32 on *bidi* home workers in Kerala). Producer co-operatives can become a purchasing co-operative to combat high prices for consumer goods, develop revolving loans schemes, locate alternative employment opportunities, or produce innovative solutions when union and management are at loggerheads (Mitter 1994:36; Jhabvala 1994:132–3).
8. Mernissi 1991:23 for Muslim societies; Lateef 1990:173–5 for India; Fakhro 1990:138, 140 for Bahrain; Warnock 1990:80 for Palestine. In Argentina, Uruguay, Chile, Brazil, Mexico and Cuba, there are strong correlations between the advent of public education and the rise of feminism (Miller 1991:35).

BIBLIOGRAPHY

Note: Books cited by surname and short title only occur in full elsewhere in the bibliography. Chinese names are generally used with family name first. In the text Chinese authors have been cited in full because the small number of Chinese family names would make them difficult to distinguish; where a name appears in the Bibliography without a comma between family and given names, that is the order which appears in the original work.

Abdalla, Raqiha Haji Dwaleh (1982) *Sisters in Affliction: Circumcision and Infibulation of Women in Africa.* London: Zed Books

Abdullah, Hussaina (1995) 'Wifeism and Activism: The Nigerian Women's Movement' in Basu, *The Challenge of Local Feminisms*

Abdulrahim, Dima (1993) 'Defining Gender in a Second Exile: Palestinian Women in West Berlin' in Gina Buijs, ed., *Migrant Women: Crossing Boundaries and Changing Identities.* Oxford: Berg

Accad, Evelyne (1991) 'Sexuality and Sexual Politics: Conflicts and Contradictions for Contemporary Women in the Middle East' in Mohanty, *Third World Women and the Politics of Feminism*

Adam, Barry D. (1986) 'Age, Structure, and Sexuality: Reflections on the Anthropological Evidence on Homosexual Relations', *Journal of Homosexuality* 11(3/4):19–33

Adolph, José B. (1971) 'The South American Macho: Mythos and Mystique', *Impact of Science on Society* 21(1):83–92

Afarq, Janet (1992) 'The Debate on Women's Liberation in the Iranian Constitutional Revolution, 1906–1911' in Johnson-Odim and Strobel, *Expanding the Boundaries of Women's History*

Agarwal, Bina (1996) 'From Mexico 1975 to Beijing 1995', *Indian Journal of Gender Studies* 3(1):86–92

Agger, Inger (1994) *The Blue Room: Trauma and Testimony Among Refugee Women: A Psycho-Social Exploration.* London: Zed Books

Ahmed, Leila (1982) 'Western Eurocentrism and Perceptions of the Harem', *Feminist Studies* 8(2):521–34

Aitchison, Jim and Theseus Chan (1994) *Sarong Party Girl.* Singapore: Angsana Books

Albrecht, Lisa and Rose M. Brewer, eds (1990) *Bridges of Power: Women's Multicultural Alliances.* Philadelphia: New Society Publishers

Alcoff, Linda (1992) 'The Problem of Speaking for Others', *Cultural Critique* 20 (Winter 1991–92):5–32

Aldunate, Raquel (1995) 'Land Mark Decision at Refugee Review Tribunal', *Sister's Say . . .* Women's Legal Service Newsletter, April:6–7

Alfaro, Rosa María (1994) 'Women as Social Agents of Communication: Social Maternity and Leadership' in Pilar Riaño, ed., *Women in Grassroots*

Communication: Furthering Social Change. Thousand Oaks, Calif. and London: Sage

Al-Khayyat, Sana (1990) *Honour and Shame: Women in Modern Iraq.* London: Al Saqi Books

Allen, Paula Gunn (1986) *The Sacred Hoop: Recovering the Feminine in American Indian Traditions.* Boston: Beacon Press

Allen, Paula Gunn (1990) 'Some Like Indians Endure' in Anzaldúa, *Making Face, Making Soul*

Allison, Anne (1994) *Nightwork: Sexuality, Pleasure, and Corporate Masculinity in a Tokyo Hostess Club.* Chicago: University of Chicago Press

Allison, Anne (1996) 'Producing Mothers' in Imamura, *Re-Imaging Japanese Women*

Alperin, Davida J. (1990) 'Social Diversity and the Necessity of Alliances: A Developing Feminist Perspective' in Albrecht and Brewer, *Bridges of Power*

Altman, Dennis (1992) 'AIDS and the Discourses of Sexuality' in R. W. Connell and G. W. Dowsett, eds, *Rethinking Sex: Social Theory and Sexuality Research.* Melbourne: Melbourne University Press

Amsden, Alice H. (1990) 'Third World Industrialization: "Global Fordism" or a New Model?', *New Left Review* 182:5–31

Ang, Ien (1995) 'I'm a Feminist But ... "Other" Women and Postnational Feminism' in Barbara Caine and Rosemary Pringle, eds, *Transitions: New Australian Feminisms.* Sydney: Allen & Unwin

Ang, Ien (1996) 'The Curse of the Smile: Ambivalence and the "Asian" Woman in Australian Multiculturalism', *Feminist Review* 52:36–49

Ann, T. K. (1987) *Cracking the Chinese Puzzles.* Hong Kong: Stockflows

Anson, Stan (1991) 'The Postcolonial Fiction', *Arena* 96:64–6

Anthias, Floya and Nira Yuval-Davis (1983) 'Contextualizing Feminism – gender, ethnic and class divisions', *Feminist Review* 62–75

Anthias, Floya and Nira Yuval-Davis (1992) *Racialized Boundaries: Race, Nation, Gender, Colour and Class in the Anti-Racist Struggle.* London and New York: Routledge

Anzaldúa, Gloria, ed. (1990a) *Making Face, Making Soul: Haciendo Caras.* San Francisco: Aunt Lute Books

Anzaldúa, Gloria (1990b) 'Bridge, Drawbridge, Sandbar or Island' in Albrecht and Brewer, *Bridges of Power*

Apffel-Marglin, Frédérique (1994) 'The Sacred Groves', *Manushi* 82:22–32

Apffel-Marglin, Frédérique and Suzanne L. Simon (1994) 'Feminist Orientalism and Development' in Wendy Harcourt, ed., *Feminist Perspectives on Sustainable Development.* London: Zed Books

Arboleda, Manuel G. and Stephen O. Murray (1985) 'The Dangers of Lexical Inference With Special Reference to Maori Homosexuality', *Journal of Homosexuality* 12(1):129–33

Arcand, Bernard (1994) *The Jaguar and the Anteater: Pornography Degree Zero*, transl. Wayne Grady. London: Verso [first published Montreal, 1991]

Ariès, Philippe (1989) Introduction to Roger Chartier, ed., *A History of Private Life* vol. 3. General eds Philippe Ariès and Georges Duby. Cambridge, Mass.: Belknap, Harvard University Press

Arizpe, Lourdes (1990) 'Forward: Democracy for a Small Two-Gender Planet' in Elizabeth Jelin, ed., *Women and Social Change in Latin America*, transl. J. Ann Zammit and Marilyn Thomson. London: Zed Books

Atkinson, Jane Monnig (1990) 'How Gender Makes a Difference in Wana Society' in Jane Monnig Atkinson and Shelly Errington, eds, *Power and Difference: Gender in Island Southeast Asia*. Stanford: Stanford University Press

Atkinson, Jeff (1995) 'Child Labour', *Horizons*, newsletter of Community Aid Abroad, 3(4):8–9

Attwood, Bain (1992) Introduction to Bain Attwood and John Arnold, eds, *Power, Knowledge and Aborigines: Special Issue of Journal of Australian Studies*. Melbourne: La Trobe University Press in association with the National Centre for Australian Studies, Monash University, Melbourne

Auluck-Wilson, Clarice A. (1995) 'When All the Women Lift', *Signs: Journal of Women in Culture and Society* 20(4):1029–38

Awekotuku, Ngahuia Te (1991) *Mana Wahine Maori: Selected Writings on Maori Women's Art, Culture and Politics*. Auckland: New Women's Press

Azim, Firdaus (1995) 'Towards Beijing' Conference, Centre for Asia Pacific Studies, Victoria University of Technology, St Albans, Vic., 9–11 February

Bacchi, Carol (1990) *Same Difference*. Sydney: Allen & Unwin

Badran, Margot and Miriam Cooke, eds (1990) *Opening the Gates: A Century of Arab Feminist Writing*. London: Virago

Ballhatchet, Kenneth (1980) *Race, Sex and Class Under the Raj: Imperial Attitudes and Policies and their Critics, 1793–1905*. London: Weidenfeld & Nicolson

Banerjee, Sumanta (1990) 'Marginalization of Women's Popular Culture in Nineteenth Century Bengal' in Kumkum Sangari and Sudesh Vaid, eds, *Recasting Women: Essays in Indian Colonial History*. New Brunswick, New Jersey: Rutgers University Press

Baranay, Inez (1995) 'The Edge of Bali' in Robyn Gerster, ed., *Hotel Asia: An Anthology of Australian Literary Travelling to Asia*. Melbourne: Penguin

Barlow, Toni E. (1994) 'Theorizing Woman: *Funü, Guojia Jiating*' in Angelo Zito, ed., *Body, Subject and Power in China*. Chicago: University of Chicago Press

Barrett, Michèle (1992) 'Words and Things: Materialism and Method in Contemporary Feminist Analysis' in Michèle Barrett and Anne Phillips, eds, *Destabilizing Theory: Contemporary Feminist Debates*. Cambridge: Polity Press

Barrett, Michèle and Mary McIntosh (1982) *The Anti-social Family*. London: Verso

Barwick, Diane E. (1970) ' "And the Lubras are Ladies Now": Victorian Aboriginal Women on Mission Stations 1860–1886' in Faye Gale, ed., *Women's Position in Aboriginal Society*. Canberra: Australian Institute of Aboriginal Studies

Basu, Amrita, ed. (1995) Introduction to *The Challenge of Local Feminisms: Women's Movement in Global Perspective*. New York: Westview Press

Basu, Rekha (1981) 'Sexual Imperialism: The Case of Indian Women in Britain', *Heresies* 12:71–3

Beall, Jo, Shireen Hassim and Alison Todes (1989) ' "A Bit on the Side"?: Gender Struggles in the Politics of Transformation in South Africa', *Feminist Review* 33:30–56

Bell, Diane (1991) 'Intraracial Rape Revisited: On Forging a Feminist Future Beyond Factions and Frightening Politics', *Women's Studies International Forum* 14(5):385–412

Bell, Diane (1996) 'Speaking of Things That Shouldn't Be Written: Cross-cultural Excursions into the Land of Misrepresentations' in Diane Bell and Renate Klein, eds, *Radically Speaking: Feminism Reclaimed*. Melbourne: Spinifex Press

Bell, Diane and Topsy Napurrula Nelson (1989) 'Speaking About Rape is Everyone's Business', *Women's Studies International Forum* 12(4):403–16

Bello, Walden and Stephanie Rosenfeld (1990) *Dragons in Distress: Asia's Miracle Economies in Crisis*. San Francisco: Institute for Food and Development Policy

Bernstein, Gail Lee, ed. (1991) Introduction to *Recreating Japanese Women, 1600–1945*. Berkeley: University of California Press

Bernstein, Gail Lee (1996) Afterword to Imamura, *Re-Imaging Japanese Women*

Bhabha, Homi K. (1986) 'Signs Taken for Wonders: Questions of Ambivalence and Authority Under a Tree Outside Delhi, May 1817' in Henry Louis Gates Jr, ed., *"Race," Writing, and Difference*. Chicago: University of Chicago Press

Bhabha, Homi (1991) 'The Postcolonial Critic – Homi Bhabha interviewed by David Bennett and Terry Collits', *Arena* 96:47–63

Bhabha, Homi K. (1994) *The Location of Culture*. New York: Routledge

Bhachu, Parminder (1993) 'Identities Constructed and Reconstructed: Representations of Asian Women in Britain' in Buijs, *Migrant Women*

Bhasin, Kamla and Nighat Said Khan (1986) *Some Questions on Feminism and its Relevance in South Asia*. New Delhi: Kali for Women

Blackburn, Susan (1993) *Practical Visionaries: A Study of Community Aid Abroad*. Melbourne: Melbourne University Press

Blackwood, Evelyn (1986) 'Breaking the Mirror: The Construction of Lesbianism and the Anthropological Discourse on Homosexuality', *Journal of Homosexuality* 11(3/4):1–18

Blackwood, Evelyn (1995) 'Senior women, model mothers, and dutiful wives: managing gender contradictions in a Minangkabau village' in Ong and Peletz, *Bewitching Women, Pious Men*

Blake, C. Fred (1994) 'Foot-binding in Neo-Confucian China and the Appropriation of Female Labor', *Signs* 19(3):676–712

Boatta, Cherifa and Doria Cherifati-Merabtine (1984) 'The Social Representation of Women in Algeria's Islamist Movement' in Moghadam, *Identity Politics and Women*

Bolt, Christine (1971) *Victorian Attitudes to Race*. London: Routledge & Kegan Paul

Bolton, Ralph (1979) 'Machismo in Motion: The Ethos of Peruvian Truckers', *Ethos* 7(4):312–42

Bonnell, Susanne (1982) 'Equal Participation by Women: The Role of Women's Councils at National and Provincial Level in Papua New Guinea', *Administration for Development* 19:30–1

Bordo, Susan (1990) 'Reading the Slender Body' in Mary Jacobus et al., eds, *Body/Politics: Women and the Discourses of Science*. New York: Routledge

Boserup, Ester (1970) *Women's Role in Economic Development*. London: George Allen & Unwin

Bottomley, Gill et al., eds (1991) *Intersexions: Gender/Class/Culture/Ethnicity*. Sydney: Allen & Unwin

Bowral, Peter (1983) 'Surrogate Procreation: A Motherhood Issue in Legal Obscurity', *Queen's Law Journal* 9:5–34

Boyle, Helen (1983) 'The Conflicting Role of Aboriginal Women in Today's Society' in Gale, Faye, ed., *We are Bosses Ourselves: The Status and Role of Aboriginal Women Today*. Canberra: Australian Institute of Aboriginal Studies.

Brady, Veronica (1994) 'The Presence which is Absence' in Duncan Graham, ed., *Being Whitefella*. Fremantle: Fremantle Arts Centre Press

Braithwaite, John (1989) *Crime, Shame and Reintegration*. Cambridge: Cambridge University Press

Brettell, Caroline B. and Carolyn F. Sargent (1993) 'Gender, Ritual and Religion' in Caroline B. Brettell and Carolyn F. Sargent, eds, *Gender in Cross-Cultural Perspective*. Englewood Cliffs, New Jersey: Prentice Hall

Brooks, Geraldine (1995) 'The Hidden World of Islamic Women', *The Australian Magazine* 25–26 February:12–23

Brownmiller, Susan (1994) 'Making Female Bodies the Battlefield' in Stiglmayer, *Mass Rape*

Brush, Lisa D. (1996) 'Love, Toil, and Trouble: Motherhood and Feminist Politics', *Signs* 21(2):429–54

Brussa, Licia (1989) 'Migrant Prostitutes in the Netherlands' in Gail Pheterson, ed., *A Vindication of the Rights of Whores*. Seattle: Seal Press

Bryan, Beverley, Stella Dadze and Suzanne Scafe (1985) *The Heart of the Race: Black Women's Lives in Britain*. London: Virago

Brydon, Lynne and Sylvia Chant (1989) *Women in the Third World: Gender Issues in Rural and Urban Areas*. Aldershot, UK: Edward Elgar

Buckley, Thomas (1993) 'Menstruation and the Power of Yurok Women' in Brettell and Sargent, *Gender in Cross-Cultural Perspective*

Buijs, Gina (1993) Introduction to Gina Buijs, ed., *Migrant Women: Crossing Boundaries and Changing Identities*. Oxford: Berg

Bulbeck, Chilla (1988) *One World Women's Movement*. London: Pluto

Bulbeck, Chilla (1991) 'Hearing the Difference: First and Third World Feminisms', *Asian Studies Review* 15(1):77–91

Bulbeck, Chilla (1994) 'Sexual Dangers: Chinese Women's Experiences in Three Cultures: Beijing, Taipei and Hong Kong', *Women's Studies International Forum* 17(1):95–103

Bullard, Nicola (1993) 'The World Agrees – Women's Rights are Human Rights', *International Women's Development Agency Report to Associates and Friends* 24(August):1–2

Bunch, Charlotte (1990) 'Making Common Cause Diversity and Coalitions' in Albrecht and Brewer, *Bridges of Power*

Burbank, Victoria Katherine (1994) *Fighting Women: Anger and Aggression in Aboriginal Australia*. Berkeley and Los Angeles: University of California Press

Burdack, Mark (1993) review of *Male Victims of Sexual Assault* by Mezey and King, eds, *Alternative Law Journal* 18(3):146–8

Burgmann, Meredith (1984) 'Black Sisterhood: The Situation of Urban Aboriginal Women and Their Relationship to the White Women's Movement' in Marian Simms, ed., *Australian Women and the Political System*. Melbourne: Longman Chesire

Butler, Judith (1990) *Gender Trouble: Feminism and the Subversion of Identity*. New York: Routledge

Butler, Judith (1993) *Bodies That Matter: On the Discursive Limits of "Sex"*. New York: Routledge

Bynam, Caroline Walker (1991) *Fragmentation and Redemption: Essays in Gender and the Human Body in Medieval Religions*. New York: Zone Books

Cahill, Desmond (1991) 'Refugees in Australia: Policy and Practice', *Asian Migrant* 2(3):81–3

Caldwell, John C. (1993) 'The Asian Fertility Revolution: Its Implications for Transition Theories' in Leete and Alam, *The Revolution in Asian Fertility*

Campbell, Beatrix (1987) *The Iron Ladies: Why Do Women Vote Tory?* London: Virago

Caplan, Ann Patricia (1979) 'Indian Women: Model and Reality. A Review of Recent Books, 1975–1979' *Women's Studies International Quarterly* 2:461–79

Caplan, Jane (1991) Afterword to Bernstein, *Recreating Japanese Women*

Carby, Hazel V. (1982) 'White Woman Listen! Black Feminism and the Boundaries of Sisterhood' in Centre for Contemporary Studies, ed., *The Empire Strikes Back: Race and Racism in 70s Britain*. London: Hutchinson

Carlitz, Katherine (1994) 'Desire, Danger, and the Body: Stories of Women's Virtue in Late Ming China' in Christina K. Gilmartin et al., eds, *Engendering China: Women, Culture and the State*. Cambridge, Mass.: Harvard University Press

Carmen et al. (1984) 'Becoming Visible: Black Lesbian Discussions', *Feminist Review* 17:53–72

Carnes, Mark C., ed. (1990) *Meanings for Manhood: Constructions of Masculinity in Victorian America*. Chicago: University of Chicago Press

Catley, Christine Cole (1991) 'Captaining the Canoe' in King, *Pakeha*

Chakrabarty, Dipesh (1994) 'Embodying Freedom: Gandhi and the Body of the Public Man in India', *Australian Cultural History* 13:100–10

Chakravarti, Uma (1990) 'Whatever Happened to the Vedic *Dasi*? Orientalism, Nationalism and a Script for the Past' in Kumkum Sangari and Sudesh Vaid, eds, *Recasting Women: Essays in Indian Colonial History*. New Brunswick, N.J.: Rutgers University Press

Chapkis, Wendy (1994a) 'Skin Deep' in Alison M. Jaggar, ed., *Living With Contradictions: Controversies in Feminist Social Ethics*. Boulder, Col.: Westview Press

Chapkis, Wendy (1994b) an interview with 'Marieme' in Alison M. Jaggar, ed., *Living With Contradictions: Controversies in Feminist Social Ethics*. Boulder, Col.: Westview Press

Charlton, Sue Ellen, Jan Everett and Kathleen Staudt (1989) Conclusion to Sue Ellen Charlton et al., eds, *Women, The State and Development*. Albany: State University of New York

Chase-Dunn, Christopher (1989) *Global Formation: Structures of the World Economy*. Oxford: Basil Blackwell

Chen Fan (1990) 'Americans and Divorce' in Wang Jianguang, *Westerners Through Chinese Eyes*

Ch'en Heng-Che (1992) 'Influences of Foreign Cultures' in Li Yu-Ning, ed., *Chinese Women Through Chinese Eyes*. New York: East Gate, Armonk

Chen Zhingming, Wang Xiao'ou and Chang Yuemin (1990) 'The Melting Pot and the Mosaic: A Comparison of Americans and Canadians' in Wang Jianguang, *Westerners Through Chinese Eyes*

Chesler, Phyllis (1988) *Sacred Bond: The Legacy of Baby M*. New York: Times Books (Random House)

Cheung, Fanny M. (1989) 'The Women's Centre: A Community Approach to Feminism in Hong Kong', *American Journal of Community Psychology* 17(1):99–107

Cheung, Fanny M. et al. (1996) 'Development of the Chinese Personality Assessment Inventory', *Journal of Cross-Cultural Psychology* 27(2):181–99

Chew, Shirley (1991) 'Searching Voices: Anita Desai's *Clear Light of Day* and Nayantara Sahgal's *Rich Like Us*' in Susheila Nasta, ed., *Motherlands: Black Women's Writing from Africa, the Caribbean and South Asia*. London: Women's Press

Chiang, Nora Lan-Hung (1994) 'A Personal Essay' in Lazarus et al., *Women's Studies, Women's Lives*

Chiang, Nora Lan-hung and Ku Yenlin (1985) 'Past and Current Status of Women in Taiwan', monograph no. 1, Taipei: Women's Research Program, Population Studies Centre, National Taiwan University

Chodorow, Nancy (1978) *The Reproduction of Mothering: Psychoanalysis and the Sociology of Gender*. Berkeley: University of California Press

Chow, Rey (1991a) *Woman and Chinese Modernity: The Politics of Reading Between East and West*. Minnesota: University of Minnesota Press

Chow, Rey (1991b) 'Violence in the Other Country: China as Crisis, Spectacle, and Woman' in Mohanty, *Third World Women and the Politics of Feminism*

Chu, Cordia M. (1992) *Reproductive Health Beliefs and Practices of Chinese and Australian Women*. Taipei and Nathan: Women's Research Program, Population Studies Center, National Taiwan University and Australian Institute for Women's Research and Policy, Griffith University, Qld.

Chua, Beng Huat (1992) 'Shopping for Women's Fashion in Singapore' in Shields, *Lifestyle Shopping*

Clammer, John (1992) 'Aesthetics of the Self: Shopping and Social Being in Contemporary Urban Japan' in Shields, *Lifestyle Shopping*

Clifford, Nicholas R. (1991) *Spoilt Children of the Empire: Westerners in Shanghai and the Chinese Revolution of the 1890s*. Hanover and London: Middlebury College Press

Collins, Jock (1988) *Migrant Hands in Distant Lands: Australia's Post-war Immigration*. Sydney: Pluto Press

Collins, Jock (1992) 'Migrant Hands in a Distant land' in Gillian Whitlock and David Carter, eds, *Images of Australia*. Brisbane: University of Queensland Press

Collins, Patricia Hill (1989) 'A Comparison of Two Works on Black Family Life', *Signs* 14(4):875–88

Collins, Patricia Hill (1990) *Black Feminist Thought: Knowledge, Consciousness, and the Politics of Empowerment*. Boston: Unwin Hyman

Coltrane, Scott (1992) 'The Micropolitics of Gender in Nonindustrial Societies', *Gender and Society* 6(1):86–107

Comaroff, Jean (1985) *Body of Power Spirit of Resistance*. Chicago and London: University of Chicago Press

Comaroff, Jean and John Comaroff (1991) *Of Revelation and Revolution: Christianity, Colonialism and Consciousness in South Africa* vol. 1. Chicago: University of Chicago Press

Connell, Robert W. (1990) 'A Whole New World: Remaking Masculinity in the Context of the Environmental Movement', *Gender and Society* 4(4):452–78

Connell, Robert W. (1991) 'Live Fast and Die Young: The Construction of Masculinity among Young Working-Class Men on the Margin of the Labour Market', *Australian and New Zealand Journal of Sociology* 27(2)141–71

Connell, R. W. (1992) 'A Very Straight Gay: Masculinity, Homosexual Experience, and the Dynamics of Gender', *American Sociological Review* 57(6):735–51

Connell, R. W. (1993) 'The Big Picture: Masculinities in Recent World History', *Theory and Society* 22:597–623

Connell, R. W. (1994) 'Masculinities: The Big Picture', seminar presented to Department of Anthropology and Sociology, University of Queensland, 28 October

Connell, R. W. (1995) *Masculinities*. Sydney: Allen & Unwin

Conway, Jill Ker (1993) 'Rethinking the Impact of Women's Education' in Jill Ker Conway and Susan C. Bourque, eds, *The Politics of Women's Education:*

Perspectives from Asia, Africa, and Latin America. Ann Arbor: University of Michigan Press

Conyebeare, Chris (1992) 'Difficulties of Women Immigrants Need Broader Understanding', *BIR Bulletin* 6:3–4

Coomaraswamy, Radhika (1986) 'Sri Lanka: Ethnicity and Patriarchy in the Third World' in Margaret Schuler, ed., *Empowerment and the Law: Strategies of Third World Women*. Washington: OEF International

Copelon, Rhonda (1994) 'Surfacing Gender: Reconceptualising Crimes Against Women in Time of War' in Stiglmayer, *Mass Rape*

Corbin, Alain (1990) 'Backstage' in Perrott, *A History of Private Life* vol. 4

Corea, Gena (1985) *The Mother Machine: Reproductive Technologies from Artificial Insemination to Artificial Wombs*. New York: Harper & Row

Cornell, Laurel L. (1991) 'The Deaths of Old Women: Folklore and Differential Mortality in Nineteenth-Century Japan' in Bernstein, *Recreating Japanese Women*

Counts, Dorothy Ayers (1993) 'The Fist, the Stick, and the Bottle of Bleach: Wife Bashing and Female Suicide in a Papua New Guinea Society' in Victoria S. Lockwood et al., eds, *Contemporary Pacific Societies: Studies in Development and Change*. Englewood Cliffs, N.J.: Prentice Hall

Courtright, Paul B. (1995) '*Satī*, Sacrifice and Marriage: The Modernity of Tradition' in Harlan and Courtwright, *From the Margins of Hindu Marriage*

Coward, Rosalind (1983) Preface to the British edition in Ann Snitow et al., eds, *Desire: The Politics of Sexuality*. London: Virago

Cowlishaw, Gillian (1988) *Black, White or Brindle: Race in Rural Australia*. Cambridge: Cambridge University Press

Cox, Elizabeth and Louise Aitsi (1988) 'Papua New Guinea' in Taiamoni Tongamoa, ed., *Pacific Women: Roles and Status of Women in Pacific Societies*. Suva: Institute of Pacific Studies of the University of the South Pacific

Crawford, Barbara E. (1984) 'Marriage and the Status of Women in Norse Society' in Elizabeth M. Craik, ed., *Marriage and Property*. Aberdeen: Aberdeen University Press

Creed, Barbara (1993) *The Monstrous-Feminine: Film, Feminism, Psychoanalysis*. London and New York: Routledge

Curthoys, Ann (1991) 'The Three Body Problem: Feminism and Chaos Theory', *Hecate* 17(1):14–21

Cusack, Dymphna (1958) *Chinese Women Speak*. Sydney: Angus & Robertson

Cusicanqui, Silvia Rivera (1990) 'Indigenous Women and Community Resistance: History and Memory: Andean Oral History Workshop (THOA)' in Elizabeth Jelin, ed., *Women and Social Change in Latin America*, transl. J. Ann Zammit and Marilyn Thomson. London: Zed Books

Daly, Mary (1978) *Gyn/Ecology: The Metaethics of Radical Feminism*. London: Women's Press

Dang Huiqiao (1995) 'The Impact of Different Attitudes Towards Infant Gender in the Tu Ethnic Group of Qinghai Province' in Tao Chungfang and Xiao Yang, eds, *Research on Women's Reproductive Health in China*. Beijing: New World Press

Daniels, Marie Cort (1991) 'Teaching Mexican Culture in Mexico from a Women's Studies Perspective', *Women's Studies International Forum* 14(4):311–20

Davidson, Cathy N. (1993) *36 Views of Mount Fuji: On Finding Myself in Japan*. New York: Penguin

• Bibliography

Davidson, Julia O'Connell (1995) 'British Sex Tourists in Thailand' in Mary Maynard and June Purvis, eds, *(Hetero)sexual Politics*. London: Taylor & Francis

Davies, Miranda (1983) Preface to Miranda Davies (comp.) *Third World – Second Sex: Women's Struggles and National Liberation* vol. 1. London: Zed Books

Davies, Miranda (1987) Introduction to Davies, *Third World – Second Sex* vol. 2

Davis, Kathy (1995) *Reshaping the Female Body: The Dilemma of Cosmetic Surgery*. New York and London: Routledge

Dawson, Gaynor (1994) 'Development Planning for Women: the Case of the Indonesian Transmigration Program', *Women's Studies International Forum* 17(1):69–81

Daylight, Phyllis and Mary Johnstone (1986) *Women's Business Report of Aboriginal Women's Task Force*. Canberra: Office of the Status of Women, Department of Prime Minister and Cabinet

de Dios, Aurora Javate (1994) 'Triumphs and Travails: Women's Studies in the Academy' in Lazarus et al., *Women's Studies, Women's Lives*

de Groot, Joanna (1996) 'Gender, Discourse and Ideology in Iranian Studies: Towards a New Scholarship' in Deniz Kandiyoti, ed., *Gendering the Middle East: Emerging Perspectives*. London: I. B. Tauris

de Lepervanche, Marie (1989) 'Women, Nation and the State in Australia' in Nira Yuval-Davis and Floya Anthias, eds, *Woman-Nation-State*. Basingstoke, UK: Macmillan

de Lepervanche, Marie (1991) 'The Family: In the National Interest?' in Bottomley et al., *Intersexions*

Denoon, Donald, with Kathleen Dugin and Leslie Marshall (1989) *Public Health in Papua New Guinea: Medical Possibility and Social Constraint, 1884–1984*. Cambridge: Cambridge University Press

Desai, Neera (1985) *Indian Women*. Bombay: Vora

Desai, Neera (1993) 'Women's Education in India' in Conway and Bourque, *The Politics of Women's Education*

Ding Xiaoqi (1991) 'Feminism in China', *Asian Studies Review* 15(1):111–13

Diprose, Rosalyn (1994) *The Bodies of Women: Ethics, Embodiment and Sexual Difference*. London and New York: Routledge

Division of the Advancement of Women, United Nations (1994) 'International Standards of Equality and Religious Freedom: Implications for the Status of Women' in Moghadam, *Identity Politics and Women*

Dixon, Kyla (1996) 'The Criminalisation of a Cruel Tradition: An Analysis of the Crimes (Female Genital Mutilations) Act (New South Wales), 1995', *Australian Feminist Studies* 11(24):277–93

Dixon-Mueller, Ruth (1993) *Population Policy & Women's Rights: Transforming Reproductive Choice*. Westport, Conn.: Praeger

Domitilia Barrios de la Chungara (1983) 'Women and organization' in Davies, *Third World – Second Sex* vol. 1

Donaldson, Laura E. (1992) *Decolonizing Feminisms: Race, Gender, and Empire-Building*. Chapel Hill and London: University of North Carolina Press

Driesen, Cynthia Vanden (1994) 'Hoju – Australia: Korean Perceptions of the Land "Down Under"' in Curtin University of Technology, *Australia in the World: Perceptions and Possibilities*. Perth: Black Swan Press

duCille, Ann (1994) 'The Occult of True Black Womanhood: Critical Demeanor and Black Feminist Studies', *Signs* (19(3):591–629

Dudgeon, Pat, Simone Lazaroo and Harry Pickett (1990) 'Aboriginal Girls: Self-esteem or Self-determination?' in Jane Kenway and Sue Willis, eds, *Hearts and Minds: Self-esteem and the Schooling of Girls*. London: Falmer Press

Duncker, Patricia (1992) *Sisters and Strangers: An Introduction to Contemporary Feminist Fiction*. Oxford: Blackwell

Duza, M. Badrud and Moni Nag (1993) 'High Contraceptive Prevalence in Matlab, Bangladesh: Underlying Processes and Implications' in Leete and Alam, *The Revolution in Asian Fertility*

Dworkin, Andrea (1983) *Right-Wing Women*. New York: Coward-McCann

Dworkin, Andrea (1994) 'Gynocide: Chinese Footbinding' in Alison M. Jaggar, ed., *Living With Contradictions: Controversies in Feminist Social Ethics*. Boulder, Col.: Westview Press

Dyer-Bennem, Susan Y. (1994) 'Cultural Distinctions in Communication Patterns of African-American Women: A sampler' in Pilar Riaño, ed., *Women in Grassroots Communication: Furthering Social Change*. Thousand Oaks, Calif., and London: Sage

Dynes, Wayne R. and Stephen Donaldson (1992a) Introduction to Wayne R. Dynes and Stephen Donaldson, eds, *Lesbianism*. New York: Garland

Dynes, Wayne R. and Stephen Donaldson, eds (1992b) *Asian Homosexuality*. New York: Garland

East Meets West Translation Group (1995) 'What Are We After?' in Wong Yuen Ling, *Reflections and Resonances*

Easthope, Antony (1990) *What a Man's Gotta Do: The Masculine Myth in Popular Culture*. Boston: Unwin Hyman

Eastmond, Marita (1993) 'Reconstructing Life: Chilean Refugee Women and the Dilemmas of Exile' in Buijs, *Migrant Women*

Eco, Umberto (1986) *Travels in Hyperreality: Essays*, transl. William Weaver. San Diego: Harcourt Brace Jovanovich

Egan, Ted (1994) 'Thinking in Australian' in Graham, *Being Whitefella*

Einhorn, Barbara (1993) *Cinderella Goes to Market: Citizenship, Gender and Women's Movements in East Central Europe*. London: Verso

Eisenstein, Hester (1996) *Inside Agitators: Australian Femocrats and the State*. Sydney: Allen & Unwin

Eisenstein, Zillah (1979) *Capitalist Patriarchy and Socialist Feminism*. New York: Monthly Review Press

Eisler, Riane (1990) 'The Gaia Tradition and the Partnership Future: An Eco-feminist Manifesto' in Irene Diamond and Gloria Feman Orenstein, eds, *Reweaving the World: The Emergence of Ecofeminism*. San Francisco: Sierra Club Books

Eitzen, D. Stanley and Maxine Baca Zinn (1992) 'Structural Transformation and Systems of Inequality' in Margaret L. Anderson and Patricia Hill Collins, eds, *Race, Class and Gender*. Belmont, Calif.: Wadsworth

Emberley, Julia V. (1993) *Thresholds of Difference: Feminist Critique, Native Women's Writings, Postcolonial Theory*. Toronto: University of Toronto Press

Emberson-Bain, 'Atu, ed. (1994) *Sustainable Development or Malignant Growth? Perspectives of Pacific Island Women*. Fiji, Suva: Marama Publications

Engle, Karen (1992) Female Projects of Public International Law: Human Rights and The Exotic Other Female. Paper presented to International Feminisms Conference, State University of New York at Buffalo, March

Enloe, Cynthia (1989) *Bananas, Beaches and Bases: Making Feminist Sense of International Politics*. London: Pandora

Enloe, Cynthia (1993) *The Morning After: Sexual Politics and the End of the Cold War*. Berkeley, Los Angeles and London: University of California Press

Errington, Frederick and Deborah Gewertz (1993) 'The Historical Course of True Love in the Sepik' in Victoria S. Lockwood et al., eds, *Contemporary Pacific Societies: Studies in Development and Change*. Englewood Cliffs, N.J.: Prentice Hall

Errington, Shelly (1990) 'Recasting Sex, Gender and Power: A Theoretical and Regional Overview' in Jane Monnig Atkinson and Shelly Errington, eds, *Power and Difference: Gender in Island Southeast Asia*. Stanford: Stanford University Press

Espín, Oliva M. (1992) 'Cultural and Historical Influences on Sexuality in Hispanic/Latin Women' in Margaret L. Anderson and Patricia Hill Collins, eds, *Race, Class and Gender*. Belmont, Calif.: Wadsworth

Ethnic Policy Unit (1993) 'Health Care in a Multicultural Society: Is "Culture" Always the Issue?', *Connexions*, Newsletter of the Ethnic Policy Unit, Program Development Branch, Queensland Health, Brisbane (July–October):1–2

Evans, Harriet (1995) 'Defining Difference: The "Scientific" Construction of Sexuality and Gender in the People's Republic of China', *Signs* 20(2):357–94

Evans, Ripeka (1994) 'The Negation of Powerlessness: Maori Feminism, a Perspective', *Hecate* 20(2):53–65

Fakhro, Munira A. (1990) *Women at Work in the Gulf: A Case Study of Bahrain*. London: Kegan Paul

Fan Cuiyu (1987) 'Group Marriage in China's Primitive Society: Marriage Before Monogamy (1)', *Women of China* January:40–1

Fang, Xiangshu and Trevor Hay (1992) *East Wind, West Wind*. Melbourne: Penguin

Fanon, Frantz (1967) *Black Skin, White Masks*, transl. Charles Lam Markmann. New York: Grove [first published 1953]

Feminist Press at the City of New York (1995) *China for Women: Travel and Culture*. New York and Melbourne: Feminist Press and Spinifex Press

Fennell, Vera and Lyn Jeffry (1992) 'To Increase the Quality of Women: A Preliminary Assessment of Women's Studies in Beijing'. Beijing: Ford Foundation

Fesl, Eve Mungwa D. (1989) 'Race and Racism: White Manoeuvres and Koori Oppression', *Social Justice* 16(3):30–4

Forman, Charles W. (1984) ' "Sing to the Lord a New Song": Women in the Churches of Oceania' in Denise O'Brien and Sharon W. Tiffany, eds, *Rethinking Women's Roles: Perspectives from the Pacific*. Berkeley: University of California Press

Foucault, Michel (1980) *The History of Sexuality* vol. 1. New York: Random House [first published 1976]

Francis, Dave (1987) 'The Great Transition' in R. J. Anderson et al., eds, *Classic Disputes in Sociology*. London: Allen & Unwin

Franco, Jean (1989) *Plotting Women: Gender and Representation in Mexico*. New York: Columbia University Press

Frankenberg, Ruth (1993) *White Women, Race Matters: The Social Construction of Whiteness*. London: Routledge

Franks, Emma (1996) 'Women and resistance in East Timor: "the centre, as they say, knows itself by the margins"', *Women's Studies International Forum* 19(1/2):155–68

French, Marilyn (1992) *The War Against Women*. London: Hamish Hamilton

Friedman, Susan Stanford (1995) 'Beyond White and Other: Relationality and Narratives of Race in Feminist Discourse', *Signs* 21(1):1–49

Frohmann, Alicia and Teresa Valdés (1995) 'Democracy in the country and the home: the women's movements in Chile' in Basu, *The Challenge of Local Feminisms*

Fry, Peter (1986) 'Male Homosexuality and Spirit Possession in Brazil', *Journal of Homosexuality* 11(3/4):137–53

Frye, Marilyn (1996) 'The Necessity of Differences: Constructing a Positive Category of Women', *Signs* 21(4):991–1010

Fujieda, Miok and Kumiko Fujimura-Fanselow (1995) 'Women's Studies: An Overview' in Fujimura-Fanselow and Kameda, *Japanese Women*

Fujimura-Fanselow, Kumiko (1995) 'College Women Today: Options and Dilemmas' in Fujimura-Fanselow and Kameda, *Japanese Women*

Fujimura-Fanselow, Kumiko and Atsuko Kameda, eds (1995) *Japanese Women: New Feminist Perspectives on the Past, Present and the Future*. New York: Feminist Press

Furth, Charlotte (1987) 'Concepts of Pregnancy, Childbirth, and Infancy in Ch'ing Dynasty China', *Journal of Asian Studies* 46(1):7–32

Gaard, Greta (1993) 'Ecofeminism and Native American Cultures: Pushing the Limits of Cultural Imperialism' in Greta Gaard, ed., *Ecofeminism: Women, Animals, Nature*. Philadelphia: Temple University Press

Gailey, Christine Ward (1996) 'Women and the democratization movement in Tonga: nation versus state, authority versus power', *Women's Studies International Forum* 19(1/2):169–78

Gale, Faye, ed. (1983) *We are Bosses Ourselves: The Status and Role of Aboriginal Women Today*. Canberra: Australian Institute of Aboriginal Studies

Gale, Fay (1989) 'Roles Revisited: The Women of Southern South Australia' in Peggy Brock, ed., *Women Rites and Sites: Aboriginal Women's Cultural Knowledge*. Sydney: Allen & Unwin

Gallin, Rita S. (1991) 'Dowry and Family in Changing Rural Taiwan', *Journal of Women and Gender Issues* 2 (January):65–86

Gandhi, Nadita and Nandita Shah (1992) *The Issues at Stake: Theory and Practice in the Contemporary Women's Movement in India*. New Delhi: Kali for Women

Ganguly, Indrani (1992) 'Cross-Cultural Body Image', *MediaMatters* 2(3):2–3 news-sheet of MediaSwitch Queensland

Ganguly, Indrani (1994) Prison or sanctuary? The family and women from non-English speaking backgrounds. Paper presented to Biennial Women's Health Conference, Darwin, Australia, October

Ganguly, Indrani (1995a) 'Exploring the Differences: Feminist Theory in a Multicultural Society', *Hecate* 21(1):37–52

Ganguly, Indrani (1995b) 'Some thoughts on feminism and racism', *Connect!* (Newsletter of The Australian Sociological Women's Association) 3(2):4

Garber, Marjorie (1992a) *Vested Interests: Cross-Dressing Cultural Anxiety*. New York and London: Routledge

Garber, Marjorie (1992b) 'The Occidental Tourist: *M. Butterfly* and the Scandal of Transvestism' in Andrew Parker et al., eds, *Nationalisms and Sexualities*. New York: Routledge

Gardner, Tracey A. (1994) 'Racism in Pornography and the Women's Movement' in Alison M. Jaggar, ed., *Living With Contradictions: Controversies in Feminist Social Ethics*, Boulder, Col.: Westview Press

Gatens, Moira (1991) *Feminism and Philosophy: Perspectives on Difference and Equality*. Cambridge: Polity Press

Gays and Lesbians Aboriginal Alliance (1993) 'Peopling the Empty Mirror: The Prospects for Lesbian and Gay Aboriginal History' in Robert Aldrich, ed., *Gay Perspectives* vol. 2. Sydney: Department of Economic History, Sydney University, with the Australian Centre for Gay and Lesbian Research

Geertz, Clifford (1995) *After the Fact: Two Countries, Four Decades, One Anthropologist*. Cambridge, Mass.: Harvard University Press

Ghvamshahidi, Zohreh (1995) 'The Linkage Between Iranian Patriarchy and the Informal Economy in Maintaining Women's Subordinate Roles in Home-Based Carpet Production', *Women's Studies International Forum* 18(2):135–51

Giddens, Anthony (1990) *The Transformation of Intimacy: Sexuality, Love and Eroticism in Modern Societies*. Cambridge: Polity Press

Gilding, Michael (1991) *The Making and Breaking of the Australian Family*. Sydney: Allen & Unwin

Gillett, Joy E. (1990) *The Health of Women in Papua New Guinea*. Goroka: Papua New Guinea Institute of Medical Research

Gilliam, Angela and Nahua Rooney (1992) 'Leaving a Record for Others: An Interview with Nahua Rooney' in Lenora Foerstal and Angela Gilliam, eds, *Confronting the Margaret Mead Legacy: Scholarship, Empire and the South Pacific*. Philadelphia: Temple University Press

Gilligan, Carol (1982) *In a Different Voice*.Cambridge, Mass.: Harvard University Press

Gilmore, David G. (1990) *Manhood in the Making: Cultural Concepts of Masculinity*. New Haven: Yale University Press

Giuffré, Giulia (1992) 'Who Do You Think You Are?' in Herne, Travaglia and Weiss, *Who Do You Think You Are?*

Goodall, Heather (1990) '"Saving the Children": Gender and the Colonization of Aboriginal Children in NSW, 1788 to 1990', *Aboriginal Law Bulletin* 2(44):6–9

Goody, Jack (1983) *The Development of the Family and Marriage in Europe*.Cambridge: Cambridge University Press

Goonesekere, Savitri (1986) 'Sri Lanka: Legal Status of Women' in Margaret Schuler, ed., *Empowerment and the Law: Strategies of Third World Women*. Washington: OEF International

Graham, Duncan (1994) Introduction to Duncan Graham, ed., *Being Whitefella*. Fremantle: Fremantle Arts Centre Press

Grahn, Judy (1986) 'Strange Country This: Lesbianism and North American Indian Tribes', *Journal of Homosexuality* 11(3/4):43–54

Gray, J. Patrick (1986) 'Growing Yams and Men: An Interpretation of Kimam Male Ritualized Homosexual Behavior', *Journal of Homosexuality* 11(3/4):55–68

Graycar, Regina and Jenny Morgan (1990) *The Hidden Gender of Law*. Sydney: Federation Press

Green, Rayna (1980) 'Native American Women', *Signs* 6(2):248–67

Greenhalgh, Susan and Jiali Li (1995) 'Engendering Reproductive Policy and Practice in Peasant China: For a Feminist Demography of Reproduction', *Signs* 20(3):601–41

Greenman, Nancy (1996) 'More Than a Mother: Some Tewa Women Reflect on Gia' in Gwendolyn Etter-Lewis and Michèle Foster, eds, *Unrelated Kin: Race and Gender in Women's Personal Narratives*. New York: Routledge

Greer, Germaine (1984) *Sex and Destiny: The Politics of Human Fertility*. New York: Harper & Row

Griffen, Vanessa (1994) 'Women, Development and Population: A Critique of the

Port Vila Declaration' in Emberson-Bain, *Sustainable Development or Malignant Growth?*

Grimshaw, Patricia (1981) 'Aboriginal Women: A Study of Culture Contact' in Norma Grieve and Patricia Grimshaw, eds, *Australian Women: Feminist Perspectives*. Melbourne: Oxford University Press

Grosz, Elizabeth (1989) *Sexual Subversions: Three French Feminists*. Sydney: Allen & Unwin

Grosz, Elizabeth (1990) *Jacques Lacan: A Feminist Introduction*. Sydney: Allen & Unwin

Gunew, Sneja (1993) 'Feminism and the Politics of Irreducible Differences: Multiculturalism/Ethnicity/Race' in Sneja Gunew and Anna Yeatman, eds, *Feminism and The Politics of Difference*. Sydney: Allen & Unwin

Gunning, Isabelle R. (1992) 'Female Genital Surgeries', *Columbia Human Rights Law Review* 23(2):189–248

Guy, Donna J. (1992) ' "White Slavery", Citizenship and Nationality in Argentina' in Andrew Parker et al., eds, *Nationalisms and Sexualities*. New York: Routledge

Habermas, Jurgen (1987) *The Philosophical Discourse of Modernity*, transl. Frederick Lawrence. Cambridge: Polity Press

Haeri, Shahla (1989) *Law and Desire: Temporary Marriage in Iran*. London: I. B. Tauris

Haj, Samira (1992) 'Palestinian Women and Patriarchal Relations', *Signs* 17(4):761–78

Hamilton, Annette (1981) 'A Complex Strategical Situation: Gender and Power in Aboriginal Australia' in Norma Grieve and Patricia Grimshaw, eds, *Australian Women: Feminist Perspectives*. Melbourne: Oxford University Press.

Haraway, Donna (1992) *Primate Visions: Gender, Race and Nature in the World of Modern Science*. London: Verso

Hardacre, Helen (1994) 'Japanese New Religions: Profiles in Gender' in Hawley, *Fundamentalism and Gender*

Hardacre, Helen and Lenore Manderson (1990) The Hall of Mirrors: Sex and the Representation of Asia. Paper prepared for the International Workshop on the Construction of Gender and Sexuality in East and Southeast Asia, University of California, Los Angeles, 9–11 December

Harlan, Lindsay (1995) 'Abandoning Shame: Mira and the Margins of Marriage' in Harlan and Courtwright, *From the Margins of Hindu Marriage*

Harlan, Lindsay and Paul B. Courtright (1995) Introduction to Lindsay Harlan and Paul B. Courtwright, eds, *From the Margins of Hindu Marriage: Essays on Gender, Religion and Culture*. New York: Oxford University Press

Harsanyi, Doina Pasca (1994) 'Romania's Women', *Journal of Women's History* 5(3):30–54

Hart, Donn V. (1992a) 'The Cebuano Bayot and Lakin-On' in Murray, *Oceanic Homosexualities*

Hart, Donn V. (1992b) 'Homosexuality and Transvestism in the Philippines: The Cebuan Filipino Bayot and Lakin-On' in Dynes and Donaldson, *Asian Homosexuality*

Hartmann, Betsy (1987) *Reproductive Rights and Wrongs: The Global Politics of Population Control and Contraceptive Choice*. New York: Harper & Row

Hartmann, Heidi (1981) 'The Unhappy Marriage of Marxism and Feminism: Towards a More Progressive Union' in Lydia Sargent, ed., *Women and Revolution: A Discussion of the Unhappy Marriage of Marxism and Feminism*. Boston: South End Press

Hassim, Shireen (1993) 'Family, Motherhood and Zulu Nationalism: The Politics of the Inkatha Women's Brigade', *Feminist Review* 43(Spring):1–25

Hatzimanolis, Efi (1993) 'Timing Differences and Investing in Futures in Multicultural (Women's) Writing' in Gunew and Yeatman, *Feminism and Politics of Difference*

Hausman, Bernice L. (1992) 'Demanding Subjectivity: Transsexualism, Medicine, and the Technologies of Gender', *Journal of the History of Sexuality* 3(2):270–302

Hawley, John S. (1994) 'Hinduism: *Sati* and its Defenders' in John Stratton Hawley, ed., *Fundamentalism and Gender*. New York: Oxford University Press

Hawley, John S. and Wayne Proudfoot (1994) Introduction to Hawley, *Fundamentalism and Gender*

Haworth, Abigail (1995) 'The World's Most Wanted Women', *She* June:15–20

Hawthorne, Lesleyanne (1994) 'National Women's Conference a Triumph', *Bureau of Immigration and Population Research Bulletin* 12:46–50

Hayden, Brian (1986) 'Old Europe: Sacred Matriarchy or Complementary Opposition?' in Anthony Bonnano, ed., *Archaeology and Fertility Cult in the Ancient Mediterranean*. Amsterdam: B. R. Gruner Publishing

Head, Lyndsay (1991) 'Culture on the Fault Line' in King, *Pakeha*

Heilbrun, Carolyn G. (1995) *The Education of a Woman: The Life of Gloria Steinem*. New York: Dial Press

Hélie-Lucas, Marie-Aimée (1987) 'Bound and Gagged by the Family Code' in Davies, *Third World – Second Sex* vol. 2. London: Zed Books

Hélie-Lucas, Marie-Aimée (1990) 'Women, Nationalism and Religion in the Algerian Struggle' in M. Badran and M. Cooke, eds, *Opening the Gates: A Century of Arab Feminist Writing*. London: Virago

Hélie-Lucas, Marie-Aimée (1994) 'The Preferential Symbol for Islamic Identity: Women in Muslim Personal Laws' in Moghadam, *Identity Politics and Women*

Hendessi, Mandana (1991) 'On *Law of Desire: Temporary Marriage in Iran*', *Feminist Review* 38:71–8

Heng, Geraldine and Janadas Devan (1992) 'State Fatherhood: the Politics of Nationalism, Sexuality and Race in Singapore' in Andrew Parker et al., eds, *Nationalisms and Sexualities*. New York: Routledge

Henry, Kristin and Marlene Derlet (1993) *Talking up a Storm: Nine Women and Consciousness-Raising*. Sydney: Hale & Iremonger

Herdt, Gilbert H. (1992) 'Semen Depletion and the Sense of Maleness' in Murray, *Oceanic Homosexualities*

Hershatter, Gail (1992) 'The Changing Discourse on Shanghai Prostitution 1890–1949', *Journal of the History of Sexuality* 3(2):245–69

Herzfeld, Michael (1985) *The Poetics of Manhood: Contest and Identity in a Cretan Mountain Village*. Princeton, N.Y.: Princeton University Press

Hewlett, Sylvia Ann (1987) *A Lesser Life: The Myth of Women's Liberation*. London: Michael Joseph

Hill, Helen (1987) 'The Gender Variable in Development Politics: Was Nairobi a Turning Point?' in Christine Jennett and Randal G. Stewart, eds, *Three Worlds of Inequality: Race, Class and Gender*. Melbourne: Macmillan

Hill, Polly (1986) *Development Economics On Trial: The Anthropological Case for a Prosecution*. Cambridge: Cambridge University Press

Hinsch, Bret (1995) 'Views of the Feminine in Early Neo-Confucian Thought' in Feminist Press, *China for Women*

Hitchcox, Linda (1993) 'Vietnamese Refugees in Hong Kong: Behaviour and Control' in Buijs, *Migrant Women*

Hite, Shere (1994) *The Hite Report on the Family Growing Up Under Patriarchy.* London: Bloomsbury

Ho, Chi-Kwan A. (1990) 'Opportunities and Challenges: The Role of Feminists for Social Change in Hong Kong' in Albrecht and Brewer, *Bridges of Power*

Hobart, Mark (1995) 'Engendering disquiet: on kinship and gender in Bali', in Karim, *'Male' and 'Female' in Developing Southeast Asia*

Hoe, Susanna (1991) *The Private Life of Old Hong Kong: Western Women in the British Colony 1841–1941.* Hong Kong: Oxford University Press

Holub, Renate (1991) 'Weak Thought and Strong Ethics: The "Postmodern" and Feminist Theory in Italy', *Annali d'Italianistica* 9:124–43

Holub, Renate (1994) 'Between the United States and Italy: Critical Reflections on Diotima's Feminist/Feminine Ethics' in Giovanna Miceli Jefferies, ed., *Feminine Feminists: Cultural Practices in Italy.* Minneapolis and London: University of Minnesota Press

Holub, Renate (1995) 'Italian "Difference Theory": A New Canon?' in Maria Marotti, ed., *Rewriting the Canon.* Philadelphia: University of Pennsylvania Press

Hondagneu-Sotelo, Pierrette and Michael A. Messner (1994) 'Gender Displays and Men's Power: The "New Man" and the Mexican Immigrant Man' in Harry Brod and Michael Kaufman, eds, *Theorizing Masculinities.* Thousand Oaks, Calif.: Sage

Honig, Emily (1992) 'Christianity, Feminism and Communism: The Life and Times of Deng Yuzhi (Cora Deng)' in Johnson-Odim and Strobel, *Expanding the Boundaries of Women's History*

Hooks, Bell (1981) *Ain't I a Woman: Black Women and Feminism.* Boston: South End Press

hooks, bell (1992) *Black Looks: Race and Representation.* Boston, MA: South End Press

Horwill, Frank M. and Sophy Bordow (1983) *The Outcome of Defended Custody Cases in the Family Court of Australia.* Sydney: Family Court of Australia

Huata, Donna Awatere (1993) 'Walking on Eggs' in Sue Kedgley and Mary Varnham, eds, *Heading Nowhere in a Navy Blue Suit and Other Tales from the Feminist Revolution.* Wellington: Daphne Brasel Associates Press

Hubbard, Dianne and Colette Solomon (1995) 'The Many Faces of Feminism in Namibia' in Basu, *The Challenge of Local Feminisms*

Huggins, Jackie (1994) 'A Contemporary View of Aboriginal Women's Relationship to the White Women's Movement' in Norma Grieve and Ailsa Burns, eds, *Australian Women: Contemporary Feminist Thought.* Melbourne: Oxford University Press

Huggins, Jackie and Thom Blake (1992) 'Protection or Persecution? Gender Relations in the Era of Racial Segregation' in Kay Saunders and Raymond Evans, eds, *Gender Relations in Australia: Domination and Negotiation.* Sydney: Harcourt Brace Jovanovich

Huggins, Jackie et al. (1991) 'Letter to the Editors', *Women's Studies International Forum* 14(5):506–7

Hunt, Lynn and Catherine Hall (1990) 'The Curtain Rises' in Perrott, *A History of Private Life* vol. 4

Hurtado, Aida (1989) 'Relating to Privilege: Seduction and Rejection in the Subordination of White Women and Women of Color', *Signs* 14(4):833–55

Hyoung, Cho (1994) 'To Grow with Women's Studies' in Lazarus et al., *Women's Studies Women's Lives*

Imamura, Anne E. (1996) Introduction to Anne E. Imamura, ed., *Re-Imaging Japanese Women*. Berkeley: University of California Press

Inden, Ronald (1990) *Imagining India*. Oxford: Basil Blackwell

Indira, M. K. (1976) *Phaniyamma*. New Delhi: Kali for Women

Irwin, Kathie (1991) 'Towards Theories of Māori Feminisms' in Rosemary du Plessis, ed., *Feminist Voices: Women's Studies Texts for Aotearoa/ New Zealand*. Auckland: Oxford University Press

Ishtar, Zoel dé (1994) *Daughters of the Pacific*. Melbourne: Spinifex Press

Iwao, Sumiko (1993) *The Japanese Woman: Traditional Image and Changing Reality*. New York: Free Press

Jacka, Tamara (1994) 'Countering Voices: An Approach to Asian and Feminist Studies in the 1990s', *Women's Studies International Forum* 17(6):663–72

Jackson, Graham (1991) *The Secret Lore of Gardening: Patterns of Male Intimacy*. Toronto: Inner City Books

Jackson, Peter A. (1996) 'The Persistence of Gender: From Ancient Indian *Pandakas* to Modern Thai *Gay-Quings*' in Chris Berry and Annamarie Jagose, eds, *Australia Queer*. Special issue of *Meanjin* 55(1):110–20

Jacobs, Jane M. (1994) 'Earth Honouring: Western Desires and Indigenous Knowledges', *Meanjin* 53(2):305–14

Jad, Islah (1995) Claiming feminism, claiming nationalism: women's activism in the Occupied Territories' in Basu, *The Challenge of Local Feminisms*

Jaggar, Alison M. (1983) *Feminist Politics and Human Nature*. New Jersey: Rowman & Allanheld

Jaggar, Alison M., ed. (1994) *Living With Contradictions: Controversies in Feminist Social Ethics*. Boulder, Col.: Westview Press

Jain, Devaki (1993) 'Healing the Wounds of Development' in Conway and Bourque, *The Politics of Women's Education*

Jain, Madhu (1992) 'The Changing Woman', *India Today* 15 July:36–43

James, Bev and Kay Saville-Smith (1989) *Gender, Culture and Power: Challenging New Zealand's Gendered Culture*. Auckland: Oxford University Press

James, Stanlie M. (1992a) Introduction to Stanlie M. James and Abena P.A. Busia, eds, *Theorizing Black Feminisms: The Visionary Pragmatism of Black Women*. New York: Routledge

James, Stanlie M. (1992b) 'Mothering: A Possible Black Feminist Link to Social Transformation?' in James and Busia, *Theorizing Black Feminisms*

James, Stanlie M. (1994) 'Challenging Patriarchal Privilege Through the Development of International Human Rights', *Women's Studies International Forum* 17(6):563–78

Jameson, Fredric (1991) *Postmodernism, or, The Cultural Logic of Late Capitalism*. London and New York: Verso

JanMohamed, Abdul R. (1986) 'The Economy of Manichean Allegory: The Function of Racial Difference in Colonial Literature' in Henry Louis Gates Jr, ed., *"Race," Writing, and Difference*. Chicago: University of Chicago Press

Jantraka, Sompop (1994) 'How Development Compromises Human Rights in Thailand' in Damien Kingsbury and Greg Barton, eds, *Difference and Tolerance: Human Rights in Southeast Asia*. Geelong, Vic.: Deakin University Press

Jayawardena, Kumar (1986) *Feminism and Nationalism in the Third World*. London: Zed Books

Jayawardena, Kumar (1995) *The White Woman's Other Burden: Western Women and South Asia During British Colonial Rule*. New York and London: Routledge

Jeffery, Patricia et al. (1989) *Labour Pains and Labour Power: Women and Childbearing in India*. London: Zed Books

Jeffrey, Robin (1992) *Politics, Women and Well-Being: How Kerala Became a 'Model'*. Basingstoke, UK: Macmillan

Jennaway, Megan (1993) Strangers, Sex and the State in Paradise: The Engineering of Balinese Tourism and its Economy of Pleasure. Paper presented to the State, Sexuality and Reproduction in Asia and the Pacific Conference, Gender Relations Project, Australian National University, 16-18 July

Jethmalani, Rani (1986) 'India: Law and Women' in Margaret Schuler, ed., *Empowerment and the Law: Strategies of Third World Women*. Washington: OEF International

Jhabvala, Renana (1994) 'Self-Employed Women's Association: Organising Women by Struggle and Development' in Sheila Rowbotham and Swasti Mitter, eds, *Dignity and Daily Bread: New Forms Economic Organising Among the Poor Women in the Third World and the First*. London and New York: Routledge

Jhamtani, Hira (1991) 'Redefining feminism as the women's movement', *Asian Studies Review* 15(1):96–100

Jogan, Maca (1994) 'Redomestication of Women in Slovenia?', *Women's Studies International Forum* 17(2/3):307–9

Johnson, Lesley (1993) *The Modern Girl: Girlhood and Growing Up*. Sydney: Allen & Unwin

Johnson, Miriam M. (1988) *Strong Mothers, Weak Wives*. Berkeley: University of California Press

Johnson-Odim, Cheryl and Margaret Strobel, eds (1992) *Expanding the Boundaries of Women's History*. Bloomington and Indianapolis: Indiana University Press

Johnston, Elliott (1991a) *Royal Commission into Aboriginal Deaths in Custody: National Report* vol. 2. Canberra: Australian Government Publishing Service

Johnston, Elliott (1991b) *Royal Commission into Aboriginal Deaths in Custody* vol. 4

Johnston, Patricia and Leonie Pihama (1994) 'The Marginalisation of Maori Women', *Hecate* 20(2):83–97

Jolly, Margaret (1991) 'The politics of difference: Feminism, colonialism and decolonisation in Vanuatu' in Bottomley et al., *Intersexions*

Jolly, Margaret (1996) '*Woman Ikat Raet Long Human Raet O No?* Women's Rights, Human Rights and Domestic Violence in Vanuatu', *Feminist Review* 52:169–90

Jones, Frank Lancaster (1991) *Ancestry Groups in Australia: A Descriptive Overview*. Wollongong, NSW: Centre for Multicultural Studies, University of Wollongong

Jones, Gavin W. (1993) 'Consequences of Rapid Fertility Decline for Old Age Security' in Leete and Alam, *The Revolution in Asian Fertility*

Jones, Mary Lucille, ed., (1993) *An Australian Pilgrimage: Muslims in Australia from the Seventeenth Century to the Present*. Melbourne: Victoria Press in association with the Museum of Victoria

Joseph, Suad (1993) 'Gender and Relationality Among Arab Families in Lebanon', *Feminist Studies* 19(3):465–86

Kabeer, Naila (1991) 'The Quest for National Identity: Women, Islam and the State in Bangladesh', *Feminist Review* 37:38–58

Kabeer, Naila (1994) *Reversed Realities: Gender Hierarchies in Development Thought*. London: Verso

Kandiyoti, Deniz (1996) 'Contemporary Feminist Scholarship and Middle Eastern Studies' in Deniz Kandiyoti, ed., *Gendering the Middle East: Emerging Perspectives*. London: I. B. Tauris

Kaplan, E. Ann (1993) 'Madonna Politics: Perversion, Repression, or Subversion? Or Masks and/asMaster-y' in Cathy Schwichtenberg, ed., *The Madonna Connection: Representational Politics, Subcultural Identities, and Cultural Theory*. Sydney: Allen & Unwin

Kaplan, Gisela (1992) *Contemporary Western European Feminism*. Sydney: Allen & Unwin

Kaplan, Gisela T. and Lesley J. Rogers (1990) 'Scientifife constructions, cultural productions: scientific narratives of sexual attraction' in Terry Threadgold and Anne Cranny-Francis, eds, *Feminine/Masculine and Representation*. Sydney: Allen & Unwin

Kappeler, Susanne (1995) *The Will to Violence: The Politics of Personal Behaviour*. Melbourne: Spinifex Press

Kardam, Nüket (1991) *Bringing Women In: Women's Issues in International Development Programmes*. Boulder, Col.: Lynne Rienner Publishers

Karim, Wazir Jahan (1995) 'Bilateralism and gender in Southeast Asia' in Wazir Jahan Karim, ed., *'Male' and 'Female' in Developing Southeast Asia*. Oxford and Washington: Berg

Karlekar, Malavika and Barbara Lazarus (1994) Introduction to Lazarus et al., *Women's Studies Women's Lives*

Kaur, Amarjit (1985) 'The Status of Women in ASEAN: Some Observations' in Harry M. Scoble and Laurie S. Wiseberg, eds, *ASEAN Perspectives on Human Rights: Access to Justice the Struggle for Human Rights in South East Asia*. London: Zed Books

Kawar, Amal (1991) 'The Intersection of Gender and Politics: Revising a Political Science Course', *Women's Studies International Forum* 14(4):305–9

Kearns, Emily (1992) 'Indian Myth' in Carolyne Larrington, ed., *The Feminist Companion to Mythology*. Hammersmith: Pandora Harper Collins

Kelkar, Govind (1987) 'Violence Against Women: An Understanding of Responsibility for their Lives' in Davies, *Third World – Second Sex* vol. 2. London: Zed Books

Kelkar, Govind (1995) 'Towards Beijing' Conference, Victoria University of Technology, St Albans, Vic., 9–11 February 1995

Kemp, Amanda et al. (1995) 'The dawn of a new day: redefining South African feminism' in Basu, *The Challenge of Local Feminisms*

Kim, Kyung-Ai (1996) 'Nationalism: an advocate of, or a barrier to, feminism in South Korea', *Women's Studies International Forum* 19(1/2):65–74

Kimmel, Michael and Michael Kaufman (1994) 'Weekend Warriors: The New Men's Movement' in Harry Brod and Michael Kaufman, eds, *Theorizing Masculinities*. Thousand Oaks, Calif.: Sage

King, Michael (1985) *Being Pakeha: An Encounter with New Zealand and the Maori Renaissance*. Auckland: Hodder & Stoughton

King, Michael, ed. (1991) *Pakeha: The Quest for Identity in New Zealand*. Auckland: Penguin

Kipnis, Andrew (1994) '(Re)inventing *Li*: *Koutou* and Subjectification in Rural Shandong' in Angelo Zito, ed., *Body, Subject and Power in China*. Chicago: University of Chicago Press

Kishwar, Madhu (1990) 'Why I do not Call Myself a Feminist', *Manushi* 61:2–8

Kishwar, Madhu (1995) 'A Code for Self-Monitoring: Some Thoughts on Action', *Manushi* 85:5–17

Klein, Anne Carolyn (1995) *Meeting the Great Bliss Queen: Buddhists, Feminists and the Art of the Self*. Boston: Beacon Press

Klein, Renate D., ed. (1989) *Infertility: Women Speak Out*. London: Pandora

Klein-Hutheesing, Otome (1995) 'Gender at the Margins of Southeast Asia' in Karim, *'Male' and 'Female' in Developing Southeast Asia*

Klug, Francesca (1989) '"Oh to be in England": The British Case Study' in Nira Yuval-Davis and Floya Anthias, eds, *Woman-Nation-State*. Basingstoke, UK: Macmillan

Knight, Alan (1994) 'Exporting Exploitation', *Arena Magazine* 8 (December/ January):21–3

Kondo, Dorinne K. (1990) *Crafting Selves: Power, Gender, and Discourses of Identity in a Japanese Workplace*. Chicago: University of Chicago Press

Kopytoff, Igor (1990) 'Women's Roles and Existential Identities' in Peggy Reeves Sanday and Ruth Gallagher Goodenough, eds, *Beyond the Second Sex: New Directions in the Anthropology of Gender*. Philadelphia: University of Pennsylvania Press

Krich, John (1989) 'Here Come the Brides: The Blossoming Business of Imported Love' in Michael S. Kimmel and Michael A. Messner, eds, *Men's Lives*. New York: Macmillan

Krishnan, Prabha and Anita Dighe (1990) *Affirmation and Denial: Construction of Femininity on Indian Television*. New Delhi: Sage

Krishnaraj, Maithreyi and Karuna Chanana (1990) *Gender and the Household Domain: Social and Cultural Dimensions*. London: Sage

Kristeva, Julia (1974) *About Chinese Women*, transl. Anita Barrows. London: Marion Boyars

Ku Yenlin (1987) 'The Feminist Movement in Taiwan', *Bulletin of Concerned Asian Scholars* 21(1):12–22

Ku Yenlin (1996) 'Selling a Feminist Agenda on a Conservative Market: The *Awakening* Experience in Taiwan' in Diane Bell and Renate Klein, eds, *Radically Speaking: Feminism Reclaimed*. Melbourne: Spinifex Press

Kumar, Radha (1995) 'From Chipko to sati: the contemporary Indian women's movement' in Basu, *The Challenge of Local Feminisms*

Kumari, Ranjana (1989) *Brides are Not For Burning: Dowry Victims in India*. New Delhi: Radiant

Kurtz, Stanley N. (1992) *All the Mothers Are One: Hindu Indian and the Cultural Reshaping of Psychoanalysis*. New York: Columbia University Press

Kwan, Margaret (1990) 'Services Rendered by the Family Planning Association of Hong Kong to Sexually Assaulted Victims' in Fanny M. Cheung et al., eds, *Research on Rape and Sexual Crime in Hong Kong*. Shatin: Centre for Hong Kong Studies, Institute of Social Studies, Chinese University of Hong Kong

Kwon, Tai-Hwam (1993) 'Exploring the Socio-cultural Explanations of Fertility Transition in South Korea' in Leete and Alam, *The Revolution in Asian Fertility*

La Marchesina, Concetta (1994) 'Working With Women in the Workplace: The Story of WICH' in Wendy Weeks, ed., *Women Working Together: Lessons from Feminist Women's Services*. Melbourne: Longman Cheshire

Lake, Marilyn (1991) 'Sexuality and feminism. Some notes in their Australian history', *Lilith: A Feminist History Journal* 7(Winter):29–45

Lâm, Maivân Clech (1994) 'Feeling Foreign in Feminism', *Signs* 19(4):864–93

Lamphere, Louise (1993) 'The Domestic Sphere of Women and the Public World of Men: The Strengths and Limitations of an Anthropological Dichotomy' in Brettell and Sargent, *Gender in Cross-Cultural Perspective*

Langman, Lauren (1992) 'Neon Cages: Shopping for Subjectivity' in Shields, *Lifestyle Shopping*

Langton, Marcia (1988) 'Aboriginal law-ways' in Barbara Hocking, ed., *International Law and Aboriginal Human Rights*. Sydney: Law Book Company

Langton, Marcia (1993) *'Well, I Heard it on the Radio and I Saw it on the Television'... An Essay for The Australian Film Commission on the Politics and Aesthetics of Filmmaking by and About Aboriginal People and Things.* Sydney: Australian Film Commission

Langton, Marcia et al. (1991) '"Too Much Sorry Business" – The Report of the Aboriginal Issues Unit of the Northern Territory' in Johnston, *Royal Commission into Aboriginal Deaths in Custody: National Report* vol. 5

Laqueur, Thomas (1989) 'Orgasm, Generation, and the Politics of Reproductive Biology' in Catherine Gallagher and Thomas Laqueur, eds, *The Making of the Modern Body: Sexuality and Society in the Nineteenth Century*. Berkeley: University of California Press

Larrain, Jorge (1989) *Theories of Development: Capitalism, Colonialism and Dependency*. Cambridge: Polity Press

Lateef, Shahida (1990) *Muslim Women in India Political and Private Realities: 1890s–1980s*. London: Zed Books

Laurie, Victoria (1994) 'Cry for the Lost Chances' in Graham, *Being Whitefella*

Lawn, Jennifer (1994) 'Pakeha Bonding', *Meanjin* 53(2):295–304

Lazarus, Barbara et al., eds (1994) *Women's Studies Women's Lives: Theory and Practice in South and Southeast Asia*. Melbourne: Spinifex Press in association with Kali for Women

Lazreg, Marnia (1990) 'Feminism and Difference: The Perils of Writing as a Woman on Women in Algeria' in Marianne Hirsch and Evelyn Fox Keller, eds, *Conflicts in Feminism*. New York and London: Routledge

Lazreg, Marnia (1994) *The Eloquence of Silence: Algerian Women in Question*. New York and London: Routledge

Lebra, Takie Sugiyama (1992) 'Self in Japanese Culture' in Nancy R. Rosenberger, ed., *Japanese Sense of the Self*. Cambridge: Cambridge University Press

Lee, In-ho (1993) 'Work, Education, and Women's Gains: The Korean Experience' in Conway and Bourque, *The Politics of Women's Education*

Lee, Lily Xiao Hong (1994) *The Virtue of Yin: Studies on Chinese Women*. Sydney: Wild Peony

Leete, Richard and Iqbal Alam (1993) 'Fertility Transition of Similar Cultural Groups in Different Countries' in Richard Leete and Iqbal Alam, eds, *The Revolution in Asian Fertility: Dimensions, Causes, and Implications*. Oxford: Clarendon Press

Lepowsky, Maria (1990) 'Gender in an Egalitarian Society: A Case Study from the Coral Sea' in Peggy Reeves Sanday and Ruth Gallagher Goodenough, eds, *Beyond the Second Sex: New Directions in the Anthropology of Gender*. Philadelphia: University of Pennsylvania Press

Lewins, Frank (1992) 'Everyday Culture in China: The Experience of Chinese Intellectuals', *China Information* 7(2):56–69

Lewins, Frank (1995) *Transsexualism in Society: A Sociology of Male-to Female Transsexuals*. Melbourne: Macmillan

Li, Huey-li (1993) 'A Cross-Cultural Critique of Ecofeminism' in Greta Gaard, ed., *Ecofeminism: Women, Animals, Nature*. Philadelphia: Temple University Press

Li Ping (1995) 'I Have Become a Feminist' in Wong Yuen Ling, *Reflections and Resonances*

Li Xiaojiang and Zhang Xiaodan (1994) 'Creating a Space for Women: Women's Studies in China in the 1980s', *Signs* 20(1):137–51

Li Zhisui (1994) *The Private Life of Chairman Mao*, transl. Tai Hung-Chao. New York: Random House

Lieh-Mak, F., K. M. O'Hoy and S. L. Luk (1992) 'Lesbianism in the Chinese of Hong Kong' in Dynes and Donaldson, *Asian Homosexuality*

Lindqvist, Cecilia (1991) *China: Empire of the Written Symbol*, transl. Joan Tate. London: HarperCollins

Linnekin, Jocelyn (1990) *Sacred Queens and Women of Consequence: Rank, Gender, and Colonialism in the Hawaiian Islands*. Ann Arbor: University of Michigan Press

Liu Yung Ho (1990) 'Miscellaneous Talks on the People of the East and West' in Wang Jianguang, *Westerners Through Chinese Eyes*

Lloyd, Genevieve (1989) 'Woman as Other: Sex, Gender and Subjectivity', *Australian Feminist Studies* 10:13–22

Longley, Kateryna O. (1992) 'Fifth World' in Sneja Gunew and Kateryna O. Longley, eds, *Striking Chords: Multicultural Literary Interpretations*. Sydney: Allen & Unwin

Louie, Miriam Ching Yoon (1995) *'Minjung* Feminism: Korean Women's Movement for Gender and Class Liberation', *Women's Studies International Forum* 18(4):417–30

Lu Danni (1995) 'Jade, Peach Blossom, and Red Soldier: Naming Chinese Women' in Feminist Press, *China for Women*

Lu Wenfu (1986) *A World of Dreams*. Beijing: Panda Books

Lucashenko, Melissa (1994) 'No Other Truth?: Aboriginal Women and Australian Feminism', *Social Alternatives* 12(4):21–4

Lucashenko, Melissa and Odette Best (1995) 'Women Bashing: An Aboriginal Perspective', *Social Alternatives* 14(1):19–22

Lucie, Patricia (1984) 'Marriage and Law Reform in Nineteenth Century America' in Elizabeth M. Craik, ed., *Marriage and Property*. Aberdeen: Aberdeen University Press

Lugones, María (1990a) 'Playfulness, "World"-Travelling, and Loving Perception' in Anzaldúa, *Making Face, Making Soul*

Lugones, María (1990b) 'Hablando Cara a Cara/Speaking Face to face: An Exploration of Ethnocentric Racism' in Anzaldúa, *Making Face, Making Soul*

Lugones, María C. and Elizabeth Spelman (1990) ' "Have We Got a Theory for You!": Feminist Theory, Cultural Imperialism and the Demand for "the woman's Voice" ' in Azizah Y. al-Hibri and Margaret A. Simon, eds, *Hypatia Reborn: Essays in Femininst Philosophy*. Bloomington: Indiana University Press

Lugones, María C. (in collaboration with Pat Alake Rosezelle) (1992) 'Sisterhood and Friendship as Feminist Models' in Cheris Kramarae and Dale Spender, eds, *The Knowledge Explosion: Generations of Feminist Scholarship*. New York and London: Teachers College Press, Columbia University

Luo Ping (1995) 'Reflections on My Impressions of Northern Europe' in Wong Yuen Ling, *Reflections and Resonances*

Lutz, Catherine A. and Jane L. Collins (1993) *Reading National Geographic*. Chicago: University of Chicago Press

Lykke, Nina, Anna-Birte Ravn and Birte Siim (1994) 'An Editorial Introduction', *Women's Studies International Forum* 17(2/3):111–16

Lyons, Lenore (1994) Report on the Feminist Reading Workshop Conducted on the AWARE Premises in December 1993. Unpublished paper

• Bibliography

Lyons-Lee, Lenore (1995) Being A Feminist Means ... Exploring the Lives of Young Women in Singapore. Paper presented to the Association of Asian Scholars, Monash University

McClintock, Anne (1995) *Imperial Leather: Race, Gender and Sexuality in the Colonial Context*. Routledge: New York and London

McColl, G. C. (1995) 'Posing: Questions About Cross-Dressing', *Meanjin* 54(1):44–53

McCreery, John L. (1993) 'Women's Property Rights and Dowry in China and South Asia' in Brettell and Sargent, *Gender in Cross-Cultural Perspective*

MacKinnon, Catharine A. (1987) *Feminism Unmodified: Discourse on Life and Law*. Cambridge, Mass. and London: Harvard University Press.

MacKinnon, Catharine A. (1989) *Toward a Feminist Theory of the State*. Cambridge, Mass.: Harvard University Press

MacKinnon, Catharine A. (1994) 'Turning Rape into Pornography: Postmodern Genocide' in Alexandra Stiglmayer, ed., *Mass Rape: The War Against Women in Bosnia-Herzegovina*. Lincoln and London: University of Nebraska Press

MacLeod, Arlene Elowe (1992) 'Hegemonic Relations and Gender Resistance: The New Veiling as Accommodating Protest in Cairo', *Signs* 17(3):533–57

MacMillan, Margaret (1988) *Women of the Raj*. London: Thames & Hudson

McQueen, Humphrey (1991) *Tokyo World: An Australian Diary*. Melbourne: Heinemann

Mahoney, Maureen A. and Barbara Yngvesson (1992) 'The Construction of Subjectivity and the Paradox of Resistance: Reintegrating Feminist Anthropology and Psychology', *Signs* 18(1):44–73

Manderson, Lenore (1992) 'Public Performances in Patpong and Explorations of the Edges of Imagination', *Journal of Sex Research* 29(4):451–75

Manderson, Lenore (1993) Intersections: Western Representations of Thailand and the Commodification of Sex and Race. Paper presented to Wenner-Gren Conference on Theorizing Sexuality: Evolution, Culture, and Development, Cascais, Portugal, 19–26 March

Mani, Lata (1988) 'Contentious Traditions: The Debate on SATI in Colonial India', *Cultural Critique* 7:119–56

Mani, Lata (1990) 'Multiple Mediations: Feminist Scholarship in the Age of Multinational Reception', *Feminist Review* 35:24–41

Marcus, Julie (1990) 'Anthropology, Culture and Post-Modernity', *Social Analysis* Special Issues Series, 27:3–16

Marcus, Julie (1992) *A World of Difference: Islam and Gender Hierarchy in Turkey*. Sydney: Allen & Unwin

Marginson, Melba (1992) 'Not For The Money' in Jocelynne A. Scutt, ed., *Breaking Through: Women, Work and Careers*. Melbourne: Artemis

Margold, Jane A. (1995) 'Narratives of masculinity and transnational migration: Filipino workers in the Middle East' in Ong and Peletz, *Bewitching Women, Pious Men*

Martin, Biddy (1992) 'Sexual Practice and Changing Lesbian Identities' in Barrett and Phillips, *Destabilizing Theory*

Martin, Jeannie (1991) 'Multiculturalism and feminism' in Bottomley et al., *Intersexions*

Martin, Susan Forbes (1993) *Refugee Women*. London and New Jersey: Zed Books

Matsui, Yayori (1995a) 'The Plight of Asian Migrant Women Working in Japan's Sex Industry' in Fujimura-Fanselow and Kameda, *Japanese Women*

Matsui, Yayori (1995b) 'Japanese Power in Asia: A Feminist Critical Analysis' in

Georgina Ashworth, ed., *A Diplomacy of the Oppressed: New Directions in International Feminism*. London: Zed Books

Mattingley, Christobel and Ken Hampton (1988) *Survival in our Land: 'Aboriginal' Experiences in 'South Australia' since 1836 told by Nungas and others*. Adelaide: Wakefield Press

Mazumdar, Sucheta (1994) 'Moving Away from a Secular Vision? Women, Nation and the Cultural Construction of Hindu India' in Moghadam, ed., *Identity Politics and Women*

Mbilinyi, Marjorie and Ruth Meena (1991) 'Introduction' *Signs* 16(4):846–7

Meenakshi (1995) 'The Hidden Hands That Lit the Sati Pyre' in Vilma Fernandes, ed., *Holding Up Half the Sky: A Collection of Incisive Writings on the Women's Question in India by Stree Jagruti Samiti*. Bombay: Stree Jagruti Samiti

Mei Yuan (1990) 'The Beauty, the Water' in Wang Jianguang, *Westerners Through Chinese Eyes*

Mencher, Joan (1993) 'Women, Agriculture and the Sexual Division of Labour: A Three-State Comparison' in Saraswati Raju and Deipica Bagchi, eds, *Women and Work in South Asia*. London: Routledge

Mernissi, Fatima (1991) *Women and Islam: An Historical and Theological Enquiry*, transl. Mary Jo Lakeland. Oxford: Basil Blackwell [first published 1987]

Mernissi, Fatima (1993) *The Forgotten Queens of Islam*, transl. Mary Jo Lakeland. Cambridge: Polity Press

Michel, Andrée (1995) 'Militarisation of Contemporary Societies and Feminism in the North' in Georgina Ashworth, ed., *A Diplomacy of the Oppressed: New Directions in International Feminism*. London: Zed Books

Mies, Maria (1986) *Patriarchy and Accumulation on a World Scale: Women and the International Division of Labour*. London: Zed Books

Mies, Maria (1993) 'Liberating the Consumer' in Maria Mies and Vandana Shiva, *Ecofeminism*. London: Zed Books

Migrant Women's Emergency Support Service, ed. (1987) *Papers from the Seminar 'Domestic Violence – A Cross Cultural Perspective'*. Canberra: Department of Immigration, Local Government and Ethnic Affairs

Miller, Francesca (1991) *Latin American Women and the Search for Social Justice*. Hanover, N.H.: University Press of New England

Mitchell, Susan (1987) *The Matriarchs: Twelve Australian Women Talk About Their Lives*. Melbourne: Penguin

Mitter, Swasti (1994) 'On Organising Women in Casualised Work: A Global Overview' in Sheila Rowbotham and Swasti Mitter, eds, *Dignity and Daily Bread: New Forms of Economic Organising Among the Poor Women in the Third World and the First*. London and New York: Routledge

Miyake, Yoshiko (1991) 'Doubling Expectations: Motherhood and Women's Factory Work Under State Management in Japan in the 1930s and 1940s' in Bernstein, *Recreating Japanese Women*

Mock, John (1996) 'Mother or Mama: The Political Economy of Bar Hostesses in Sapporo' in Imamura, *Re-Imaging Japanese Women*

Moghadam, Valentine M., ed. (1994) *Identity Politics and Women: Cultural Reassertions and Feminisms in Perspective*. Boulder, Col.: Westview Press

Moghadam, Valentine M. (1996) 'The Fourth World Conference on Women: Dissension and Consensus', *Indian Journal of Gender Studies* 3(1):93–102

Mohanty, Chandra Talpade (1992) 'Feminist Encounters: Locating the Politics of Experience' in Barrett and Phillips, *Destabilizing Theory*

Mohanty, Chandra Talpade et al., eds (1991) *Third World Women and the Politics of Feminism*. Bloomington and Indianapolis: Indiana University Press

Molony, Barbara (1995) 'Japan's 1985 Equal Opportunity Law and the Changing Discourse on Gender', *Signs* 20(2):268–302

Momsen, Janet Henshall (1991) *Women and Development in the Third World*. London and New York: Routledge

Monk, Janice et al. (1991) 'Introduction: reaching for global feminism in the curriculum', *Women's Studies International Forum* 14(4):239–47

Moore, Clive (1993) 'The Abominable Crime: First Steps Towards a Social History of Male Homosexuals in Colonial Queensland, 1859–1900' in Robert Aldrich, ed., *Gay Perspectives II: More Essays in Australian Gay Culture*. Sydney: Department of Economic History, University of Sydney, with the Australian Centre for Gay and Lesbian Research

Moore, Henrietta L. (1994a) *A Passion for Difference: Essays in Anthropology and Gender*. Cambridge: Polity Press

Moore, Henrietta (1994b) '"Divided We Stand": Sex, Gender and Sexual Difference', *Feminist Review* 47(Summer):78–95

Moraes-Garecki, Vanda (1991) 'Domesticity and Latin American Women in Australia' in Bottomley et al., *Intersexions*

Moreton-Robinson, Aileen (1992) 'Masking Gender and Exalting Race: Indigenous Women and Commonwealth Employment Policies', *Australian Feminist Studies* 15:5–24

Morgan, Derek (1985) 'Making Motherhood Male: Surrogacy and the Moral Economy of Women', *Journal of Law and Society* 12(2):219–43

Morgan, Robin, ed. (1984) *Sisterhood is Global*. New York: Anchor Press/Doubleday

Morrow, Betty Hearn (1994) 'A Grass-Roots Feminist Response to Intimate Violence in the Caribbean', *Women's Studies International Forum* 17(6):579–92

Mort, Frank (1987) *Dangerous Sexualities: Medico-Moral Politics in England Since 1830*. London and New York: Routledge & Kegan Paul

Mukherjee, Bharati (1973) *The Tiger's Daughter*. London: Chatto & Windus [first published 1971]

Mumford, Kevin J. (1992) '"Lost Manhood" Found: Male Sexual Impotence and Victorian Culture in the United States', *Journal of the History of Sexuality* 3(1):33–57

Murray, Stephen O., ed. (1992) *Oceanic Homosexualities*. New York and London: Garland

Murray, Alison (1993) Dying for a Fuck: Commercial Sex, State Ideology and Implications for HIV/AIDS in Indonesia. Paper presented to the State, Sexuality and Reproduction in Asia and the Pacific Conference, Gender Relations Project, Australian National University, 16–18 July

Muse, Corey J. (1991) 'Women in Western Samoa' in Leonore Loeb Adler, ed., *Women in Cross-Cultural Perspective*. New York: Westport

Myers, Fred R. (1986) *Pintupi Country, Pintupi Self: Sentiment, Place and Politics Among Western Desert Aborigines*. Washington, London and Canberra: Smithsonian Institution Press and Australian Institute of Aboriginal Studies

Nagata, Judith (1995) 'Modern Malay women and the message of the "veil"' in Karim, *'Male' and 'Female' in Developing Southeast Asia*

Nain, Gemma Tang (1991) 'Black Women, Sexism and Racism: Black or Antiracist Feminism?', *Feminist Review* 37:1–22

Nakikus, Margaret et al. (1991) *United Nations Development Programme: Papua New Guinea, Women in Development Sector Review*. Port Moresby: United Nations Development Program

Nam, Jeong-Lim (1994) 'Reforming Economic Allocation in the Family: The Women's Movement and the Role of the State in South Korea', *Women's Studies International Forum* 18(2):113–23

Nanda, Serena (1990) *Neither Man Nor Woman: The Hijras of India*. Belmont, Calif.: Wadsworth Publishers

Nandan, Satendra (1992) 'Artists and Islands in the Pacific' in Gunew and Longley, *Striking Chords*

Nasta, Susheila (1991) Introduction to Susheila Nasta, ed., *Motherlands: Black Women's Writing from Africa, the Caribbean and South Asia*. London: Women's Press

Nelson, Cynthia (1992) 'The Voices of Doria Shafiq: Feminist Consciousness in Egypt, 1940–1960' in Johnson-Odim and Strobel, *Expanding the Boundaries of Women's History*

Nelson, Sarah M. (1993) 'Diversity of the Upper Paleolithic "Venus" Figurines and Archaeological Mythology' in Brettell and Sargent, *Gender in Cross-Cultural Perspective*

Nelson, Topsy Napurrula (1991) 'Letter to the Editors', *Women's Studies International Forum* 14(5):507

New South Wales Law Reform Commission (1988) *Artificial Conception*. Sydney: NSW Law Reform Commission

Ng, Vivien W. (1987) 'Ideology and Sexuality: Rape Laws in Qing China', *Journal of Asian Studies* 46(1):57–70

Nicholas, Ralph W. (1995) 'The Effectiveness of the Hindu Sacrament (*Samskāru*): Caste, Marriage and Divorce in Bengali Culture' in Harlan and Courtwright, *From the Margins of Hindu Marriage*

Nicolaescu, Madalina (1994) 'Post-Communist Transitions: Romanian Women's Responses to Changes in the System of Power', *Journal of Women's History* 5(3):117–28

Niederer, Barbara (1995) 'Women in Chinese Script' in Feminist Press, *China for Women*

Njeuma, Dorothy L. (1993) 'An Overview of Women's Education in Africa' in Conway and Bourque, *The Politics of Women's Education*

Nkrumah, Juliana (1996) 'Female Genital Mutilation: A Development Issue' in Margaret Winn et al., eds, *Women Sexuality Culture*. Sydney: Women's Studies Centre, University of Sydney

Nolte, Sharon H. and Sally Ann Hastings (1991) 'The Meiji State's Policy Toward Women, 1890–1910' in Bernstein, *Recreating Japanese Women*

Noonuccal, Oodgeroo (1989) 'Towards a Global Village in the Southern Hemisphere'. Nathan: Institute for Cultural Policy Studies, Division of Humanities, Griffith University

Norton, Anne (1992) 'Gender, Sexuality and the Iraq of Our Imagination', *Middle East Report* 21(6):26–8

Nowicka, Wanda (1994) 'Two Steps Back: Poland's New Abortion Law', *Journal of Women's History* 5(3):151–5

Oaks, Laury (1994) 'Fetal Spirithood and Fetal Personhood: The Cultural Construction of Abortion in Japan', *Women's Studies International Forum* 17(5):511–23

Obbo, Christine (1989) 'Sexuality and Economic Domination in Uganda' in Nira

Yuval-Davis and Floya Anthias, eds, *Woman-Nation-State*. Basingstoke, UK: Macmillan

Obbo, Christine (1992) 'HIV Transmission: Men are the Solution' in James and. Busia, *Theorizing Black Feminisms*

O'Brien, Mary (1981) *The Politics of Reproduction*. London: Routledge & Kegan Paul

O'Brien, Mary (1989) *Reproducing the World: Essays in Feminist Theory*. Boulder, Col.: Westview Press

O'Harrow, Stephen (1995) 'Vietnamese women and Confucianism: creating spaces from patriarchy' in Karim, *'Male' and 'Female' in Developing Southeast Asia*

Odeh, Lama Abu (1993) 'Post-Colonial Feminism and the Veil: Thinking the Difference', *Feminist Review* 43(Spring):26–37

Oduol, Wilhelmina and Wanjiku Mukabi Kabira (1995) 'The mother of warriors and her daughters: the women's movement in Kenya' in Basu, *The Challenge of Local Feminisms*

Odzer, Cleo (1994) *Patpong Sisters: An American Woman's View of the Bangkok Sex World*. New York: Blue Moon Books/Arcade Publishing

Oey-Gardiner, Mayling (1991) 'A commentary from an Indonesian perspective', *Asian Studies Review* 15(1):100–7

Ofei-Aboagye, Rosemary Ofeibea (1994) 'Altering the Strands of the Fabric: A Preliminary Look at Domestic Violence in Ghana', *Signs* 19(4):924–38

Office of the Status of Women, Department of the Prime Minister and Cabinet (1995) *Australian National Report to the United Nations Fourth World Conference on Women*. Canberra: Commonwealth of Australia

Ogle, Greg (1994) 'An Alternative Trade', *Social Alternatives* 13(3&4):17–19

Ogundipe-Leslie, 'Molara (1992) 'African Women, Culture and Another Development' in James and Busia, *Theorizing Black Feminisms*

Oldenburg, Veena T. (1994) book review: 'May You Be the Mother of a Hundred Sons: A Journey Among the Women of India', *Manushi* 84:39–43

Ong, Aihwa (1987) *Spirits of Resistance and Capitalist Development: Factory Workers in Malaysia*. New York: Albany State University and New York Press

Ong, Aihwa (1995) 'State versus Islam: Malay families, women's bodies and the body politic in Malaysia' in Aihwa Ong and Michael G. Peletz, eds, *Bewitching Women, Pious Men: Gender and Body Politics in Southeast Asia*. Berkeley and Los Angeles: University of California Press

Oppel, Frances (1994) 'Irigaray's Goddesses', *Australian Feminist Studies* 20:77–90

Orfini, Kristina et al. (1991) 'Nations of Families' in Antoine Prost and Gérard Vincent, eds, *A History of Private Life* vol. 5, transl. Arthur Goldhammer. Cambridge, Mass.: Belknap, Harvard University Press

Otto, Dianne (1996) 'Holding Up Half the Sky, But For Whose Benefit? A Critical Analysis of the Fourth World Conference on Women', *Australian Feminist Law Journal* 6(March):7–28

Ounei, Susanna (1987) 'Kanak Women: Out of the Kitchen into the Struggle' in Davies, *Third World – Second Sex*. London: Zed Books

Ounei, Susanna (1992) 'For an Independent Kanaky' in Lenora Foerstal and Angela Gilliam, eds, *Confronting the Margaret Mead Legacy: Scholarship, Empire and the South Pacific*. Philadelphia: Temple University Press

Ounei, Susanna (1995) 'New Caledonia' in International Commission of Jurists, ed., *Women and the Law in the Pacific*. Geneva: International Commission of Jurists

Paidar, Parvin (1996) 'Feminism and Islam in Iran' in Deniz Kandiyoti, ed., *Gendering the Middle East: Emerging Perspectives*. London: I. B. Tauris

Pala, Achola O. (1977) 'Definitions of Women and Development: an African Perspective', *Signs* 3(1):9–13

Pallotta-Chiarolli, Maria and Zlatko Skrbis (1994) 'Authority, Compliance and Rebellion in Second Generation Cultural Minorities', *Australian and New Zealand Journal of Sociology* 30(3):259–72

Parashar, Archana (1992) *Women and Family Law Reforms in India: Uniform Civil Code and Gender Equality*. New Delhi: Sage

Parashar, Archana (1993) The Indian State, Religious Personal Laws and Women's Struggle for Equality. Paper presented to the State, Sexuality and Reproduction in Asia and the Pacific Conference, Gender Relations Project, Australian National University, 16–18 July

Parker, Lynette (1993) Witches, Bees and IUDs: Sexuality and Fertility Control in Bali. Paper presented to the State, Sexuality and Reproduction in Asia and the Pacific Conference, Gender Relations Project, Australian National University, 16–18 July

Parker, Richard (1988) 'Youth, Identity and Homosexuality: The Changing Shape of Sexual Life in Contemporary Brazil', *Journal of Homosexuality* 17(3/4):269–89

Parker, Richard (1986) 'Masculinity, Femininity, and Homosexuality: On the Anthropological Interpretation of Sexual Meanings in Brazil', *Journal of Homosexuality* 11(3/4):155–63

Pathak, Zakia and Rajan, Rajeswari Sunder (1992) '"Shahbano"' in Judith Butler and Joan W. Scott, eds, *Feminists Theorize the Political*. New York: Routledge

Peletz, Michael G. (1995) 'Neither Reasonable Nor Responsible: Contrasting Representations of Masculinity in a Malay Society' in Ong and Peletz, eds, *Bewitching Women, Pious Men*

Peña, Manuel (1991) 'Class, Gender and Machismo: The "Treacherous-Woman" folklore of Mexican Male Workers', *Gender and Society* 5(1):30–46

People's Republic of China (1994) 'The Report of the People's Republic of China on the Implementation of the Nairobi Forward-Looking Strategies for the Advancement of Women', *Beijing Review* 37(43):7–28

Peredo, Petite O. (1991) 'United States Military Bases And Their Impact On Women in the Philippines' in Lenora Foerstel, ed., *Women's Voices on the Pacific*. Washington: Maisonneuve Press

Perrott, Michelle, ed. (1990) *A History of Private Life* vol. 4, transl. Arthur Goldhammer. Cambridge, Mass.: Belknap, Harvard University Press

Perrott, Michelle and Anne Martin-Fugier (1990) 'The Actors' in Perrott, *A History of Private Life* vol. 4

Perrott, Michelle and Roger-Henri Guerrand (1990) 'Scenes and Places' in Perrott, *A History of Private Life* vol. 4

Petchesky, Rosalind Pollack (1986) *Abortion and Woman's Choice: The State, Sexuality and Reproductive Freedom*. London:Verso

Petrova, Dimitrina (1994) 'What Can Women Do to Change the Totalitarian Cultural Context?', *Women's Studies International Forum* 17(2/3):267–71

Pettman, Jan (1988) 'Whose Country is it Anyway? Cultural Politics, Racism and the Construction of Being Australian'. Working Paper No. 39, Canberra: Research School of Pacific Studies, Australian National University.

Pettman, Jan (1991) 'Racism, sexism and sociology' in Bottomley et al., *Intersexions*

Pettman, Jan (1992) Women, Nationalism and the State: Towards an International

Feminist Perspective. Paper presented at the Fourth Australian Women's Studies Association Conference, Sydney, October, forthcoming as an occasional paper in Gender and Development Studies, Asian Institute of Technology, Bangkok.

Pettman, Jan Jindy (1996) *Worlding Women: A Feminist International Politics.* Sydney: Allen & Unwin

Pheterson, Gail (1990) 'Alliances Between Women: Overcoming Internalized Oppression and Internalized Domination' in Albrecht and Brewer, *Bridges of Power*

Pietilä, Hikka and Jeanne Vickers (1990) *Making Women Matter: The Role of the United Nations.* London: Zed Books

Plumwood, Val (1993) *Feminism and the Mastery of Nature.* London and New York: Routledge

Poivre, Pierre (1993) 'Description of Cochinchina, 1749–50' in Li Tana and Anthony Reid, eds, *Southern Vietnam under the Nguyễn: Documents on the Economic History of Cochinchina (Đàng Trong), 1602–1777.* Singapore: Institute of Southeast Asian Studies

Pollard, Alice (1995) Paper presented to 'Towards Beijing' Conference, Centre for Asia Pacific Studies, Victoria University of Technology, St Albans, Vic., 9–11 February

Potiki, Roma (1991) 'Confirming Identity and Telling the Stories: A Woman's Perspective on Māori Theatre' in Rosemary du Plessis, ed., *Feminist Voices: Women's Studies Texts for Aotearoa/New Zealand.* Auckland: Oxford University Press

Probert, Belinda (1989) *Working Life.* Melbourne: McPhee-Gribble

Probyn, Elspeth (1993) *Sexing the Self: Gendered Positions in Cultural Studies.* London and New York: Routledge

Proctor, Robert (1988) *Racial Hygiene: Medicine Under the Nazis.* Cambridge, Mass.: Harvard University Press

Radl, Shirley Rogers (1983) *The Invisible Women: Target of the Religious Right.* Laurence: Delta.

Raheja, Gloria Goodwin (1995) '"Crying When She's Born and Crying When She Goes Away": Marriage and the Idiom of the Gift in Pahansu Song Performance' in Harlan and Courtwright, *From the Margins of Hindu Marriage*

Rajan, Rajeswari Sunder (1990) 'The Subject of Sati: Pain and Death in the Contemporary Discourse on Sati', *Yale Journal of Criticism* 3(2):1–28

Rajan, Rajeswari Sunder (1993) *Real and Imagined Women: Gender, Culture and Post-Colonialism.* London: Routledge

Raju, Saraswati (1993) Introduction to Saraswati Raju and Deipica Bagchi, eds, *Women and Work in South Asia.* London: Routledge

Ram, Kalpana (1991a) '"First" and "Third World" feminisms: a new perspective?', *Asian Studies Review* 15(1):91–6

Ram, Kalpana (1991b) *Mukkuvar Women: Gender, Hegemony and Capitalist Transformation in a South Indian Fishing Village.* Sydney: Allen & Unwin

Ram, Kalpana (1996) 'Liberal Multiculturalism's "NESB Women": A South Asian Post-colonial Feminist Perspective on the Liberal Impoverishment of "Difference"' in Ellie Vasta and Stephen Castles, eds, *The Teeth are Smiling: The Persistence of Racism in Multi-cultural Australia.* Sydney: Allen & Unwin

Ramusack, Barbara N. (1990) 'Cultural Missionaries, Maternal Imperialists, Feminist Allies: British Women Activists in India, 1865–1945', *Women's Studies International Forum* 13(4):309–22

Ramusack, Barbara N. (1992) 'Embattled Advocates: The Debate Over Birth

Control in India, 1920–1940' in Johnson-Odim and Strobel, *Expanding the Boundaries of Women's History*

Randall, Margaret (1994) *Sandino's Daughters Revisited: Feminism in Nicaragua*. New Brunswick, N.J.: Rutgers University Press

Ranke-Heinemann, Uta (1991) *Eunuchs for the Kingdom of Heaven: Women, Sexuality and the Catholic Church*. London: Penguin

Rarua, Kathleen (1988) 'Vanuatu' in Taiamoni Tongamoa, ed., *Pacific Women: Roles and Status of Women in Pacific Societies*. Suva: Institute of Pacific Studies of the University of the South Pacific

Rasbridge, Lance (1996) 'An Anthropological Approach to Cambodian Refugee Women: Reciprocity in Oral Histories' in Gwendolyn Etter-Lewis and Michèle Foster, eds, *Unrelated Kin: Race and Gender in Women's Personal Narratives*. New York: Routledge

Razack, Sherene (1994) 'What is to Be Gained by Looking White People in the Eye? Culture, Race, and Gender in Cases of Sexual Violence', *Signs* 19(4): 894–923

Reagon, Bernice Johnson (1983) 'Coalition Politics: turning the Century' in Barbara Smith, ed., *Home Girls: A Black Feminist Anthology*. New York: Kitchen Table, Women of Color Press

Reay, Marie (1975) 'Politics, Development and Women in the Rural Highlands', *Administration for Development* 5:4–13

Régnier-Bohter, Danielle (1987) 'Imagining the Self: Exploring Literature' in Antoine Prost and Gérard Vincent, eds, *A History of Private Life* vol. 5, transl. Arthur Goldhammer. Cambridge, Mass.: Belknap, Harvard University Press

Reist, Melinda Tankard (1995) 'China's One-Child Policy' in Feminist Press, *China for Women*

Rele, J. R. and Iqbal Alam (1993) 'Fertility Transition in Asia: The Statistical Evidence' in Leete and Alam, *The Revolution in Asian Fertility*

Remy, John (1990) 'Patriarchy and Fratriarchy as forms of Androcracy' in Jeff Hearn and David Morgan, eds, *Men, Masculinities and Social Theory*. London: Unwin Hyman

Renteln, Alison Dundes (1992) 'Sex Selection and Reproductive Freedom', *Women's Studies International Forum* 15(3):405–26

Research Institute of All China Women's Federation and Research Office of Shaanxi Provincial Women's Federation (1991) *Statistics on Chinese Women (1949–1989)*. Beijing: China Statistical Publishing House

Revel, Jacques et al. (1989) 'Forms of Privatization' in Roger Chartier, ed., *A History of Private Life* vol. 3. Cambridge, Mass.: Belknap, Harvard University Press

Rich, Adrienne (1984) *On Lies, Secrets and Silence: Selected Prose 1966–1978*. London: Virago

Rigg, Julie and Julie Copeland, eds, (1985) *Coming Out! Women's Voices, Women's Lives: A Selection From ABC Radio's Coming Out Show*. Melbourne: Nelson in association with the Australian Broadcasting Corporation

Risseeuw, Carla (1988) *The Fish Don't Talk About the Water: Gender Transformation, Power and Resistance Among Women of Sri Lanka*. Leiden: E. J. Brill

Robertson, Claire (1996) 'Grassroots in Kenya: Women, Genital Mutilation, and Collective Action, 1920–1990', *Signs* 21(3):615–42

Robertson, Jennifer (1991) 'The Shingaku Woman: Straight from the Heart' in Bernstein, *Recreating Japanese Women*

Robinson, Kathryn (1996) 'Of Mail-Order Brides and "Boys' Own" Tales: Representations of Asian-Australian Marriages', *Feminist Review* 52:53–68

Rodd, Laurel Rasplica (1991) 'Yosano Akiko and the Taishō Debate over the "New Woman"' in Bernstein, *Recreating Japanese Women*

Rogers, Barbara (1980) *The Domestication of Women: Discrimination in Developing Societies*. London: Kegan Paul

Rolls, Eric (1992) *Sojourners: The Epic Story of China's Centuries-Old Relationship with Australia*. Brisbane: University of Queensland Press

Roman, Leslie G. (1993) 'White is a Color! White Defensiveness, Postmodernism, and Anti-racist Pedagogy' in Cameron McCarthy and Warrean Crietchlow, eds, *Race Identity and Representation in Education*. New York: Routledge & Kegan Paul

Ropp, Paul S. (1993) 'Love, Literacy, and Laments: Themes of Women Writers in Late Imperial China', *Women's History Review* 2(1):107–41

Rosa, Kumudhani (1994) 'The Conditions and Organisational Activities of Women in Free Trade Zones: Malaysia, Philippines and Sri Lanka, 1970–1990' in Sheila Rowbotham and Swasti Mitter, eds, *Dignity and Daily Bread: New Forms Economic Organising Among the Poor Women in the Third World and the First*. London and New York: Routledge

Roscoe, Will (1994) 'How to Become a Bedarche: Toward a Unified Analysis of Gender Diversity' in Gilbert Herdt, ed., *Third Sex, Third Gender: Beyond Sexual Dimorphism in Culture and History*. New York: Zone Books

Rosemberg, Fúlvia (1993) 'Education, Race and Inequality in Brazil' in Conway and Bourque, *The Politics of Women's Education*

Rosenberger, Nancy R., ed. (1992) *Japanese Sense of the Self*. Cambridge: Cambridge University Press

Rosenberger, Nancy R. (1996) 'Fragile Resistance, Signs of Status: Women Between State and Media in Japan' in Imamura, *Re-Imaging Japanese Women*

Ross, Ellen (1995) 'New Thoughts on "the Oldest Vocation": Mothers and Motherhood in Recent Feminist Scholarship', *Signs* 20(2):397–413

Ross, Loretta J. (1992) 'Abortion: 1800–1970' in James and Busia, *Theorizing Black Feminisms*

Rouche, Michel (1987) 'The early Middle Ages in the West' in Paul Veyne, ed., *A History of Private Life* vol. 1, transl. Arthur Goldhammer. Cambridge, Mass.: Belknap, Harvard University Press

Rowbotham, Sheila (1992) *Women in Movement: Feminism and Social Action*. London: Routledge

Rowe, William and Vivian Schelling (1991) *Memory and Modernity: Popular Culture in Latin America*. London: Verso

Rowland, Robyn, ed. (1984) *Women Who Do and Women Who Don't Join the Women's Movement*. London: Routledge & Kegan Paul

Rowland, Robyn (1988) *Woman Herself: A Transdisciplinary Perspective on Woman's Identity*. Melbourne: Oxford University Press

Rowland, Robyn (1992) *Living Laboratories: Women and Reproductive Technologies*. Melbourne: Sun Books

Rozario, Santi (1991) 'Ethno-religious communities and gender divisions in Bangladesh: Women as boundary markers' in Bottomley et al., *Intersexions*

Ruan, Fang-fu and Yung-mei Tsai (1992) 'Male homosexuality in Contemporary Mainland China' in Dynes and Donaldson, *Asian Homosexuality*

Rubin, Gayle (1975) 'The Traffic in Women: Notes on the "Political Economy" of Sex' in Rayna R. Reiter, ed., *Towards an Anthropology of Women*. New York: Monthly Review Press

Rushdie, Salman (1988) *The Satanic Verses*. London: Viking

Russell, Diana (1996) 'US Pornography Invades South Africa: A Content Analysis of *Playboy* and *Penthouse*' in Diane Bell and Renate Klein, eds, *Radically Speaking: Feminism Reclaimed*. Melbourne: Spinifex Press

Russell, Pamela (1993) 'The Palaeolithic Mother-Goddess: Fact or Fiction?' in Hilary du Cros and Laurajane Smith, eds, *Women in Archaeology: A Feminist Critique*. Canberra: Department of Prehistory, Research School of Pacific Studies, Australian National University

Saadawi, Nawal el (1980) *The Hidden Face of Eve*. London: Zed Books

Saadawi, Nawal el (1983) *Woman at Point Zero*, transl. Sherif Hetata. London: Zed Books [first published 1975]

Sacks, Karen (1979) *Sisters and Wives: the Past and Future of Sexual Equality*. Westport, Conn.: Greenwood Press

Said, Edward W. (1985a) *Orientalism*. London: Penguin [first published 1978]

Said, Edward W. (1985b) 'Orientalism Reconsidered', *Cultural Critique* 1:98–107

Said, Edward W. (1995) 'East Isn't East', *Times Literary Supplement* 3 February:3–6

Salomon-Nékiriai, Christine (1996) 'Men and Women in New Caledonia: A Smouldering Antagonism' in Margaret Winn et al., eds, *Women, Sexuality, Culture*. Sydney: Women's Studies Centre, University of Sydney

Sambo, Dalee (1994) 'Cultural Rights' Presentation at the Women, Power and Politics Conference, 8–11 October, Adelaide Convention Centre, organised by the Women's Suffrage Steering Committee and Conference Committee

Sánchez-Ayéndez, Melba (1992) 'Puerto Rican Elderly Women: Shared Meanings and Informal Supportive networks' in Margaret L. Anderson and Patricia Hill Collins, eds, *Race, Class and Gender*. Belmont, Calif.: Wadsworth

Sand, Reena et al. (1994) 'Modern Day Marriages', *Femina* 23 January 1994:7–20

Sanday, Peggy Reeves (1981) *Female Power and Male Dominance: On the Origins of Sexual Inequality*.Cambridge: Cambridge University Press

Sandoval, Chela (1991) 'U.S. Third World Feminism: The Theory and Method of Oppositional Consciousness in the Postmodern World', *Genders* 10(Spring): 1–24

Sangari, Kumkum and Sudeshi Vaid (1990) 'Recasting Women: An Introduction' in Kumkum Sangari and Sudesh Vaid, eds, *Recasting Women: Essays in Indian Colonial History*. New Brunswick, N.J.: Rutgers University Press

Sartre, Jean-Paul (1965) Preface to Frantz Fanon, *The Wretched of the Earth*, transl. Constance Farrington. London: Penguin [first published 1961]

Sawer, Marian and Abigail Groves (1994) *Working From the Inside: Twenty Years of the Office of the Status of Women*. Canberra: Australian Government Publishing Service

Sawer, Marian and Marian Simms (1993) *A Woman's Place: Women and Politics in Australia* 2nd edn. Sydney: Allen & Unwin

Schädler, Monika (1995) 'Economic Reforms and Rural Women' in Feminist Press, *China for Women*

Schmidt, Elizabeth (1991) 'Patriarchy, Capitalism, and the Colonial State in Zimbabwe', *Signs* 16(4):732–56

Schultz, Vicki (1992) 'Women "Before" the Law: Judicial Stories about Women, Work, and Sex Segregation on the Job' in Judith Butler and Joan W. Scott, eds, *Feminists Theorize the Political*. New York: Routledge

Screech, Timon (1993) 'Race and Gender? Human Categorisation in Japan' in Sunil Gupta, ed., *Disrupted Borders: An Intervention in Definitions and Boundaries*. London: Rivers Oram Press

Scutt, Jocelynne A., ed. (1988) *The Baby Machine: Commercialisation of Motherhood*. Melbourne: McCulloch

Seager, Joni (1993) *Earth Follies: Coming to Feminist Terms with the Global Environmental Crisis*. New York: Routledge

Sedgwick, Eve Kosofsky (1990) *Epistemology of the Closet*. Berkeley and Los Angeles: University of California Press

Segura, Denise A. and Jennifer L. Pierce (1993) 'Chicanaó Family Structure and Gender Personality: Chodorow, Familism, and Psychoanalytic Sociology Revisited', *Signs* 19(1):62–91

Seidman, Steven (1994) *Contested Knowledge: Social Theory in the Postmodern Era*. Cambridge, Mass.: Blackwell

Sen, Amartya (1990) 'More Than 100 Million Women Are Missing', *New York Review* 20 December:61–6

Shaaban, Bouthaina (1988) *Both Right and Left Handed: Arab Women Talk About Their Lives*. London: Women's Press

Shaanxi Provincial Women's Federation (1991) *Shaanxi Women 1949–1989*. Xian: Shaanxi Travel and Tourism Publishing House

Shaheed, Farida (1994) 'Controlled or Autonomous: Identity and the Experience of the Network, Women Living Under Muslim Laws', *Signs* 19(4):997–1019

Shaheed, Farida and Khawar Mumtaz (1993) 'Women's Education in Pakistan' in Conway and Bourque, *The Politics of Women's Education*

Shahidian, Hammed (1991) 'The Education of Women in the Islamic Republic of Iran', *Journal of Women's History* 2(3):6–38

Shami, Seteney et al. (1990) *Women in Arab Society: Work Patterns and Gender Relations in Egypt, Jordan and Sudan*. Oxford and Paris: Berg and United Nations Educational, Scientific and Cultural Organization

Shang Rongguang (1990) 'The Americans I Know: Not Much Different from Us Chinese' in Wang Jianguang, *Westerners Through Chinese Eyes*

Sharpe, Jenny (1993) *Allegories of Empire: The Figure of Woman in the Colonial Text*. Minneapolis: University of Minnesota Press

Shields, Bob, ed. (1992) *Lifestyle Shopping: The Subject of Consumption*. London: Routledge

Shiva, Vandana (1988) *Staying Alive: Women, Ecology and Development*. London: Zed Books

Shoemaker, Nancy (1991) 'The Rise and Fall of Iroquois Women', *Journal of Women's History* 2(3):39–57

Shreve, Anita (1989) *Women Together, Women Alone: The Legacy of the Consciousness-Raising Movement*. New York: Viking Penguin

Shukrallah, Hala (1994) 'The Impact of the Islamic Movement in Egypt', *Feminist Review* 47(Summer):15–32

Sievers, Sharon (1993) 'Recent Historical Scholarship on Japanese Women', *Journal of Women's History* 4(3):190–8

Silman, Janet (1987) *Enough is Enough: Aboriginal Women Speak Out*. Toronto: Women's Press

Silverberg, Miriam (1991) 'The Modern Girl as Militant' in Bernstein, *Recreating Japanese Women*

Simson, Ina (1995) 'Love, Marriage, and Violence: Sexuality in China' in Feminist Press, *China for Women*

Singh, Parlo (1994a) 'Generating Literacies of "Difference" from the "Belly of the Beast"', *Australian Journal of Language and Literacy* 17(2):92–100

Singh, Parlo (1994b) The Colonial Legacy of Regulating Third World Women as the Alluring Other. Unpublished paper

Singh, Renuka (1990) *The Womb of Mind: A Sociological Exploration of the Status-Experience of Women in Delhi*. New Delhi: Gangpura

Singhal, Uma and Nihar R. Mrinal (1991) 'Life Stages in the Development of the Hindu Woman' in Leonore Loeb Adler, ed., *Women in Cross-Cultural Perspective*. New York: Westport

Sinha, Mrinalini (1994) 'Reading *Mother India*: Empire, Nation and the Female Voice', *Journal of Women's History* 6(2):6–44

Smedley, Agnes (1995) 'Silk Workers' in Feminist Press, *China for Women*

Smith, Linda Tuhiwai (1994) 'In Search of a Language and a Shareable Imaginative World: E Kore Taku Moe E Riro I A Koe', *Hecate* 20(2):162–74

Smith, Sidonie (1993) *Subjectivity, Identity and the Body*. Bloomington, Indiana: Indiana University Press

Smith-Rosenberg, Carroll (1983) 'The Female World of Love and Ritual: Relations between Women in Nineteenth-Century America' in Elizabeth Abel and Emily K. Abel, eds, *The Signs Reader: Women, Gender and Scholarship*. Chicago: University of Chicago Press [article first published 1975]

Snitow, Ann (1990) 'A Gender Diary' in Marianne Hirsch and Evelyn Fox Keller, eds, *Conflicts in Feminism*. New York and London: Routledge

Soares, Vera et al. (1995) 'Brazilian feminism and women's movements: a two-way street' in Basu, *The Challenge of Local Feminisms*

Sontag, Susan (1979) *I, etcetera*. New York: Random House

Spivak, Gayatri Chakravorty (1987) *In Other Words: Essays in Culture and Politics*. New York: Methuen

Spivak, Gayatri Chakravorty (1992) 'The Politics of Translation' in Barrett and Phillips, *Destabilizing Theory*

Spivak, Gayatri Chakravorty (1994) Paper presented to 'Culture/Sex/ Economies Conference', School of Law and Legal Studies, La Trobe University, Melbourne, 16–18 December

Stacey, Judith (1990) *Brave New Families: Stories of Domestic Upheaval in Late Twentieth Century America*. New York: Basic Books HarperCollins

Starke, J. G. (1988) 'Surrogate Motherhood and the Appeal in the Baby M Case', *Australian Law Journal* 62(5):324–7

Steady, Filomina Chioma (1992) 'Women and Collective Action: Female Models in Transition' in James and Busia, *Theorizing Black Feminisms*

Stearns, Peter N. (1990) *Be a Man! Males in Modern Society*. New York: Holmes & Meier [first published 1979]

Steinhoff, Patricia G. and Kazuko Tanaka (1994) 'Women managers in Japan' in Nancy J. Adler and Dafna N. Islaili, eds, *Competitive Frontiers: Women Managers in a Global Economy*. Cambridge, Mass.: Blackwell

Sternfeld, Eva (1995) 'A Stone Age Matriarchy: The Yangshao Culture' in Feminist Press, *China for Women*

Stiglmayer, Alexandra (1995) 'The Rapes in Bosnia-Herzegovina' in Alexandra Stiglmayer, ed., *Mass Rape: The War Against Women in Bosnia-Herzegovina*. Lincoln and London: University of Nebraska Press

Stimpson, Catharine R. (1988) *Where the Meanings Are*. New York: Methuen

Stivens, Maila (1985) 'The Private Life of the Extended Family: Family, Kinship and Class in a Middle Class Sydney Suburb' in Lenore Manderson, ed., *Australian Ways: Anthropological Studies of an Industrialised Society*. Sydney: Allen & Unwin

Stivens, Maila (1994) 'Gender at the Margins: Paradigms and Peasantries in Rural Malaysia', *Women's Studies International Forum* 17(4):373–90

Stivens, Maila (1996) *Matriliny and Modernity: Sexual Politics and Social Change in Rural Malaysia*. Sydney: Allen & Unwin

Stoller, Robert J. (1968) *Sex and Gender or The Development of Masculinity and Femininity*. New York: Science House

Stone, Lawrence (1990) *Road to Divorce: England 1530–1987*. Oxford: Oxford University Press

Stone, Linda and Caroline James (1995) 'Dowry, Bride-Burning, and Female Power in India', *Women's Studies International Forum* 18(2):125–34

Strathern, Marilyn (1988) *Gender of the Gift*. Berkeley: University of California Press

Sun, Lung-kee (1991) 'Contemporary Chinese Culture: Structure and Emotionality', *Australian Journal of Chinese Affairs* 26:1–25

Sybylla, Roe (1990) 'Old Plans, New Specifications: A Reading of the Medical Discourse of Menopause', *Australian Feminist Studies* 12:95–107

Sykes, Roberta (1975) 'Black Women in Australia: A History' in Jan Mercer, ed., *The Other Half: Women in Australian Society*. Melbourne: Penguin

Sykes, Roberta B. (1990) 'Black Women and the Continuing Struggle for Resources' in Dale Spender, ed., *Heroines: A Contemporary Anthology of Australian Women Writers*. Melbourne: Penguin

Szaszy, Dame Mira (1993) 'Opening My Mouth' in Sue Kedgley and Mary Varnham, eds, *Heading Nowhere in a Navy Blue Suit and Other Tales from the Feminist Revolution*. Wellington: Daphne Brasel Associates Press

Tan, Amy (1990) *The Joy Luck Club*. London: Minerva (Octopus Publishing)

Tan, Amy (1991) *The Kitchen God's Wife*. New York: G. P. Putnam's Sons

Tan, Cheng Imm (1994) 'Thinking about Asian oppression and liberation' in Elena Featherstone, ed., *Skin Deep: Women Writing on Color, Culture and Identity*. Freedom, Calif.: Crossing Press

Tanaka, Kazuko (1995) 'The new feminist movement in Japan, 1970–1990' in Fujimura-Fanselow and Kameda, *Japanese Women*

Tavakoli-Targhi, Mohamad (1994) 'Women of the West Imagined: The *Farangi* Other and the Emergence of the Woman Question in Iran' in Moghadam, *Identity Politics and Women*

Teng, Jin Hua Emma (1990) 'Religion as a Source of Oppression and Creativity for Chinese Women', *Journal of Women and Gender Issues* 2(January):165–94

Terry, Les (1995) '"Not a Postmodern Nomad": A Conversation with Stuart Hall on Race, Ethnicity and Identity', *Arena Journal* 5:51–70

Tharu, Susie and K. Lalita (1991) *Women Writing in India: 600 BC to the Present* vol. 1. New York: Feminist Press

Thobani, Sunera (1992) 'Making the Links: South Asian Women and the Struggle for Reproductive Rights', *Canadian Woman Studies/Cahiers de la Femme* 13(1):19–22

Thomas, Nicholas (1989) 'Domestic Structures and Polyandry in the Marquesas Islands' in Margaret Jolly and Martha Macintyre, eds, *Family and Gender in the Pacific: Domestic Contradictions and the Colonial Impact*. Cambridge: Cambridge University Press

Thomas, Nicholas (1992) 'Fear and Loathing in the Postcolonial Pacific', *Meanjin* 2:265–76

Thomas, Nicholas (1994) *Colonialism's Culture: Anthropology, Travel and Government*. Cambridge: Polity Press

Thubron, Colin (1987) *Behind the Wall: a Journey Through China*. London: Heinemann

Tobin, Joseph (1992) 'Japanese Preschools in the Pedagogy of Selfhood' in Rosenberger, *Japanese Sense of the Self*

Tomaševski, Katarina (1995) *Women and Human Rights*. London and New Jersey: Zed Books

Topley, Marjorie (1975) 'Marriage Resistance in Rural Kwangtung' in Margery Wolf and Roxanne Witke, eds, *Women in Chinese Society*. Stanford: Stanford University Press

Townsend, Janet (1993) 'Housewifisation and Colonisation in the Colombian Rainforest' in Janet Henshall et al., eds, *Different Places, Different Voices: Gender and Development in Africa, Asia and Latin America*. London and New York: Routledge

Traue, Jim (1991) 'A Citizen of the Polis with a Library Card and Borrowing Rights' in King, *Pakeha*

Travaglia, Joanne and Elizabeth Weiss (1992) 'A Girl's Guide to Bomboniere' in Karen Herne, Joanne Travaglia and Elizabeth Weiss, eds, *Who Do You Think You Are? Second Generation Immigrant Women in Australia*. Sydney: Women's Redress Press

Trinh, Minh-ha T. (1987) 'Difference: "A Special Third World Women Issue"', *Feminist Review* 25:5–22

Trinh, Minh-Ha T. (1992) *Framer Framed*. New York and London: Routledge

Trinh, Minh-ha T. (1993) 'All-owning Spectatorship' in Gunew and Yeatman, *Feminism and Politics of Difference*

Trombley, Stephen (1988) *The Right to Reproduce: A History of Coercive Sterilization*. London: Weidenfeld & Nicolson

Truong, Thanh-dam (1990) *Sex, Money and Morality: Prostitution and Tourism in Thailand*. London: Zed Books

Truong, Thanh-Dam (1994) 'Passage to Womanhood and Feminism: Bridge over Troubled Water' in Lazarus et al., *Women's Studies Women's Lives*

Tsui, Elaine Yi-lan (1990) 'Are Married Daughters "Spilled Water"? – A Case Study of Working Women in Urban Taiwan', *Journal of Women and Gender Studies* 1(January):1–37

Tuivaga, Jesse (1988) 'Fiji' in Taiamoni Tongamoa, ed., *Pacific Women: Roles and Status of Women in Pacific Societies*, Suva: Institute of Pacific Studies of the University of the South Pacific

Underhill-Sem, Yvonne (1994) 'Blame it All on Population: Perceptions, Statistics and Reality in the Population Debate in the Pacific' in Emberson-Bain, *Sustainable Development or Malignant Growth?*

United Nations (1991) *The World's Women 1970–1990: Trends and Statistics*. New York: United Nations

United Nations (1995) *The World's Women 1995: Trends and Statistics*. New York: United Nations

United Nations Information Centre in Sydney for Australia, New Zealand and the South Pacific (1995) *Beijing Declaration and Platform for Action* adopted by the Fourth World Conference on Women: Action for Equality, Development and Peace, Beijing, 15 September

Uno, Kathleen S. (1991) 'Women and Changes in the Household Division of Labor' in Bernstein, *Recreating Japanese Women*

Valeri, Valerio (1990) 'Both Nature and Culture: Reflections on Menstrual and Parturitional Taboos in Huaulu (Seram)' in Jane Monnig Atkinson and Shelly Errington, eds, *Power and Difference: Gender in Island Southeast Asia*. Stanford: Stanford University Press van den Berghe, Pierre L. (1979) *Human Family Systems: An Evolutionary View*. New York and North Holland: Elsevier

Vargas, Virginia (1993) 'Academia and the Feminist Movement in Latin America' in Mary Kennedy et al., eds, *Making Connections: Women's Studies, Women's Movements, Women's Lives*. London and Washington: Taylor & Francis

Vasta, Ellie (1991) 'Gender, Class and Ethnic Relations: The Domestic and Work Experiences of Italian Migrant Women in Australia' in Bottomley et al., *Intersexions*

Vicinus, Martha (1985) *Independent Women Work and Community for Single Women 1850–1920*. London: Virago

Vickers, Jeanne (1991) *Women and the World Economic Crisis*. London and New Jersey: Zed Books

Vickers, Jeanne (1993) *Women and War*. London: Zed Books

Violence Against Children Study Group (1990) *Taking Child Abuse Seriously: Contemporary Issues in Child Protection Theory and Practice*. London: Unwin Hyman

Voice of People Awakening (1995) 'Dowry Murders: Macabre Yet "Modern"' in Vilma Fernandes, ed., *Holding Up Half the Sky: A Collection of Incisive Writings on the Women's Question in India by Stree Jagruti Samiti*. Bombay: Stree Jagruti Samiti

Walby, Sylvia (1990) *Theorizing Patriarchy*. Oxford: Blackwell

Walker, Alice (1989) *The Temple of My Familiar*. London: Penguin in association with the Women's Press

Walker, Alice (1990) 'Definition of Womanist' in Anzaldúa, *Making Face, Making Soul*

Walker, Kath (1988) later known as Oodgeroo of the tribe Noonuccal, *Kath Walker in China*. Brisbane: Jacaranda

Wallace, Michele (1990) *Invisibility Blues: From Pop to Theory*. London: Verso

Walthall, Anne (1991) 'The Life Cycle of Farm Women in Tokugawa Japan' in Bernstein, *Recreating Japanese Women*

Wang Jianguang, ed. (1990) *Westerners Through Chinese Eyes*. Beijing: Foreign Languages Press

Wang Jaixiang (1991) 'A Chinese view on feminism', *Asian Studies Review* 15(2):177–80

Wang Jiaxiang (1996) 'What are the Chinese women facing after Beijing?' Sixth International Interdisciplinary Congress on Women, Adelaide, 21–26 April

Ware, Vron (1992) *Beyond the Pale: White Women, Racism and History*. London: Verso

Waring, Marilyn (1988) *Counting for Nothing*. Wellington: Allen & Unwin and Port Nicholson Press

Warner, Marina (1994) *Managing Monsters: Six Myths of Our Time: The 1994 Reith Lectures*. Vintage: London

Warnock, Kitty (1990) *Land Before Honour: Palestinian Women in the Occupied Territories*. Basingstoke, UK: Macmillan

Watanabe, Kazuko (1994) 'Militarism, Colonialism, and the Trafficking of Women: "Comfort Women" Forced into Sexual Labor for Japanese Soldiers', *Bulletin of Concerned Asian Scholars* 26(4):3–17

Watson, Irene (1992) 'Surviving as a People' in Jocelynne A. Scutt, ed., *Breaking Through: Women, Work and Careers*. Melbourne: Artemis

Watson, Lilla (1994) keynote address at the Australian Women's Studies Association Conference: Women and the Politics of Change. Australian Women's Research Centre, Deakin University, Geelong, 4–6 December

Watson, Rubie S. (1993) 'The Named and the Nameless: Gender and Person in Chinese Society' in Brettell and Sargent, *Gender in Cross-Cultural Perspective*

Watson-Franke, Maria-Barbara (1993) 'The Lycian Heritage and the Making of Men: Matrilineal Models for Parenting', *Women's Studies International Forum* 16(6):569–79

Wee, Vivienne (1995) 'Towards Beijing' Conference, Centre for Asia Pacific Studies, Victoria University of Technology, St Albans, Vic., 9–11 February

West, Guida (1990) 'Conflict and Cooperation among Women in the Welfare Rights Movement' in Albrecht and Brewer, *Bridges of Power: Women's Multicultural Alliances*. Philadelphia: New Society Publishers

West, Lois A. (1992) 'Feminist Nationalist Social Movements: Beyond Universalism and Towards a Gendered Cultural Relativism', *Women's Studies International Forum* 15(5/6):563–79

Whitam, Frederick L. (1992) 'Bayot and Caliboy: Homosexual–Heterosexual Relations in the Philippines' in Murray, *Oceanic Homosexualities*

White, Caroline (1993) '"Close to Home" in Johannesburg: Gender Oppression in Township Households', *Women's Studies International Forum* 16(2):149–64

White, Tyrene (1994) 'The Origins of China's Birth Planning Policy' in Christina K. Gilmartin et al., eds, *Engendering China: Women, Culture and the State*. Cambridge, Mass.: Harvard University Press

Whiting, Pat (1972) 'Female Sexuality: Its Political Implications' in Michelene Wandor, comp., *The Body Politic: Women's Liberation in Britain*. London: Stage

Wikan, Unni (1992) 'Man Becomes Woman: Transsexualism in Oman as a Key to Gender Roles' in Dynes and Donaldson, *Asian Homosexuality*

Williams, Walter L. (1993) 'Amazons of America: Female Gender Variance' in Brettell and Sargent, *Gender in Cross-Cultural Perspective*

Winkler, Robin and Margaret van Keppel (1984) *Relinquishing Mothers in Adoption*. Melbourne: Institute of Family Studies

Winter, Bronwyn (1994) 'Women, the Law, and Cultural Relativism in France: The Case of Excision', *Signs* 19(4):939–74

Wirrpanda, Margaret (1987) 'Aboriginal Activist' in Gloria Frydman, ed., *Protesters*. Melbourne: Collins Dove

Wolchik, Sharon (1994) 'Women in Transition in the Czech and Slovak Republics: The First Three Years', *Journal of Women's History* 5(3):100–7

Wolf, Margery (1975) 'Women and Suicide in China' in Margery Wolf and Roxanne Witke, eds, *Women in Chinese Society*. Stanford: Stanford University Press

Wong, Aline K. (1994) 'Feminism and Women's Studies: A View from Singapore' in Lazarus et al., *Women's Studies Women's Lives*

Wong, Nellie (1991) 'Socialist Feminism: Our Bridge to Freedom' in Mohanty, *Third World Women and the Politics of Feminism*

Wong Yuen Ling, ed. (1995) *Reflections and Resonances: Stories of Chinese Women Involved in International Preparatory Activities for the 1995 NGO Forum on Women*. Beijing: Ford Foundation

Wood, Briar (1993) 'The Trials of Motherhood: The Case of Azaria and Lindy Chamberlain' in Helen Birch, ed., *Moving Targets: Women, Murder and Representation*. London: Virago

Wu Ping (1990) 'Behind the Black Suit, White Shirt and Red Tie' in Wang Jianguang, *Westerners Through Chinese Eyes*

Xiao Ding (1987) 'Sex Therapy Chalks Up Successes', *Women of China* April:16–17

• Bibliography

Xiao Yang et al. (1995) 'An Analysis of Induced Abortions' in Tao Chungfang and Xiao Yang, eds, *Research on Women's Reproductive Health in China*. Beijing: New World Press

Xie Lihua (1995) 'How Do We Face the World – Some Thoughts on Making Contacts' in Wong Yuen Ling, *Reflections and Resonances*

Xie Shihao (1990) 'Americans from A to Z' in Wang Jianguang, *Westerners Through Chinese Eyes*

Xing Jiao (1990) 'Americans Around Me' in Wang Jianguang, *Westerners Through Chinese Eyes*

Yahp, Beth (1992) *The Crocodile Fury*. Sydney: Angus & Robertson

Yamaguchi, Masanori (1995) 'Men on the Threshold of Change' in Fujimura-Fanselow and Kameda, *Japanese Women*

Yang, Anand A. (1992) 'Whose Sati? Widow-Burning in Early Nineteenth-Century India' in Johnson-Odim and Strobel, *Expanding the Boundaries of Women's History*

Yasmeen, Samina (1991) 'Hearing the difference: Pakistani feminism', *Asian Studies Review* 15(1):108–10

Ye Sang (1996) *The Year the Dragon Came*. Brisbane: University of Queensland Press

Yeatman, Anna (1993) 'Voice and Representation in the Politics of Difference' in Gunew and Yeatman, *Feminism and Politics of Difference*

Yeatman, Anna (1995) 'Interlocking Oppressions' in Barbara Caine and Rosemary Pringle, eds, *Transitions: New Australian Feminisms*. Sydney: Allen & Unwin

Yeganeh, Nahid (1993) 'Women, Nationalism and Islam in Contemporary Political Discourse in Iran', *Feminist Review* 44:3–18

Young, Iris Marion (1990) *Throwing Like a Girl and Other Essays in Feminist Philosophy and Social Theory*. Bloomington and Indianapolis: Indiana University Press

Young, Robert C. (1995) *Colonial Desire: Hybridity in Theory, Culture and Race*. Routledge: London and New York

Young, Susan and Ros Madden (1992) 'Characteristics of Women Migrating to Australia and their Migration Decisions' *BIR Bulletin* number 6:5–10

Yu, Lucy C. and Lee Carpenter (1991) 'Women in China' in Leonore Loeb Adler, ed., *Women in Cross-Cultural Perspective*. Westport, Conn.: Praeger

Yue, Audrey (1996) 'Colour Me Queer: Some Notes Towards the NESBian' in Chris Berry and Annamarie Jagose, eds, *Australia Queer*. Special issue of *Meanjin* 55(1):110–20

Yuval-Davis, Nira (1989) 'National Reproduction and "the Demographic Race" in Israel' in Nira Yuval-Davis and Floya Anthias, eds, *Woman-Nation-State*. Basingstoke, UK: Macmillan

Yuval-Davis, Nira (1996) 'Women and the biological reproduction of "the nation"', *Women's Studies International Forum* 19(1/2):17–24

Zack, Naomi (1993) *Race and Mixed Race*. Philadelphia: Temple University Press

Zafar, Fareeha (1994) 'A Feminist Activist in Pakistan' in Lazarus et al., *Women's Studies Women's Lives*

Zhang, Naihua with Wu Xu (1995) 'Discovering the positive with the negative: the women's movement in a changing China' in Basu, *The Challenge of Local Feminisms*

Zhou Lishing (1990) 'A Chinese View of the English Mentality' in Wang Jianguang, *Westerners Through Chinese Eyes*

Zhu Xiaodong (1995) 'Age and Experience Are No Longer Obstacles' in Wong Yuen Ling, *Reflections and Resonances*

Ziellinska, Eleonora and Jolanta Plakwicz (1994) 'Strengthening Human Rights for Women and Men in Matters Relating to Sexual Behavior and Reproduction', *Journal of Women's History* 5(3):91–9

Zinn, Maxine Baca (1989) 'Chicano Men and Masculinity' in Michael S. Kimmel and Michael A. Messner, eds, *Men's Lives*. New York: Macmillan

INDEX

Aboriginal Australians, *see* Indigenous Australians
abortion, 5, 28, 101, 103, 104, 106, 111, 126, 170
Africa, gender relations in, 20, 40, 42, 71, 81–2, 113, 121–2, 197, 198, 200; *see also* Kenya, gender relations in; South Africa, gender relations in
African-American gender relations 67–8, 103, 115–16, 140, 178, 197–8, 210
agency, 70, 92–6, 109–10, 112
agriculture, 121, 225 n.3
aid, 17, 175, 186–8
alliances, women of colour with men, 68
Ang, Ien, 94, 219–20
Anzaldúa, Gloria, 53
Aotearoa, gender relations in, 20, 29, 60–1, 116–17, 156, 162
Australia, gender relations in, 54, 80, 87, 100–1, 103, 114, 116, 151, 156, 162–3, 171–2, 182–4, 193–5, 209–10, 218, 225 n.2
Awekotuku, Ngahuia te, 29, 61, 116, 162

Bangladesh, gender relations in, 106
Besant, Annie, 48
Bhabha, Homi, 53
body image cross-culturally, 162–3, 213–14
brideprice, 120–2
Buddhism, 24–5, 137, 150, 177, 182
Butler, Josephine, 24

Canada, gender relations in, 103, 208–9
Caribbean, gender relations in, 39, 92, 107, 203
China, gender relations in, 3, 5–6, 24–6, 49–52, 57, 65, 76–7, 92, 107–9, 123, 124, 126–7, 139, 142, 150, 197, 199, 200, 206–7
Chow, Rey, 25, 48–52, 64, 168, 217
Christianity, 30, 100, 103–4, 117, 123, 131–2, 136, 138, 171, 177
citizenship rights, 72, 119
class, 8–9, 142, 145, 172, 205; *see also* inequality between women

collectivism/community versus individual, 68–9, 72–3, 74–9, 93–5, 114, 116, 203–4; *see also* individualism
Collins, Patricia Hill, 67, 140
colonialism, 3, 9, 21, 22, 37, 39, 90, 145, 160, 168, 170, 208; *see also* imperialism
colonialism, white women's role in, 24, 168; *see also* maternal imperialism
colonisation, 18, 19, 23–6, 31, 33, 35, 38, 46–7, 102, 115–16, 197
Confucianism, 25, 27, 52, 64, 76, 78, 190
consciousness-raising, 61–2
Convention on the Elimination of All Forms of Discrimination Against Women, 70–1
cosmetic surgery, 84–5, 213
Cuba, gender relations in, 34, 42, 105
Cusack, Dymphna, 49–50

declension narratives, *see* matriarchial societies
debt forgiveness, 172
Descartes, René, 44, 132
desire, 51–2, 58
development, 19, 41–2, 48–9, 110, 169, 173, 174–5, 186, 187
development, third and first world compared, 41–3
divorce, 164–5, 214
domestic workers, 38, 168, 178–9
dowry, 88–9, 120–2, 201, 202
dowry burnings compared with violence in USA, 89
dualism in western thought, 6, 16, 18, 33, 44–52, 53, 80, 119, 129, 131, 132, 138, 148, 154, 155, 159, 217, 218; *see also* orientalism
dualism, less marked in non-western thought, 52, 151, 170
duCille, Ann, 219

eating patterns, 58
education, 172, 196–7

education and links to fertility, 105, 106, 111; *see also* literacy
Egypt, gender relations in, 81, 82–3, 225 n.3
Emberley, Julia, 72, 82–4, 205
Enloe, Cynthia, 168
equality before the law, 71, 73, 75–7, 109, 113; *see also* rights
equality, critique of, 75–8, 162, 172, 200, 206–7, 212
ethnocentrism, 53, 69, 170, 184, 223–4 n.4; *see also* racism
eugenics, 102–3, 106

fatherhood, 100–1, 113
family planning, *see* population policies; reproductive rights and choices
family relations in the west, 59–60, 69, 214
family relations beyond the west, 64–5, 69, 146; *see also* motherhood; mother–son bonds; mothers-in-law
Fanon, Frantz, 52–3, 55, 68
fashion, 33, 58, 59, 213–14
femininity, feminist constructions of, 159; *see also* sexualities
feminism
  and postcolonialism, 14–15, 72
  and postmodernism, 12–13, 15
  and psychoanalysis, 11–12, 94, 99–100, 128, 135–6
  and socialism, 34
  Arab, 30, 32
  Chinese (includes Taiwan and Hong Kong), 6, 25–6, 76, 107, 199, 200–1
  critique of western, 9, 68, 76–7, 94, 98–9, 100, 129–30, 170, 192, 194–5, 198, 201, 204, 209, 211–20
  eco-feminism, 11, 49, 93, 118
  Filipino, 203–4
  Indian, 23–4, 88, 91–2, 102, 164, 198
  Italian, 98
  Japanese, 27–8, 190, 198, 203–4
  Latin American, 203
  liberal, 7–8, 175, 179
  maternal, 11, 48, 93, 119
  marxist, *see* feminism, socialist
  radical, 7, 82, 85, 93–4, 100, 126, 222 n.2
  socialist, 8–9, 100, 168, 171, 179, 199, 217–18
  South African, 201
  western definition, 4–5
fertility, 40–1, 101–12
fifth world women, *see* migrant women on gender and ethnic relations in country of migration

First Nations (Canada), gender relations in, 72, 208–9
footbinding, 25, 50
Foucault, Michel, 131, 148
fourth world women, 35; *see also* First Nations (Canada), gender relations in; Indigenous Australia, gender relations in
Freud, Sigmund, 133
fundamentalism, 30

Gandhi, Mahatma, 23
Ganguly, Indrani, 58, 67, 88, 93, 124, 125, 130, 142, 143, 146, 162–3, 189, 194, 195, 212, 213, 221
gender, *see* sex
genital mutilation, 80–7, 170
global economy, *see* international economy
Great Britain, gender relations in, 115, 134–5, 182–3, 192, 195–6
Gunning, Isabelle, 84–5, 87, 173

hijab, *see* veiling
Hinduism, 46, 88, 90–1, 137, 138, 143–4, 157
homosexuality, 148–54, 157–8
Hong Kong, gender relations in, 25, 75, 140, 152, 177, 179, 197
hooks, bell, 29, 140
Huggins, Jackie, 47
human development index, female, 41–2, 43
humanism, 12, 14, 47, 54, 155, 158, 207
hybridisation, hybrid identities, 52–4, 56, 63, 68, 160–5, 183, 195–6, 207, 209–10

imperialism, 19, 187; *see also* colonialism
independence movements, *see* nationalism
India, gender relations in, 21, 23–4, 40, 48, 72–3, 88–92, 102, 106, 121, 130, 142, 146, 157, 163–4, 168, 191, 197, 201–3, 225 n.8
Indigenous Australia, gender relations in, 47, 81, 103, 114, 116, 166, 178, 204, 209, 212, 223 n.3
individualism, 57–8, 59–60, 63, 67, 94–5, 109, 143, 214
individualism contrasted with relationality, 65–6, 128
individualism, critique by women from beyond the west, 61–2; *see also* collectivism/community versus individual
Indonesia, gender relations in, 32, 106, 179, 187

inequality between women, 9–10, 41–3, 55; *see also* class
infibulation, *see* genital mutilation
international division of labour, 17, 167–8, 176–88
international economy, 35, 101, 186
international movements/traffic in women, 167–8, 196
Irwin, Kathie, 61
Islam, 30, 79, 86, 136, 181; *see also* Muslim nations, gender relations in
Iwao, Sukimo, 52, 164

Japan, gender relations in, 26–8, 52, 62, 77, 92, 111, 112, 118–19, 142, 144–5, 146, 153, 157–8, 164–5, 182, 183, 190–1
Jayawardena, Kumari, 23–4, 28–9, 55–6

Kenya, gender relations in, 105–6, 118–19
Kerala, gender relations in, 106, 142, 225 n.7
Kishwar, Madhu, 198, 201
Korea, gender relations in, 38, 105, 109, 112, 176, 177, 182, 196
Kristeva, Julia, 49–51, 139, 148

labour, paid, *see* workforce, women in
labour, unpaid, 174–6
Lacan, Jacques, 135
Latin America, gender relations in, 34, 72, 106, 113, 117–18, 145, 151, 153, 189, 203, 225 n.3, 225 n.8
Lazreg, Marnia, 31, 82
lesbianism, 81, 114–15, 126, 133, 150, 151, 152, 156, 159, 164, 170, 171, 201
life expectancy, 41, 42
literacy, 41, 169, 196–7; *see also* education

maternal imperialism, 24, 187; *see also* colonialism, white women's role in
matriarchal societies, 19–21, 26, 27, 124
matrilineality, 19, 106, 123–4
matrilocality and patrilocality, 124–5, 126, 138
Mao Zedong, 26
marriage relations, 164–5
marriage resisters, 126–7
masculinities, 115–16, 129, 132, 134–5, 146, 150–1, 165
masculinities, racialised, 141–7, 182–5
Mayo, Katherine, 24, 55
Mernissi, Fatima, 86
Mies, Maria, 121, 217–18
migrant women on gender and ethnic relations in country of migration, 35, 54, 86–7, 95, 103, 114, 115, 162–3, 184–5, 188, 208, 218
migrant women's experiences, 191–4

Mill, John Stuart, 21
Mohanty, Chandra Tolpade, 10, 19, 68, 129, 176
mother–son bonds, 141–7
motherhood, 16, 17, 107, 112–19; *see also* reproductive choices and rights
motherhood, men's attitudes to, 99–100, 134–5, 150
motherhood, status in the west, 97–8, 119, 132
motherhood, status beyond the west, 119, 125, 127–8, 142–7, 163, 214
motherhood, status on bearing a son, 125–6
motherhood and sisterhood compared, 97–9
mothers-in-law, 125, 126, 143
mothers of the disappeared, 117–18
Muslim, definition, 223 n.3
Muslim nations, gender relations in, 21, 30, 31–3, 46, 62, 71, 73–5, 82, 86–7, 100, 112, 113, 153, 158, 171, 173–4, 181, 191, 225 n.8; *see also* Islam
multiculturalism, 193

nationalism, nationalist movements, 21, 23–4, 26, 28–9, 31
Native American nations, gender relations in, 20, 151
Nehru, Jawaharlal, 23
New Zealand, *see* Aotearoa
non-government organisations, 187–8

one-child policy, 107–9, 189
Ong, Aiwha, 33, 178
Oodgeroo Noonuccal, 49, 191
orientalism, 46–53, 55, 58, 80, 82, 141, 146, 184, 194, 208, 223 n.6; *see also* dualism
other, idealising non-western other, 47–52, 207
other, speaking about western other from beyond the west, 3, 24, 212–14
other, western feminists speaking for, 208–11

Pacific Island nations, gender relations in, 20, 39, 124, 137, 157, 175, 178, 181; *see also* Papua New Guinea, gender relations in; Samoa, gender relations in; Vanuatu, gender relations in
Papua New Guinea, gender relations in, 42, 92–3, 122, 123, 134, 150, 176
patrilocality, *see* matrilocality and patrilocality
Philippines, gender relations in, 110–11, 118, 152–3, 179, 181–2, 184–5
Plumwood, Val, 44–6, 55–6
politics, women in, 43, 117–18, 173, 217–20

polygamy, 81, 94, 192
population policies, 28, 101–10
pornography, 139–40, 144–5, 164, 191
postcolonialism, 14, 188
postmodernism, 12–13, 53, 155, 158–9, 165–6
poverty, 169, 171, 172, 186
psychoanalysis, 58, 61–2, 63, 147, 162
prostitution, *see* sex work
public patriarchy, 60
purdah, *see* veiling

racism, 38, 80, 102, 103, 115, 182–4, 194, 215, 220; *see also* ethnocentrism
racism in the white women's movement, 204
Ram, Kalpana, 51, 87, 95, 121, 124, 137, 160
rape, *see* violence
rape in war, 190–1
Rathbone, Eleanor, 24
Reagon, Bernice Johnson, 219
refugees, 189–91
reproductive rights and choices, 5, 16, 101, 104, 108, 110–12
reproductive technologies, 89, 94–5, 100, 105, 107, 125–6, 201
reproduction and social security, 109
rights, 5, 16, 44, 70–9, 86, 88, 93–5, 101, 104, 110, 122, 133, 153, 170, 172–3, 217–18; *see also* equality
Rich, Adrienne, 9, 29, 219
Roy, Raja Rammohan, 23, 90
Rubin, Gayle, 121

Saadawi, Nawal el, 82–4
Said, Edward, 20, 46, 208
Samoa, gender relations in, 65, 200, 224 n.6
sati, 23, 88–92
second world, *see* socialist countries
self, non-western constructions of, 62–3, 64–7
self, western constructions of, 154–5
sex preference, 125–6
sex tourism, 182–4
sex workers, 144, 179–85
sexology, 133–4, 140
sexual discourses in the west, 131–4
sexual identities, 12, 16–17, 21, 28, 60, 93–4, 129, 130–6, 148–9, 151–6, 160–1, 165–6
sexual identities, centrality in the west, 155, 158–9, 165–6
sexual relations across ethnic lines, 52, 72, 78, 99, 133, 182–5, 192, 214
sexualities, racialised, 129–30, 140, 183–4

sexualities, western compared with non-western, 130, 183–5, 211–14
Shah Bano, 73
Shintoism and gender relations, 137
Shiva, Vandana, 48, 217–18, 225 n.3
Singapore, gender relations in, 106–7, 163, 177, 179, 184, 222 n.1
Singh, Parlo, 54, 68–9, 207, 214
socialist countries, gender relations in, 34, 50, 101, 140, 223 n.4; *see also* Cuba, gender relations in
Southeast Asia, gender relations in, 21–2, 39, 42, 113, 137–8, 155, 156, 176–80; *see also* Indonesia, gender relations in; Philippines, gender relations in; Singapore, gender relations in; Thailand, gender relations in
South Africa, gender relations in, 117, 122, 140
Spivak, Gayatri, vi, 10, 101, 130, 188, 211
statistics, critique of national, 39–40, 175
submission, *see* other, idealising non-western other
suffrage, 27, 29, 43
suicide, 89, 92
surrogacy, *see* reproductive technologies

Tanaka, Kazuko, 28
Taiwan, gender relations in, 76, 77, 140, 177, 180, 200
Thailand, gender relations in, 22, 154, 181–4
third genders, 157–60
third world, 35–44, 186, 204
third world, definition, 34, 35
torture, 189
tradition, traditionalism and women's status, 23, 29–30, 31–2, 49, 54, 87, 91, 122, 123, 129, 170, 223 n.2
traditional societies, gender relations in, 20, 72, 98, 124
transsexualism, 155–6
Trinh Minh-ha, 35, 53, 207

United Nations and status of women, 70–1, 104, 110, 168–73, 175–6, 182–4, 187, 190, 197
United Nations Decade for Women, 82
United Nations World Conference of Women in Beijing, 69, 109, 168, 169–73
United States, gender relations in, 5, 77–8, 95, 100, 103, 104, 111, 115–16, 152, 156, 164, 192–3, 224 n.3

Vanuatu, gender relations in, 71, 122–3, 224 n.6

Vietnam, gender relations in, 20, 44, 55, 93, 189
veiling, 30–3
violence, 71, 86, 88, 94, 115, 122–3, 126, 140, 170, 177, 178, 184, 185, 187, 202, 208–9

Walker, Alice, 68, 196
Wang, Jiaxiang, 6, 76, 79, 108–9, 161, 199
whiteness, 3, 45, 47, 54, 56, 214–16
womanism, 68

women's liberation 61; *see also* feminism
women's movements, 42, 168, 177–8, 199–204, 225 n.7; *see also* feminism
women's studies, 11, 28, 197–9
workforce, women in, 27, 28, 38, 41, 43, 126–7, 173–85, 193–4; *see also* domestic workers, sex workers
world-travelling, 84–5, 170, 173, 184, 198–9, 211, 212–13, 220–1

Yahp, Beth, 138